CW01338009

REBELLION
IN THE
MIDDLE
AGES

REBELLION
IN THE
MIDDLE AGES
FIGHT AGAINST THE CROWN

MATTHEW LEWIS

PEN & SWORD
HISTORY

AN IMPRINT OF PEN & SWORD BOOKS LTD.
YORKSHIRE – PHILADELPHIA

First published in Great Britain in 2021 by
PEN AND SWORD HISTORY
An imprint of
Pen & Sword Books Ltd
Yorkshire – Philadelphia

ISBN 978 1 52672 793 0

A CIP catalogue record for this book is available from the British Library.

Typeset in Times New Roman 11/13.5 by
SJmagic DESIGN SERVICES, India.
Printed and bound in the UK by CPI Group (UK) Ltd.

Pen & Sword Books Limited incorporates the imprints of Atlas, Archaeology,
Aviation, Discovery, Family History, Fiction, History, Maritime, Military, Military
Classics, Politics, Select, Transport, True Crime, Air World, Frontline Publishing,
Leo Cooper, Remember When, Seaforth Publishing, The Praetorian Press,
Wharncliffe Local History, Wharncliffe Transport, Wharncliffe True Crime and
White Owl.

For a complete list of Pen & Sword titles please contact
PEN & SWORD BOOKS LIMITED
47 Church Street, Barnsley, South Yorkshire, S70 2AS, England
E-mail: enquiries@pen-and-sword.co.uk
Website: www.pen-and-sword.co.uk

Or
PEN AND SWORD BOOKS
1950 Lawrence Rd, Havertown, PA 19083, USA
E-mail: Uspen-and-sword@casematepublishers.com
Website: www.penandswordbooks.com

Contents

Introduction

There are few things more terrible than a failed rebellion.
Nothing better guarantees the establishment in perpetuity of
the perceived injustices that led to revolt than their successful
defence.

Throughout the Middle Ages, from the Norman Conquest of 1066 until the Battle of Bosworth in 1485, rebellions in England came almost like clockwork. Around every fifty years between these convenient bookend dates the incumbent monarch would be forced to fend off a challenge of some kind. These rebellions must have been in each case an act of faith or utter desperation because the chances of success against a king and his massed force of arms, wealth, castles and knights were always lower than any rebel might like.

Each point of crisis for a monarch and his nation had very particular causes and aims. Sometimes it was a nobleman, an erstwhile friend of the king who had fallen from favour or been tempted to reach a little too far from his exalted position. On occasion, it was the more general populace who would be driven to seek the correction of a keenly felt injustice or the lifting of too heavy a burden placed across their collectively broad shoulders. Even the church might be a source of resistance to the royal will, particularly during the centuries that saw attempts to balance and rebalance the relationships between kings and popes.

We remain fascinated by the individuals thrust up before us as ringleaders or instigators of these moments of national, sometimes international, crisis. In some, we can see noble motives compelling them to act against the ultimate authority in the land. These hallowed few take on the aspect of the folk hero, the altruistic rebel obliged to react for the benefit of others despite the personal cost. They are the Robin Hood figures. These rebels fit perfectly with a view of the medieval world as intrinsically, fundamentally and inherently unfair. It surely was just that to the minds of later folk, who consider themselves more civilised and socially evolved. Quite what a thirteenth-century husbandman would make of the twenty-first-century obsession with twenty-four-hour availability to employers and strangers from around the globe, of screen time replacing conversation and of messaging the person sitting next to you in your living room rather than speaking to them is rarely given any consideration. It is our projection backwards of our own beliefs, bias and understanding, both of our world and theirs, that will often define these rebels as hero or villain.

I have always tried to shun a Hollywood notion of historical figures as either wholly good or entirely consumed by evil. Real life does not divide so neatly into goodies and baddies in an eternal struggle for supremacy. Nowhere has it been more challenging to resist the temptation to turn stories into would be movie scripts than in detailing rebellions against the crown. It lends itself to the portrayal of one side as just and the other as equally, irreconcilably unjust. I have tried to put down my bucket of popcorn and set aside my oversized bag of pick and mix sweets. Each crisis point had complex causes and every person who elected or felt compelled, or indeed was forced, to offer rebellion and resistance was driven by a mosaic of often conflicting motivations. These can be hard to pick out, piece together and, to the twenty-first-century mind, understand. For almost all, it must have been a difficult decision to reach that rebellion against the monarch was the right, or only, path available. It must have been so because the cost of failure was so high – invariably mortal.

The willingness to pay this ultimate price, or at least to wittingly risk incurring it, only adds to the mystique that surrounds rebellions in a swirling fog of misdirection and romance. Most would have been aware that they ventured not only their status, where it was something valuable, and their lives, which to all were worth protecting, but the lives and livelihoods of those they loved. Entire families could be ruined, and where the rebel was a nobleman, he embarked on his undertaking fully aware that he might die, by execution if not in the act of revolt, but also that his family may well be dispossessed. His legacy, a vital part of the outlook of any baronial patriarch, would be the loss of the family's titles, lands and fortune. Why would someone take that gamble, with the odds so stacked against them, unless forced to it by some noble burden?

If a rebellion was given odds like a football match is today, few would back the rebel, though the potential pay-out might look alluring. If medieval politics was a casino, those entering did so at their own risk, as a large sign would warn them, and in the full knowledge that every game was rigged. The king was the house. The crown dealt the cards and set the rules, which might be changed at any moment. It could be this sense of injustice that causes one hopeful player to throw his chips in and turn over the table in outraged frustration. Still, in doing so, his aims are more likely to be restricted to anguish at his personal loss than a desire to help his fellow patrons and any future customers.

Religious resistance to the crown is easy to hold up as spiritual supremacy over a corrupt, grubby, secular world. The man at the casino who never gambles doesn't exist. Churchmen provided the lubrication for medieval government. At lower levels, they were the literate clerks who could keep records and draft documentation. They wrote the letters that conveyed the king's will and crammed into his household with no less ambition than those outside religious orders. Bishops and archbishops often acted as close advisors to kings and existed at the centre of the nation's political life as much as its spiritual one. The seesaw that balanced secular and ecclesiastical duties was easily tilted toward the former, exposing them as every bit as worldly as the men they feigned to turn their noses up at around the court.

The Roman Catholic Church spent much of the first half of the period on which this book focuses trying to elbow its way into the temporal lives of its flock. Popes and kings ground against each other as both claimed rights they coveted either as ancient, valuable or prestigious. Neither side wished to concede ground. There was some conflict within the church. The rise of monkish orders committed to cloistered life was itself a rebellion against the embracing of worldly power and authority by senior members of the clergy. Bernard of Clairvaux helped forge the Cistercian order that shunned political influence and demanded a life within the walls of an abbey. Yet, he was one of the most politically influential figures of the twelfth century, who regularly left his cloister to preach and wrote to censure kings, nobles, popes and clergymen alike. Behind much of the church's manoeuvring lay the desire to unify Western Christendom to facilitate crusades to the Holy Land. Successive popes sought to impose themselves as a higher political authority to end conflict on the Continent, but only so that they could export it to the east. Even the religious rebel may not be all that he appears.

Perhaps the most shocking, and also least prevalent, source of revolt was the general public. There were only two explosive points of popular unrest during the period. It is worthy of consideration whether these were more or less threatening to the crown and its government than noble revolt. What it lacked in financial and political backing it could compensate for in numbers with a catchy, appealing complaint. These were the sparks that might not look like much but could ignite the tinder-dry discontent of an entire population. Huge national events that might make or break a senior nobleman would likely have little or no bearing on the common man, woman or child. Their preoccupation lay with tending the fields, making it to market with enough produce to sell, feeding the family through the winter and meeting the exacting requirements of religious obligations that should help their soul to Heaven. These are not the stories and struggles that make headlines in history, and if something distracted enough people from their daily toils to constitute a rebellion, it points to a deep-seated and keenly felt problem.

Medieval rebellion had to be against the crown, but this presented problems of its own that were all but impossible to overcome. The king was appointed and approved by God. To criticise and challenge the monarch's authority was to dare to question God's plan. This is why a challenge to the crown was often cloaked beneath complaints against the monarch's ministers and advisors, whose deficient or evil counsel was the only possible reason the king might be behaving badly. The king was, obviously, being led astray. When these ministers were blamed, it was as a proxy for the king, because few dared directly censure God's anointed monarch. Aside from the religious aspect of doing so, it made rebellion openly treasonous, whereas denouncing advisors made it seem reasonable, noble and for the benefit of the king and country.

The real question this book seeks to answer is whether there is any thread that knits these regular rounds of uprisings into a tapestry that tells a broader tale. The regularity with which they occurred might hint at some overarching problem or theme that makes them predictable. If so, the failure to resolve the root cause might appear hubris on the part of successive monarchs, a symptom of a conviction that they were above the mistakes of their predecessors. If no strand connects the cycle of revolts, then they may be no more than a symptom of a societal structure that placed one man, apparently unassailably, at the pinnacle by an accident of birth. The potential that revolt is a natural state of the human condition cannot be ignored either.

Rebellion neither began nor ended between the Norman Conquest and the dawn of the Tudor era in England. It is a global and eternal phenomenon. As I write, a portion of the world is convulsing in response to the murder of George Floyd in Minneapolis, USA. Just yesterday, the statue of Edward Colston was toppled in Bristol and unceremoniously dumped into the sea, where the lives of so many enslaved people, traded by Colston for money, were lost. Rebellion is alive today. It is never more than lightly sleeping, one eye open to the next injustice or opportunity. Not all aims are noble, and not all rebels share an objective. The search for justice and parity, irrespective of colour, culture, sexuality, religion, wealth or anything else seems to this writer to be one of the few genuinely noble causes, a banner we can all take up together to demand change. I struggle to see violence as an answer in any situation, yet what will follow is a series of violent clashes that caused innumerable deaths. Violence has often been the key that has unlocked the door to change. Perhaps it is for those on the other side of the door to open it and avoid violence.

Martin Luther King Jr once said that rioting is the language of the unheard. It is always easier to blame the rioter than to wonder what we have failed to hear. In the current climate, that is how I think I define white privilege; to be deaf to the calls of inequity you do not see or feel because of the colour of your (my) own skin. As I watch the development of the Black Lives Matter movement today, I find myself wondering how it will have turned out by the time you read this. Did anything change? I hope so. This book is, in part, about the sweeping under the carpet of serious political, social and economic issues and the volcanic pressure that such dismissals will inevitably, and repeatedly, create. When I set out to write it, I looked around at famous quotes from history about rebellion. I then tried to think up a few of my own. Vanity, perhaps, leading me to test whether I could do better. This is one from the list I cobbled together that seems relevant as I write today:

Few ever want to rebel. It is usually a final destination on a long journey. When you have been prevented from leaving the train at every station, the end of the line is the only stop remaining.

Chapter 1

Hereward the Exile

Under the weight of tyranny, exercising one's freedom is an act of rebellion.

In the aftermath of the Norman Conquest of England, King William I did not sit comfortably upon his throne. His coronation offered portents of the troubles to come. On 25 December 1066, William was crowned at Westminster Abbey by Aldred, Archbishop of York as his soldiers prowled the streets of London, armed and mounted against the threat of unrest. Inside the abbey, the gathered Norman and English barony were keen to show their loyalty to the new regime and responded enthusiastically to the call to give ascent to William's rule. Aldred demanded the cry from the English in their tongue as Geoffrey, Bishop of Coutances asked the Normans in attendance in their native French. There was a clamour to show consent, and the din inside the abbey of competing voices and languages drew the attention the guards stationed outside.

Believing that William was under some kind of threat, the soldiers set fire to buildings to cause a general alarm. It worked, but only drew looters alongside those who tried to fight the fire. The nobles and other guests within the abbey began to panic and flee. The clergymen alone remained at the altar to tremulously complete the coronation rites as the king found it increasingly impossible to hide his own fear. It was a chaotic beginning to Norman rule in England, and the monk-chronicler Orderic Vitalis noted that it sowed the seeds of English resistance, as 'they waited for some future opportunity of revenge'.[1] William soon faced problems in Yorkshire, leading to the vicious Harrying of the North that saw entire communities laid waste, carving scars that lasted for generations. One man above all others came to symbolise this English desire for vengeance against their new, cruel Norman masters, but he was not entirely what he has been remembered as.

Hereward has been known by many epithets. The most famous is perhaps *the Wake*, which first appears in the Peterborough Chronicle towards the end of the fourteenth century.[2] There is disagreement about the origin of this appellation. One theory gives its meaning as 'the Watchful',

1

perhaps relating to his remarkable ability to escape the blades of would-be killers. Another explanation is that the Wake family, who gained control of land in Bourne previously belonging to Hereward, gave it to him in an attempt to tie themselves to him dynastically. There is no clear answer to this mystery. In his 1865 novel, Charles Kingsley christened Hereward the Wake as *Last of the English* in a work that propelled the eleventh-century rebel to the status of romantic national hero, throwing off the yoke of Norman oppression. Even this is a smokescreen to suit nineteenth-century imperial nationalism. What evidence remains suggests that Hereward was of Danish descent, a member of an Anglo-Danish class that lived alongside the Anglo-Saxons after Viking incursions and sporadic Scandinavian rule in England.

The real identity and family background of Hereward remain unclear. It was long held that he was the son of Leofric, Earl of Mercia and his wife Godgifu, better known as Lady Godiva. Leofric and Godgifu did have a wayward son, Ælfgar, who was exiled in 1055 'without any kind of guilt', according to *The Anglo-Saxon Chronicle*. Fleeing to Ireland, Ælfgar returned with troops and found an ally in King Gruffydd of Wales. Together, they moved against the forces of King Edward the Confessor and caused severe damage around Hereford, putting the army of Ralph the Timid, Earl of Hereford to flight. In the wake of this destruction, it was diplomatically decided 'that earl Ælfgar be inlawed and his earldom be given him and all that had been taken from him'.[3] The exploits of Ælfgar either became muddled with, or were used to give authenticity to, Hereward's story.

It is possible that the connection to Earl Leofric grew from a suggestion that Leofric of Bourne might have been Hereward's father, but there is no evidence for such a man. This theory may stem from the possibility that a priest named Leofric penned an early, Old English account of Hereward's adventures on which the later, Latin *Gesta Herewardi* was based. *Ingulph's Chronicle of the Abbey of Crowland*, understood to be a later pen using the voice of the earlier Abbot Ingulph, is clear that Leofric of Bourne was Hereward's father. He is portrayed as 'a nobleman, the lord of Bourne and of the adjoining marshes, Leofric by name, a person of high lineage, and renowned for his military prowess'. Leofric of Bourne is described as a kinsman of Ralph the Timid, Earl of Hereford, the same man who had been defeated by Ælfgar, son of Earl Leofric. To further muddy the waters, Earl Ralph was married to Godgifu, a sister of King Edward the Confessor who shared a name with the more famous wife of Earl Leofric. *Ingulph's Chronicle* continues:

This Leofric, by his wife Ediva, who was of like noble blood (being granddaughter in the fifth degree of the mighty duke Oslac, who formerly lived in the time of king Edgar), had a son, Heward by name, at this period a young man remarkable for his strength of body. He was tall in person, and a youth of singular beauty, but too fond of warfare, and of a spirit fierce and uncontrolled beyond expression.[4]

Leofric of Bourne has proven impossible to track down in the historical record. It seems feasible that in casting about for a background for such a heroic figure, a tangle of names and events caused Hereward to be identified incorrectly. A link with Earl Leofric, by virtue of the similar exploits of the earl's son Ælfgar, provided a root in fact and a firm Anglo-Saxon heritage. The assertion Hereward was the son of Leofric of Bourne may have been derived from muddled information that led to the creation of this hitherto elusive local magnate as Hereward's father. There are good reasons for the use of these figures in connection to Hereward. To create him as a national hero, he needed to be English or Anglo-Saxon. He also required some noble connection to explain his prowess, leadership and success. Surely no unknown commoner of lowly heritage could be capable of the feats ascribed to Hereward. The jumble of Leofric, Earl or Lord of Bourne, Godgifu, Countess of Mercia or of Hereford ultimately turns out a Hereward suitably noble and English for the task of resisting the Norman takeover of England. There is, though, another, more convincing identity for Hereward.

Inguplh's Chronicle provides another family connection for Hereward which is at odds with being a son of Leofric of Bourne, but which offers a compelling alternative heritage. On two occasions, the writer refers to Brand, Abbot of Peterborough as a paternal uncle of Hereward. The mentions are almost innocuous. The first describes Hereward looking for someone capable of legally knighting him and settling on 'his uncle, Brand by name, who was at that time abbat of Burgh'.[5] A little later, the death of Abbot Brand is recorded, and he is further identified as 'Brand, abbat of Burgh, the before-named uncle of Herward'.[6] In the original Latin, Brand is described as Hereward's *patruus*, paternal uncle, rather than *matruus*, a maternal uncle. Brand is a prominent enough figure for his brothers to be identified, and there were four of them: Asketil, Siric, Siworth, and Godric. The supposed ages of these brothers mean that the oldest, Asketil, is the most likely candidate for being Hereward's father. It would also make sense that Asketil would have inherited and passed his lands to Hereward.

The five brothers were the sons of Toki of Lincoln, a wealthy man with enough spare land to give some to Peterborough Abbey. Toki was himself the son of Auti, another rich man from Lincoln. What is most striking about these names is that they are clearly of Danish descent. The family was almost certainly part of an Anglo-Danish class that settled in England and prospered in the old Danelaw areas to the north and east. Only the youngest of Toki's sons, Godric, has an English name, hinting that he had married an English wife who had been allowed to name their final son. Asketil Tokison had held land at Scotter, Scotton and Raventhorpe. By the time of the compilation of Doomsday, he retained much of his land from his brother Brand, Abbot of Peterborough. Having previously held it from King Edward and then King Harold, it seems likely it was gifted to the abbey and leased back to keep it out of Norman hands. Asketil held a total of twenty-six carucates, the Danelaw's equivalent of a hide, in Lincolnshire, making him a significant landowner and explaining his description as a king's thegn. A thegn was a pre-Conquest equivalent of a baron, a powerful local lord with a direct link to the king, often acting as a councillor to the monarch. This explanation of Hereward's lineage provides a rich, landed connection to which he, as the son of Asketil, was heir. The Danish link makes sense of a portion of Hereward's exploits, too, in which a Danish army feature strongly.[7] Whoever Hereward was, and whatever his heritage, he was to leave a profound mark on England's new Norman masters.

The story of Hereward's astounding adventures is related in *De Gestis Herewardi Saxoni – The Exploits of Hereward the Saxon*. He appears in other sources, but *De Gestis* was compiled, perhaps originally by the priest Leofric, to relate Hereward's tale. The writer explains that he has recorded the events because: 'We think it will encourage noble deeds and induce liberality to know Hereward, who he was, and to hear of his achievements and deeds, and especially to those who are desirous of living the life of a soldier.'[8] By the age of 18, Hereward was a notorious tearaway and something of a spoiled brat. Frequently

> his hand was against every man, and every man's hand was against him'. He was renowned locally as a bad loser, so that 'when the youths of similar age engaged in wrestling and other sports of a like nature, if he could not gain a triumph over them all, and his fellows did not offer him the laurel crown as the reward of victory, he would very often obtain with the sword that which by the mere strength of his arm he was unable.[9]

Both *De Gestis* and *Ingulph's Chronicle* agree that this behaviour led to clamorous complaints about Hereward. His father, eventually having enough of his son's 'youthful pranks' and 'acts of excessive violence against his neighbours', appealed to King Edward the Confessor to exile his own son.[10] At 18, Hereward the Outlaw was driven from his home by the king's orders, given at his father's request. Thus began the experiences that would craft the young rebel into a national hero. Hereward went south and west, first into Cornwall where he started to carve out his military reputation. He confronted a local tyrant named Ulcus Ferreus (Iron Sore) who was attempting to marry the daughter of a local prince. The two men traded insults and ended up in a duel to the death which Hereward, the younger man, won. When the prince's men arrived, they apprehended Hereward for killing the man who would be their lord's son-in-law, and there were calls for his execution. The prince hesitated, not displeased by what Hereward had done, and his daughter eventually helped Hereward slip out of the region, complete with a sword given to her by Ulcus Ferreus as a gift. She provided Hereward with letters of safe conduct and recommendation to the king of Ireland and begged him to remember her always.[11] Already, he was transforming from a local troublemaker into a righter of wrongs.

Hereward was welcomed by the king's son, who pleaded with the young firebrand to stay a while. Hereward was itching to leave, news having reached him that his father was dead and his mother had been left trying to manage Hereward's inheritance. War was on the horizon as the duke of Munster challenged the king of Ireland, and Hereward's reputation caused the prince to offer him a place at the front of his army. When the time came for battle, Hereward 'drew up the lines and led them'. He and his men, 'in the midst of the enemy's wedges, killing to the right and left', reached the duke's tent. Dispatching the two guards, Hereward asked the duke for his surrender. When he refused to concede, Hereward ran him through, taking the duke's sword and trumpet to show his army that their commander had fallen. Effectively winning the battle, Hereward was hailed as a hero. During the year that followed, men flocked to be trained by Hereward, and he assembled a crack unit with which he put down all resistance to the prince's father.

With his star climbing ever higher, Hereward received a message from his Cornish princess. She had been abducted and was in Ireland, about to be forced into marriage to the son of a local lord, despite now being engaged to the king's son. The prince sent messengers, but they were arrested. Hereward used dye to turn his blond hair black and his beard red and set out to attend the wedding. He managed to get into the celebrations posing as a traveller, and when he learned that the prince's messengers were to have their right eyes cut out, he ambushed their captors, freed them, killing the lord in the melee. Returning the bride to the prince, Hereward sealed his reputation in Ireland.

Attempting to return to Cornwall, Hereward found himself thrown off course by storms and was eventually shipwrecked in Flanders. Captured by scouts, he was suspected of being part of an invasion force and imprisoned. He gave his name as Harold, and as concern about his motives subsided, he became involved in military efforts in the area and immediately impressed. The handsome warrior caught the eye of a noble lady named Turfrida, who fell in love with Hereward. Her admirer was unimpressed, and when the two men met at a tournament, Hereward defeated him and sent his horse as a gift to Turfrida. As their romance grew, Hereward took part in a campaign to a geographically unknown place named as Scaldemariland. The purpose of the action was to enforce a tribute owed by the region to the count of Flanders, and it was the count's son, Robert, who led the army.

Hereward is credited with inspiring Robert's men 'in light-hearted fashion', and the first clash was won. The people of Scaldemariland rose again to try and drive out their attackers and as they gained ground, they insisted that Robert should be handed over as leader of the army. The only other named individual was Hereward, 'the master of the soldiers', along with the tribunes of each company of the army. If these men were surrendered for execution, the rest would be permitted to leave unharmed.[12] Refusing to surrender, Hereward, in a possible Spartan reference, took 300 men and went in disguise towards the enemy camp, posing as ambassadors returning from a journey laden with gifts. As the clamour to claim the best prizes grew, Hereward sprang the trap, slaughtering many and chasing the rest back to their camp.

Next, Hereward directed a plan to lure the enemy army into a valley, feigning a retreat so that the enemy gave chase, then wheeling around with 1,000 cavalrymen and 600 men-at-arms to cut them off from their camp. They were herded together and picked off with javelins and other missiles all afternoon until darkness fell. Finally, Hereward selected 600 men and directly attacked the enemy camp during the night, killing many and wounding more. The tactics employed by Hereward had utterly confounded the enemy, and he was singled out as the prime cause of the campaign's victory. The *Gesta* raved that 'It was a complete surprise and as far as the enemy was concerned, beyond all their experience in warfare.'[13] Scaldemariland agreed to pay double the tribute it had previously defaulted on to win peace. Hereward's reputation was sealed. He was a warrior of great renown, a master tactician, and clever beyond the limits of his allies and enemies alike. He was all set for a return to England and a showdown with the man who had conquered the kingdom in Hereward's absence.

How much of this might be true is hard to discern. The campaigning and fighting is of the kind that was probably taking place in Europe throughout the period. Scaldemariland could be located in Zeeland (Holland). The *Vita S. Willibrordi* seems to describe the same campaign, an attack based on non-payment of taxes, from the perspective of the attacked. The son of the count of Flanders could be Robert the Frisian, second son of Baldwin V and later count himself. It seems likely that Hereward was transposed into some conflicts that had a basis in fact to cultivate his reputation and give him a background that would explain his actions on his return to England. Those setting down Hereward's tale needed a place to start, a way to explain his dramatic eruption onto the stage of English politics after the Norman Conquest. The confusion with Earl Leofric's son Ælfgar gave an authentic Anglo-Saxon flavour to the story. Mixing Hereward up in real local disputes across Ireland and the Low Countries added to the palpable sense of the forging of a genuine hero. Here was a new Beowulf, a hero who can outsmart his enemies, but who will crush them if brought to a fight. Ironically, the real Hereward was probably closer to the Scandinavian Beowulf than an Anglo-Saxon, usually used to mean English, hero.

Hereward had been absent from England when Duke William of Normandy invaded in 1066, defeating King Harold at the Battle of Hastings and taking the crown of England for himself. It seems likely that Hereward's journey back home falls around the year 1068. His motive for returning is two-fold, according to the *Gesta*. He had 'a strong desire to visit his father's and his country which by then was subject to the rule of foreigners and almost ruined by the exactions of many'. His second, much more altruistic and heroic reason was that if 'any of his friends or neighbours were still alive, he felt he would like to help them'.[14] On his return to his ancestral lands, Hereward is met with disaster. His father has died, his brother killed the day before Hereward's arrival, and Normans have snatched their properties. Hereward, stung by outrage and guilt, crept into his former home in the dark of night and slew the Normans within.

Now firmly in opposition to the new regime, Hereward gathered forty-nine men to his side quickly, and his numbers were swollen in the days that followed by 'fugitives, and condemned men as well as those that had been disinherited'.[15] As this band began to look to Hereward as their leader, he was nagged by the thought that he had never been knighted, a step he felt would qualify him to lead. Both the *Gesta* and *Crowland* state that Hereward travelled to Peterborough Abbey to be knighted by Abbot Brand, who *Crowland* calls Hereward's uncle, while a monk knighted his companions.[16] The *Gesta* adds the detail that even this was part of Hereward's rebellion. The Normans believed that a man knighted by a member of the clergy was not a true knight, so even as Abbot Brand gave him his sword and belt, Hereward was offering a challenge to the Norman ideals seeking to swamp England. There is doubt about whether Hereward was ever truly knighted, or whether this flourish was added to make him a more worthy and acceptable opponent to the Norman barons and new king of England than a mere thegn. The visit may well have taken place to renew the bonds that had existed between Peterborough Abbey and Hereward's father, Brand accepting Hereward as his man along with the rest of his band. Having obtained the rank of knight, if indeed he did, Hereward returned briefly to Flanders to visit his wife and two men described as his nephews, Siward the White and Siward the Red. During his stay he was invited to take part in a local tournament, impressing once more with his skill and strength.

Immediately after this, Hereward, having recruited more men to his cause, sailed back to England, taking his wife, Turfrida, with him. This second return may well have been in late 1069. No sources note Hereward as being involved in the revolt that year that ultimately led to the Harrying of the North. Edgar the Ætheling, who had been proclaimed the new Anglo-Saxon king in the wake of Hastings, became entangled in a plot to raise the country against William, aided by a Danish contingent. King Sweyn II of Denmark, a nephew of Cnut the Great, joined Edgar with a large contingent of Danish warriors, but the invasion ultimately floundered when William paid Sweyn off. In response to the betrayal, William descended on the region with a ferocity that left the area scarred for generations. Orderic Vitalis found himself unable to defend the king's behaviour. 'Never did William commit so much cruelty; to his lasting disgrace, he yielded to his worst impulse, and set no bounds to his fury, condemning the innocent and the guilty to a common fate.'[17] This outrage could have sparked Hereward's swift return to England, to act as the Conqueror's conscience and an avenging blade for the increasingly oppressed English.

The precise sequence of events that followed Hereward's return is difficult to unpick from contradictory sources. He and his followers seem to have quickly acquired a reputation as brigands around Peterborough and Ely. The country was ripe for rebellion, but William had crushed its will, so those able to continue to resist were found in small pockets and characterised as violent robbers. With Normans increasingly taking the lands of Anglo-Saxon men, there was no shortage of dispossessedand offended fighting men who could be harnessed to a cause. Hereward's story becomes inextricably linked to the Isle of Ely, a spit of solid land in a marshy region that was unpassable to any who did not know the terrain and its safe paths. It was nature's castle, providing a home to those seeking to escape the new stone monoliths erupting from the countryside to impose the Norman king's will.

In 1070, William made a move that was designed to cut off resources to those stubbornly resisting his authority. Monasteries and abbeys were 'plundered' by the king.[18] Their wealth was removed as an increasing number of Norman appointees replaced bishops and abbots who either died or were removed from office on charges of corruption.[19] In a time before banks, monasteries and abbeys could be used to deposit cash, plate and jewels. William, realising that those opposing him were probably using these institutions as a funding mechanism, cut it off from them.[20] Peterborough Abbey was one of those that received attention, quite possibly because of Hereward and his men's links to the abbey and Abbot Brand. *The Anglo-Saxon Chronicle* records that Hereward's uncle Brand died on 27 November 1069. The death, and appointment of a Norman, Turold, as the new abbot may also have been behind Hereward's decision to return to England to protect the abbey he was pledged to serve. Unwilling to accept what was happening, Hereward and his men attacked Peterborough Abbey.

The Anglo-Saxon Chronicle notes for the year 1070 that 'the monks of Peterborough heard say that their own men were wishing to plunder the monastery, namely, Hereward and his band, because they heard that the king had given the abbacy to a French abbot named Turold'. One of the wardens gathered together all of the gospels, copes, robes and anything else easily portable and fled to Turold during the night. The next day, Hereward and his men fell on Peterborough Abbey. When the monks refused to let them in, they began to set fire to the surrounding buildings. Eventually, they managed to break into the abbey and stole all that they could remove, including books, a gold crown from the head of a statue of Jesus, two golden shrines and nine silver ones. Leaving laden with the abbey's treasures, the men insisted 'they did this because of their loyalty to the monastery.'[21] Chroniclers, who were monks, would never accept the looting of one of their houses, yet there is some insistence, at least from the attackers, that the action was justified. If William had already seen to it that the money and goods of local Anglo-Saxon men had been removed, Hereward might have sought to take what he and his men were owed from the abbey's treasures rather than see them fall into Norman hands forever. *Ingulph's Chronicle* adds that Abbot Turold summoned the powerful Ivo Taillebois to avenge the abbey, but that he was taken prisoner in a pitched battle and ransomed for a handsome fee.[22]

The writer of *The Anglo-Saxon Chronicle* is also confident that Hereward was allied to the Danish forces brought by King Sweyn II, which would further reinforce the likelihood that Hereward was of Anglo-Danish descent. After the attack on Peterborough, where one surviving version of the narrative was penned, Hereward is noted as withdrawing or returning to the Isle of Ely. It is now, according to the writer, that King William comes to 'an agreement' with King Sweyn, paying him and his Danes to leave, and allowing them to take with them all the plunder they have gained.[23] If the timing is correct, it would have been a devastating blow to Hereward's operations, suddenly depriving him of an army. The increasing threat of the Anglo-Danish community joining forces with Sweyn and his invasion offered a powerful incentive to William to divide them. It would explain the favourable terms Sweyn was able to extract.

The Isle of Ely was a natural fortification, and so became a magnet to those opposed to William who saw their efforts floundering. If Hereward had not already been based at Ely, it was a fitting place to hide once his Danish allies had deserted him. Ely provided a focal point for the dispossessed, dissatisfied and outlawed alike. The two most senior figures noted as arriving on the Isle were earls Edwin and Morcar. Edwin had been Earl of Mercia since 1057, succeeding his father, Ælfgar. Edwin's younger brother Morcar was Earl of Northumberland, a title he had gained when King Harold Godwinson's brother Tostig had been exiled. Edwin and Morcar had supported efforts to make the Anglo-Saxon claimant Edgar the Ætheling king after Hastings but had quickly submitted to William when the cause appeared lost. In 1068, the brothers tried to raise a revolt in Mercia but lost their nerve when William moved against them. Edwin and Morcar's father was the same Ælfgar whose story may have provided some colour to Hereward's own, a confusion added to by Ælfgar's sons' involvement with Hereward at Ely. The brothers made for Ely as it became the epicentre of resistance to Norman rule, sneaking away from the royal court 'because King William wanted to put them in prison'.[24] The abbot there, Thurstan, was sympathetic because his own position was under threat as William tried to replace him with a Frenchman. Whether Edwin and Morcar's presence attracted Hereward or vice versa is unclear, but William must have been relieved that all his enemies were packing themselves together in one place. It made them easier to find and deal with, even if that place was the Isle of Ely.

The *Gesta* asserts that those already seeking sanctuary at Ely heard of Hereward's return to England and asked him to join them. After 'assuring him that he would in every way be most highly esteemed among them',

Hereward was made 'leader and commander-in-chief of these men'.[25] William saw his chance to encircle all remaining resistance and strangle it. Gathering his army, the new king marched towards Ely, and the stage was set for a final showdown. The romantic and heroic nature of the resistance offered by Hereward and his companions is summed up in a speech the *Liber Eliensis* claims Hereward gaveto galvanise his men.

> Now, brothers, be zealous for the liberty of your country and give your souls for the heritage bequeathed to you by your fathers, since we have been made trash and an object of contempt in the sight of all neighbouring kingdoms and regions, and it is better for us to die in war than look upon the evil afflictions of our race and our saints.[26]

When he arrived, William selected a spot called Alrehede to launch his assault. The fens that surrounded Ely were narrowest around here, pinched to just four furlongs, about half a mile. William ordered the construction of a causeway across which his army could march. It seemed a simple solution to the problem of reaching solid ground on the Isle. Trees were swiftly felled and lashed together to form a series of platforms. Sheepskins were carefully sewn up and inflated to provide buoyancy. In no time, a floating path across the impassable marshes was created, and the Normans rushed across.

It was a disaster. As the enthusiastic Normans piled onto the causeway, vying to be the first to reach the enemy, it collapsed beneath them. All those caught between Alrehede and Ely were dragged down into the marsh and drowned. Locals were able to pull clothing and weapons from the waters in the area for decades afterwards.[27] William left guards to prevent the rebels leaving the Isle, but withdrew to Brampton himself, stung by the loss of so many knights. Unbeknownst to the king, one Norman had survived, scrabbling onto the dry land of Ely. Dada was a trusted knight who was close to William. He was taken straight to Hereward, and rather than execute his foe, Hereward gave him a tour of the Isle. Dada was shown the defences erected around the Isle to protect it from assault. He was able to see the sheer number of men on the Isle, bristling with weapons and ready to fight any who made it across the marshes. The knight was even made welcome at a feast as Hereward's guest. After this, he was released, taken back across the fens to the king to report what he had witnessed.

When Dada reached William, he dutifully reported the scale of the opposition they faced and counselled the king to find terms to avoid conflict with the honourable Hereward. On hearing the knight's report, William 'contemplated making peace with them, for he was aware that the Isle of Ely was protected both by nature and by very brave men'.[28] As the king wavered, others amongst his counsellors were outraged. If, they warned, William allowed this resistance to go unchallenged or unpunished, it would encourage the whole kingdom to oppose him. Ivo Taillebois, who may already have been embarrassed by Hereward after the raid on Peterborough, assured the king that he knew of a woman who could singlehandedly bring down the rebels.

While William mulled over his options, Hereward snuck off the Isle and into the king's court. Disguised as a potter, he trimmed his hair and beard and put on a shabby, travel-worn coat. Hereward lodged with a widow at Brampton, where the woman employed by Taillebois also happened to be staying. Assuming he was an uneducated rustic, their plan was discussed in Latin, all understood and committed to memory by the potter in the corner. Next, Hereward wandered through the town pretending to sell pots until he managed to talk his way into the royal kitchens. Someone there almost recognised Hereward and had him sent to the king's hall as a spectacle. All marvelled at the resemblance, though they concluded he was significantly shorter than the mighty Hereward. After this distraction, the potter was sent back to the kitchens where the royal servants continued to make him an object of fun. They threatened to shave his head and pull out his beard before trying to blindfold him. They planned to scatter his pots around the floor and see how many he would break as he blindly stumbled. When Hereward refused to go along with them, one of the men punched him, and Hereward immediately returned the blow with devastating force. As the others moved against him, Hereward grabbed a fire iron and fended them off. A guard appeared, alerted by the ruckus, and tried to put the violent potter in fetters. Hereward took the soldier's sword and ran him through, killing several others as he made his escape.

Pursued into the night, Hereward evaded the Norman soldiers. When they were finally too exhausted to continue to chase, Hereward ambushed one, carelessly wandering alone, and disarmed him. The man was sent back to the court with instructions to explain to William all that had taken place: that Hereward had been in his kitchens, that the potter they thought looked like a shorter version of Hereward was the man himself, and that he had escaped. William was impressed when he heard the tale. He announced that he admired Hereward as 'a man of noble soul and a most distinguished warrior'.[29] The light-hearted response and compliments may point to grudging respect, but probably also covered up a deepening rage and seething determination to defeat Hereward. It certainly helped William make up his mind. He ordered fresh preparations for an assault on Ely.

The king instructed all local fisherman to bring their boats to Cotingelade (Cottenham Lode). There, they were loaded up with materials to be transported to Alreheche, the new sight of the Norman offensive. Hereward, now disguised as a fisherman, joined the convoy and watched all day as the Norman army toiled away crafting mounds that rose above the water level and siege machines to help them cross and breach the Isle. As evening fell and the tired Normans set down their tools to rest their aching bodies, Hereward set fire to everything they had built. As William watched it burn, he felt his face glow red, not with the heat, but the embarrassment of being tricked by Hereward again. He ordered his men that the rebel leader was to be brought before him alive, though whether this was to be shown respect or for the extraction of revenge was not disclosed.

The Normans renewed their efforts, erecting new mounds and palisades to make the area defensible as well as a platform for an assault. Wherever the men of Ely saw a Norman causeway approaching solid ground, they threw up defensive walls to prevent access to the Isle. It took eight days before William's forces were ready to launch a fresh offensive. Hereward's interference had made them cautious, and the tactics of those on the Isle slowed their progress further. The assault began with the production of the woman Ivo Taillebois had assured the king would win the day. Apparently against William's better judgement, and perhaps signalling his increasing desperation, he allowed Ivo to send his witch to the top of one of the wooden towers. The woman began to hurl abuse at those across the water on the Isle, berating them for their defiance. Next, she called out incantations designed to bring about their downfall before turning her back on them in disdain. The witch repeated her spell two more times, and when she had finished, there was a terrifying sound. Loud cracks rent the air and sent waves of panic through the watching Norman army. The alarm grew as they realised it was not the witch's spell causing the horrible noise.

During the ritual, Hereward and his men had been carefully making their way to selected spots in the marshes around the Norman constructions. As the witch completed her third cycle, they set fire to the reeds where they hid. The wind drove the flames towards the Normans, and as the heat intensified, brushwood and willow cracked noisily as it burned. The soldiers panicked and fled, but many were engulfed by flames, others falling into the treacherous pools to be dragged down by their armour. Still more were picked off by Hereward's archers. The witch, gripped by the same fear of the terrifying noise and the growing inferno, fell from her tower and lay dead on the ground. 'And thus,' *the Liber Eliensis* recorded, 'she who had come for the infliction of death upon other people, herself perished first, dead from a broken neck.'[30]

13

King William despaired of ever winning the Isle of Ely and bringing the rebels sheltered there to heel. He moved his court to Cambridge Castle, where he ordered the seizure of all the lands of the monastery at Ely beyond the Isle. The measure worked more fully than any assault. The monks flew into a desperate panic and sent word to the king that they wished to sue for peace. They offered to arrange access to the Isle of Ely for William and his army without Hereward's knowledge if the king would reverse his decision. Abbot Thurstan assured William that the people of the Isle would fall into line. They relied on Thurstan for guidance, and their morale was already low. The aftermath suggests the truth of an arrangement of this kind. The monastery was fined heavily for its defiance, but otherwise left alone, and the residents of the Isle suffered no vengeance from William either.

Although the fate of Earl Edwin is unclear, only the *Liber Eliensis* claims he was still at Ely by this point. Other writers report that he was killed travelling north to try and enlist the help of the king of Scots against William. There are suggestions that his own men betrayed him to the Normans, or that he was trapped by the tide near to the Wash and killed. Earl Morcar, though, was still at Ely. He appears to have been tempted by the offer of a pardon from William if he would give up and leave the Isle peacefully. Morcar, 'weakly listening to false representations', left Ely and appeared before the king 'in peaceable guise'.[31] He was immediately arrested and thrown into a prison cell. On his deathbed in 1087, William ordered the release of Morcar, along with other prisoners, but the new king, William Rufus, had the earl rearrested. He was imprisoned at Winchester, and his final fate is unrecorded. It is safe to assume he died in captivity at some point after 1087.

Finally, William was making progress in dealing with Ely and the rebels it sheltered. The *Gesta* reports that one of the monks, Alwinus, warned Hereward that his brothers were planning to betray the rebels and let William onto the Isle. A furious Hereward threatened to burn the church down, but Alwinus calmed him. Instead, the monk suggested he should plan for his escape in case William and the Normans did arrive. Agreeing, Hereward gathered boats at one of the wider stretches of water and called all his men to join him.[32] By the time William gained peaceful access to the Isle of Ely, Hereward had slipped away. The king had won part of the battle, but his greatest adversary had eluded his grasp once more. After fleeing Ely, Hereward took refuge in the Brunneswald. Although there has been confusion that Brunneswald might mean the woods around Bourne, this appears to be an effort to associate Hereward with that area again.

The Brunneswald was an ancient forest in Northamptonshire, around Newton Bromswold and about fifty miles west of Ely.

Unwilling to let go of his prey, William sent an army in pursuit of Hereward. At one point, the fugitives reversed the shoes on their horses to try and disguise their tracks.[33] Men began to flock to Hereward in his new woodland refuge, providing an early model for the later legends of Robin Hood. The Norman army was relentless, and eventually, when he thought he had enough men around him, Hereward decided they would have to confront the more numerous force. Laying his plans for the battle, the *Gesta* describes its hero 'in everything always leading the way'. Using the shelter provided by the trees, he employed guerrilla tactics to negate the numerical advantage of the Normans. Under cover of arrow fire, his men charged from the tree line, harried the Norman force and then vanished back to the security of the forest. The disorientated Normans endured the sporadic assaults for nine hours before they gave up and retreated, utterly unable to lay a blow on Hereward's men.[34]

Amongst those taken captive during the fighting was the abbot of Peterborough, who already had cause to dislike Hereward. All of the prisoners were well treated before being ransomed and released unharmed. Abbot Thorold immediately granted away large chunks of the abbey's lands to any knight who would accept the terms of service for holding it. The only requirement imposed was to hunt down Hereward. Feeling that his previous mercy and goodwill had been sorely repaid, Hereward launched another assault on Peterborough, burning the town, looting the Abbey and taking Thorold prisoner again. According to the *Gesta*, Hereward had a vision in his sleep that night. He saw 'a man of indescribable form, old, terrible of aspect, in all his clothing more remarkable than anything he had seen or imagined, threatening him with a great key which he carried in his hand'. Was it, perhaps, Saint Peter, who shared a name with the church that was the focus of Hereward's destruction? The man ordered Hereward to return all that he had taken or face a terrible death the next day. When he awoke, the fear-stricken Hereward freed Thorold, gave him back all the Abbey's treasure and left Peterborough in a hurry.[35]

On their way back to the Brunneswald, Hereward and his men became inexplicably lost during the night. A dog suddenly appeared amongst them and, lacking a better option, they followed it. When they came across the road again, strange fairies' lights attached themselves to their lances and could neither be removed nor extinguished. When dawn finally broke, the lights faded away, and the dog they had been following was revealed to be a wolf. The wild animal had led them to precisely where they had been trying to reach, and all thanked God for what they could only think was a miracle. Hereward had heeded the warning sent to him and restored himself to God's good grace. It was a worrying sign that things were beginning to go wrong, though. Driven from Ely, pursued by a Norman army, and incurring the Lord's displeasure was a stark contrast to Hereward's previous flamboyant and seemingly blessed successes. Hereward himself was conscious of what he felt had caused his change of fortune. It was at this time his wife, Turfrida, was reported to have become a nun at Crowland Abbey. Hereward had been unashamedly pursuing the rich and beautiful wife of an earl, and Turfrida had turned her back on him. This, Hereward insisted, was the turning point of all his good fortune.[36]

Suddenly willing to abandon his resistance, Hereward offered to appear before King William to negotiate terms for peace. When he arrived at court with forty of his tallest, strongest men, all presented in their finest arms and armour, William seemed impressed. They were lodged in the next town, just in case any trouble broke out, but when William went to watch Hereward's men march, his nobles were furious. They managed to convince a giant of a man named Ogger to challenge Hereward to a fight. Hereward was tall and strong, but Ogger was bigger. Exactly who he was is uncertain, but there was an Odger the Breton listed in Doomsday as a significant landowner in the area. Ogger taunted Hereward, who refused to be drawn into a fight. Eventually, the goading worked, and the two men met to fight a duel. They fought for hours, Hereward frequently suggesting that they end the pointless clash. Ogger took the protestations as a sign of weakness, or tiredness, or fear, and continued to attack. In the end, Hereward realised he had no option but to defeat his giant opponent, and so increased his effort level enough to overcome Ogger. It was far from easy, though, and Hereward's right arm was seriously wounded.[37]

The Norman lords, who had arranged the confrontation, ran to William to complain about Hereward's violence. The king was convinced to arrest Hereward, and he was given into the custody of Robert de Horepol. Hereward would languish in chains for a year at Bedford Castle. Some of the senior Anglo-Norman nobility, including the earl of Warenne, Robert Malet and Ivo Taillebois, always counselled William never to release Hereward from custody. Eventually, it was decided that Hereward would be handed over to Ivo Taillebois, a man with an axe to grind. Robert de Horepol protested. He had perhaps become fond of Hereward, as did all who spent any time with him. It may have been merely a rivalry with Taillebois, but whatever the reason, de Horepol seems to have tipped Hereward's men off about the transfer. When the exchange was being made, Hereward's companions burst onto the scene to free him. Hereward ordered that de Horepol and all his men were to be spared because they had treated him well. When Robert went before William to explain what had happened, he spoke up for his former prisoner, arguing that Hereward had been unjustly arrested while relying on the king's peace. He also delivered a message from the escapee. Hereward wished William to know that he was still willing to offer homage to the king in return for his father's lands. William agreed, accepting Hereward's submission and granting him the lands of his father on condition that 'henceforth he must be willing to cultivate peace, not folly, if he wished hereafter to retain the king's friendship'.[38]

> Thus Hereward the famous warrior, in many places proved and well known, was received into favour by the king, and with his father's lands and possessions lived afterwards for many years, faithfully serving King William, and wholly devoted to his neighbours and friends. And so at last he rested in peace, and upon his soul may God have mercy.[39]

Hereward's rebellion was over. He had earned the respect of William the Conqueror and recovered some of the status his family had enjoyed in Anglo-Saxon England. Given William's fearsome military reputation, anyone who, even for a while, got the better of him was worthy of note. Hereward's reputation grew in the centuries that followed until legend became layered on myth to create a national hero. Hereward the Wake, the last of the English, became the embodiment of fierce Anglo-Saxon resistance to the yoke of an oppressor. He was a prototype for later legendary figures like Robin Hood; evading the authorities, executing daring raids, getting the better of cruel men, romancing noble ladies, all to selflessly stand against tyranny.

It is both difficult and simple to see why the story of Hereward has evolved into the figure remembered by history. The difficulty lies in the disparity between the Hereward of fireside stories and the real historical figure. An Anglo-Saxon hero, he was far more likely to have been of Danish descent, part of the Viking settlement that followed Cnut. An Anglo-Dane who had made his home among the Anglo-Saxons. *The Last of the English* is a romantic notion applied, like the title *the Wake* with a healthy dose of bleary-eyed hindsight. The selflessness of Hereward's cause is also a later interpretation. Although chroniclers were keen to paint him as a popular hero, they were writing later, and the monks penning the accounts had a complaint about William's treatment of religious houses. The frequent references to the removal of abbots and seizure of treasure for the royal coffers attest to their abhorrence. Hereward seemed a suitable vehicle to offer William a little bit of a comeuppance.

In reality, Hereward's motives were not so altruistic, though they were clear and easy to understand. The cause of Hereward's initial outrage on his return from Europe was the seizure of his inheritance on the death of his father. The lands that he had expected to acquire were instead given to Norman interlopers as the spoils of victory. Having killed those he found at his ancestral home, Hereward became an outlaw. His final reconciliation with William came only when the Norman king agreed to let Hereward take possession of his inheritance. The months of rebellion and outwitting William were not born of some desire to improve the lot of those struggling beneath the yoke of Norman oppression. It was about land and money. The motive is entirely understandable, and perhaps part of the reason William reached terms with the rebel leader was that he was in danger of becoming something else. The longer Hereward frustrated the king, the more attractive his cause would look. It was at risk of becoming something romantic.

After his escape from custody, the need to end his resistance was magnified further. If Hereward could not be caught and punished, he at least had to be prevented from embarrassing William further and encouraging others to rebel. Once Hereward had what he wanted, he laid down his weapons and lived the remainder of his days in peace as a vassal of the Norman king. It was in the years that followed that Hereward's story, repeated, embellished, and slipping into the realms of myth, became a tale of English resistance to Norman rule. Hereward's exploits came to symbolise something beyond mere personal interest and greed, much as the legend of Robin Hood would.

The simplicity of Hereward's appeal lies in this amorphous version of his story. Stripped of selfish motivation, he became a vehicle for the complex feelings in England about the Norman Conquest. Monks who committed his story to writing probably made far more effort to dig through to an authentic version of Hereward than minstrels and wandering storytellers would. For both, and those listening or reading, Hereward became a vehicle for working through what the Norman Conquest meant for those at the sharp end. He had walked a fine line by defying the king, but not defeating him. A match for the Conqueror, Hereward found a way to live in peace on terms both could accept. Ultimately, Hereward won because he got what he had wanted all along, and William had been forced to give it to him. The victory was in choosing to stop fighting, accepting the new order and taking up a place within it. The Conquest was only successful because Hereward allowed it to be. In his role as a native, Anglo-Saxon or

Anglo-Danish landowner, Hereward came to represent the entire nation. His victory became that of all England. The Normans had not really conquered England. The English had allowed them to rule, as much on terms set by the English as by the Normans. It was a fantasy through which a crushing defeat and occupation could be rebranded and made palatable.

For those nobles who dominated England in the centuries that followed, Hereward offered a path to smooth integration with English society as it changed over the decades and centuries that followed Hastings. If Hereward, that immovable pillar of English resistance, could accept Norman rule and show that it could be a comfortable canopy to live under, so could everyone else, without a loss of honour. Nowhere is the use of Hereward plainer than in his adoption by the Wake family, Anglo-Norman landowners in Bourne. By declaring Hereward one of their own, they staked a claim to a perceived Anglo-Saxon heritage and an empathy with Hereward's cause that made their acceptance in the local area much easier.

The Conquest only succeeded because the English allowed it to do so. As Norman families became integrated into English society, as Hereward's Danish forebears had, they developed a desire to identify themselves with their new home. As the Channel became an increasingly divisive border and Continental lands drifted from English control, Anglo-Normans sought local English heroes to identify with. Hereward represented a fierce independence, a determined resolution to have, and to fight for, what was wrongfully taken. The English would, periodically, take that attitude back across the Channel in the centuries that followed, attempting to conquer and re-conquer lands they claimed should have always been theirs, sometimes to devastating effect. Hereward sums up all that the English think of as quintessentially English. Yet he was an Anglo-Danish rebel, presented as the pinnacle of English military and tactical ability, adopted by a Norman family as an ancestor. Alongside the defiance, uncrushable will, strength and cunning, it is perhaps a mixed heritage, a wilful refusal to accept the superiority of others and a need to create victory from any defeat that makes Hereward, and all of us, English.

Chapter 2

The Anarchy

*If a house be divided against itself, that house
cannot stand.*

Mark 3:25

After Hereward reached his terms with the Conqueror, there was an uneasy
peace in England. The social and administrative changes that followed
the Norman conquest radically altered the kingdom but became the new
legal and political landscape. William I was succeeded by his second son,
William II, known as William Rufus, in 1087. The oldest surviving son
Robert was given the duchy of Normandy, the family's patrimony, and the
youngest, Henry, was bequeathed cash with which to make his way in the
world. Rufus ruled for thirteen years until his death in 1100. His military
success mingled with a lack of the expected social graces of a king to create
a complex reputation. By the time he was hit by an arrow during a hunting
trip to the New Forest, Rufus was unpopular, primarily due to his ability to
extract money from his nobles and the church.

Robert, Duke of Normandy, who had the senior claim to the throne of
England, was on his way back from the Holy Land when his brother died.
Henry, who had been literally on the scene, rode with all haste to Winchester,
secured the royal treasury there, then sped to London to have himself crowned
at Westminster Abbey. King Henry I met the predictable backlash from his
brother head-on, and the two spent the first years of Henry's reign at war.
Robert was eventually captured at the Battle of Tinchebray on 28 September
1106. He would pass his remaining twenty-eight years as his little brother's
prisoner in England and Wales. As Duke of Normandy as well as King of
England, Henry reunited the territories his father had held under one ruler.
Landowners who held properties on both sides of the Channel had a preference
for a single ruler since it avoided the question of divided loyalties highlighted
by the fighting between Robert and Henry. Supporting one meant defying the
other and inevitably placed lands on one side of the Channel at risk of seizure.

Henry I ruled for thirty-five years. Viewed with hindsight as a time
of peace and prosperity, the youngest son of the Conqueror was a hard

ruler who spent much of his time at war, primarily in Normandy. His reign was irreparably scarred by the White Ship Disaster of 25 November 1120. Although Henry holds the record for the most illegitimate children fathered by an English or British monarch with at least twenty-four, he had only one son and one daughter who were legitimate. Matilda, the elder child, was married at the age of 8 to Holy Roman Emperor Henry V in 1110. William Adelin was 17 when he and a clutch of his companions made a fateful, drunken crossing of the Channel. Henry's ship had sailed first, and the young courtiers were to join William on board the White Ship. Its master boasted of its speed, and the intoxicated young men and women on board shoved to get the oars and encouraged the captain to try and overtake the king's ship. Having barely set sail, they hit a rock, tearing a hole in the hull and swiftly sinking the White Ship. Only a butcher survived the wreckage, and a boy was forced to break the news to Henry when no one else dared. The distraught king was forced to deal with a succession crisis amid his grief.

Henry's response was to cause his nobles to swear oaths that they would recognise and support his daughter Matilda, who now styled herself Empress (though she was not technically eligible to use the imperial title). When the Holy Roman Emperor died in 1125, the widowed Matilda was remarried in 1128 to Geoffrey, son of the count of Anjou. Matilda was furious. Geoffrey was ten years her junior at 15, and she viewed him as a definite step down in prestige, refusing to drop the title of her first husband. Her father had no sympathy. When Matilda left Geoffrey, Henry sent her right back again. The king knew that female rule was problematical, to say the least. He hoped for a grandson that would allow his nobles to see beyond Matilda, who would only be a caretaker at most. Henry was 60 when the marriage took place, and although in robust health, he knew time was running out. With every passing year, he was less likely to live long enough to hand his crown to a grown-up grandson.

It was five years into the marriage before a child arrived. Named Henry for his grandfather, it was what the king had been hoping for. Another son, Geoffrey, followed the next year and Matilda was soon pregnant for the third time. The king, though, would not live to see his third grandson born. Henry died on 1 December 1135 in Normandy, on the brink of open warfare with his daughter and son-in-law. Empress Matilda's pregnancy and the ongoing issues on the Norman border meant that she was unable to move to claim her inheritance. Instead, she was forced to rely on the oaths given by her father's nobles. Just as Henry had done in 1100, another moved swiftly to make his own bid. The fact that he was a *he* is significant. Stephen of Blois, Count of

Boulogne was Henry I's favourite nephew. The son of Henry's sister Adela, Stephen had been raised at Henry's court, making a good impression on his uncle and being showered with lands in England and Normandy.

Stephen claimed that on his deathbed, Henry had bequeathed his kingdom and duchy to his nephew because of the growing rift with Empress Matilda. He took ship from Boulogne and managed to have himself crowned King of England on 22 December, just three weeks after Henry's death. For many in England, there was a strong appeal to Stephen. He was well known to them, unlike the distant Empress Matilda. It was believable that Henry had disinherited his daughter as their relationship crumbled. Stephen even produced witnesses to swear that it was true. As law and order broke down in the wake of Henry's death, a king was needed to restore the king's peace, and Stephen pledged to do it swiftly. The Scots were already across the border in the north, and fear was increasing that they might march south unopposed. A king was needed to raise and lead an army. Quickly. Perhaps beyond all these reasons, or excuses, Stephen was something Empress Matilda could never be. Henry had known female rule would be a difficult sell. There were inherent problems with leading armies and requiring noblemen to be subservient to a woman. England, like many other medieval kingdoms, had not really grappled with those questions yet, and for most, they were best avoided. Stephen solved all the problems of Henry's arrangements for the succession, and so was warmly welcomed.

Normandy initially turned to Stephen's older brother Theobald, Count of Blois, offering him the duchy. Like England, there was little appetite to have Empress Matilda in charge. When news reached them that Stephen had been crowned King of England, the Norman nobility dropped Theobald, who slunk away scalded, in favour of keeping one lord on both sides of the Channel. Stephen quickly pushed the Scots back, his lightening manoeuvres around the kingdom becoming a trademark that constantly caught his enemies unawares. All seemed to have gone incredibly well for Stephen. Empress Matilda still made no real move, and one chronicler gave him a glowing reference: 'For this same man was by far the dearest of all his nephews to King Henry the peacemaker, not only because of the close family relationship but also because he was peculiarly eminent for many conspicuous virtues.'[1]

Empress Matilda, though, had not forgotten what she was due. Her husband Geoffrey would begin slow, careful efforts to gain control of Normandy. He never showed any interest in England, wary of overreaching himself, and in Normandy, he was more concerned with his own claim as the duchy's conqueror than his wife's as its rightful ruler. The problems that would soon dog England and Normandy were highlighted as early as 1136. Baldwin de Redvers, a landowner in south-west England, seized the castle at Exeter. The townsfolk appealed to Stephen that Baldwin was 'loudly threatening fire and sword against all who did not yield to his presumption'.[2] Stephen duly arrived with Robert, Earl of Gloucester amongst his force. Robert was the oldest and favourite illegitimate son of Henry I. He had given homage to Stephen despite the claims of his half-sister the empress. After months of siege, the castle surrendered, and Stephen allowed those within to leave. Baldwin next took Carisbrooke Castle on the Isle of Wight, but when Stephen appeared at Southampton with an army, the recalcitrant rebel fled across the Channel.

Baldwin sought out Geoffrey and offered to help win Empress Matilda's inheritance. Nobles and wealthy landowners always rebelled from time to time. There was nothing new in that. The problem in 1136 was the existence of an alternative monarch to whom allegiance could be transferred. Stephen was unable to effectively punish and cut off those who opposed him because they had a ready-made home for their disaffection at Empress Matilda's court. In the spring of 1137, Stephen felt confident enough of his control in England to travel to Normandy. His younger brother Henry, Bishop of Winchester had been sent ahead and had witnessed the problems dogging the duchy in the absence of a leader. Empress Matilda and her husband Geoffrey had been raiding the southern borders every year since 1134, leaving homes in ashes and people in fear. A severe drought such as 'no one in our times has witnessed before' also threatened the duchy, though it appears to have been a widespread problem.[3] *The Anglo-Saxon Chronicle* reported similar misery in England at the same time.[4]

The positive note was that Stephen had not been required to visit Normandy to assert his right to rule or his dominance. The duchy had readily accepted the king of England as the new duke of Normandy without a passing thought to Empress Matilda's claim. The constant assaults conducted by her husband can hardly have nurtured warm feelings toward the wife of the Angevin count. In truth, Stephen's swift action in England had won Normandy, with the barons' preference for a single ruler. Now, they needed to see some of the other side of Stephen's work in England. They required those threatening their borders to be firmly pressed back. There were some formalities to deal with first. Stephen met with his brother Theobald on 25 March. Any lingering resentment about missing out on Normandy, and perhaps even England, to his little brother, was softened by a pension of 2,000 marks a year. Stephen then met King Louis VI of France to receive recognition of his right to rule Normandy as a fief of the

French crown. Stephen's son Eustace performed the homage required since kings were averse to submitting to other kings. A peace was also agreed that would leave Stephen free to deal with Count Geoffrey.

In May 1137, Angevin forces attacked Exmes and headed towards Caen. The direction was significant because Caen was the Norman seat of Robert, Earl of Gloucester, Empress Matilda's half-brother. Despite the suspicion that the move was a signal of an arrangement that Robert would defect, Caen held firm. Whether this was at Robert's instruction or contrary to it is not known, but the earl may have judged that the time was not yet right to rally to his sister's cause. Stephen ordered a muster at Lisieux, planning to defy the accepted traditions of twelfth-century warfare by trying to force a pitched battle. Convention advised against the unpredictability of a confrontation, in which greater numbers and advantageous terrain were still no guarantee of victory. A nobleman who was captured risked financial ruin to ransom himself, and there was no certainty of avoiding death, even if it was rarely the aim of the enemy. No such thought was given to the general soldiery who were unlikely to be worth ransoming. Siege warfare was the preferred method of engagement; a tactical game of brinkmanship and attrition with clearly defined rules of engagement and ways to bring it to an end. When a scuffle broke out between some Norman soldiers and Flemish mercenaries, it was all the excuse many Norman barons needed to walk away from the muster. Embarrassingly, Stephen was forced to chase his own men in a bid to convince them to return, but they would not.

Stephen agreed a two-year truce with Count Geoffrey that at least brought some respite to Normandy. The tour of 1137 was to be Stephen's only visit to Normandy throughout his reign, but it had been relatively successful. He had been unable to win over barons nervous at the thought of a pitched battle, but that was a cultural caution he would have faced anywhere. Theobald had been placated, and Louis had formally recognised Stephen's right to rule Normandy. There would be two years of peace to end four years of border raids, giving the duchy time to recover from the ravages of assaults and the problems caused by the drought. There was also caution to be taken from the visit too. The issue with Count Geoffrey, and by extension with Empress Matilda, had not been resolved, merely put off for another time. Robert of Gloucester was under increasing suspicion which risked driving him into his sister's camp if, as Stephen suspected, he was not already waiting for the right time to declare for her. The Norman barons had not been willing to bend to Stephen's will where it conflicted with their own ideas of accepted military tactics. Normandy was bound to Stephen by the crown of England, a tie that might slip all too easily. Trouble in England drew Stephen away in November, making it clear which was considered the more important. The monk-chronicler Orderic Vitalis was unimpressed by Stephen's brief visit and lack of tangible success in the duchy. Many doubtless shared his view.

Problems escalated for Stephen just after Whitsun 1138. Earl Robert would later claim that he had been the target of an assassination attempt while he had been in Normandy with the king. The leader of the bid to take his life had supposedly been William of Ypres, one of Stephen's Flemish mercenary captains. Whether the attempt was real or not, or whether it was a literary device to package up the slow disintegration of the relationship between the two men, it was Robert's excuse to make his move. The earl issued a *diffidatio* – a formal revocation of the homage he had given to Stephen. Technically, the statement meant Robert was no longer Stephen's vassal and therefore both beyond his control and incapable of committing treason against the king. It neatly cleared the way for Robert to return to the oath he had given previously to support his half-sister on their father's death without the loss of honour involved in rebelling against a liege lord. The touchpaper was ignited, and Bedford soon exploded into rebellion. Earl Robert remained in Normandy but sent word to all his men in England to begin active opposition to the king. Stephen marched to Robert's stronghold at Bristol Castle but soon realised the fortress was all but impossible to take.

There was already division amongst those with Stephen, too. At Bristol, some counselled him to pursue a siege no matter how long it took or what it cost. They advised him to blockade the River Avon to prevent supplies reaching the city, and even to dam it to try to flood Bristol. Others almost immediately told the king he had no hope of taking the fortress. Trying would waste time and money, and the failure would prove more embarrassing for every day he had tried his hardest. Without the benefit of hindsight, Stephen was forced to weigh the contradictory opinions being offered. He elected to abandon Bristol and instead aimed to make some quick attacks on softer targets in the hope that it would discourage those considering joining the rebels. Castle Cary was snatched from Ralph Lovel and Harptree Castle was taken from William FitzJohn, but the problems created by the focus on Bristol, and Stephen's decision to leave it alone, would not go away. Earl Robert now represented an ability to stand against Stephen successfully, and a location the king deemed impenetrable from which those opposed to his rule might challenge him. Bristol was offered up as a magnet to any who wished to stand against Stephen. A king would always face dissent. His security lay in his ability to bring his nobility to heel swiftly, effectively, and ideally with a resolution all could accept. More worrying for Stephen was the fracture appearing within his court. There was suspicion that those who had advised leaving Bristol alone had done so out of sympathy for Earl Robert and that meant for his half-sister, Empress Matilda.[5] Already, as the king cast his eye around those he needed to trust, he was wondering who was really with him and who was waiting for the right moment to swap cause. The real poison of Earl Robert's *diffidatio* and Empress Matilda's refusal to ignore her rights was beginning to work on the body of Stephen's kingdom. Those who opposed him had a viable rival to whom they could give their allegiance. With his ability to discipline his barons compromised by their ability to simply switch their support to Empress Matilda, he was hamstrung. A heavy hand would drive more to Matilda's cause. A soft one would open up the kingdom to chaos and anarchy.

To add to Stephen's problems, King David of Scotland crossed the River Tees in July 1138 to stake a claim to swathes of northern England. The chronicler Henry of Huntingdon voiced the traditional fears of those in the north when the Scots rampaged across the border: 'They ripped open pregnant women, tossed children on the points of their spears, butchered priests at the altars, and, cutting off the heads from the images on crucifixes, placed them on the bodies of their victims.'[6] With the king kept busy in the south-west, the resistance to the Scots invasion was delegated to Thurstan, Archbishop of York. It was an interesting move that not only took the sting out of competing local rivals who might vie for superiority within the army but cast the campaign as something of a crusade against the large Pictish contingent in David's force.

Thurstan arrayed his army at Northallerton, some thirty miles north of York, where he would make his stand. A cart was placed on top of a hill with a ship's mast mounted to it. On the pole were displayed banners of St Peter, local saints St John of Beverley and St Wilfrid of Ripon as well as other conspicuous religious symbols. The image of the coming fight as a holy crusade on English soil was heightened to a peak. Three hours after the fighting began on 22 August 1138, a reported 11,000 Scots had been killed with just a handful of English casualties. David's son Prince Henry had tried to lead a valiant cavalry charge, 'heedless of what his countrymen were doing', but it failed as the Scots army crumbled.[7] The English saw no need to pursue the fleeing Scots, and many were found by locals wandering lost in woods and fields, where they were killed on sight. King David fled back across the Scots border. Disparagingly known locally as the Battle of Bagmoor because of the amount of baggage the Scots army was forced to abandon, the victory became more widely remembered as the Battle of the

Standard. Despite Stephen's absence, it represented a tangible demonstration of his authority in the north as well as his ability to delegate effectively.

Stephen's wife, Queen Matilda, was also proving a firm buttress to her husband's rule. The daughter of the count of Boulogne, she, like her namesake Empress Matilda, was a niece of King David of Scotland, making David's assertions that he invaded England only to champion his family's rights ring a little less clear. While Stephen was occupied in the west by Earl Robert and Thurstan was driving away David's threat, Queen Matilda was also busy. She oversaw a siege at Dover Castle, arranging the assault on the land side as her family in Boulogne sent ships to blockade it from the sea. Earl Robert had thought Dover Castle would make an ideal landing point for an invasion of England, but he was denied the foothold by the queen's sterling work. The monk Orderic Vitalis, who wrote a chronicle of Normandy and its affairs, was clear that Dover Castle fell only because of the queen's efforts. Although the opposition that sprang up in all fronts was a severe problem for Stephen, he could take comfort in the abilities of those he trusted. The delegation of his authority to tackle geographically dispersed threats was remarkable and stood his cause in good stead. The trials the king faced were not lost on the anonymous writer of the *Gesta Stephani*. 'It was like what we read of the fabled hydra of Hercules; when one head was cut off two more grew in its place.' Stephen rushed about his kingdom with an army always in tow, resolutely facing every threat that emerged, 'and like another Hercules he always girded himself bravely and unconquerably to endure each'.[8]

Earl Robert found the going harder than he hoped, and support for his half-sister proved hard to come by. There was no excited flocking to the cause he now espoused, but rather 'Robert found that in England the nobles were either hostile or gave no help.'[9] When the Second Lateran Council met in April 1139 to try to resolve the issues surrounding a schism, Empress Matilda tried to win papal support for her claim to Stephen's throne. Ulger, Bishop of Angers was sent to make the case for Matilda's rights in Normandy and England. It was claimed that Stephen had defrauded Matilda of her inheritance and that the oaths given to her before her father's death held precedence over the fealty received by Stephen when he became king. Geoffrey may have been willing to try to press his wife's claims as a result of the failures of his military efforts, though he would never show any concerted interest in England. His real concern was the conquest of Normandy. Having tried and found it all but impossible, sending Bishop Ulger represented an effort to adjust his tactics and press his wife's claim to be the legitimate heir to Normandy. If it worked, he would get the duchy in any case as her husband. It was, Geoffrey concluded, worth a go. For Empress Matilda, it represented an opportunity to take her complaint onto the international stage. Unseating a crowned king, with all of the religious significance of a coronation behind him, was all but impossible, but the duchy of Normandy remained attainable. Even if she were not successful, she would at least ensure her cause was not forgotten.

Stephen sent Arnulf, Archdeacon of Sées to offer his response. When Arnulf took the floor, he made the shocking claim that Empress Matilda was illegitimate and therefore could not be her father's heir. Rather than try to counter the arguments set forth by Ulger, Stephen's camp simply bypassed them all and launched a direct assault on Matilda's capability to rule. Illegitimacy had become more of a barrier to power than it had been in the days of William the Conqueror, who had himself been a bastard. This was even more acutely true in the case of a crown, with all the religious significance attached to kingship. Earl Robert might have been a viable, even preferable, candidate to succeed his father, but his status as an illegitimate son had always been understood, not least by Robert himself, to be an absolute bar. The allegation was not invented for this moment. It was a rumour that had been in circulation for many years. The story was that Henry I's wife Matilda of Scotland had been a confirmed nun during her time at Wilton Abbey in the care of her aunt Christina. When Henry became king, he had abducted Matilda from the abbey to marry her, thereby giving his kingship the Anglo-Saxon credentials offered by Matilda's descent from the House of Wessex. Since she had been a nun, Henry could not legally marry Empress Matilda's mother, making their children illegitimate. Gilbert Foliot, abbot of Gloucester, was present at the proceedings and would later write that he was unsure whether the charge was valid or not, but stated that in his belief, the blessing bestowed at the wedding by the archbishop of Canterbury removed any stain of impropriety anyway.[10]

Pope Innocent II, faced with a delicate dilemma that risked upsetting one powerful faction or the other, and which spoke directly to the sanctity of kingship, tried to sidestep the issue. Although he sent written confirmation of Stephen's titles as King of England and Duke of Normandy, he did not actually try the case but threw it out. This meant that Empress Matilda's claim was not dismissed or ruled to be faulty in any way. Stephen was reinforced because Rome had already recognised his kingship and was unwilling to open the papacy up to accusations of making mistakes. In reality, Innocent made the problem worse, because both sides could claim a victory and neither had lost. English and Norman politics was a lamb sacrificed to Rome's need to appear unimpeachable and disinclination to upset powerful temporal lords. In this case, the fact that Geoffrey's father was currently sitting on the throne of Jerusalem was not far from Innocent's mind.

The unsatisfactory outcome at the papal court led Empress Matilda to radically adjust her tactics. Rebellion by proxy, through her husband or half-brother, had failed. Legal avenues had offered no succour. All that remained was rebellion in person. In September 1139 she launched an invasion of England. For four years, she had sat tight while her husband tried to press her claims militarily and failed. She had endured the flimsy vacillations of the pope that had allowed her to be branded illegitimate before the case had been tossed aside unresolved. Never devoid of the resolute spirit of adventure her father had been praised for, Empress Matilda decided to take matters into her own hands. A man, deprived of his rights and taking to the field to fight for them, would have garnered admiration, praise and followers. Things were different for a woman, though.

In August, Baldwin de Redvers, the first rebel against Stephen's rule, landed in the south-west. The plan was to use his connections there to secure Wareham Castle as a landing spot for the empress. Wareham sat nestled in a natural bay in Dorset, opposite Bournemouth and Poole. It was almost directly south of Bristol, so offered easy access to the emerging centre of her cause as well as a line of communication and supply back to her husband. Baldwin's old friends let him down, though. He was pressed back to Corfe, and though he managed to secure that castle, it was too far inland to be any use as a bridgehead. Undaunted, Empress Matilda amended her plans. On 30 September, she arrived at Arundel Castle near Worthing on the south coast with Earl Robert. Arundel was held by William d'Aubigny, Earl of Sussex (sometimes referred to as Earl of Arundel). William was married to Adeliza of Louvain, the young widow of Henry I. A year younger than Matilda, Adeliza was the dowager queen and the empress's stepmother. It is unclear whether William and Adeliza knew the controversial visitors were coming or what their purpose was. Adeliza perhaps hoped to offer her services to find a resolution to the tension between the cousins. If Matilda hoped her presence would ignite the faintly smouldering embers of her cause in England, she was in for a sharp disappointment.

The mountainous problems a woman faced in trying to claim power were neatly highlighted by the writer of the *Gesta Stephani*. He explained that Earl Robert 'landed at the castle of Arundel, as though he were merely to be a guest there and was admitted with a strong body of troops'.[11] All eyes were on Earl Robert. As the man, he was perceived as the military threat that had landed. There were concerns that he might launch his own bid for the throne, and that was deemed a much more significant threat to Stephen than Empress Matilda was. Earl Robert, for reasons he never explained, consistently rejected the notion. Whether because he felt bound by his oath to the empress or because he was pragmatic enough to understand that his illegitimacy would always prevent a successful claim, it was not an option he entertained. The problem was diverting everyone else's attention to the real reason they had come to England.

Almost as soon as they arrived, Earl Robert left Arundel to head west. His departure was well-timed, perhaps deliberately so, because Stephen arrived outside Arundel Castle with his characteristic speed. It was a disappointment to the empress that her cause was not widely embraced once she had landed. Stephen's appearance with an army reinforced his control of England, but he found himself confronted with an awkward problem. Earl Robert was a legitimate target, a former subject who had renounced his allegiance and now invaded Stephen's kingdom. But Robert was gone. Inside the castle was someone who was laying claim to Stephen's crown, and his duchy across the Channel, without an army, and a guest of one of Stephen's barons. It was ideally set up to bring the matter to an end once and for all. Except for one thing. Stephen's opponent was a woman. Attacking a lady, who was also his cousin and the daughter of the last king, was dishonourable and risked incurring criticism. Stephen was stopped in his tracks. What followed attracted the criticism of contemporaries and later observers alike.

Empress Matilda was permitted to leave Arundel under a safe-conduct. Stephen's brother Henry, Bishop of Winchester was tasked, along with Waleran, Count of Meulan, with escorting Matilda west. The apparent generosity was, in fact, a response to Stephen's chivalric duty. William of Malmesbury explained that if the supply of an escort is required, 'it is not the custom of honourable knights to refuse to anyone, even their bitterest enemy'.[12] Empress Matilda was not a valid target for Stephen to attack, and the only proper response was to assist a lady in need. The arrangement has been viewed ever since as a display of Stephen's weakness and foolishness. However, had he assaulted Arundel Castle to get to Empress Matilda, he would have been viewed as a dishonourable, unchivalrous tyrant. The solution was not without its benefits. Stephen had faced threats in all corners of his domains before. Shepherding all of his opponents together in one place, even if it was the impenetrable Bristol, stopped them flanking him or seeking to spread their rebellion further. Once Matilda was with Earl Robert, she was also standing beside a viable target and would lose the protection Arundel had afforded her. Matilda's own dissatisfaction with the aftermath of her landing is displayed by the lack of time she spent at Bristol. She quickly moved to Gloucester, where the castellan Miles of Gloucester welcomed her, allowing her to take possession of a symbolically important royal castle that proudly and loudly proclaimed her intentions.

The arrival of Empress Matilda in England marked the real ignition point of the dynastic conflict for the crown. The dynamic of two rulers, both claiming to be legitimate and demanding the fealty of the country's barons, was problematic. Stephen was king, both in fact, as demonstrated by his ability to govern and raise men, and in law, having undergone a coronation and received papal confirmation. Empress Matilda claimed the throne as her right, as the heir to her father, the previous king, and based on the binding oaths sworn to her by the English barons. Even the pope had sidestepped the question of who was right and who was wrong. Now, the nobility of England were forced to try to confront the problem. Stephen's reign has been dubbed The Anarchy, the first civil war in post-Conquest England, but who were the rebels?

Stephen was sure that as a properly selected and anointed king, Empress Matilda, her half-brother Earl Robert and anyone who joined them at Bristol were outlaws. Empress Matilda insisted that Stephen was a usurper and that the oaths sworn to her before her father's death took precedence over those offered later to Stephen. To her and those who followed her cause, Stephen and his men were rebels. For the barons, it was a tricky process of balance. A few, like Earl Robert and Miles of Gloucester, nailed their colours firmly to Matilda's standard. Most, however they might have felt in private, remained publicly loyal to Stephen. As king, it was he who could deprive them of lands, try them in his courts, and ruin their families if they stepped out of line. However the wider barony felt about Matilda's cause, it was simply too flimsy and too riddled with unanswerable questions to make the leap to her side. A misogynistic, patriarchal society wondered whether a woman was able to rule. A queen, as the wife of a king, had a specific role, a set of expectations, and a framework of power within which to operate. A female king was something different. Men would be forced to make themselves subservient to a woman. One of a king's primary roles was to lead armies into battle. A woman could not discharge that critical function. If Earl Robert was her military leader, then was he, in reality, closer to being king than she would be? Until these issues were resolved, few would be willing to renounce their allegiance to Stephen and join Empress Matilda. The decision was made even easier by the muted response her arrival produced, in part because of those central problems.

The king could not ignore the presence within his borders of a rival who claimed his throne, however her cause stalled and misfired. Stephen had delegated authority to a local level after the victory at the Battle of the Standard. He created earls in York, Derby, Worcester, Bedford, and Pembroke. Their responsibilities were primarily military, maintaining peace and order in their region. Two men became central pillars of Stephen's government. The Beaumont twins came from a family that held power on both sides of the Channel. Robert had acquired their father's English earldom at Leicester and Waleran the Norman title Count of Meulan. Their brother Hugh had become earl of Bedford, and other relatives were rising sharply in political and ecclesiastical offices. The presence of a rival began to cause problems for Stephen even amongst those loyal to him as they spied opportunities for further advancement at the expense of others who stood in their way.

Roger, Bishop of Salisbury set out to attend the king's court on a warm morning in June 1139, just before Empress Matilda's landing. He was worried. Although he was uncertain why, the idea of the journey made him nervous.[13] Roger had risen high in the service of the last king since he had impressed Henry as a priest in Caen. Plucked up and propelled to high office as lord chancellor once his patron took the throne, Roger had become bishop of Salisbury, and had run the country in Henry's frequent absences. A pioneer of the Exchequer form of finance, his ability and position brought influence and wealth. His family reaped the rewards. One nephew became bishop of Lincoln and another bishop of Ely and treasurer. Despite his close association with Henry I and oaths sworn to his daughter, Bishop Roger was quick to recognise Stephen as king. He claimed that Henry's failure to consult about Matilda's second marriage to the count of Anjou had been in direct breach of a condition of the oaths of allegiance to her.

The claim of Henry's daughter to Stephen's throne placed Bishop Roger under suspicion. Alongside this, the bishop's family stood in the way of the further rise of the Beaumont faction. The emerging conflict offered the opportunity to sow seeds of doubt and clear a path for those ruthless enough to take it. The *Gesta Stephani* suggests Bishop Roger was planning to put his considerable weight behind Matilda when the moment was right.[14] As tensions heightened on all sides, a flashpoint drew ever closer. Whether Roger was worried about making his journey to court because he was plotting, or because he knew the Beaumont twins were whispering in Stephen's ear, or because uncertainty breeds paranoia is unclear. His fears caused him to travel with a sizeable armed retinue, which only made things appear worse. The spark was a brawl in an Oxford tavern over lodging space. Roger's soldiers quarrelled with the men of Alan, Count of Brittany, and though the bishop's contingent drove off their rivals, one of their number was left dead, and Stephen reacted sharply to the breach of peace within his court. There were rumours that Waleran Beaumont had planned the scene to get Roger into trouble.[15] If so, it worked.

Bishop Roger and his nephew Alexander, Bishop of Lincoln, were arrested. Roger's other nephew Nigel, Bishop of Ely, had not arrived yet, and when news of the arrests reached him, he fled to his uncle's castle at Devizes. A row immediately erupted about the arrests. Stephen's brother Henry, Bishop of Winchester, complained that it was for canon law to judge men of the church, not the king or any secular authority. Others argued that Roger had built castles 'in defiance of the canon law' and so deserved to lose them.[16] Stephen was quick to characterise the arrests as political measures; he was disciplining men as his servants and castellans, not as bishops, for purely secular offences. The king demanded that the bishop hand over his castles, a standard practise in Normandy but not in England. Roger refused. Stephen laid siege to Devizes and eventually Roger ordered his nephew to surrender. Nigel returned to Ely but quickly sought to use the Fens as a base for rebellion, just as Hereward had done a century earlier. Stephen stormed the Isle of Ely with a devastating effectiveness that had evaded William the Conqueror. Nigel was forced to flee. He found his way to the empress at Bristol, 'where all those who attacked the king had assembled as though it were a receptacle of filth'.[17]

The arrest of the bishops marked a turning point in Stephen's reign. The suspicion that the king had orchestrated the whole affair with the Beaumont twins made others wary of his intentions and his integrity. On the other hand if, as some clearly suggested, Roger was plotting against the king, Stephen had to deal with him. The conflict of jurisdiction between the crown and Church was a hot coal throughout Europe, but Stephen added it to the mounting list of problems he faced. The arrival of Empress Matilda within a few months must have confirmed many of Stephen's suspicions. His swift arrest and seizure of a man as prominent as Bishop Roger just might have been the show of strength and authority that made men think twice about standing against him when the opportunity presented itself. If Stephen was aware of an impending threat from Matilda and Robert, then this was a well-timed pre-emptive strike to remind men in England what they had to lose by making an enemy of the king.

The spring of 1140 brought a demonstration of another emerging problem in a kingdom that endured two claimants to its crown. Robert Fitz Hubert was a Flemish mercenary engaged by Earl Robert. Fitz Hubert managed an unexpected victory for the empress's cause when he besieged and took Devizes Castle, the very place Stephen had taken from Bishop Roger the previous summer, on 26 March. The bright light reaching Bristol was quickly snuffed out when Fitz Hubert promptly refused to hand over the castle. William of Malmesbury, ensconced within an abbey located uncomfortably close to all of this violence and treachery, knew of Fitz Hubert. He was, William complained, 'the cruellest of all men within the recollection of our age' and would boast that he had burned down churches with monks locked inside before threatening to do the same to William's own Malmesbury Abbey. Fitz Hubert was known to enjoy tying prisoners to a stake in the hot sun, smearing them in honey, and trying to find any insect that would bite or sting them.

Fitz Hubert decided he could use the division and uncertainty in England to carve out something for himself. Devizes had been easy to take. Why hand it over when he could keep it for himself? The proud new lord of Devizes sent to Flanders for knights to act as a bodyguard and planned how he might expand his newly won fiefdom. Setting his sights on nearby Marlborough Castle, Fitz Hubert made little secret of his plans to attack it. The castellan there, John Fitz Gilbert, known as John the Marshal and father to the famous William Marshal, had no intention of waiting for Fitz Hubert to make his move. John went on the offensive and managed to capture Fitz Hubert, ransoming the mercenary to Earl Robert, whose trust Fitz Hubert had betrayed. Earl Robert took his prisoner to the walls of Devizes Castle and threatened to hang him unless the garrison surrendered. Those within refused, and Fitz Hubert was strung up, meeting an end for which William of Malmesbury felt little sympathy. 'Wondrously was God's judgment exercised upon a sacrilegious man, in that he earned so shameful an end not from the king, to whom he was an enemy, but from those whom he seemed to favour.'[18] Earl Robert was unable to shake the garrison from Devizes, though Stephen's new earl of Wiltshire soon bribed them out.

At Whitsun 1140 a meeting was arranged at Bath between the two sides. Stephen's brother Bishop Henry, who had been appointed papal legate to England, was the driving force behind the search for a solution. Earl Robert and others attended to represent Empress Matilda, and Stephen sent his wife Queen Matilda and Theobald, Archbishop of Canterbury to lead his delegation. Little record of the meeting survives, though William of Malmesbury claimed the empress offered to put the matter before the church for a final judgement and Stephen refused.[19] Given the pope's attitude to the issue, it was an odd offer from Matilda. She may have believed the church was sympathetic to her claims, and this was why the pope had not explicitly ruled against her. If Stephen's refusal to submit to any question about his claim had prevented a ruling against an anointed king, she perhaps hoped to tempt him to take the risk. Stephen would have been a fool to agree. Even if he had no concern that the church might favour his cousin, acknowledging ecclesiastical supremacy was out of the question, as the issues surrounding Bishop Roger's arrest had demonstrated. The meeting broke up with no resolution, the intractability of the problem at hand the only thing upon which both sides could agree.

The cold war began to intensify as summer crept over England. Stephen appointed Alan of Brittany, who was already earl of Richmond, to the office of earl of Cornwall in an effort to assert some authority in the south-west. In response, Reginald de Dunstanville, another of Henry I's illegitimate sons, was appointed earl of Cornwall by the empress. William of Malmesbury is insistent that it was Earl Robert who conferred the office on his half-brother. He was perhaps still grappling with the idea that a woman could do such a thing.[20] In August the simmering confrontation warmed along with the weather. Earl Robert led an assault on Bath but was unable to take it. In a radical change of tactic, he then took a small force all the way to Nottingham in the East Midlands and burned it, making no effort to take the town or the castle.

Although it appears random, there may have been an ulterior motive behind Earl Robert's foray to the eastern Midlands. One of Stephen's most powerful and independently-minded subjects was seething quietly, but running out of patience. The earl of Chester, who goes by the fabulous name of Ranulph aux Gernon – Ranulph the moustaches – was unhappy with Stephen's settlement with Scotland. After the Battle of the Standard, it may have been tempting to impose a punishing peace treaty on King David, but that would have left him looking for an excuse to reignite hostilities and undo it. Stephen had enough problems and favoured a more even, acceptable, and hopefully thereby permanent agreement. David was given control of lands in the north, and his son Prince Henry was created earl of Northumbria as well as earl of Huntingdon. Part of the deal saw David take possession of Carlisle and Cumberland, which Ranulph claimed as part of his patrimony. Ranulph decided in late 1140 to ambush Prince Henry on his way back to Scotland from Stephen's court, but he was thwarted when the king accompanied the young man. Ranulph then switched his attention to the East Midlands.

Ranulph's wife and his sister-in-law, the wife of his half-brother William de Roumare, travelled to Lincoln Castle to visit the lady there. They passed a pleasant day being suitably entertained, and in the late afternoon, Earl

Ranulph arrived with three attendants to escort the ladies back home. Seeing nothing amiss, the guards ushered the earl inside and had him led into the castle to find his wife. Once deep within, Ranulph and his men overpowered their escort, found weapons and subdued the skeleton guard on duty. At Ranulph's signal, William led an army into Lincoln and was let into the fortress. The two men set about making themselves comfortable and subduing the city.

Stephen had barely made it back to London from Scotland when a frantic delegation arrived from Lincoln to complain that Ranulph and William were terrorising the residents. They begged the king to come to their aid quickly, and Stephen duly pulled back on his riding boots. The royal army arrived in Lincoln on 6 January 1141 and laid siege to the castle. Ranulph managed to slip away and head back to Cheshire to raise men from his Welsh lands, but he also now decided to take advantage of Stephen's broader problems. The complication for the king was that Ranulph's wife, who was now amongst those under siege within Lincoln Castle, was Maud of Gloucester, the daughter of Earl Robert. Ranulph appealed to his father-in-law for help in rescuing his wife, and Earl Robert was honour-bound to help his daughter. He needed no encouragement to move against Stephen by this point anyway.

Earls Robert and Ranulf gathered their forces and met on the road to Lincoln. It was Stephen's turn to be caught unawares by the speed of his enemies, and as news of a much larger army than had accompanied the king began to trickle, then rush, into Lincoln, many advised him to run. Stephen refused; his father's poor reputation for having fled Antioch in the Holy Land preventing him from accepting what might have been wise council. The empress's cause had proven hard to snuff out, huddled as her forces were behind the impenetrable walls of stout castles. Siege warfare was getting Stephen nowhere and time would only embolden his enemies and cause doubt to creep into the minds of those who, for now, remained loyal to him. Pitched battles were still incredibly rare in the mid-twelfth century. They were too unpredictable, paying ransoms if captured was exorbitantly expensive, and there was always the risk of serious injury or death. Contemporary wisdom advised against battle, preferring the carefully structured order of siege warfare that allowed for a peaceful resolution. Everyone understood the rules. Battle was random. Stephen and Robert were both ready to roll the dice, and no one could dissuade them.

Henry of Huntingdon was a canon at Lincoln when the two sides clashed.[21] He describes Earl Robert's army arriving on 2 February 1141 having been forced to traverse 'a marsh which was almost impassable'.[22]

The Foss Dyke, often made marshy by the swollen River Witham, would have blocked Robert's approach to the north of the city. There was tactical sense to making the challenging crossing. A flat plain outside Lincoln's north wall offered the ideal spot for a battle, and an approach from the south meant crossing the River Witham itself by a narrow bridge and then fighting uphill into the city. The early effort to approach from the north made what would follow easier.

Although Robert and Ranulph had gathered a larger army, that was only because Stephen had been planning a siege that required a small force. The king was joined by the earls of Worcester, Northampton, Hertford, York, and Richmond. Hugh Bigod, who would soon become earl of Norfolk, was also present and Stephen had brought his trusted mercenary captain William of Ypres. These nobles represented about a quarter of the available earls in England at the time, but also seems to reflect Stephen's desire to use local military officials. Each of these men was drawn in from regions surrounding Lincoln, so the failure of others to attend should not be taken as a sign that they abandoned the king. The armies arrayed in the traditional three battles; the vanguard, the centre, and the rearguard. William of Ypres led the king's vanguard and opened the assault against 'a wild band of Welshmen' that formed Earl Robert's front lines. The Welsh were driven back by William of Ypres's cavalry, but as they broke and fled, Earl Ranulph charged and caught the horsemen unawares. William's men were thrown into chaos, and it was their turn to run. Some chroniclers accuse William and others of cowardice for abandoning the king. Henry of Huntingdon is more sympathetic, allowing that William saw almost immediately that it was hopeless to try to fight, and, 'perceiving the impossibility of supporting the king, he deferred his aid for better times'. William reasoned that discretion was the better part of valour and that if they were all captured or killed, there would be no one to fight for Stephen another day.

From the relative safety of his cloisters, Henry of Huntingdon could hear the clanging of swords. If he looked toward the fighting, he was able to make out the flashes of sunlight caught for an instant on swinging swords. Shouts and screams echoed around the hills and filled his ears too. Earl Robert's cavalry charged relentlessly at the knot of men that was packed tightly around the king but shrank with each assault. Some were crushed beneath the heavy hooves of the destriers. Others were sent crumpled to the dirt by a sword blow, while still more were dragged away to be ransomed later. In the heart of the brave resistance stood Stephen. Many who tried to come close to him fell under the blows of his heavy battle axe so that it eventually shattered on one man. Drawing his trusty sword, Stephen went to work with this until it too broke under the crushing strikes he delivered. Left unarmed, one of the attackers rushed in and grabbed the king by his helmet, yelling 'Here, here; I have the king!' Robert of Torigni recorded that Stephen had fought 'like a lion, grinding his teeth and foaming at the mouth like a boar', but his capture spelt disaster.[23]

In the aftermath of the fighting, Lincoln was sacked for its support of the king. Those citizens who had turned out to bolster Stephen's numbers were hunted through the streets as they tried to return home. Houses were plundered and burned, and even churches were looted in the heat of victory. Anyone who considered the broader implications of the outcome as they watched Stephen led away as Earl Robert's prisoner must have been fearful of what it might mean to have the king a captive of his enemies. The only thing anyone knew for certain was that God, who decides the victor of any battle, had turned His back on King Stephen. As he was escorted along the way to Gloucester to be put before his cousin Empress Matilda, the king must have worried what his future held. If he had one.

Earl Robert treated his prisoner with deference and respect, but as soon as they arrived in Gloucester, all such niceties vanished. Empress Matilda was furious that her cousin had snatched what had rightfully been hers and kept her from her inheritance for six years now. From Gloucester, Stephen was bundled down to Bristol and placed in 'close custody' behind the castle's impenetrable walls.[24] As he languished in his cell, any freedoms slowly withdrawn, Stephen might have been put in mind of the fate of his oldest maternal uncle. After his capture at the Battle of Tinchebray in 1106, Robert Curthose had spent the next twenty-eight years as his little brother's prisoner until his death in 1134. As news of what had happened at Lincoln spread like wildfire across the kingdom and reached Normandy, most were convinced Stephen would remain confined 'until the last breath of his life'.[25] The reign of King Stephen was over. In an instant, those painted by Stephen as insurgents had become the establishment, and by direct consequence, those associated with Stephen were at risk of being marked as rebels. Political pragmatism and the desperate rearrangement of allegiances lay behind the fact that 'the greater part of the kingdom at once submitted to the countess'.[26] What, everyone was left wondering, would come next?

One person who was absolutely certain what was going to happen next was Empress Matilda. Fortune, and God, had gifted her what she had been trying to secure for six years. Papal courts had failed to recognise Matilda's claim. Her invasion had made little real impact, but now Robert had delivered her inheritance at the point of his sword. In early March, a month after the Battle of Lincoln, Empress Matilda made contact with Stephen's brother

Henry, Bishop of Winchester to gain entry into his city, which was still the site of the royal treasury. She did not rush at her objective. Despite the long wait, and her fury with Stephen that must have extended to his brother, the empress took her time to take the correct steps in the proper order. At a meeting at Wherwell on 2 March 1141, Bishop Henry was offered full control over appointments to ecclesiastical offices and a voice in all the political decisions of the new regime. In return, he would recognise Matilda as 'lady of England'.[27]

The title Empress Matilda had settled on played a part in the slow progress she made. Doubtless, as her son would do, she was keen to avoid the headlong rush that had been the lingering uncertainty around both her father's and cousin's kingship. She could take her time because it was rightfully hers. Neither she nor her followers could ignore the focus that would be placed on her position as a female ruler. A queen held a very specific role with particular connotations. Most notably, a queen was the wife of a king. Her political power was limited and flowed directly from her husband. This was not a connection Matilda sought to emphasise. Geoffrey was making inroads into Normandy in the wake of Stephen's defeat, but he was not doing so in his wife's name. In England, Matilda had no intention of looking like her husband's representative. There had been a suggestion before her father's death that she might only act as regent for her young son, Henry, but she was keen to sweep aside that idea too. England was hers. She could deal with Normandy later.

Henry I had been at pains to associate his rule with England's Anglo-Saxon heritage more closely than his father's conquest. His daughter looked to history for a solution too. Æthelflæd, the eldest daughter of Alfred the Great, had used the title Lady of the Mercians when she had ruled the kingdom of Mercia between 911 and 918. The resurrection of this style not only re-anchored Henry I's dynasty in the misty nostalgia of the Anglo-Saxon past but directly aligned the empress with a previous female ruler who had exercised authority successfully in her own right. The delay in Matilda's move to Winchester and towards a coronation masked the uncertainty about how she should present herself to her new subjects. The senior amongst them were all men, who had no experience or terms of reference for submission to a woman. Any uncertainty about her status and authority risked undermining what had been won. The solution was Matilda, Lady of the English, and it is this polished and confident bearer of sovereignty who arrived outside Winchester in early March 1141.

The lady of the English was met at the gates of Winchester by a formal delegation led by Bishop Henry. The castle and royal treasury were given over to her, and a clerk named Turstin placed the crown into Matilda's possession. The people welcomed the empress in the streets before she was escorted to the cathedral, with Bishop Henry at her right hand and the bishop of St David's on her left. After the formalities had been observed, all held their collective breath as they waited for the first indication of who their new ruler was and what she would do. Matilda's camp was not alone in trying to work out how she would wield the power that was now hers. It was into this ingrained trap of the impossible balancing of need and expectation that the empress fell immediately. If she behaved in the manner expected of a woman, she would expose herself as weak and her rule as fundamentally flawed. Her subjects would be looking to Geoffrey as her husband or Earl Robert as her military commander for a clearer idea of what they required in an overlord. The empress took what must have felt like the lesser of two evils. She followed the example of her father.

The anonymous writer of the *Gesta Stephani* was quick to voice his distaste for the experience. Matilda 'at once put on an extremely arrogant demeanour instead of the modest gait and bearing proper to the gentle sex'.[28] Those who had been at Stephen's side in opposing her cause received rough treatment. Many were 'received ungraciously and at times with unconcealed annoyance', while 'others she drove from her presence in fury after insulting and threatening them.'[29] Henry of Huntingdon is equally damning in his assessment that the empress 'was elated with insufferable pride'.[30] This shock and disgust at Empress Matilda's attitude, and the accompanying sympathy it was meant to generate for the men treated so sorely, was the open wound Matilda was struggling to address. In her place, a man who came down heavily on those who had fought to deny him his rights would be applauded as strong and just. Matilda was, instead, unwomanly, arrogant, and ungracious. Just as she had not been able to win a military victory for her cause, she found herself cut off from a political one by the simple but inescapable virtue of her sex. The situation became all the more tangled with the arrival of Theobald, Archbishop of Canterbury.

Whether by the design of Bishop Henry, who was keen to secure his own position and assert the authority of his role as papal legate, or of Archbishop Theobald, the primate had not been in Winchester for the arrival of Empress Matilda. If he had chosen to stay away, he soon offered a reason why, which may also have been a warning shot across Bishop Henry's bow from the moral high ground. Theobald insisted it was not proper to transfer his allegiance from Stephen to Empress Matilda 'without consulting the king'.[31] The archbishop, several bishops and some of the lay nobility were permitted to make the journey to Bristol to consult with

Stephen in his prison cell. With 'a courteous permission to change over as the times required' from the king, Theobald returned to offer his recognition to Matilda as Lady of the English.[32] Once more, her victory was exposed as hollow by the insistence that a man, her vanquished opponent, languishing in chains in her dungeon, must permit her to take his crown. Stephen's agreement is interesting. He may have recognised the political reality of his situation and accepted what others were trying to resist. However, by allowing the transfer of fealty, he created a situation in which it could be as easily shifted back to him if he should find a way out of his prison.

Bishop Henry summoned a Legatine Council to Westminster. As Empress Matilda recovered from the celebration of Easter Sunday at Oxford, the church gathered on Monday to try and smooth out the kingdom's problems. In a blistering attack on his brother's character and kingship, Henry admitted he had been wrong to support Stephen. As with all moments when power is in the process of transfer, there were opportunities to be grabbed, and Henry made an audacious move. Amongst the explanation of his personal errors, the bishop asserted that Empress Matilda's rights had been discussed by the clergy, 'whose special prerogative it is to choose and consecrate a prince'.[33] The throwaway statement represented a claim to authority over the appointment of rulers that the church in England had not possessed before. It was in line with the empress's experiences in Germany, and Henry perhaps saw a chance to advance the status of the church in England.

If Bishop Henry had not entirely abandoned his brother, it was also the laying of a foundation for his return. As Archbishop Theobald had established that it was possible to transfer allegiance to an ascendant de facto ruler, so he had caused acknowledgement that fealty could be withdrawn from the loser. In positioning the church as the vehicle to select a monarch, Bishop Henry also created the necessary mechanism by which the church deselected an existing ruler. One day, that might be to Stephen's benefit. Another signal that Henry was working to keep the flame of his brother's cause burning came when he summoned the citizens of London to the Legatine Council. When Stephen had been accepted as king in 1135, he had made an agreement with London to support their causes if they offered him their backing. The Londoners arrived in Winchester to not only stake their claim to be a commune, a status that would provide the city with greater independence, but also to insist on Stephen's release in return for recognising Matilda. If nothing else, it was clear that the capital, where the empress aimed to be crowned, was not yet entirely on board.

The final piece of what looks suspiciously like Bishop Henry's puzzle came with the arrival of a clerk named Christian. Bishop Henry refused

41

to read the message he brought, so Christian read it aloud to the meeting. It was a plea from Queen Matilda that her husband be released and restored as king. The meeting broke up immediately after Christian had read the missive, but an important point had been made. Queen Matilda, in championing her husband's cause and requesting merciful intervention from men of power was behaving precisely as a woman was expected to. It was a sharp contrast to Empress Matilda's efforts to impose herself in the mould of a male ruler. Although on the surface he had abandoned and condemned his brother, Bishop Henry had both opened the door for Stephen's return and played up to the greatest fears of the nobility about Empress Matilda's rule. Stephen offered the comfort of traditional normalcy. Empress Matilda brought radical change. Bishop Henry was, perhaps, relying on the lack of desire for such a departure from the status quo.

The Legatine Council ended on 10 April 1141. It took until 24 June for Empress Matilda to negotiate permission to enter London. It was hardly a positive sign for her. The empress appointed several earls, mirroring Stephen's decentralisation of power. Baldwin de Redvers was rewarded for his early support of Matilda with the earldom of Devon. William de Mohun became earl of Somerset, Hugh Bigod was created earl of Norfolk, and Aubrey de Vere was appointed earl of Oxford. Central to the emerging stand-off with London with Geoffrey de Mandeville. Geoffrey had been created earl of Essex by Stephen and was confirmed in the post by Empress Matilda. Critically, he was also the castellan of the Tower of London. Like so many others embroiled in the civil war, Geoffrey's aims are hard to perceive with certainty and whether or not he was a rebel to either side is impossible to tell. He extracted good terms for offering his support to Empress Matilda, preventing a loss of titles and offices. The population of London was less keen to abandon Stephen, so Geoffrey was placed at odds with the people surrounding him. Although it is possible he used his pivotal position in London to improve his lot, it is every bit as likely that he recognised the unavoidable fact that Empress Matilda was in charge, and she was coming to London. With the church and a large portion of the nobility now behind her, resistance, however principled, risked ruin.

The balancing act many of the nobility were forced to perform was perfectly displayed when Waleran Beaumont, Count of Meulan and Earl of Worcester, transferred his allegiance to Empress Matilda. The Beaumont twins had been the core of Stephen's support, and Robert Beaumont, Earl of Leicester, kept faith with the deposed king. Waleran, whose earldom lay on the border of the empress's stronghold in the south-west, and who had significant lands in Normandy now under threat from Geoffery, Count of

Anjou, hedged the family's bets. The arrangement was almost certainly made after discussions with his brother. This way, there was a foot in each camp that could protect the other if and when a final outcome was reached. Bridges were built, but none were burned.

King David came south to join in his niece's triumph. He was confirmed in his earldom of Huntingdon, but the relationship quickly became tense. The *Gesta Stephani* insists Empress Matilda upset David, Earl Robert and Bishop Henry by refusing to rise when they entered her company. She also began to ignore their advice (or direction) and 'arranged everything as she herself thought fit and according to her own arbitrary will'.[34] Such behaviour in a new king would have been considered strong and admirable, but in a woman, it drove home the uncomfortable novelty of the situation. Fractures were made worse when David tried to impose his chancellor William Cumin as the new bishop of Durham. The chapter at Durham wrote horrified letters to the empress and Bishop Henry. The latter immediately wrote back supporting the monks and forbidding Cumin to take the post unless properly elected. Empress Matilda then fired off her own letters recognising Cumin as bishop-elect and instructing the chapter to accept him, denying their right to a free election. When she also confirmed David's possession of chunks of northern England, it looked to those in the north as though the lady of the English had no interest in part of her new kingdom.

When Empress Matilda was finally welcomed into London in June, she was on the very brink of completing her victory. As preparations were made for the coronation that would solemnify her position and provide it with protection from challenge, she could reflect that she was about to achieve what no woman had ever done by becoming Lady of the English, a queen regnant of the realm of England. This moment had been six years in the making, crafted from adversity, won on the battlefield, and moulded by political will against institutional resistance. Then, it all went wrong. For once, the problem was nothing to do with Matilda's sex, but with her ill-timed, heavy-handed decision to take some degree of vengeance on the city of London. However much they had resisted, the people of London celebrated Empress Matilda's arrival when it came. Many saw it as the end of the troubles and the advent of a settled peace. Within days, the Lady of the English would be crowned at Westminster Abbey, and the business of her rule would begin, with whatever challenges the new experience would bring.

Unwilling to wait for that moment, Empress Matilda summoned the wealthiest men of London and ordered them to pay a huge tribute to her. They pleaded that the recent upheavals had left them short of cash, but promised that when things had settled down under her rule, they would gladly pay whatever taxation was required of them. Enraged, Empress Matilda's temper snapped and 'with a grim look, her forehead wrinkled into a frown, every trace of a woman's gentleness removed from her face', she 'blazed into unbearable fury'.[35] London had, she retorted, given vast sums to Stephen to help him resist her. Why, then, should she reduce her demands on them now? The simple answer was that her timing was abysmal. She made an aggressive move against the most powerful city in England while she was still vulnerable. The writer of the *Gesta Stephani* chooses once more to point out the unwomanly spectacle of a lady trying to wield a man's power, reducing it to physical comments on her furrowed brow, wrinkled face and stern, manly countenance.

To make matters even worse, Queen Matilda selected this moment to make her next interjection. Stephen's wife is described by the *Gesta Stephani*, in stark contrast to her cousin the empress, as 'a woman of subtlety and a man's resolution', applying male characteristics to the queen to emphasis her strengths even as he did the same to pour scorn on the empress.[36] As she had done at Winchester, the queen reminded the powerful men of England how a woman could act within a recognisable framework. She asked for Stephen's freedom, but not the return of the crown, or any of his lands. All that she asked for beyond her husband's release was the confirmation of their son Eustace as heir to her family's lands and titles in Boulogne, which he should have held through Queen Matilda's father. The request sounded entirely reasonable, but Stephen's release was not something the empress could countenance. Asking for her father's inheritance to pass to her son was a clear signal from Queen Matilda that she felt a woman could not rule. It was an unsubtle way of asking the great men of the kingdom if they were really willing to accept female authority; a question many were still posing themselves. Sandwiched between these unpalatable requests was the claim to inheritance that any baron held sacred. The laws of inheritance were supposed to be beyond royal interference. The Boulogne lands and titles were rightfully Eustace's. Denying them would send a shiver of terror through the already uncertain nobility, but granting them meant acknowledging the damaging aspects of the queen's request; Stephen's freedom and the inappropriateness of female rule.

Bishop Henry carefully suggested that what Queen Matilda requested for Eustace was just. This moment was perhaps the culmination of his efforts to keep Stephen's cause alive from within the empress's court. Enraged, Empress Matilda hurled abuse at the queen's messengers, refused to grant any part of their mistress's request and sent them scurrying from her court.[37] Bishop Henry withdrew. William of Malmesbury, who was sympathetic to Earl Robert and therefore to Empress Matilda's cause, believed she had fatally wounded her own hopes. He wrote that the barons became disaffected because they 'had kept their faith with her but she had broken hers, being unable to show restraint in the enjoyment of what she had gained'.[38] Empress Matilda was handing men the excuse they sought to reconsider their allegiance to her.

As the empress sat down to a feast prepared to celebrate the impending coronation, Queen Matilda struck her deadliest blow yet. An army, led by Stephen's mercenary captain William of Ypres, who had not abandoned his patron after fleeing the Battle of Lincoln, appeared on the south bank of the River Thames. As they began to assault the opposite side of the river, London quickly descended into panic. Empress Matilda had not yet resolved the open question of how a female ruler would raise and deploy an army. Allowing a man to take command risked creating a perception that he was the real monarch. Into this uncertainty, Queen Matilda poured an army she had raised in the names of her imprisoned husband and disinherited son. The queen answered the question her cousin had left dangling; a woman raised an army in right of her husband. This was what men knew and were comfortable with. By denying the empress time to set out her own policy on the matter, the queen doubled Empress Matilda's problems. The citizens of London, who had also remained loyal to Stephen, threw open the gates to the city and joined the army that filled the streets 'like thronging swarms from beehives'.[39]

Caught unawares, the empress and her guests were forced to leap from their laden tables and leave the hot food behind as they fled for their lives. Empress Matilda was driven from the capital in an indecorous hurry just before she was to be crowned. She had, perhaps, contributed to her own downfall by mistiming her assault on the wealthy residents of London, but there was a strong feeling that female rule was still a leap too far, into a dark abyss of uncertainty. When Queen Matilda provided the opportunity to push the idea away, it was snatched at by all but those closest to Empress Matilda. Bishop Henry had rushed back to Winchester, where he laid siege to the castle. The empress followed with what remained of her army, but as she entered the city through one gate on 31 July, Bishop Henry coolly mounted his horse and rode out of another, making for his bishop's palace at nearby Wolvesey. As her army poured into Winchester and set about lifting the siege, she may have missed the glaring parallel to Stephen's position at Lincoln six months earlier.

Once the empress's forces had made their way to besiege the bishop's palace at Wolvesey, the queen and William of Ypres snapped the trap shut, snaring Empress Matilda between an unwelcoming castle and a hostile army. William of Malmesbury complained that many earls took the chance to abandon Empress Matilda.[40] King David remained at her side, as did Earl Robert and the earls of Cornwall, Devon, Somerset, Hereford, Warwick, and Chester, though the latter was both 'late and ineffectual', attracting suspicion that his heart was no longer with Empress Matilda.[41] Queen Matilda had recruited the earls of Surrey, Northampton, Hertford, and Essex; Geoffrey de Mandeville rising to the call to re-join the king's cause. A contingent of Londoners swelled the ranks of Stephen's supporters too, not satisfied with chasing the empress from their city.

Over the weeks that followed, there were daily clashes, but no decisive gains were made. Finally, on 14 September, Earl Robert had decided their cause was flagging and was likely to fail first. He led an attack against the queen's army that provided cover for the empress to retreat. Escorted by her half-brother Reginald, Earl of Cornwall, and the loyal Brian Fitz Count, Matilda was forced to flee with such haste that she rode astride her horse, like a man. It was some fifty miles before they found some safety at Devizes to the north-west. Here, Empress Matilda, exhausted and 'nearly half-dead', was transferred to a litter for the rest of the journey into the safety of Gloucester.[42] Her problems, though, had only just begun.

As bedraggled men stumbled into Gloucester, they brought the worst possible news. In Winchester, Earl Robert had bravely provided the distraction that saved his sister but found himself unable to make his escape. Forced to make a stand at Stockbridge, Robert had been captured and was now a prisoner at Rochester Castle. The king's faction immediately set about negotiating a prisoner exchange. Earl Robert refused to agree to anything behind his sister's back, no matter how they flattered, and then threatened him. They offered him control of the government, second only to the king in authority. When he would not accept, he was threatened with being sent to Boulogne. His calm response was that before he reached Boulogne, Stephen would be in Ireland. Earl Robert did make one mistake, which was compounded by his sister. In insisting Stephen, as a king, was worth more than a mere earl, he elevated the position of the supposedly deposed monarch and weakened the empress's claim. Matilda was so desperate to get Robert back to her side that she tripped over herself to recognise Stephen's status.[43]

In November 1141, an agreement was reached, and the two prisoners were exchanged. Within eleven months, England had been turned upside down and inside out. It might have appeared that, as winter set in, the chessboard had been reset to its position before the Battle of Lincoln, but it was not that simple. Empress Matilda had been within a hair's breadth of becoming the first queen regnant of England. She had contributed to throwing away the chance with some 'haughty' and ill-timed lashing out, but ultimately the men forced to recognise the political fact of her ascendancy had always been uncomfortable with the notion. They were desperately seeking a reason to repudiate the idea of female rule and a chance to return to Stephen, or perhaps any other man qualified and capable to rule. Empress Matilda had made it easier than she might have done, but her actions may well have simply hastened the inevitable.

Normandy was all but lost to Stephen but was not gained for Empress Matilda. Count Geoffrey had been hard at work during Stephen's captivity and was now duke of Normandy. Doubtless, it was a problematic loss for Stephen, but it also left him free to focus exclusively on England. Although restored to his throne, Stephen's kingdom was fractured. The south-east and Midlands were loyal to the king, and his authority stretched as far north as York. Beyond that, King David held sway, and there was little resistance to his rule now. In the south-west and along the Welsh borders, Empress Matilda still had a firm grip that defied every effort to loosen it. In the east, Hugh Bigod, Earl of Norfolk, was perhaps the most genuine rebel of the Anarchy. He never seems to have been particularly behind Empress Matilda's cause but was frequently disobedient to Stephen. He had played a key role in Stephen's accession, giving testimony that on his deathbed Henry I had appointed Stephen as his heir. Perhaps he felt the rewards he was due had been slow to come. Hugh had, and would continue to, frequently raise men and attack towns and castles for his own ends.

In the early months of 1142, Empress Matilda took a step she had been trying to avoid. She agreed to send to her husband for help. One contemporary noted the sense of doing so, 'it being his duty to maintain the inheritance of his wife and sons in England'.[44] The reference to her sons is perhaps not accidental at this moment. The pitfalls of trying to place Matilda on the throne of England had been exposed for all to see. Appealing to Geoffrey was an admission of defeat, but there was an effort to insist his intervention would not be on his own behalf. Associating her sons with her efforts harked back to the belief some had held that Matilda was only ever intended to be a caretaker for Henry I's grandsons. A regency under her might be less unappealing than direct female rule and may cause some to reconsider the oaths they had previously made to protect Henry's line. It also took away whatever sting her sex or personality had injected into the matter. If nothing else, it served as a threat that the opposition to Stephen and his dynasty would rumble on into the next generation at least.

Geoffrey agreed to help if Earl Robert would go to him and give details of the situation. Robert was hesitant but made the crossing to Normandy after some persuasion. He had been right. Geoffrey used Robert to tighten his hold on Normandy but gave no real support to the efforts in England.

The only small bit of hope Earl Robert managed to return to England with was Empress Matilda's oldest son, the 9-year-old Henry. The boy had not seen his mother in three years, and it perhaps points to the relative safety of the civil disputes in England that Geoffrey sent his son and heir to gain experience in that arena. In France, Louis VII had just attacked the town of Vitry-en-Perthois as part of an ongoing dispute with Stephen's older brother Theobald, Count of Blois. The assault only ended after Louis was horrified that 1,300 had been locked inside a church and burned to death. Compared to that, England's prolonged internal squabbling seemed civilised and safe. As Earl Robert had feared, though, he returned to discover that Stephen had been making the most of his absence. Wareham, the critical port from which Robert had departed, had been taken, cutting the empress's lines of communication. Matilda herself was under siege by Stephen at Oxford Castle. Seeing his chance to end the matter once and for all, Stephen dug in and committed to seeing the siege through, no matter what.[45]

Robert sailed back to England with some 300 knights, many raised from his Norman lands, but some supplied by Geoffrey after the news of his wife's perils reached them. Little Henry's inclusion was intended to provide a rallying point for his mother's wavering adherents. The earl landed at Wareham and lay siege to the castle, perhaps hoping to draw Stephen away from Oxford as well as regain the vital fortress. Stephen had learned from his experience at Lincoln and was rumoured to have around 1,000 knights with him at Oxford. Earl Robert called a muster at Cirencester for 29 November, frantically trying to gather any man willing to fight for the empress. As the winter snow began to fall, Earl Robert led his army eastward, but they would never reach Oxford.

The castle at Oxford was teetering on the brink of surrender. Supplies had been exhausted, the cold was biting, and it was clear to all that those within could not hold out much longer. In an act of personal bravery and defiance that perfectly encapsulates Empress Matilda, she took matters into her own hands. As the thick winter darkness fell one evening, she took two hand-picked men and slipped out of one of the castle's postern gates. The three figures wore white cloaks that offered camouflage against the blanket of snow covering the ground and carefully stepped across the frozen River Thames that ran past the castle. Next, the trio picked their way through Stephen's camp, evading the guards on watch. After that, they trudged six more miles or so in the dark to reach the safety of Wallingford just before morning. Writers quickly agreed it was miraculous, but were uncertain why God had chosen to help Empress Matilda. Either her cause was the right one, or God was not yet done punishing England with civil war.

Stephen, refusing to be demoralised by the empress's escape, took the surrender of Oxford Castle and led his army to Wareham to lay siege once more to the castle there. It proved well-defended, and the king withdrew to Wilton to strengthen the fortress as a base of operations. Earl Robert promptly led his army to Wilton and arrayed it for battle. Perhaps acquiescing to his insistent advisors, Stephen pulled back from a fight. It was not a decision the king liked being forced to make, however wise it was. Into the uncertainty it created, and the fear of looking weak Stephen suddenly felt acutely, some dripped the poisonous rumour that Geoffrey de Mandeville was plotting against the king again. The events of 1141 had left Stephen concerned about the loyalties of some, if not all, at his court. Geoffrey had been quick to accept Empress Matilda after the Battle of Lincoln, though equally swift to return to Stephen's cause when Queen Matilda raised forces against her cousin. As he had done with Bishop Roger in 1139, Stephen allowed himself to become convinced Geoffrey de Mandeville was about to betray him. At Michaelmas 1143, in a replay of four years earlier, a scuffle broke out that led to Geoffrey being accused of treason. The earl laughed off the charge, but his reaction was seen as an admission of guilt. He was placed under arrest, only offered his freedom in return for handing over the Tower and castles at Saffron Walden and Pleshey.

Once freed, Geoffrey predictably flew into revolt. He did not, as Stephen must have feared, head west into the arms of the empress. Instead, he went to the Isle of Ely, by now a renowned centre for rebellion. He took control of territory around the Isle at Ramsey, Wood Walton, Benwick, and Chatteris before sacking Cambridge. Hugh Bigod was quick to make contact with Geoffrey, and the two men combined their efforts to cause trouble for Stephen. It is at this point that *The Anglo-Saxon Chronicle* offers its famous lament on the state of England during Stephen's reign. 'Wheresoever men tilled, the earth bare no corn, for the land was ruined by such deeds; and they said openly that Christ and his saints were asleep. Such and more than we can say we endured nineteen winters for our sins.'[46] This doleful passage came from the quill of a monk at Peterborough Abbey, just thirteen miles north-west of Ramsey. It possibly reflects the terror and doom experienced by men living usually quiet, cloistered lives when peril and worldly disputes reach their threshold more than almost two decades of constant sorrow and struggle. It may also speak to the growing concern that all of this would never end.

Stephen was forced to install garrisons to encircle Geoffrey and Hugh's revolt, making him uncharacteristically static. Ranulph, Earl of Chester, spotted an opportunity he deemed too good to ignore and snatched Lincoln Castle again. The king arrived in the city in May 1144 to set about taking it back, perhaps a little wary of a repeat of history. The siege was short-lived because, during construction, a collapse killed eighty of Stephen's men, suffocating them in the trenches they had dug.[47] The king was so upset he immediately abandoned the effort and withdrew. A bad omen was not something likely to encourage Stephen to linger in Lincoln. He sped south instead to relieve the siege at Malmesbury Castle before attacking Tetbury. When Earl Robert arrived with an army and offered battle, Stephen slipped away.

Geoffrey de Mandeville had used Stephen's absence to move against the small garrisons meant to hem him in. He was assaulting Burwell Castle in August when he was injured. The wound quickly turned septic and on 16 September 1144, he died. Geoffrey had been excommunicated for taking control of Ramsey Abbey and so passed away out of favour with the church. Denied burial on holy ground, his family had his body placed in a lead coffin until they managed to convince the Knights Templar to accept it. It was held in an unconsecrated area at the Old Temple until the pope absolved Geoffrey and his body was buried at the New Temple in 1163 beneath the effigy his son commissioned and which remains today. Geoffrey had been hugely powerful and wealthy, an experienced soldier and administrator, and his removal as a threat to Stephen owed more to providence than planning, but nevertheless, Stephen could count it a much-needed victory.

As one problem was resolved, another took its place, Stephen still confronted by threats that resembled the hydra that had challenged Hercules. His brother Bishop Henry fell out violently with William de Pont de l'Arche, a former close ally to Henry I who had control of the royal castle and treasury at Winchester. William appealed immediately to Empress Matilda for help when it was clear he stood no chance against the king's rich brother. The weakness of her cause was exposed once more when she was unable to send the knights and captain for which William pleaded. Keen not to miss the chance both to recruit one of her father's trusted men and to undermine Bishop Henry, Empress Matilda hired mercenaries under the command of Robert Fitz Hildebrand and despatched them to Winchester. Robert was warmly welcomed at the castle and soon became friendly with William. It was not only William who made Robert feel at home, though. His wife took a shine to Robert that was reciprocated enthusiastically. The couple began an affair and, in no time at all, had placed

William in chains in his own dungeon. Robert made his peace with King Stephen and Bishop Henry as he enjoyed William's home, his wealth and his wife. Matters got worse for the empress's cause when Earl Robert's son Philip was placed in charge of Cricklade Castle, just thirteen miles north-east of Stephen's outpost at Malmesbury. Philip launched a campaign to retake Oxford but found himself unable to defeat Stephen. In a dramatic shock to all observers, Philip duly gave his fealty to Stephen, his father's mortal enemy, and began working for the king's side.

In early 1146, a fresh round of peace talks between King Stephen and Empress Matilda was arranged. In the build-up, Earl Robert's son Philip captured his own uncle Reginald, Earl of Cornwall. When the earl protested that he had been relying on the truce and safe-conduct surrounding the talks, Stephen ordered Philip to release his uncle, demonstrating that chivalry and honour had not been abandoned a decade into Stephen's contested rule. When Empress Matilda insisted on her right to the throne, and Stephen equally predictably refused to surrender his crown, the talks broke down. The nobility were becoming increasingly disillusioned with what was proving to be an irresolvable problem for the whole kingdom. It may be at this moment that many of the senior barons began to consider taking matters into their own hands. Not to perpetuate or escalate the conflict, but to mitigate the damage it was doing.

Ranulf, Earl of Chester, had been lured back to Stephen's side by a compromise that saw him retain control of Lincoln Castle. As it had with Bishop Roger and then Geoffrey de Mandeville, the new relationship soon soured, and Ranulf was ordered to hand over all of the castles he held from the king. In the argument that ensued, the earl was accused of treason and lost his temper. Ranulf was forced to agree to the demands, but as soon as he left the king's court, he unsurprisingly marched directly to Lincoln was a large force. Ranulf lost a lot of men trying to take Lincoln and failed. He attacked Coventry next in his rage, and though Stephen was wounded, the king was victorious once more, and Ranulf was driven away.

At the same time as Ranulf was targeted, Gilbert Fitz Richard, Earl of Hertford, was also arrested. Gilbert was required to hand over all of his castles to obtain his freedom, but once released, he fled to Ranulph, who was his uncle. Stephen was playing a dangerous game in alienating powerful men. Gilbert had shown no signs of disloyalty since being created earl by Stephen in 1138, and one of his other uncles was Gilbert de Clare, Earl of Pembroke. There is insufficient evidence to understand whether these men deserved Stephen's suspicion, or whether paranoia had begun to creep into all of the king's relationships with his nobility. Stephen was into his fifties now, and the relentless pace of his reign must have been taking a toll. The one certain thing was the attention he began to pay to the future of his dynasty.

Stephen's oldest son and heir was Eustace. His date of birth is so uncertain that in 1147 he might have been anywhere between 12 and 20. Stephen provided him with an impressive retinue of knights, plenty of lands to support him, and had Eustace invested as Count of Boulogne. As he grew inexorably older, Stephen turned his attention to a French tradition, used to strengthen dynastic claims, which had never been introduced to England. The Capetian kings of France would have their heir crowned during their own lifetime, creating a junior king already perfectly placed to succeed on the death of his father. This, Stephen began to think, would provide his family with the security that had proved so elusive. The sacred act of coronation had afforded Stephen untold protection during his reign and captivity. It could do the same for his son and prevent all-out war on Stephen's death. The problem for Stephen was that everyone else saw that as a problem.

Part of the reason Stephen shifted his focus to his son's position was the arrival in England in 1147 of the now 14-year-old Henry, son of the empress and Geoffrey, now undisputed duke of Normandy as well as count of Anjou. News of the boy's arrival spread like wildfire through England, with reports that he had brought thousands of men, and had thousands more ready to make the crossing behind him. He was burdened by vast sums of money that he was keen to disperse amongst any who would join his cause against Stephen.[49] Everyone panicked. Then relaxed. It was a lie.

Young Henry had come with no backing from his father, no cash, and barely a handful of men with no way to pay them. They made for Cricklade Castle but were brushed away. An assault of Purton Castle failed with equal speed. Henry's men began to drift away from him, realising the campaign was doomed, and they were not going to get paid. Embarrassed, the youthful adventurer asked his mother for funds to pay his men. She refused. He turned to Earl Robert, his uncle and mentor during his last brief visit to England. Robert also turned his back on Henry, suggesting that his invasion had been without the approval of anyone else, a spirited but doomed expedition. Fearing the dishonour of leaving his army unpaid, Henry turned to King Stephen for assistance. It was a bold and brash move, but it had a basis in the code of chivalry that guided military men. Henry was family, even if he was openly in opposition to Stephen, and the king was in a position to protect the young man from losing his honour. Even without these considerations, the cash Stephen sent Henry offered political benefits. It would see both

Henry and a band of dissatisfied, unpaid mercenaries leave English shores. It would drive home the weakness of the cause Henry hoped to represent in the near future, and if nothing else, it would create a small well of goodwill. Henry would owe Stephen.

On 31 October 1147, Earl Robert died while planning the next military phase of Empress Matilda's efforts. Like his father, he had remained active to the end, almost reaching 60 years of age. It was a crushing blow to the empress, whose cause had stalled in the wake of the eventual failures of 1141. In the early months of 1148, she made her preparations and slipped away from England, never to return. Any efforts to win back her father's inheritance would now rest on the young, inexperienced, and to date unsuccessful Henry. After nine years, and with the loss of her beloved, loyal half-brother, Empress Matilda saw that her time actively driving the narrative in England was over, but she had not given up altogether.

Although this was better news than Stephen could have hoped for, all was not going as well as he wished. The church, with express papal instructions, was refusing to crown Eustace. The king was furious and frustrated at every turn. There seemed to be a sense that crowning his son would perpetuate the questions and legal objections swirling around the English throne. It was precisely the protection that Stephen sought for Eustace and their dynasty that increased resistance to the move. There was a growing sense that on Stephen's death, it was all up for grabs and one way or another, there would be a final resolution. In 1149, when Henry turned 16, he made another daring venture into Stephen's kingdom, this time traversing it to have the honour of knighthood, a prerequisite to kingship, bestowed on him by his great-uncle, King David of Scotland. Henry managed to convince David and Earl Ranulf to join him in an attack on York, but Stephen's swift arrival thwarted them. As Henry rushed south towards the safety of Bristol, Eustace almost caught him at Dursley Castle in Gloucestershire, but the newly knighted lad slipped through his fingers.

Henry gained a victory against Eustace at Devizes, when he was able to gather enough men to press Eustace back. In the wake of this positive moment, though, Henry left England again. Part of the reason for his success was that Earl Ranulf and Hugh Bigod had been causing trouble, keeping Stephen away. It was clear that his cause was nowhere near strong enough to defeat the fully arrayed might of Stephen's crown. Something else was happening at around the same time, too. After a decade of active civil war that had defied every effort to bring it to an end, and which was no further forward than it had been at its beginning, the barons took matters into their own hands. Stephen's reign, usually referred to as the Anarchy, acquired the name in reference to the lawlessness and breakdown in royal authority it has always been assumed to have facilitated. Evil, selfish lords ran amok in the vacuum of power, persecuting poor folk for their own malign pleasure and gain. This image is unfair.

The first *conventio* recorded was made between Ranulf, Earl of Chester, and Robert Beaumont, Earl of Leicester. The document was a contractual agreement that aimed to establish a *finalis pax et concordia* – a final peace and concord – between them. It was agreed that the earls had no desire to be at war with each other but acknowledged that their respective masters (Henry for Ranulf, and Stephen for Robert) were in conflict. They agreed that if they should be ordered onto the field of battle against each other, neither would move against the other with any more than twenty knights. Both men would refuse to allow their liege lord to launch assaults against the other from their private lands or castles. They also promised to give fifteen days' notice of any intention to attack the other's lands. Furthermore, the two men made a pact of mutual support, promising to come to the assistance of the other against all men but their liege lord.[49]

More of these arrangements quickly followed. Ranulf made similar agreements with Robert de Ferrers and William Peverel of Nottingham. Robert agreed on terms with Roger, Earl of Hertford, and his own twin brother Waleran Beaumont, Earl of Worcester. It seems likely that other similar mechanisms were being adopted by the barony too. Although it is hard to assess how well the terms might have held up to pressure from either Stephen or Henry, the very fact that opposing noblemen were seeking such arrangements demonstrates that they had now had enough of the seemingly eternal cycle of disputes. Ultimately, as landowners, barons profited from peace, not lawlessness. Getting the harvest in successfully, safely making it to market and selling produce kept them prosperous. In the long term, at least, anarchy was to their detriment, and it is telling that it was the barons who took the first steps towards ending the civil war.

Back in Normandy, Henry raised an army in September 1151, but the sudden death of his father Geoffrey caused him to rush south and abandon the attempt. In April 1152, another muster was ordered at Lisieux. This time, it was news of the annulment of the marriage of Louis VII of France and Eleanor of Aquitaine that distracted Henry. The 19-year-old duke of Normandy and count of Anjou again charged south, and on 18 May, he married the 30-year-old duchess of Aquitaine. Henry tried once more in June 1152, but a renewal of the alliance between Louis, now furious at Henry's marriage to Eleanor, which made him a greater landowner in France than the king of France, and Eustace dragged him away.

After two years of trying, Henry sailed from Barfleur in January 1153. He took with him 140 knights and 3,000 men-at-arms in thirty-six ships.[50] His allies in England were desperate, pleading that they could not hold out any longer, and Henry determined that this year must see a conclusion to the matter. After gathering his English support, Henry attacked Malmesbury. King Stephen duly arrived with an army, and the two sides confronted each other across an impassable, rain-swollen river. Stephen was unable to reach Malmesbury, and the tactically important castle fell to Henry. A truce was agreed during Lent and Henry moved from Bristol to Gloucester, where he held an Easter court at which he made much of adopting the title Duke of Aquitaine to add to his already impressive collection. After Easter, Henry marched his army across Worcestershire, Warwickshire, Northamptonshire, and into Derbyshire, where he took Tutbury Castle. When Robert Beaumont, Earl of Leicester, joined the assault on Tutbury, it was clear he had now abandoned Stephen. When Henry's army arrived outside Warwick Castle, it was immediately surrendered by the lady within, Gundreda de Warenne. Her husband, Roger de Beaumont, Earl of Warwick, was with Stephen, and when news of his wife's actions reached court, he dropped dead in shock and disgrace.

Henry next targeted the relief of Wallingford Castle. He assaulted Stephen's counter-castle at Crowmarsh, and the king arrived quickly with his son Eustace. The two sides faced off across the River Avon, but neither was willing to make the first move again. The desire of the nobility on both sides to avoid a fight was evident for all to see. The *Gesta Stephani* observed that 'the leading men of each army, and those of deeper judgement, were greatly grieved and shrank, on both sides, from a conflict that was not merely between fellow countrymen, but meant the desolation of the whole kingdom'.[51] Stephen and Henry met at the narrowest part of the river. Both lamented the unreliability of their nobles, but the two men made little effort to force a confrontation. Perhaps Stephen's kindness in helping Henry five years earlier had created an unwillingness to instigate battle now. Perhaps too, both men knew they would expose problems with loyalty in their ranks if they tried. Still, there was only one crown, and two men claiming it.

The direction of the conflict took a dramatic turn on 17 September 1153. Eustace had been infuriated by his father's unwillingness or inability to finish things off. He left court and took an army into the field, laying waste to Bury St Edmonds and the region around Cambridge. His plan was to bring Henry to battle and end the matter once and for all. Suddenly, and unexpectedly, on 17 September, Eustace died. All of his fury went with him, along with his father's plans for the future. Stephen had another son, but William would consistently make it clear he had no interest in the crown. All of a sudden, personal tragedy opened the door to lasting peace. King David of Scotland had passed away in May, predeceased by his son and succeeded by his 12-year-old grandson Malcolm IV. Scotland had its own internal issues that reduced its focus on the English dispute. The stars appeared to be aligning, finally.

On 6 November 1153, Stephen and Henry were persuaded to meet face to face at Winchester to try and settle the war. After almost twenty years of Stephen's reign, a solution emerged from the discussions. Stephen's son William would receive the county of Boulogne and all of the lands in England and Normandy his father had held before becoming king. He was already married to Ada de Warenne, one of the richest heiresses in England, so could look forward to a comfortable life away from the trials of kingship. Stephen recognised Henry's hereditary right to the throne. He had little to gain by perpetuating the conflict which was likely to end in Henry's accession on Stephen's death anyway. In return, Henry conceded that Stephen should reign for the rest of his natural life, recognising the sanctity of his kingship which would, ultimately, transfer to Henry. The final flourish was Stephen's adoption of Henry as his son, meaning that the king was still able to appear at least to be leaving his crown to his own heir, as well as the heir to Henry I.[53]

Early in 1154, Stephen and Henry held a series of joint courts. At the third of these in Oxford on 13 January, the nobility swore fealty to Henry. After several more joint sessions around Canterbury and Dover, Henry celebrated Easter in England and then left for Normandy. He had responsibilities across the Channel and perhaps felt that remaining in England risked getting under Stephen's feet and causing him to reconsider his decision. Stephen took himself on a slow, leisurely progress around his newly quieted kingdom. It was perhaps his first chance to simply enjoy being a king of a land at peace. Stephen was almost 60 and had spent nineteen years rushing about his realm confronting constant threats on several fronts. On 25 October 1154, able to relax at last, he passed away at Dover. He died a king, undisputed in the end, a fate many had not predicted for him. Mirroring his mother's refusal to be rushed to claim his blood right, Henry lingered in Normandy until 7 December, when he sailed from Barfleur. He was crowned at Westminster Abbey on 19 December 1154, beginning the Plantagenet dynasty that would shape England over the three centuries that followed.

The Anarchy was over. King Stephen had spent two decades viewing the claims first of his cousin Empress Matilda and then her son Henry as rebellious. The empress considered Stephen the great rebel who had stolen her inheritance. Eventually, Stephen would recognise Henry's claim and Henry would acknowledge Stephen's right, but quite where the real revolt stemmed from was still a matter of contention. The central question was how the right to the crown of England was passed from one king to another. In France, the crowning of an heir during the king's lifetime solved the uncertainty, but nothing like it ever crossed the Channel to England successfully. For all of Henry I's efforts to secure his bloodline, his own snatching of the throne from his older brother haunted his legacy and undid all of his work even before his body was cold. The central question from 1135 onwards boiled down to whether possession of the crown could ever be overridden by a claim, however good. For all of the charges that Stephen was a weak king who oversaw two decades of regressive war in England, he had demonstrated the power of the office of king. His success doubtless also highlighted the issues faced by a woman attempting to take up power in her own right, but the act of coronation had proven indissoluble and an absolute. Once anointed, a king could not be unmade.

The role of the nobility is critical during this period too. Presented with a situation in which their allegiance could be passed between two masters, some made the most of it. If there was one ruler, nobles were encouraged to behave themselves by the threat of sanctions, but if they were able to transfer their fealty to another candidate, there was no compulsion to accept whatever they did not like. By the same measure, a ruler in Stephen's position had no leverage to maintain discipline and order amongst his nobles. Hugh Bigod, Earl of Norfolk, seems to have cared little for Empress Matilda's cause, but was almost constantly in rebellion against Stephen for his own ends. Ranulf, Earl of Chester, shifted his allegiance between Empress Matilda and King Stephen to suit his own desire to make gains. Most of the barons were forced by political reality to play a careful balancing game. With no idea how the conflict might end, they needed to take immense care to protect themselves and their heirs. Alienating either side risked the loss of all their lands and possessions but failing to declare conclusively for one side bore the same risk.

Geoffrey de Mandeville had been a powerful man who had caused Stephen no harm prior to 1141. As the empress approached London with Stephen a prisoner, he secured his possessions and accepted the new political reality rather than fight against it. By the time of the Rout of Winchester, Geoffrey was back within Stephen's army, yet in the aftermath of his return, Stephen found himself unable to trust Geoffrey ever again fully. Eventually, he would drive one of his wealthiest subjects into revolt and an early grave. Others, including the Beaumont twins, seem to have deliberately spread their risk by placing a foot in each camp, allowing one to back the winner, whoever it may be. The other would be protected from the fallout. This kind of uncertainty only perpetuated the conflict and made a resolution harder to find.

Ultimately, the most striking aspect of King Stephen's reign as a long period of rebellion is that it was the nobility who grew tired of it first and sought to force an end to the fighting. The barony was the most likely place to look for revolt against the crown, but when two rivals claimed the throne, the impact on the country was devasting over a prolonged period. Landowners grew wealthy through peace. A brief rupture offered the chance to make smash-and-grab gains, but over years that drew out into decades, it prevented them from making a profit from their possessions. It was this that ultimately convinced the nobility to take steps to protect and insulate themselves from the effects of the civil war. Their withdrawal of active military support, in turn, compelled Stephen and Henry to find terms. Eustace's death was the catalyst to the final settlement, but neither side could continue a war in which no one would fight. The peaceful end to the Anarchy owed much more to the barons traditionally seen as selfishly and maliciously prolonging and intensifying it than to those tasked with ruling England. In the mid-twelfth century, the monarch was the rebel against the peace that it was their duty to maintain in the kingdom. The saviours came from the unlikely ranks to the barony who suffered from the failure.

Chapter 3

The Becket Affair

*Rebellion itself is never noble nor an end. Accepting the price
that must be paid to indulge in revolt is noble.
Paying it is the end.*

King Henry II would oversee a vast amalgamation of territories that might
be considered to constitute an empire. By the time he became King of
England, he was already Duke of Normandy in northern France, Duke
of Aquitaine, the vast province sprawled through southern France to the
Mediterranean, and Count of Anjou, which included the county of Maine
and linked Normandy to Aquitaine. Henry controlled more of the kingdom
overseen by King Louis VII of France than was directly ruled from Paris.
If that had not been enough to make Louis nervous and suspicious, Henry
had obtained Aquitaine by marrying Eleanor of Aquitaine within weeks of
the annulment of her marriage to Louis. The couple had made the match
without Louis's permission, a sanction they should have sought since he
was liege lord to both. Personal resentment was layered on top of wariness
to forge a relationship in white heat that required tempering to prevent it
from becoming brittle. Now that Henry was a king too, it added another
element to an already complicated situation.

In England, Henry found that all of the problems of the Anarchy vanished
in an instant. As Stephen's appointed heir and the son of Empress Matilda,
he unified the warring factions and allowed the barony to unite behind him.
King David of Scotland had died May 1153, eighteen months before Henry
came to the English throne. David's son Henry had predeceased him, and
the crown passed to David's grandson, Malcolm IV, who was just 12 years
old when he became king. Faced with a minority government, Scotland
was no longer in a position to challenge England for the lands in northern
England that David had snatched and retained. Henry simply demanded
them back, and Malcolm's ministers, terrified at the prospect of upsetting
a new king who was accumulating territories with alarming ease, handed
them over as the price for peace. With Normandy already under his belt, all
of the problems of dissecting the Anglo-Norman lands were immediately set

aside too. Henry's dynasty would become known as the Plantagenet family. The name appears nowhere in writing until 1460, more than three centuries after his accession. It is taken from Henry's father Geoffrey of Anjou's penchant for wearing a sprig of the broom plant as a badge. The Latin name for a sprig of broom is *planta genista*, which became Plantagenet. The dynasty's foundation mythology wove a story of Henry's swift and easy triumph in the wake of civil war but glossed over the alignment of stars that precipitated his astonishing rise and establishment of security.

One man rose to astonishing pre-eminence at the side of his master. His humble beginnings belied great talent and a driven yet likeable personality that was more than sufficient to make up for an education that was extensive yet appeared somewhat lacking. Thomas Becket shot to prominence and became so useful to Henry that the king sought to use to Becket to resolve a problem that had seemed beyond his reach. It was a spectacular failure in Henry's illustrious career and led to one of medieval England's most famous moments. So little is known of Thomas Becket's humble beginnings that even his year of birth is uncertain. It may have been 1119 but is usually accepted as 1120. The date, however, is known, falling on 21 December, St Thomas's day. It was for this Feast Day of St Thomas the Apostle that the parents named their new baby. He was baptised the same day at St Mary Colechurch, hinting that he may have been feared sickly or too weak to survive. Any fears were soon allayed as the baby began to thrive.

Thomas's parents were Gilbert Beket, a successful merchant, and his wife, Matilda. Both were of Norman extraction and had come to London to make their fortune. At the time of Thomas's birth, Gilbert and Matilda appear to have had three, and possibly four, daughters. They lived in Cheapside, an up-and-coming area of London increasingly populated by wealthy members of the merchant and aldermen classes. Although Gilbert used the surname Beket, it is unclear where that originated from or whether it was a hereditary family name as we might recognise it today. Thomas appears not to have used it during his career, usually referring to himself during his years as a clerk as Thomas of London. It was common for those within the profession to be identified by the place of their birth or employ, but it is also possible that Thomas shed the name Beket in a deliberate attempt to cast a shadow over his origins. For ease, Thomas Becket will be used to denote Gilbert's son.

In many ways, Thomas's education was unspectacular, but sufficient to equip him for whatever career may have awaited him. Some of his biographers in the immediate aftermath of his death would claim that his mother Matilda was the driving force that encouraged him academic attainment. As a successful merchant on the up in London society, his father too understood the need to be numerate and literate. Thomas was enrolled at Merton in 1130, aged 10. The school was some distance from home, around fifteen miles away, out of the city. The reason for its selection by Thomas's parents is unclear but may have been pragmatic. Merton was a school run by Benedictine monks; a fashionable order far more interested in worldly affairs than some others who took solace in their cloisters. Thomas could learn practical applications for the skills and knowledge he would accrue, which would prepare him for a profession. Entry into Merton would require Thomas to adopt the tonsure, the shaved crown common to all clerks, and he may well have taken minor orders, though these would not restrict him later from marriage or a secular career. One other potential benefit of a placement at Merton was a connection to the bishop of Winchester, within whose diocese Merton sat. Henry of Blois had been appointed in 1129 and was a nephew of King Henry I. None could have foreseen that five years later, Bishop Henry's brother Stephen would sweep to the throne in the wake of Henry I's death, but the king was fond of his nephews from Blois. Pushing Thomas into the orbit of someone so close to the king might bring additional benefits, but it is also clear that as an only son, a career in the church was unlikely to be the long-term plan for young Thomas.

At some point, and for reasons that are unclear, Thomas was withdrawn from Merton and placed into one of London's grammar schools, closer to home. The notion that Thomas's parents were directing his path towards avenues of power and promotion is supported during this period of his youth by a connection to Richer II of Laigle. Richer was of noble Norman descent; his great-grandfather Engenulf had been killed at Hastings fighting for William the Conqueror. It is possible that Gilbert or Matilda had a connection to Richer from their Norman home, or that they were actively seeking to create such links, because Richer lodged with the Beket family while visiting London. Richer appears to have taken a liking to young Thomas and took him into the countryside as part of his household, exposing him to the noble pursuits of hunting and hawking that would remain a lifelong passion for Thomas.

The sketchy information available suggests that Thomas next travelled to Paris to continue his education. There was not yet a university in the city, but its schools were already famed as the best in Northern Europe when Thomas arrived around 1140. The heady atmosphere attracted serious academics, and Thomas's time there may have reflected his parents' efforts to broaden his horizons and opportunities. Like much of Thomas's younger years, his time in Paris is shrouded in mystery, though it was undoubtedly another chance to move in lively and influential circles that facilitated the creation of powerful connections. Whatever drove the visit to Paris, it appears to have been brief. He was back in London just after he turned 21 in December 1141. That year had been seismic, seeing Stephen's capture at the Battle of Lincoln, Empress Matilda's reception into London and expulsion on the eve of her coronation, and the Rout of Winchester. London had been central to all of the uncertainty and brinkmanship, and it was to this that Thomas returned. It is possible that his time in Paris was cut short by the death of his mother, who many writers believed to have been the driving force behind his studies. With her influence removed, Thomas gave up on the idea. Other biographers would link the end of his time as a student to financial problems suffered by his father. Either way, he was dragged into the reality of beginning a career of some kind.

His experiences throughout this eclectic education would provide Thomas with a robust platform. Nowhere is he recorded as an excellent or in any way notable scholar during this period. It is possible that despite his parents' best efforts, Thomas lacked the focus and drive to make the most of the opportunities provided for him, at least in academic terms. What is clear is that his personality more than filled any gap in scholarly attainment. The scraps of physical descriptions provided by biographers hint at a tall, slender young man, whose good looks matured well over the years. He was considered elegant and amiable.[1] His education and early training had equipped him to move within clerical circles, and his personality eased his passage among men of power and influence. Those who wrote of Thomas's life shortly after his death were members of the church, men such as Edward Grimm, William Fitz Stephen, and William of Canterbury. For them, Thomas's lack of distinguished academic reputation and his worldly interests was problematical. That may explain why they are somewhat brushed under the carpet, though it may have equally served the biographers' ends to focus on these aspects as a contrast to accentuate Thomas's later Damascene conversion.

Having begun work for a London financier named Osbert, who was a relative of Thomas, he soon transferred to the household of the archbishop of Canterbury. Theobald of Bec had been chosen for the office by King Stephen in 1138. Many sources hint that Stephen's brother Henry, Bishop of Winchester coveted the position, but there is little evidence to support that view. Theobald hailed from the same region of Normandy as Thomas's family. Though there has been speculation that there may have been some distant relationship between them, such a connection remains elusive. Whatever link existed was exploited to gain Thomas a place in Theobald's household. Although Gilbert may have been the driving force behind securing the placement, there is no reason to suppose it was not Thomas's own work. He was 21, well-educated in primarily clerical, ecclesiastical circles and in need of a stable career.

Exposure to the money houses of London in late 1141 and early 1142 would have highlighted the fragility of the market. Empress Matilda had, just months before Thomas's return, been received by the city only to place enormous financial demands on the merchants and money lenders. The outcome of the conflict between Stephen and Matilda was still far from certain. Stephen was well-liked by London, but Empress Matilda would always have a fraught relationship with the authorities and wealthy men of the capital. It points to a degree of risk aversion in Thomas that he turned away from the volatile but potentially lucrative markets of London. Gilbert may have counselled his son to seek more security, but after a brief taste, Thomas was ready for something else. The Church offered a secure, if unprofitable and unspectacular, career path. It was involved in the machinations of the conflict but detached from it and largely shielded from any fallout. If this is an aspect that appealed to Thomas, it may offer an insight into his personality.

However he arrived within the household of the archbishop of Canterbury, it was a move that was to define Thomas's life. The clerk made steady progress, acquiring offices and incomes around England that made him comfortable. The later claim that he had been plucked from nothing for high office is slightly disingenuous, as he would have received an annual income that was not to be sneezed at. His first post appears to have been at the church at Bramfield in Hertfordshire. From various bishops who were former colleagues or acquaintances, and from Archbishop Theobald, he would add appointments at churches including St Mary-le-Strand in London, Otford in Kent, and prebends at cathedrals in London and Lincoln.[2] This gathering of posts over thirteen years hints at another of Thomas's personality traits; he was charming and affable as well as competent. It was this that would lead to his change of direction in 1154.

As the Anarchy was being drawn to a close with the coronation of King Henry II at Westminster Abbey on 19 December 1154, Thomas was set on a new career path. By the end of January 1155, Thomas was witnessing the new king's documents as his chancellor. The office was the most senior ecclesiastical post in the royal household, commanding the largest salary of 5s a day. The chancellor was not yet the governmentally significant office it would become, not least under Thomas's stewardship. It balanced control of the royal chapel and its religious services with oversight of the *scriptorium*, the king's writing office that produced the considerable volume of letters, warrants and writs that expressed the royal will. Thomas's appointment was at the recommendation of Archbishop Theobald, who had been a driving force behind the compromise that had presented the throne to Henry. Theobald must have trusted Thomas, both to serve Henry well, since his performance would reflect on his patron, and to represent Theobald and the church within the royal household.

What none could have foreseen was the bond that would develop between Henry and Thomas. Theobald was aware of his protégé's charm and easy manner, and the confidence these provided allowed him to recommend Thomas to the post. Over the years that followed, the two men, despite the gulf between them, or perhaps because of it, became firm friends. Henry was born to power and had accrued even more through good fortune and sheer will. Thomas was a merchant's son with a solid but unspectacular background. Henry was 21 when he became king. Thomas was 34. Beneath this veil of disparity, there was plenty to draw the two men together. Henry had risen far beyond what might have been his by birth. Thomas, too, had persevered with his education and selected a career path that had propelled him into the king's household and presence. Henry would always shun the more refined trappings of his exalted rank, preferring travelling clothes to fine robes, the mud of the road to scented oils. In Thomas, the king saw something he could be a little jealous of; a lack of expectation placed on him, an ability to behave as he wished. Henry saw a man rising through his own ability; a kindred spirit. Thomas's charm oiled the gears of friendship that spanned rank, and like so many low-born successful servants of monarchs, Thomas quickly developed a knack for knowing what his master wanted and delivering it.

There are numerous examples of jocularity between the two men, though it was always edged with a reminder of who was really in charge. William Fitz Stephen, one of Thomas's companions and earliest biographers, told one story of the king and his minister riding through the streets on a bitterly cold winter's day. Henry spotted an old man in rags who was clearly freezing cold. The king asked Thomas whether it would be an act of charity to offer a warm cloak to such a sorry figure. 'It would indeed,' Thomas replied, adding 'and right that you should attend to it my king.' They approached the elderly man, and Henry asked him if he would like a cloak. Assuming he was being mocked, and failing to recognise the king, the old man ignored the offer until the king reached across and took a handful of Thomas's new scarlet and grey cloak. With the garment clasped tightly at his throat, Thomas was forced to resist, and a scuffle broke out that brought the king's men running.

Fitz Stephen is adamant that in the end, Thomas allowed the king to win and wrestle the cloak from him. It was passed to the old man, and as the royal party went on their way, Henry's men mocked Thomas, offering him their cloaks.[3]

Although the incident displayed an ease and closeness in their relationship – how many men could physically wrestle the king? – it was also evident for all to see that Thomas was the punchline of Henry's jokes. Thomas was frequently the polished face of Henry's kingship, performing the displays of ostentation that held no interest for the king, and Henry took his opportunities to remind Thomas not to get too big for his boots. He would often ride his horse directly from the hunt into Thomas's great hall where he was hosting a feast, dismount in the middle of the room, vault the table laden with food and sit in a chair with his muddy boots on the table.[4] Alongside the close relationship such incidents provide glimpses of, each also shows that Henry was always sure to assert his ultimate dominance and that Thomas was continually willing to accept it.

In 1158, Henry opened negotiations to marry his oldest son, Prince Henry, to a daughter of the French king Louis VII. King Louis had remarried after his split from Eleanor of Aquitaine, who was now Henry's wife. Part of the reason for the end of their marriage had been the birth of two daughters, but no son to succeed Louis. His second marriage to Constance of Castile had produced one daughter to date. As he approached 40, Louis began to panic that his male line might fail. An alliance with Henry would keep his most powerful subject, and potential rival, in line, and would provide Henry with the possibility of adding the French crown to the family's holdings if Louis should die without a male heir. Henry knew that he had to dazzle the rich French king, not as his subject, but as his equal, a fellow king. Such a display was of no interest to Henry, but it was necessary, so Thomas was tasked with representing the king of England. Alongside getting him out of something he did not want to do, Henry could make a statement to Louis by sending a household servant to begin the negotiations.

Thomas arrived in the heat of the Paris summer with a glittering entourage. Led by 250 footmen who sang through the streets, the procession caused jaws to drop. An impressive collection of hounds and their handlers followed, and after them came eight wagons, each pulled by five horses, each horse ridden by a monkey, and every wagon guarded by a large mastiff chained to it. Two of the wagons were packed with barrels of beer, the others with impressive finery. Twenty-eight packhorses followed the wagons weighed down with gold, silver, cloth, coin, and books. Behind the horses came 100 squires, each holding a shield in one hand and in the other the reins to a large warhorse, upon each of which sat a gleaming, armoured knight. Next appeared the sons of noblemen in Thomas's care, his clerks, stewards, and servants. Finally, at the rear of this astonishing cavalcade, rode Thomas, the chancellor. He was the climax of the whole display. William Fitz Stephen wrote that the whole of Paris was amazed by the exhibition, and Henry's absence even added to the moment. On the lips of all Parisians was a similar sentiment: 'What a magnificent man the king of England must be if his chancellor travels in such great state.'[5] Perhaps there was more to using Thomas than a lack of will on Henry's part.

When Henry decided to press his claim gained via Eleanor to the county of Toulouse in early 1159, Thomas was noted as the mastermind behind the campaign. He brought a large retinue of knights, and Thomas drove increased tax revenue in Normandy to fund the effort. Henry led a vast host into Toulouse, but when Louis VII appeared to defend Count Raymond V, he halted at the thought of attacking his liege lord. It was a dangerous move for Henry in several ways, but Thomas pressed for an offensive. Instead, Henry withdrew and left command of the army to his chancellor. Thomas managed the move out of Toulouse. Becket had co-ordinated great alliances and income streams to make the campaign possible, and its failure was made his too since the king would take no blame for a mistake. Nevertheless, the pair continued their effective and mutually beneficial relationship for two more years before arriving at the moment that would set them irreparably at odds.

On 18 April 1161, Theobald of Bec, Archbishop of Canterbury died peacefully. He was in his early seventies and had sat on the throne of Canterbury for twenty-three years. His efforts to guide the kingdom through the upheavals of Stephen's reign had been even-handed, and his negotiation of the compromise between Stephen and Henry was critical to ending the conflict. Henry II had relied on Theobald to offer experience and wisdom, and there was a sense the country had benefitted from a strong tie between the church and the crown. Finding a replacement could be a pivotal moment in Henry's reign, and so the king did not hurry himself. Taking care over the decision was not the only reason for delay. It was traditional for the king to enjoy the revenues of the feudal lands held by a vacant bishopric. The man tasked with overseeing Canterbury's estates was the chancellor, Thomas Becket, and Henry was pocketing a handsome income. It was perhaps this efficiency that nurtured the seed of an idea in the king's mind.

During the early months of 1162, Thomas was summoned to attend the king at Falaise, along with the justiciar, Richard de Lucy. Henry had been on the Continent for several years and needed to catch up with his senior ministers from time to time. As soon as Thomas arrived, he was pulled aside by the king and told 'You do not yet fully know the cause of your mission.' Thomas frowned, wondering what task Henry had in mind for him. He did not have to speculate for long. 'It is only well,' Henry told him, 'that you should be archbishop of Canterbury.' After a stunned silence, Thomas began the protestations that he knew would accompany Henry's decision. The chancellor had risen to the highest office at court but had never even been ordained as a priest. He was 40 years old, and though he had worked for a time in the household of the archbishop, he had no experience to recommend him to the highest ecclesiastical office in the land. Thomas knew all of the objections, and as he looked down at his expensive clothes, he asked Henry, 'How religious, how saintly, is the man whom you would appoint to that holy see, and over so renowned a monastery!'[6]

The king was adamant. He told Richard de Lucy to go back to England with Thomas and placed his own son and heir, Prince Henry, into their care to add royal weight to their visitation upon Canterbury. Thomas was to go there and have himself elected archbishop. Henry cared little for how it was done, but they were to see his command fulfilled. Resigned that arguing would achieve nothing, Thomas crossed the Channel and made his way to Canterbury. The advantages of the desired appointment were clear to Henry. Thomas had proven himself capable and efficient in all that he had turned his hand to. There was no reason to suspect that he would fail to make the same success of his new task. Any lack of experience was mitigated by his time in Theobald's household, the high regard the late archbishop had held Thomas in, and his career at the heart of royal administration. Beyond all of this was one central consideration. Thomas had shown himself to be pliant. He excelled at all that he did, but would always, as their jocular relationship demonstrated, bend to Henry's will. At a time when the church across Europe was trying to redefine its relationship with secular princes and insert itself into the business of states, Henry saw a chance to resist. He had modelled his kingship on that of his grandfather, Henry I, and he had given no quarter to the church's demands to be given powers traditionally reserved for the king, including the right to invest bishops and archbishops. Now, Henry II could imagine the coup of having his man, a friend whose aims were aligned with his own, in charge of the English Church.

One person saw the danger. Empress Matilda advised her son against the appointment of Becket to Canterbury. She had no axe to grind with Thomas, but experience warned her of the folly of her son's policy. She had seen first-hand how wrong it could go. Her first husband, Emperor Henry V, had believed he could establish control over the church in Germany by appointing his closest advisor Adalbert to the vacant archbishopric of Mainz. As soon as he had been confirmed in office, Adalbert accused Henry V of eroding the rights of the church and worked tirelessly against his former master. When Matilda heard of her son's plan, she warned him of the alarm bells it rang.[7] In a signal of his own increasing sense of independence and the associated waning of his mother's influence, Henry ignored her. He was looking to restrain the fingers of Church interests that were working their way further into secular affairs across his holdings. In Normandy, Henry had the perfect mechanism. He resurrected the Decrees of Lillebonne, created in 1180 by his great-grandfather William the Conqueror and reissued by Henry I in 1107.[8] The Decrees laid out the precise extent of Church authority in Normandy and forbade any expansion of those rights without the express consent of the duke. In England, Thomas was to be his vehicle to control the church.

On 23 May 1162, Thomas stood outside the closed door of a packed chamber in London. The fact that he had been proven right was little consolation against the impending rage of a king who would not be opposed. At Canterbury a few weeks earlier, the monks had been advised by the king that Thomas was his preferred candidate to be their archbishop, but that they were free to elect whomever they wished. The monks had rejected Thomas outright and made it clear they were unimpressed by the idea.[9] Henry had asked nicely, but he would not be refused. A free election would have removed any question over Thomas's appointment and had been the king's preferred outcome. When the monks of Canterbury were ordered to appear in London, they knew pressure was about to be applied. On a dais sat the 7-year-old Prince Henry, lending royal authority to proceedings he can hardly have understood. The justiciar led the gathering and ecclesiastical weight was added by Henry of Pisa, a cardinal recruited in Normandy by Henry to support his aims. From outside the room, Thomas could hear letters from the king being read aloud to the gathering. The monks were now instructed to elect Thomas. Some felt it would be wise to do as Henry commanded, but others continued to resist, 'saying that Thomas is in no wise a person fitted for such a station, a man of mark though he may be among lay powers'.[10]

Gilbert, Bishop of Hereford led those opposed to the appointment, while Hilary, Bishop of Chichester and Henry, Bishop of Winchester made the case for accepting the king's wishes. The abbot of Canterbury suggested one of his monks for the post as others shied away from denying Henry what he demanded. The deadlock was broken by Cardinal Henry of Pisa. With a speech that offered little doubt as to the likely consequences of challenging royal authority, he counselled the monks to elect Thomas, and they duly did so, some still reluctantly.[11] Thomas was summoned, the doors swung open to him, and he was told that he had been elected Archbishop of Canterbury. The chancellor pleaded to be excused the honour because his workload was already too great. Richard de Lucy stepped forward with a letter from the king that released Thomas from all his offices and duties so that he was free to become archbishop. It is easy to see Thomas's reluctance as theatre, a show of reticence. Still, if he understood the extent of the king's plans and the position in which he would be placed, jammed between the rock and the hard place, it would be understandable if he sought a last-minute reprieve. When Bishop Henry pleaded with Thomas to accept, expressing his regret at his role in his brother's reign and offering Saint Paul as an example of one who withstood the church for a time, only to become its strongest pillar, Thomas relented. The meeting closed, and Thomas left the chamber Archbishop Elect of Canterbury.

On 2 June Thomas was ordained as a priest, and on the following day, he was consecrated as Archbishop of Canterbury by Henry, Bishop of Winchester. The honour was denied Roger de Pont L'Évêque, Archbishop of York, a former colleague and rival of Thomas's in Theobald's household, because he continued to deny Canterbury's supremacy over York. It was now that a sudden transformation came over Thomas. He wore the black cappa, a long, wool-lined robe that reached the ground, with a short surplice over it. Shunning the glittering finery of an archbishop, he looked to all the world like an Augustian monk and would dress this way for the rest of his life. Some contemporaries claimed that he began to wear the uncomfortable, self-punishing hair shirt from this point too.[12] Henry had got what he wanted. Almost immediately, he would regret not listening to his mother's warnings.

The reason for Thomas's Damascene conversion at the moment of his consecration is a mystery he took to the grave. His contemporaries, and those who wrote their thoughts were all monks and clerks, believed the religious experience changed him in an instant. Hagiographers were keen and quick to see God's hand at work. The weighty moment of investiture as not only a servant of God but as his highest-ranking representative in England (subject to York's protestations) would be sufficient to leave a mark on any but the most cynical. What Henry had failed to comprehend was that Thomas had risen to his position at the king's right hand with a conscientious and meticulous devotion to excelling at those tasks placed before him. Why, Henry might have asked himself, would he approach the role of Archbishop of Canterbury differently, or with any less commitment? What Henry lost sight of was the fundamental transformation in their relationship. If he believed friendship and service to the king was what Thomas valued most, he had miscalculated. Not only that, but he had forced Thomas to accept a new master, one beyond Henry's control. The new archbishop had always taken service to his master seriously. Thomas was now a servant of God.

Aside from this profound aspect to his religious awakening, which his friends were always keen to highlight, there were other possible explanations. Thomas had enjoyed the perks of his position at the king's right hand, living a lavish lifestyle and providing the pomp and display for which Henry had no time. All of that was being ripped away. Archbishops could certainly live as luxuriously as any great temporal magnate, but it was a dereliction of their role to do so. The conscientious Thomas may well have felt that he was being punished despite his excellent service. Not only was he explicitly removed from all of his offices, but he was set up to take the king's side in a conflict between the crown and the church now under Thomas's care. Beyond this, Henry handed Thomas the opportunity for a parity the king had always denied his chancellor. Low-born servants were useful to kings because they held nothing of their own. Everything they possessed, all of their incomes and prestige, remained firmly in the king's palm, to be taken away at any moment. Their skill and ability could be firmly harnessed because of their lack of independent means. Henry lifted that yoke from Thomas's shoulders by shifting him from the king's control to that of the church. Henry wanted his friend there because the church was not under the crown's influence. The danger was that once made archbishop, neither was Thomas. Detached from Henry's direct control, Thomas was free to perform the role of archbishop however he saw fit, not as Henry directed. It is just possible too that Thomas's dramatic conversion was driven in part by an entirely human desire for revenge. Not only had Henry taken away all that Thomas had worked for, but had presented his straight man, the butt of his jokes, with a freedom to act that he had never possessed before.

As the ship transporting Henry II and Queen Eleanor glided into Southampton's harbour in January 1163, the couple were pleased to see their oldest son, Prince Henry, now a month short of his eighth birthday, at the head of those assembled to greet them. Henry had been away from England for four and a half years. His dominance over the Norman Church had been swiftly and decisively established. A desire to replicate the triumph in England, as well as to fill the governmental gap left by Thomas's move, drew the king back to his realm. Behind the prince, in his long, black robe, looking like a late afternoon shadow, stood Thomas. Prince Henry had entered the archbishop's household and developed a personal fondness for his father's friend that would endure all that was to follow. If Thomas's entry into Paris in 1158 had been a shining statement of Henry's glory, his muted appearance at the dock was a stark contrast.

Unaware of any issue, Henry's first priority was to deal with a rebellion in Wales. In a swift and decisive campaign, Rhys, Prince of Deheubarth was captured and brought to England as Henry's prisoner. At a court held at Woodstock on 1 July, Henry ordered Rhys, along with other Welsh princes and Malcolm, King of Scots, who had all been summoned to attend, to swear fealty to him. The relationship between the king of England and these other rulers was finely but ambiguously balanced. Usually, it was accepted that the English king was the most powerful ruler on the British Isles, but peace rested on an understanding rather than extraction of an explicit expression of this. Henry, never fond of ambiguity, felt confident enough to take the risk. The leaders, seeing no other way out of Woodstock, gave their homage through gritted teeth, seething with embarrassment. Malcolm, who had provided military support to Henry in Toulouse, slunk back north with their previously friendly relationship soured. The Welsh princes returned home and immediately jumped into open rebellion.

One other contentious matter at Woodstock caused Henry to furrow his brow. He renegotiated the crown's deal with the sheriffs. These local officers were responsible for collecting taxes and delivering a fixed, contracted amount for their region to the Exchequer. Anything above that agreed sum a sheriff was able to raise was his to keep. Henry felt they were managing to take too much, which meant the Exchequer could get more. The sheriffs collectively decided it was easier to allow Henry to take a little of their cream. After all, there was still plenty left for them. One dissenting voice, claiming the king had no right to the money he sought to extract, was the new Archbishop of Canterbury. It had nothing to do with Thomas, but he stuck his nose in anyway, in opposition to the king. Henry might have thought it was a ploy; an effort on Thomas's part to distance himself and make it known he was not the king's man so that when he submitted the church to the king, it would look less suspicious. What other explanation could there be? The archbishop had no interest in this matter, nothing to gain or lose from the arrangement. With hindsight, this was the first moment Thomas exposed himself as the king's opponent; a tentative toe dipped into the tempestuous pool of revolt.

As winter fell, Henry began his move against the church. In parallel, he sought to have his son Prince Henry crowned in the French Capetian tradition to ensure the succession. It was perhaps these two finite and short-term aims that caused Thomas some concern amongst his other considerations. Government was a continual challenge, a never-ending process. Thomas was assured of a long and varied career there provided he could keep Henry's confidence. If he was archbishop simply to crown a boy, then hand control of the church to the king, what was he to do then? He was in his early forties and would effectively be put out to pasture if he gave the king what he wanted. There must have been a great deal swirling around Thomas's mind as Henry gathered the great men of his kingdom at Westminster on 1 October 1163. The king was certain he was about to get all that he wanted. He would soon be disabused of that belief.

Henry launched a scathing attack on the privileges claimed by the church. He complained that the institution asserted its jurisdiction over the clergy without possessing the processes to deliver justice. The king even pointed to a new practice of thieves disguising themselves as clerics to join bands of travellers, only to rob them.[13] Somehow, he positioned the crime as the church's fault because until they could be proven not to be real monks, the church claimed authority to deal with them. All too often, and all too literally, Henry complained that inadequate systems and slack sentencing allowed people to get away with murder. As king, it was his responsibility to maintain justice, and if the church could not do it, he would. Henry sat back and waited for his pliant archbishop to hand a chunk of the church's independence to the king. Thomas rose and expressed his sympathy for the king's concerns. Then, he dropped his bombshell.

As Archbishop of Canterbury, Thomas was unable to allow the degradation of the church's rights. Henry paused. Was this, like the display at Woodstock, part of the game? Thomas, surely, was merely giving the appearance that he would not give in to the king too easily. It allowed Henry to explain the basis for his demand. The king sought to restore rights his grandfather had enjoyed, as he had done ever since his accession, and which had been permitted to slip during the upheavals of Stephen's reign. He insisted that members of the clergy arrested for crimes such as theft, arson, and murder were to be handed over to his judges for trial and punishment in the same manner as the laity. Henry awaited Thomas's submission. Instead, the archbishop drew a breath and calmly refused. He explained to the king that ecclesiastics ought to be tried by ecclesiastical courts. If found guilty of such a serious crime, they would be ejected from their order. In that manner, if they should re-offend, they would then, and only then, be subject to the king's justice.[14] Thomas was negotiating with the king. This had not been the plan.

Henry's temper frayed, and he demanded his rights. The bishops, who must have feared they knew what the king had planned when he had appointed Thomas, were stirred by an unexpected hope and rallied to support their archbishop. Anger was fuelled by embarrassment as bishops gathered around Thomas to reinforce his position. Henry was attacking the church, but it had found an unforeseen champion, who 'endeavoured by every possible means to keep the ecclesiastical power and dignities intact'.[15] The king stormed out of the meeting and away from the capital. He spent Christmas 1163 at Berkhamsted, a manor he had gifted to Thomas when he had been chancellor. Snatching it back, Henry displayed his dissatisfaction with the archbishop by celebrating the holy festival there. The king took the chance to re-evaluate his plans, and in January 1164, he made a fresh, more modest attempt to bring the church under his control.

A council of the church's leading men was summoned to the royal hunting lodge at Clarendon in Wiltshire. The king presented them with a document entitled the Constitutions of Clarendon and told them to sign it.[16] The articles set out the relationship between the king and the church. Disputed appointments to ecclesiastical posts were to be settled by the king's justices. If a person accused of a crime claimed the benefit of clergy, it would be for the king's judges to decide whether that person would face trial in an ecclesiastical or a lay court. If it were referred to the church, the justices would retain a right to follow up the matter to ensure proper rigour had been applied to the inquiry, trial, and punishment. The right to appeal to Rome, which Henry felt had got out of hand, was to be curtailed. An appeal could only leave the kingdom with the king's express permission. Within the realm, appeals would follow a set structure, from archdeacon to bishop, to archbishop, and ultimately to the king. The crown was to sit at the pinnacle of the appeal process, controlling the gateway to Rome.

What Henry was seeking to achieve was an English equivalent of the Decrees of Lillebonne in Normandy. It had been easy to enforce that document in Normandy, and Henry felt that lacking an English parallel to lean on was the blockage in his kingdom. The Constitutions were carefully positioned to represent a collection of rights previously held by the king of England. There was little within them that should have been contentious: Henry wanted written confirmation of the rights the crown had always held. No more, no less. This issue of the links between lay rulers and Rome was widespread within Europe. The Church had, for decades, been trying to homogenise its relationship with the bickering states of Europe primarily to facilitate a clearer focus on crusading and the Holy Land. Spats between rulers and internal problems often prevented key figures enlisting in crusading efforts, or at least provided an excuse to fail to join. The problem with Rome's efforts to place itself as an umbrella across the disparate nations of Europe was that it necessarily infringed on what secular rulers considered their inviolable rights. Henry was concerned to clarify his prerogatives within his territories, just as other rulers were. Normandy had been brought into line quickly, and he had thought England would fall easily with Thomas in place. The Constitutions of Clarendon represented a step back from Henry's original plan by insisting on what he could demonstrate ought to comprise his rights.

Thomas stood to address the gathering. He accepted the Constitutions and the king's rights detailed within them. Henry relaxed. Thomas had overplayed the act of defending the church but was now falling into line. The other bishops looked on, horrified, as their worst fears were realised. The king's face fell as the archbishop began to speak again. The English clergy would accept the Constitutions 'saving their orders and the honor of God and of the Holy Church in all respects'.[17] The caveat was the equivalent of recognizing the Constitutions but retaining a right to ignore them completely. The document was designed to curtail ecclesiastical independence, and Thomas offered to sign it while asserting that the church's rules and service to Rome would always stand above it. Henry erupted with fury. He thrust a copy of the Constitutions into Thomas's hand and demanded that he accept it without condition. The bishops swung again from hope to horror as Thomas took it, only to turn around and tell them, 'Courage, brethren! by means of this writing we shall be enabled to discover the evil intentions of the king, and against whom we ought to be on our guard.'[18]

The meeting broke up, and no one was happy. Henry was furious, but the bishops were left bewildered by their erratic leader. They were used to measured and careful dealings with the crown, particularly when opposing its aims. Theobald had exemplified this quiet diplomacy, walking a fine line of providing guidance and support to the king while guarding the rights of the church. Thomas was openly defying the king, shouting and waving papers about in a manner that could only make things worse. If they had feared he would be the king's puppet as archbishop, this was almost worse. That Becket himself was conflicted was demonstrated when he placed himself under a strict penance, denying himself Mass until he had consulted Pope Alexander.[19] The pope, who was based in France as a result of a schism that had seen the rise of an antipope in Italy, tried to mediate. He needed Henry's support and was concerned about a rift between the church and one of Europe's most powerful rulers.

Rotrou, Archbishop of Rouen was dispatched to mediate, but Henry insisted he would only countenance a reconciliation if Alexander himself confirmed the Constitutions of Clarendon. Alexander would not gift away Church authority. Henry sent representatives to request that Roger, Archbishop of York, Thomas's former rival in Theobald's household and now his adversary in the ongoing dispute between England's archdiocese, be appointed legate. The pope was unwilling to add to the contentious problems between Canterbury and York but made an astounding offer instead. Alexander would make King Henry himself papal legate to England. To the king's frustration, there was an infuriating caveat. Henry could be the pope's representative in England with authority over the church provided he 'do nothing offensive to the archbishop of Canterbury'. Henry turned the messengers around and sent them back to Alexander with their letters.[20]

In October, Henry changed tack. He took a dangerous course that stirred memories of the fate of Roger, Bishop of Salisbury, at King Stephen's hands in 1139. Thomas was ordered to appear before the king at Northampton to answer charges of misconduct in public office and contempt of court. Thomas responded by informing the king that as Archbishop of Canterbury, he was beyond the king's jurisdiction. Given Henry's purpose in having Thomas elected to the office, it was an inflammatory reply. Henry snapped back that Thomas was not being summoned as an archbishop but as a baron, and if he refused to answer the summons, he would face secular reprisals. On Thursday 6 October, Thomas arrived in Northampton to find his lodgings filled with the king's servants.[21] He installed himself at St Andrew's Priory and the next morning rode to the castle. Henry made the archbishop wait, and when Thomas offered the kiss of peace as a greeting, Henry pointedly refused it. Thomas asked for permission to visit the pope in Sens before answering Henry's charges, something he must have known would further infuriate the king, to which Henry bellowed in response, 'You shall first answer me.'

The king launched into a charge that Thomas had denied justice to John, the king's marshal, in the archbishop's court. John laid claim to a piece of land that Thomas held and had tried to bring the case in Thomas's court but been denied a fair hearing. Thomas shrugged the charge off. John, he insisted, had arrived at his court with a bundle of papers, and then immediately turned around and left again. Henry, Thomas asserted, had staged the incident as a pretence for the current charade. Unperturbed, Henry ordered his barons to find Thomas guilty and fine him £500. When the archbishop retired for the evening, he took to his bed, telling his servants he was ill. When word of this reached the king, he ordered Thomas to return and answer charges of financial malpractice during his time as chancellor. Thomas sent back word that he was unprepared to deal with matters of which he had no prior notice, reminding the king that on his election as archbishop, Thomas had been discharged from all secular offices in a document that included a pardon for any and all debts and charges relating to those offices. Besides, Thomas added, he was too ill to travel back to the castle. Henry sent the earls of Leicester and Cornwall to check the archbishop's claims, and they were convinced of his ailment. Thomas was excused from attending immediately, and his suspicions must have been confirmed when members of the royal household visited to warn him that he faced arrest and possible execution if he continued to resist the king.

After weighing his options, Becket rode back to the castle on 13 October. Dressed in his black robes, he carried his archepiscopal cross before him, emphasising that he was going to the king as Archbishop of Canterbury, not as his vassal. At the castle gates, Thomas dismounted and walked into the hall, still bearing his cross. He found the room packed with a variety of people there to petition the king and quietly took his seat amongst them. After a short time, Gilbert, formerly bishop of Hereford and now transferred to London, spotted Thomas. Pushing his way through the crowds, Gilbert chastised Thomas for daring to come before the king brandishing a cross as though it were a weapon. He tried to grab it but found himself unable to prise it from Thomas's powerful grip. Henry, Bishop of Winchester, intervened to diffuse the embarrassing spectacle of senior clergyman physically brawling in public. Gilbert, frustrated at being unable to overpower Thomas, turned on the elderly bishop of Winchester and berated him for interfering in the king's business. Next, Roger, Archbishop of York joined the group to warn him to set down his cross or face the king's much sharper sword. Henry needed Thomas there as a secular individual, and this overt display of his ecclesiastical office defeated the king. Aware of what he was doing, Thomas coolly advised Roger, 'If the king's sword carnally slays the body, my sword pierces spiritually, and sends the soul to hell.'

The bishops now changed their approach and pleaded with Thomas to bring an end to this terrible situation by resigning his see and throwing himself on the king's mercy. Unwilling to give up the armour of his office, Thomas declined. The king now sent several knights to summon the archbishop into the royal presence. Henry demanded once more that Thomas account for his time as chancellor, specifically accusing him of embezzling £30,000 in silver and failing to repay £1,000 the king had lent him for the Toulouse campaign. Thomas's response to the serious accusations of fraud on a colossal scale was predictable. He had always rendered full accounts to the king during his time as chancellor. Besides, the archbishop reminded the king, he had been excused all debts and charges on his election to Canterbury.

Henry, who must have expected the reply, instructed the gathered barons to move to judgement on Thomas 'who, being my liege-man, refuses to take his trial in my court'. Ushered out of the hall, Thomas awaited the inevitable guilty verdict as he tried to work out what to do next. When the earls of Leicester and Cornwall emerged and approached the archbishop, he raised his hand. Before they could speak, he forbade them to deliver the news that he was to be arrested and imprisoned on pain of excommunication. As they hesitated and decided to return to the hall to relay this development to the king, Thomas stood up and walked out of the crowded waiting area. Climbing onto his horse, he rode to the city gates. They were locked, but one of Thomas's servants found the keys and opened them as the porter stood on and watched, uncertain what he should do.

At St Andrew's Priory, Thomas instructed the monks to lay on a feast for all the poor folk they could find. He made up a bed before the altar and took some rest, clearly still feeling unwell, as his household made preparations for him to leave. As night fell, Thomas left the crowded Priory, which would take time to search if anyone came looking for him and rode hard for Lincoln. He took only three companions; two monks and a servant and used the name Dereman as he travelled. From Lincoln he rode south, travelling by night and resting in the houses of friends and sympathisers during the day. At Sandwich on the south coast, the archbishop and his small company took ship at night across the Channel, landing at dawn in Flanders and making all haste to the court of Louis VII, King of France. Becket arrived to find Gilbert, Bishop of London, and William, Earl of Arundel, already there. Henry had asked Louis to eject Becket from his lands and to petition the pope, still within Louis's kingdom, to ignore the wayward archbishop.

Henry had misjudged Louis. The French king had no intention of passing up an opportunity to cause discomfort and embarrassment for a man who was a political threat. The more Gilbert and William protested, the warmer the reception Becket received. At the request to advise the pope to ignore the archbishop, Louis sent word to Alexander that if he valued French backing in the schism, he would receive Thomas and hear his case. Alexander, having little option, obliged. At this, Henry sent Roger, Archbishop of York, the bishops of Winchester, London, Chichester and Exeter, along with William, Earl of Arundel, and a host of his barons to the papal court at Sens. They demanded that Becket be handed over to face Henry's judgement as a secular servant of the king. Alexander had no choice but to refuse. He could never hand an archbishop over to a king. To do so would be to acknowledge the superiority of secular law over the benefit of clergy, the denial of which was precisely what had begun this saga. Prepared for the pope's reticence, the delegation asked for two legates to be despatched to England so that Henry could show them the truth of the charges laid against Thomas. Wary of how easily some of his cardinals could be bribed and flattered by Henry, Alexander declined. As the party rode away from Sens, they tried to work out how they would break the news to the king.

Thomas prostrated himself before Pope Alexander and pleaded that he was being persecuted for trying to uphold the rights of the church. He gave the pope the copy of the Constitutions of Clarendon that Henry had forced on him. When it was read aloud to the gathered cardinals, they all agreed that the archbishop had done the right thing. Alexander proclaimed a perpetual damnation on the Constitutions and ordered the excommunication of anyone who tried to uphold them. Henry responded by effectively breaking England from the Roman Church. No member of the clergy was permitted to leave English shores without a letter from the justiciar. Anyone trying to return without an additional letter of permission from the king would be arrested. Any person attempting to bring into the realm any edict or notice from Pope Alexander or the archbishop of Canterbury was to be seized and proclaimed a traitor. Anyone observing an interdict or other instruction originating outside England would be banished from the kingdom immediately along with all their family, their goods and lands forfeit to the crown. St Peter's Pence, the contribution made by the English Church to the papacy, was to be collected still but delivered to the Exchequer. Henry's plan in 1164 that had seemed so simple had blown up in his face. He had control over the English Church, but had caused an enormous rift within it, driving its leading figure into exile, exposing the weakness of his relationship with the French king, and he had been snubbed by the pope.

Henry tried to discourage others from following Becket's example by extending punishment for his disobedience to his family. Unable to get his hands on Thomas, it also provided the king with an outlet for his simmering frustration. Anyone with the faintest blood relation to the archbishop was jostled out of Henry's kingdom, 'even infants crying in the cradle'. Some saw tyranny in the persecution. 'What art thou doing, thou tyrant? What madness is it that hath overcome thee, that thou shouldst thus drive away from thy kingdom those who have done thee no injury, and in whose mouths no guile has been found? There is no reason why the issue of the banished, so long as they observe the laws, should not live in the city!'[22] Having erupted in the aftermath of Thomas's, to Henry's mind at least, betrayal, the king tried to carry on with the immense task of ruling his sprawling territories. The effort to define his relationship with the church in England had been only one aspect of Henry's relentless workload. He would make efforts to ignore his exiled archbishop, and that was perhaps an active policy decision. Thomas would toil endlessly to keep his situation at the forefront of political discourse. It was this oxygen that Henry denied his chancellor. For all Thomas felt he knew the king of England, Henry had spent years working closely with his chancellor too. Each could predict the other's moves and moods. If Henry saw in Thomas a showman who thrived on attention and spectacle, then he would remove the spotlight.

Like a fly buzzing just beyond reach, Thomas became a persistent irritation to Henry. He used the allies he had identified to full effect. Pope Alexander wrote to Empress Matilda to ask her to encourage her son to find peace. The pope literally told on the king of England to his mom. The empress, obviously unimpressed at being placed into such a position, reluctantly sent a letter to Thomas. Having warned her son of the dangers of promoting Thomas, the empress took no delight in being proven right. Nor did she place any blame on her son. Thomas, she was at pains to point out, was in the wrong, and it was Thomas who ought to seek reconciliation. Having informed the archbishop that the pope had instructed her 'to interfere' in the matter, Matilda laid out the problem. Henry had been nothing but kind and gracious to Thomas, showing him faith and favour. This rebellion, she sniped, was no way to repay the king. The onus was on Thomas to undo what he had done, though the king's mother warned, 'I plainly tell you, that you cannot recover the king's favour except by great humility and most evident moderation'.[23] These were not qualities for which Thomas was well-known.

It was not until 1166 that Henry attempted to tackle the problem of his wayward archbishop head-on again. Thomas had taken refuge at the Cistercian abbey at Pontigny just south-east of Paris. Here, he had been joined by those expelled from Henry's lands on account of their connection to him. Despite being hosted at the abbey at the express request of Pope Alexander, Henry fired off an angry letter. He informed the abbot that if his organisation continued to shelter the rebel archbishop, the king would expel all Cistercians from England and take their lands into royal hands. Rather than force his host to make an impossible choice, Thomas packed up and left.[24] If Henry felt he had gained a victory, he had, inexplicably, underestimated Becket again. The archbishop took his luggage and persecuted entourage to Louis's court, where he was warmly greeted with excitement. From Henry's perspective, Thomas had moved deeper into the viper's nest and was even further beyond the reach of the king of England. Louis gave Thomas lodgings at St Columba's Abbey in Sens. Still south-east of Paris, it remained nestled safely away from Henry's Continental holdings. To Louis's delight, Thomas began to excommunicate English ministers, simultaneously asking the pope to place England under an interdict. Alexander wrote to Henry, asking him to return to the devotion to the church that 'seems in some measure to have waxed cool'. The king must, Alexander insisted, cease his efforts to 'render subject to your power that which belongs to Jesus Christ' and 'leave to the ecclesiastics all ecclesiastical matters'.[25]

The pope also wrote to Gilbert, Bishop of London, to encourage him to lead Henry to the path of reconciliation. Gilbert offered the king's response that he had no wish to be at odds with the church. Although he recognised the pope's authority, he turned Thomas's weapon around, by adding the caveat of 'saving always the dignity of himself and of his kingdom'. On the question of Becket's predicament, Henry insisted it was all of the archbishop's own making. He had chosen to leave England, and so he was free to return whenever he was ready to face Henry's charges. Pleading for moderation, Gilbert explained that an interdict or a sentence of excommunication laid against the king would only make matters worse and deepen the crisis. The apparently reasonable warning that Henry might try to reduce papal influence in England further and bend the church to his own will was more likely a stark warning from Henry than the concerned conjecture of the clergy.[26]

Never one to retreat from an approaching storm, Thomas penned his own letter to Henry.[27] He hoped his advice would 'contribute to the salvation of your soul and to my acquittal', making the two matters appear as one; Henry could not be saved without resolving his disputes with Thomas. The archbishop had been wrestling with the impossible problem of deciding between the competing demands of temporal and spiritual concerns. He had concluded that he must follow God since his soul was at risk if he failed in his obligations to the church. Thomas missed no opportunity to remind Henry that he would always be below the church in power and authority. The king could inflict temporary, physical pain, but God held sway over the eternal being. Neither man was willing to back down, and Thomas had found a platform that offered him, at least in the archbishop's mind, parity with his former master. Their authority was derived from different paths to the same source, but Henry's, Thomas insisted, was not greater than the archbishop's.

The stalemate persisted. Henry spent the campaigning season of 1167 subduing Aquitaine and Brittany. He also lost his mother in September. She was 65 and had provided her son with unswerving support, even if he had sought to shake off her influence. With the colder months that prevented military activity, he returned his focus to Thomas. Henry held court at Argentan between 29 November and 5 December. During the week, two cardinals sent by Alexander passionately pleaded with the king to find a way to be reconciled with Becket. As part of the negotiations, Henry secured assurances that Thomas would not be permitted to place England under interdict but gave no ground. Alexander made Thomas a papal legate, increasing his authority in the face of Henry's belligerence. Prevented from moving against England as a whole and refraining from targeting the king directly, the archbishop offered a display of his new power against his adversary Gilbert, Bishop of London. Thomas explained that he had endured Gilbert's 'extravagances' for too long and excommunicated the bishop. Gilbert was to be prevented from receiving communion 'lest by coming into contact with you, the Lord's flock may be contaminated to its ruin'. Gilbert was the king's most vocal supporter within the English church, and Thomas's targeting of him was a thinly veiled warning to other bishops, but also to the king. The archbishop also wrote to the chapter in London instructing them to enforce Gilbert's exclusion from services, and to Robert, Bishop of Hereford. Robert was a close associate of Gilbert, but instead of threatening him or imposing sanctions, Thomas made him the most senior officer of the church in England during the archbishop's absence. He forwarded a list of those to be treated as excommunicated, including the archdeacon of Canterbury, the joint-justiciar Richard de Lucy, and Earl Hugh Bigod.[28] There may have been a plan to divide and conquer by drawing those supporting Gilbert and the king into Thomas's orbit while demonstrating what happened to those who opposed his authority.

At the beginning of 1168, Henry was required to face more unrest in Aquitaine. It was a source of constant frustration to Thomas that Henry had so much else to deal with across his dominions. The archbishop had been left with nothing but his current predicament. He continued to write letters and tell his tale to any who would listen, but to the king, he was just one vexing problem among many. Much of the year was spent trying to balance the relationship between Henry and Louis. Henry insisted on freedom to act within the vast holdings he nominally held as Louis's liegeman. The English king's military effectiveness on French soil was unnerving for Louis and looked ever more like a threat. Conferences broke down, and Louis began to try to split Henry's holdings apart, interfering in Brittany and infuriating Henry. Eventually, realising his policy was in danger of backfiring and causing Henry to focus his hostility more fully on the French crown, Louis arranged peace talks at Montmirail for January 1169.

The two kings settled several matters at Montmirail, including the status of Brittany as subservient to Normandy. Brittany would be held by Henry's third son Geoffrey as duke. Prince Henry was to do homage to Louis for Normandy and Anjou. Henry's second son, Richard, would do homage for Aquitaine. The steps were designed to provide Louis with confirmation of his lordship without Henry being forced to do personal fealty to a fellow king. It was all going perfectly. Then Thomas Becket arrived. The emerging détente between Henry and Louis was not in Thomas's interests unless he could use the harmony to resolve his own plight. Thomas offered to be fully reconciled to the king, before adding that he would never consider himself subject to the will or judgement of any layman, including the king. Henry stormed out of the meeting. The frustration of other leading figures with the archbishop was beginning to match Henry's. Thomas rode away from Montmirail with Louis, tearing down all of the goodwill that had been built up. That had, perhaps, been Becket's plan.

When Henry and Louis next met at Montmartre in November 1169, Becket again inserted himself into the meeting. Henry refused to give the archbishop the kiss of peace, and it was clear that Becket was not going to go away or give in. Precisely what had made Thomas such a valuable chancellor made him an implacable rebel. Having settled various issues from Aquitaine to Brittany, Henry moved into Normandy and re-evaluated his tactics in dealing with his former friend. The king sent word to the archbishop in early 1170 that he wished to meet at Caen in western Normandy to try and find a final resolution. Although for Thomas it meant leaving the protection of Louis's lands, he agreed and began the journey to Caen. Somewhere along the road, Thomas learned that Henry was not at Caen. The king was no longer even in Normandy, or on this side of the Channel. Henry's new tactic was a proactive effort to embarrass Thomas and demean his authority, which was precisely what Thomas had been doing to Henry. The king had returned to England to begin plans for the coronation of his oldest son, Prince Henry. The move offered dynastic security, but the crowning of a king was the preserve of the archbishop of Canterbury. Arranging it in Thomas's absence was a direct challenge to his power within the English church.

By June 1170, Henry was putting the finishing touches to his plans for the coronation. He had not rushed but instead had given Thomas time to stew on it. Prince Henry had left Caen on 5 June. When Henry, Bishop of Winchester had tried to join the party, he had been delayed by the joint efforts of Eleanor of Aquitaine and the constable of Normandy. It transpired that Bishop Henry had been furnished with letters from the pope forbidding the coronation and had been instructed to smuggle them into England in the prince's party. Henry had calculated his final decision to cause maximum devastation. The coronation was not to be undertaken by the archbishop of Canterbury, nor by Robert, Bishop of Hereford, appointed by Thomas as the senior clergyman in his absence. The honour had been handed to Roger, Archbishop of York. Roger and Thomas had a personal rivalry that dated back decades. More than that, Henry offered recognition of York's pre-eminence at a time when Canterbury was fiercely advocating York's subservience to the southern archepiscopal seat.

On Sunday 14 June 1170, Henry the Younger, who would now become known as Henry the Young King, was crowned at Westminster Abbey, aged 15. On the following day, William, King of Scots, his brother David, and all the earls and barons of England swore fealty to Henry the Young King, saving only their loyalty to his father. Henry had tricked Thomas, rubbed his nose in it, and slammed the door in his face. Now, he would open the door again, just a crack, and see how Thomas reacted. The moment was so perfectly staged that it seems entirely likely it was designed by Henry and Louis at Montmartre. As troublesome as Thomas was to Henry, he was becoming tiresome to Louis, the pope and everyone else. Henry was a mighty ruler. Louis and Pope Alexander were pragmatic enough to see that isolating and endlessly infuriating him was not a long-term policy that would meet anyone's aims. Louis had enjoyed his use of Becket to annoy his rival. Alexander had been pushed into a corner by his need to defend the church, but it was Thomas who was drawing the affair out. He refused to move an inch and was frustrating the peace between Henry and Louis that the pope needed to resolve the schism and focus on the Holy Land. Frankly, everyone was getting a bit bored of Thomas's constant, and loud, whining too.

King Louis took offence that his daughter Margaret, who was married to Henry the Young King, had been left in Caen and excluded from the coronation ceremony. He gathered an army and marched to the Norman border. Henry left England in the care of his son and crossed the Channel to face the threat. The two kings met at Fréteval to try and find a peaceful solution. Henry immediately offered to repeat the coronation the following year, this time with Margaret at her husband's side. Louis was satisfied. At the last moment, just as Henry planned, Thomas bustled into Fréteval. Henry was acutely aware that without papal approval and the involvement of the archbishop of Canterbury, his son's coronation was open to suggestions that it was invalid. He needed Thomas and Alexander to get the job done properly, so the coronation had perhaps been little more than a rehearsal in Henry's mind. What Henry had counted on was Thomas's inability to resist the afront to the dignity of his office. He had been correct. The hint of a wider plan can be seen in the intelligence that Bishop Henry had been carrying papal letters. The tip-off, perhaps, came from Louis, or even Alexander himself. Either way, Thomas was dragged to the negotiating table for the first time on terms other than his own.

Henry repeated his offer of another coronation. As well as involving Margaret, Henry would allow Thomas to officiate if they could drop all the issues pulling them apart. Faced with the realisation that he was outstaying his welcome in France and losing sympathy fast, as well as risking the dignity of his archdiocese, Thomas accepted. Henry believed he had won when the archbishop meekly submitted in his desperation to return home. He ought to have known Thomas better. When the king and archbishop met again at Amboise in October, there was no friction. A third date was arranged when they would join together at Rouen and travel back to England together. Henry had been ill in August, seriously enough to have made his will. When he recovered, he made a pilgrimage to the Shrine of Our Lady at Rocamadour in Aquitaine. He wrote to Thomas that being so far south would prevent him from making their rendezvous at Rouen, adding that he had heard rumours Louis meant to stir up trouble as soon as he crossed the Channel too. How true the excuse was is unclear, and Henry may have wished to stay away from Thomas until the coronation was completed to avoid the risk of any renewal of their hostility.

Thomas set sail for England. When he received word that a delegation of bishops was gathering to meet him at Dover, he redirected his ship to land at Sandwich. He rode swiftly to Canterbury, where he was jubilantly welcomed by the monks, though Thomas chastised them for contributing to the prolonging of his breach with the king.[29] Seeking to make the most of Henry's absence, Thomas set about establishing his authority from his base at Canterbury. The archbishop's first act was to excommunicate all those bishops who had been involved in the coronation of Henry the Young King. In dismay, they fired off letters to King Henry to complain that Thomas had not come timidly to be reconciled. If Henry had believed he had won and tricked Thomas into doing what the king wanted, the flurry of letters that reached him at the Christmas court in Bur-le-Roi, near Bayeux, represented the realisation of his mistake. What happened next has become one of the most famous moments in medieval history, as hotly debated in the weeks that followed as it is 850 years later.

What is beyond doubt is that Henry was furious at Thomas's behaviour. The precise wording of his eruption has changed in the various retellings of the episode ever since. History has long placed the phrase 'Will no one rid me of this turbulent priest?' into the king's mouth.[30] William of

Newburgh, a contemporary chronicler, noted only that Henry 'grew angry and indignant beyond measure, and losing the mastery of himself, in the heat of his exuberant passion, from the abundance of his spirit, poured forth the language of indiscretion'.[31] Edward Grim, a monk of Canterbury who was with Thomas through what would ensue, recorded the king's words as they were reported to him. The Latin phrase is now usually translated as 'What miserable drones and traitors have I nurtured and promoted in my household who let their lord be treated with such shameful contempt by a low-born cleric!'[32] The words matter because the question of Henry's intent would become central to the controversy that followed from them.

Four knights rose from the feast, each confident that their master had issued what amounted to an instruction. Reginald FitzUrse, Hugh de Morville, William de Tracy, and Richard le Breton rode to the coast, crossed the Channel, and made directly for Canterbury. As the knights burst into Thomas's room on 29 December 1170, they found him eating a meal. They demanded that he undo the sentences of excommunication placed on those who had been doing the king's bidding. Thomas coolly informed them that the judgement of a higher power could not be undone at the whim of a lesser authority. It is impossible that Thomas was unaware of the incendiary nature of his comments. The knights lurched into threats of violence, but Thomas waved them away, unconcerned. In a fit of pique, the men clattered out of the cathedral to recover the weapons they had set aside before entering.

The frightened monks gathered around Thomas, trying to convince him to move from the cloisters to the high altar to better protect him from the threat of violence. Edward Grim was one of those monks, and he was at Thomas's side when the angry knights returned brandishing their swords. He would set down his eyewitness account of the dramatic scene.[33] The knights had come without the king's knowledge but had not come alone. A large force was stationed outside the cathedral to support them. The subdeacon, named by Grim as Hugh the Evil-clerk, led the knights to Becket before the altar. As most of the monks formed a knot around their archbishop, others ran to bar the doors to prevent the soldiers outside from entering. Thomas called them back, telling them that they stood in God's house, not a fortress, and God would provide more protection than closed doors could.

'Where is Thomas, traitor of the king and kingdom?', roared one of the knights. When no answer came, he bellowed louder, 'Where is the archbishop?' The monks were becoming fretful in their tight huddle as the four brandished their swords. Pushing the brethren gently aside, Thomas emerged from the centre of the group, assuring the knights calmly, 'Here I am, not a traitor to the king but a priest.' When Thomas asked what they wanted of him, the knights demanded again that he absolve the excommunications he had imposed. Thomas shrugged off the order. The men had done no penance, so could not be forgiven. With that came a threat to Thomas's life: 'Then you will now die and will suffer what you have earned.' The archbishop was unflustered. He had served a king with a short temper. He had been a military man and taken part in campaigns. His nerve held well against the menace. 'I am prepared to die for my Lord', he assured the knights before forbidding them to harm anyone else in the cathedral.

At this defiance, the knights lost what remained of their control. They grabbed the archbishop and tried to drag him from the building. Now nearly 50, Thomas clung to a pillar so tightly the four could not move him. Thomas rebuked one of the knights, Reginald FitzUrse, who the archbishop claimed owed him allegiance. Reginald screamed back that he owed no man allegiance above that which he owed the king. With this, Thomas released his grip on the pillar, pressed his hands together, leaned forward, and began to pray loudly. Some of the monks, who had scattered to hide from the shocking violence, rushed back to the archbishop, suddenly emboldened to protect him. Reginald, blinded by rage, raised his sword above his head and swung it down, shaving skin from Thomas's head and slicing into Edward Grim's arm as he tried to protect the archbishop. Edward managed to keep his arm above Thomas's head until a second blow severed it clean off and crashed into Becket's head. A third caused the archbishop's knees to buckle, and he crumpled to the floor. Edward heard him mutter, 'For the name of Jesus and the protection of the church I am ready to embrace death.'

As the knights pressed in around the prone figure, a fourth sword swing crunched through bone and sliced the top of Thomas's skull off. The sword shattered as it hit the stone floor of the cathedral in a pool of blood. In a final act of betrayal, Hugh the Evil-clerk stepped forward and placed his foot across the back of Thomas's neck, causing his brains to pour into the puddle of blood. 'We can leave this place, knights,' Edward heard him crow, 'he will not get up again.' Edward stood, his own severed arm bleeding profusely, utterly stunned by the shocking violence and the gory scene left before him. He had just watched an archbishop of Canterbury hacked to death before the altar within Canterbury Cathedral.

Becket's murder made Henry II an international pariah. It took three days for news of what had happened to reach him. The king shut himself away for three days amid fear for his health and his sanity. He may have racked his brain for the words he had shouted out during the drunken feasting. Had he ordered Becket's murder without really meaning to? It was a personal disaster that placed his immortal soul at risk. Politically, it was catastrophic. Criticism was not slow to come. King Louis wrote in shock and outrage to Pope Alexander of 'a cruelty so unheard-of'. He demanded 'the sword of St Peter be unsheathed to avenge the martyr of Canterbury'. If Louis had participated in the scheme to lure Thomas back to England, this cannot be what he believed would happen. He seized on the opportunity to turn the Christian world against Henry, though. William, Archbishop of Sens, also called on the pope to take action in what was quickly beginning to look like crusading fervour. Theobald, Count of Blois, an ally of Louis, added his weight to the demands for an immediate remedy, expressing to Alexander a hope that 'God would both instil into you a wish for vengeance, and the power of obtaining it.'[34]

Alexander resisted calls to act against Henry. The king made efforts both to stay out of the way and to ingratiate himself to the pope. Henry moved into Ireland to subdue the territory and bring it into line with the structures and governance of the Roman church. It was May 1172 before Henry returned to Normandy to face judgement. On 17 May he met papal representatives at Savigny. Over the next five days, as they travelled the thirty miles south to Avranches, a deal was made. The Compromise of Avranches was the price of Henry's rehabilitation. All English bishops were to be absolved of any promises made to observe the Constitutions of Clarendon. Although he retained a right to protect Crown interests against ecclesiastical interference, it was the first time in his life Henry had given up on a privilege he claimed had been his grandfather's. At the church of St Andrew the Apostle in Avranches, Henry stood before the altar, placed his hand on the bible and swore that he had never meant for the archbishop of Canterbury to be killed. Two papal legates then absolved him of any blame in the murder. Among the requirements placed on Henry was that he should take the cross and journey to the Holy Land the following year. This was the primary reason Alexander wished to be generous to Henry; to kickstart a new crusade under Europe's most capable and experienced military leader.

Unhappy at the leniency shown to the king of England, Louis and his allies began to stir up trouble. Henry did not leave for the Holy Land in 1173 because threats from the French king kept him busy. Alexander had failed to foresee this complication. Things were going badly for Henry. Louis tried to lure Henry back to England by sponsoring a Scots invasion from the north. That would clear the way for Louis to attack Normandy as soon as Henry was gone. Unused to being unable to resolve his problems swiftly and in his own favour, Henry suddenly saw something clearly.

Landing at Southampton in July 1174, the king rode the 100 miles east to Canterbury. As the Cathedral came into view on 11 July, Henry dismounted, removed his riding boots, and walked the rest of the way barefooted. By the time he approached the cathedral doors, Henry's feet were cut and bloodied. Leaving smeared footprints along the aisle, the king came before Thomas's tomb and fell to his knees. Crying openly before the monument, Henry prayed for forgiveness, pleading his sorrow at the death of the archbishop, but also at the murder of a friend he had let down.

Rising, Henry walked to the gathered, bemused monks. Getting back onto his knees, he removed his shirt and lay prostrate on the ground, face down. He insisted that the monks whip him, physically punish his sins with scourging. None would lay the first blow until Henry pleaded with them. Lining up, each monk of Canterbury struck the king of England across the back with a stick. Getting up stiffly, Henry returned to Thomas's tomb and passed the entire night kneeling there in prayer, surrounded by the monks. On the morning of Saturday 12 July, the king solemnly mounted his horse and rode to London to face the impending disasters closing in around him. He was about to discover that he was no longer alone, and he would experience true power that was not his own.

At London, news arrived in the middle of the night that William, King of Scots had been captured and was a prisoner at Richmond Castle. From all that anyone could work out, the unexpected development had taken place at the very time Henry had been kneeling before Thomas's tomb begging for forgiveness. William of Newburgh summed up the sentiment that spread like wildfire through England and across the Continent: 'the divine power overthrew his most mighty enemy the king of Scots, in the extreme confines of England: so that the reward of that pious work might not seem to have followed the work itself, but rather to have attended it, so that no man might be suffered to be in suspense on this point'. Henry had been absolved by God Himself, through Thomas, and the demonstration of God's power was plain for all to see. Alexander had canonised Thomas on 21 February 1173, just two years after his murder, in recognition of both his martyrdom and the cult that had sprung up around the archbishop. Finally reconciled, God and His saints were on Henry's side again.

Thomas Becket's tomb would become a focal point for pilgrimage for centuries after his death. In 1175, Henry would pay his former friend another visit, accompanied by his son Henry the Young King, who would retain a strong affection for his erstwhile mentor. King Louis VII of France would cross the Channel to pray at Saint Thomas's shrine after a vision instructed him to do so to heal his son, Philip, from a serious illness.

Having waited so long and married three times to get himself a male heir, Louis was unwilling to take any chances and did as he was told. When Philip made a full recovery, Thomas's reputation was further sealed. If his powers were appealed to by kings, then everyone wanted to call on him to intercede. The vast income generated by the rapidly growing cult of the saint-archbishop made Canterbury even more wealthy.

A rebellion against the king by the church was both mundane and novel. The two institutions ground against each other throughout Europe. The friction caused by papal desires to extend authority into temporal matters, whether to bring cohesion to Christian Europe or to increase influence frequently sparked into flames. The German emperors were invariably at odds with the pope and excommunicated so often the sentence began to lose its bite. Temporal princes were defiant in the face of popes stretching their fingers into ancient rights and questioning whether they ought to belong to ecclesiastical powers. All of that was part of a settling process; something tectonic that caused quakes before settling and finding another fissure to explore. English kings had fallen out with archbishops of Canterbury before too. Anslem had been exiled after quarrelling with William Rufus. Even Thomas's predecessor Theobald had been driven from England by King Stephen. Thomas was not the first, even in living memory, and he would not be the last. What happened within Canterbury Cathedral on 29 December 1170 transformed an ongoing power battle into something much closer to a moment of rebellion. Perhaps that was no accident.

The relationship between the church and temporal rulers was always underpinned by shared beliefs. Popes were acutely aware that they did not exist beyond the world around them, so had to keep princes on their side. That was particularly true at times of schism or when there was a drive for a crusade. Rulers were restrained by their need to ensure their soul's passage to Heaven, and the perception that God approved of their temporal authority. The reason Thomas began to seem an embarrassment to both sides was his utter refusal to find a compromise. What Henry had seen as Thomas's strengths in the role of chancellor, his efficiency, drive, and commitment, became the core problems in his archbishop. It had not been impossible to foresee if Henry's mother had warned him of the dangers of blurring the lines between ecclesiastical and temporal power. All his contemporaries remarked on the transformation Thomas underwent when he became archbishop. Where commentators, invariably monks, looked for miracles, there were other potential explanations.

Thomas had protested at Henry's efforts to have him elected archbishop. He, like Empress Matilda, perhaps saw the conflict of interests it would bring. The chancellor had excelled and risen high through dedication to the tasks he undertook, and there was little reason to suspect he would approach leading the church in England in any other way. As the butt of Henry's jokes and jibes, Thomas may have built up a well of resentment against the king that found a spring in his new authority, disconnected as it was from Henry's control. Only just into his forties, he might also have felt betrayed by the king's manoeuvre. Thomas had never wanted to be a priest. He may have taken minor orders as a clerk in Theobald's household, but he had never done anything that prevented him taking temporal office, becoming personally wealthy, or marrying and having a family. For whatever reason, he had not begun a family yet, but that does not mean he never wanted to. Taking up the post of Archbishop of Canterbury closed all of those doors to him. He would undoubtedly be rich and could expect to live a lavish lifestyle, but none of it would be his own. The point of Henry giving him the post was for Thomas to hand control of the church to the king. After that, he would have no real purpose; he would gift away all the power he had just obtained and spend the rest of his life, potentially running into decades, in obscurity doing a job he had never wanted. He risked being remembered as the worst archbishop of Canterbury ever, the one who betrayed the church, and Thomas was not a man who wished to be seen doing a bad job of anything.

It seems likely that Thomas saw a revolt against Henry and all of the personal and professional turmoil it would bring as an unavoidable consequence of his appointment. He tried to get out of it, but Henry insisted. What lay in Thomas's heart is impossible to discern now. The weight of the office may have changed his mindset; he was God's man now, not Henry's. Bitterness and the chance for some degree of vengeance may have burned within him. Inability to perform a role other than to the best of his ability could have prevented him from caving in to Henry. The realisation that this post was effectively a retirement he did not want, the dooming of his reputation and his life, could have caused him to fight back. Perhaps the most likely explanation is a swirling combination of all of these factors, coming together in a perfect storm to force the church to collide with the king of England head-on. As the crisis progressed, it must have become apparent to Thomas that he was losing support. Louis had found it amusing to infuriate his rival, but Thomas was beginning to get in the way of efforts to find peace with Henry. The pope, tangled in the problems of a schism that made his position fragile, unusually subject to the whim of temporal princes, felt he could only back Thomas so far, however right he was.

It can hardly have escaped Thomas's notice that he was being played by 1170. If he failed to see that Henry the Younger's coronation was a ploy to catch his attention and drag him to the negotiating table, the offer to let him repeat it must have rung alarm bells. Henry failing to make their meeting to return to England together was the final straw. How far Thomas was willing to go may still have been open to question, but he decided that the fight had to be continued from within England. If Louis and the pope were faltering, Thomas was not. His actions, from the moment he left Normandy, demonstrate that reconciliation was not on his agenda. Thomas avoided his suffragan bishops when they gathered to meet him at Dover. They were, he must have believed, too much Henry's men. On arriving at Canterbury, the archbishop set about chastising his monks and excommunicating Henry's ministers, including bishops. Thomas must have known the reaction his provocative attitude would draw. Whether he dreamed that four armed men would arrive to threaten him is less clear than his determination to ramp up the tension.

The knights' comportment presented another opportunity to Thomas. His cool response to the physical threats fits with another pattern of behaviour. Edward Grim, in writing his account of the archbishop's death, saw that Thomas was aligning himself with the arrest and death of Christ. When he insisted that the knights harm no one else, Thomas was recreating the appeal by Jesus in the Garden of Gethsemane that 'If you are looking for me, then let these men go'.[36] Thomas had, perhaps, seen an opportunity to win an eternal victory if he was brave enough to take it. Aware that Henry still planned to try him as a secular baron, Thomas's refusal to leave the cathedral ensured that he faced his fate as archbishop of Canterbury. The physical resistance to being dragged outside shows the importance of remaining within the body of the church. When the knights become irate, Thomas does nothing to calm them but instead enrages one of them further. There is an interpretation of Judas's role in the betrayal of Christ to the Romans that casts Judas as an unwilling actor in what Christ knows must happen. Thomas's words to Reginald could offer a similar hint. The archbishop reminds Reginald that he owes Thomas allegiance, but was he insisting on one last service from the knight?

The lengths to which the archbishop might have gone cannot be untangled now. Is it beyond the realms of possibility that Thomas planted one or more men at Henry's court in Normandy that Christmas? He knew his actions would be inflammatory, and he may well have guessed Henry's reaction. The king may have been genuine in his insistence that he had not ordered or even meant Becket's murder. If Reginald owed the archbishop some fealty, he and his companions might have been sent to await the inevitable reaction as their excuse to do as Thomas ordered. The certainty and haste with which they acted offers some support to this theory. Thomas could have reacted the way he did because this was his plan. The archbishop all but dared Reginald to kill him before leaning forward and stretching out his neck, as if preparing to be sacrificed. Had Thomas, realising that traditional avenues of dissent were running toward dead ends, decided on a radical new course?

Rebellions against the crown had proven hard to bring to success, whatever the aims of rebels had been. The church becoming so tightly entangled in revolt was unusual, but so was everything about Thomas Becket and his rise to the post of Archbishop of Canterbury. Where secular and ecclesiastical interests met, there was usually care taken to leave room to compromise and move on, but Henry and Becket's feud left no such civilised space. Henry was obsessed with securing the rights he claimed, and Thomas knew it. Neither would back down. Thomas sought to prevent Henry eroding the rights of the church, and in the aftermath of his death, Henry backed down to regain the favour of the pope. The Constitutions of Clarendon were buried with the archbishop who was murdered resisting them. The protection provided to Thomas by his role within the church, separate from Henry's sphere of direct influence, insulated him from the sanctions usually available to a king to deal with rebels. It was no accident that Henry tried his best to deal with his former friend as a secular servant rather than a religious leader. Thomas's refusal to shed the protection of his vestments frustrated Henry's plans and prevented him from ending the archbishop's challenge. Ultimately, Thomas found a way to successfully rebel against the king, but at the cost of his life.

Chapter 4

The Eaglets

*Power that is kept beyond reach, or waits for the passage of
time, will always look the more appealing the farther away it
feels, and make the son a rebel against the father.*

Henry II got his wish to see his son and heir crowned in his own lifetime, to
secure the succession and protect his dynasty. On 27 August 1172, Henry the
Young King and his wife Margaret were crowned at Winchester Cathedral
by Rotrou, the ageing archbishop of Rouen, to correct any deficiency in
the previous ceremony. Once more, Henry was to discover that getting
everything he desired was not all it promised to be. In the regular cycles
of rebellion, remaining on the throne for a prolonged amount of time made
it more likely that a new source of revolt was always only just around the
corner.

In January 1173, the first sign of trouble emerged. Henry betrothed his
6-year-old youngest son John to Alice, the daughter of Humbert, Count of
Maurienne. Humbert had no sons yet, so John stood to inherit Maurienne
in south Aquitaine and Humbert promised them a parcel of lands even if
he did eventually produce a male heir. When asked in return what John's
prospects were, Henry assured Humbert that John would receive the
traditional appanage of a younger son of Anjou; the castles of Chinon,
Loudun, and Mirebeau. Henry the Young King took the opportunity to
pick a fight and flex his muscles against his father. The presence of a senior
and junior king of England was novel, with none of the precedent for a
relationship that existed in France. Henry the Young King asserted that
his father had no right to alienate lands without consulting his junior king
and refused to recognise the arrangements with Humbert. The young man
was on shaky ground, but his point was not really about ownership of three
castles.

Chinon, Loudun, and Mirebeau had been the inheritance of Henry II's
younger brother, so the arrangement seemed sound. Since the castles were
in Anjou, Henry had made the deal as Count of Anjou, not as King of
England, and the king had never given any indication that his territories in

France were subservient to the English crown. Indeed, he explicitly held them from Louis VII as a vassal of the French Crown. England provided Henry with his most exalted title and parity with Louis when it suited him, but there was no way in which Henry ruled a cohesive empire managed from London. His son's real issue was something altogether different. The Young King's brothers were, he mused, in a better position than him. Richard had been invested as Count of Poitou and Duke of Aquitaine, where he would succeed their father and was already wielding a good deal of authority under their mother's wing. Geoffrey was 15, and as soon as he reached the age of majority, which might be within the year, he would become Duke of Brittany. However small the provision made for John, it cast a magnifying glass over the Young King's position. Just as planned.

After the coronation of Henry and Margaret, the young couple had visited her father in Paris. Louis planted the seed of an idea that he hoped could be nurtured into a rift within his rival's family.[1] Louis casually enquired as to what his son-in-law was going to get now he was junior king, and how soon it might be heading his way. Young Henry was embarrassed that he could offer no indication of his immediate prospects. He was 18 and began to reflect that his father had been just 16 when he had been handed Normandy by his own father. The young man had a crown, but no power or land of his own. Even his household was packed with men chosen by his father. Feigning surprise, Louis wondered whether his son-in-law should just ask his father for something. After all, what harm could it do? One commentator, Roger of Howden, saw the danger clearly. 'For no trust is there in associates in rule, and all power is averse to a partner therein.'[2]

Father and son got into a blazing row. As far as Henry II was concerned, his son would get everything one day, and that should be enough. As he looked at his younger brothers, Henry the Young King was consumed by embarrassed jealousy and wanted something tangible right away. The two kings could not be reconciled. The younger stormed out of Limoges and back to Paris, where he was eagerly welcomed by Louis. Displaying a naivety that might have been behind his father's concern, Henry the Young King lapped up the attention his father-in-law lavished on him. Louis summoned a council and encouraged his barons to offer support to young Henry in gaining what he wanted. Henry, in return, promised never to be reconciled to his father without the agreement of Louis and the French barons. It was an extraordinary arrangement. Henry the Young King, began to promise land and incomes to Louis's men if he succeeded, giving away what he did not own. He even offered Northumberland to William, King of Scots.

Henry II returned to England as a storm cloud gathered around Normandy. The duchy was self-destructive when at peace and might not rise in support of a duke who was increasing taxation. The one way to ensure Normandy would act was to expose it to a threat of invasion. Nothing in Norman history better guaranteed a prompt and violent reaction. While Henry organised resistance in England, Louis positioned his pawns around Normandy. When the invasion came, Normandy duly reacted just as Henry had hoped. Louis was delayed for a month by a siege at Verneuil that made no progress. The Breton attack from the west faltered before it got going. Providence intervened for Henry when the eastern arm of the assault was halted by the death of Matthew, Count of Boulogne. He was struck by a crossbow bolt, and his death caused his older brother Philip, Count of Flanders to pack up and go home. Matthew had been his heir and the dynastic risk of the campaign now outweighed any potential advantage. Spying the moment he had waited for, Henry crossed the Channel and sent his mercenaries to reinforce the defence of Normandy. Louis and his allies were driven out of the duchy and returned to Paris to lick their wounds.

Henry the Young King had been supported in his uprising by his siblings Richard and Geoffrey. There was also a strong suspicion that Eleanor of Aquitaine had not only approved of her sons' actions but had been the driving force behind the rebellion. There was no evidence to support such a charge, but chroniclers were always happy to find a woman to blame for the folly of men. King Henry set out generous terms for his sons if they would meet him at Gisor to agree on peace. The Young King would receive castles and income in either England or Normandy, whichever he preferred, as well as the same in Anjou. Richard would have castles and income from Aquitaine, and Geoffrey would become Duke of Brittany as soon as it could be arranged. When they met, Robert, Earl of Leicester, who had joined the Young King's cause, disrupted the meeting by hurling abuse at Henry II and even placing his hand on his sword as a signal of aggression.[3] As a rebel baron, Robert's position was made more precarious by peace between father and son. It is easy to see Louis greasing the wheels of continued discord too.

In England, the arrangements Henry had made meant that the trap snapped shut on rebellion there too. Robert, Earl of Leicester crossed the sea soon after the meeting at Gisor broke up in disarray. Meeting with Hugh Bigod in Norfolk, he led an army against the royal forces. When they met at the Battle of Fornham on 17 October 1173, Robert was defeated 'in the twinkling of an eye' and captured.[4] One of the other prisoners taken during the fighting was Petronilla de Grandmesnil, the wife of Earl Robert.

Chroniclers recorded in astonishment that not only had Petronilla convinced her husband to give battle but had ridden beside him encased in armour to join the fight. When she fell from her horse into the river, a royalist knight hauled her out and took her into custody.[5] The revolt was a failure, or Henry's response to it was measured perfection.

One outcome of this episode was a rift between Henry II and his wife Eleanor of Aquitaine. As their three oldest sons returned to Louis's court, she left Aquitaine, appearing to aim for Paris. Adding to the perception that Eleanor lay behind their sons' revolt, Henry had her picked up on the road and taken into custody. There was no investigation into the queen's motives or actions. Henry, perhaps, was unwilling to air dirty laundry in public, but Eleanor would remain under comfortable house arrest for the remainder of her husband's life. What drove Eleanor to seek out her former husband cannot be known. Though it appeared an admission of her culpability, the notion that she might have been trying to intercede with her sons to restore unity should not be ignored. Her long imprisonment is testament to the difficulty in finding peace among her family again.

1174 saw a repeat of the previous year's tactics. Henry was lured out of Normandy by fresh unrest in England, and as soon as his back was turned, Louis invaded Normandy. It was at this moment that Henry made his fateful pilgrimage to Becket's tomb at Canterbury, instantaneously transforming his fortunes. His authority restored in England and the king of Scots added to his list of captives, Henry sailed back to Barfleur. Louis had been laying siege to Rouen, the Norman capital, but Henry's arrival, reinvigorated by God's renewed favour, was enough to cause the French king to withdraw again. When peace was finally agreed between Henry, Louis, and the Young King, Richard was excluded from it because he was causing trouble in Poitou to the south. Henry chased his 17-year-old son down, and when they met, Richard submitted to his father in floods of tears.[6] Peace was made by the submission of the sons to their father, and Henry recognised his sons' grievances by providing each with some castles and an income. When the Christmas court met at Argentan in 1174, Henry's sons were all in attendance, though his wife remained absent.

On 18 September 1180, King Louis VII of France died, succeeded by the son he had waited so long to produce, Philip. Although the relationships between Henry and his sons remained fractious and tense, they had found ways to co-exist. For Henry the Young King, still lacking a real direction and purpose, the tournament circuit, with all of its danger, glory, and opportunity for riches, had beckoned. Part of the appeal may well have been his father's disapproval of the mock battles, but the Young King carved out a niche and a chivalric reputation for himself. Philip and Young Henry became firm friends, and Henry II, who had done all he could to support the new young King of France, was dismayed to see the continuation of Louis's tactics. The view that Henry was unable to delegate, to release his firm grip on power, is not the full picture. Richard had been given almost free rein in Poitou and Aquitaine for years. Geoffrey was in control of Brittany. The unwillingness to hand over responsibility was restricted to Henry the Young King. Either Henry II had never come to terms with the reality of a junior king, or he saw something in his 27-year-old oldest son that gave him cause for concern.

The Christmas court of 1182 at Caen saw more family ructions. Richard refused to offer his older brother homage for Aquitaine, insisting he understood it would be separate from England and the rest of the family holdings. The adjustment might have been the result of continued friction between the brothers that Henry saw storing up problems for the future. When Richard was finally convinced to do as he was told, Henry the Young King suddenly refused to accept his fealty. Richard stormed out. Henry the Young King and Geoffrey pursued Richard. Basing themselves at Limoges, they made no effort to seek peace with Richard, instead rallying Aquitainian rebels and whipping them up to fight their duke. When their father arrived with an army to try and resolve the tension, the soldiers in Limoges opened fire with their crossbows, one striking the king's horse in the head. As Henry withdrew, there was general condemnation of the Young King for failing to take any action against the men who had nearly killed his father.[7]

Shortly afterwards, perhaps in response to the outrage, Henry the Younger came before his father. Geoffrey, though, continued to rampage around Aquitaine, many believing he did so with the Young King's approval. When the two met again, Henry the Young King seemed distraught at his own failings and inability to restore order in Aquitaine. He fell to his knees and swore to take the cross and travel to the Holy Land. His father sought to dissuade him, fearing it would be the death of his son. Amid heightened emotion, the Young King asked his father to forgive those who had rebelled with him, and the tearful father agreed.[8] As soon as Henry the Young King left his father, he fell back into revolt, killing one of Henry's messengers. As finding a resolution seemed increasingly impossible, Henry the Young King was suddenly struck down by illness. At Martel, south of Limoges, dysentery wracked the young man's body. Aware of how serious his condition was, the Young King sent word to his father, asking him to visit. Although the king's instinct was to rush to his son's deathbed, his counsellors urged caution. Henry instead sent a ring as a token of his forgiveness.

On 11 June 1183, Henry the Young King died aged 28. His father was distraught, despite the endless problems he had caused. Richard was suddenly heir to all his father held in a readjustment of the inheritance plans. When Henry told Richard to hand Poitou over to John, Richard flatly refused to give up the post he had held for most of his life. In truth, all Richard really wanted was Aquitaine. With Geoffrey up to his neck in recent rebellions, the 17-year-old John was becoming the focus of his father's thoughts.

Through 1184, the problem of a new settlement persisted. Henry challenged John to take Poitou from Richard by force. It was an unfair test of a young man with no land or money, sent to fight an older brother with a wealth of military experience. Geoffrey lent Breton support to John, but Richard retaliated by assaulting Brittany in Geoffrey's absence. In November, Henry summoned all three of them to England. The excuse was the election of a new archbishop of Canterbury, but in reality, he needed to find a resolution. Richard had acquired his mother's love for Aquitaine and shared her commitment to the retention of its independence. The combined efforts of Geoffrey and John had demonstrated that the militarily gifted Richard could not be removed by force. In November, Henry sat down to try and resettle what had proven a problematic mess, but one that everyone understood.

Richard would not be prised out of Aquitaine. It is unclear whether he hoped for the English Crown and his father's other holdings too, but his focus on Aquitaine and its independent status suggests his duchy was sufficient. John was emerging as his father's favourite son, but possibly only because he had not yet rebelled, having been too young and lacking a powerbase. Henry had secured the possibility that John could be created Lord of Ireland to provide his youngest son with a tricky training ground as well as an inheritance beyond what most fourth sons might hope for. The simplest and least disruptive solution was also the most dangerous. Despite his unreliability, propelling Geoffrey into the space left by his oldest brother offered the best answer, while remaining a long way from ideal. Geoffrey was already Duke of Brittany, giving him political and military experience. Brittany was a vassal state of Normandy, so shifting Geoffrey to become heir to England, Normandy and Anjou would make little difference. Interestingly, after a dozen years in secluded captivity, Eleanor was involved in the discussions. She had not seen her sons for years, and it was a signal either of a softening of Henry's attitude or the hardness of the problem confronting him that he now turned to Eleanor for help.

There was no formal announcement of a new settlement. Henry was made cautious by his sons' treacheries but trying to establish what would happen when he died was unavoidable. The possibility that this was the trial arrangement agreed at the end of 1184 is supported by what happened when Henry's sons left England. John was knighted at Windsor by his father before being packed off to Ireland to try and get to grips with his new lordship. Richard returned to Poitou, and Geoffrey moved into Normandy. In early 1185, Henry received an astonishing request. His grandfather, Baldwin, had left Anjou for the Holy Land to marry the heiress to the throne of Jerusalem. Now in dire need of a new champion, Heraclius, the patriarch of Jerusalem travelled all the way to England to ask Henry to become the new king of Jerusalem. It was a testament to Henry's immense reputation in Christian Europe that he was sought out. His family connection to the Holy Land also made him a leading candidate, but although Henry was careful not to offer offence, he declined the request. Those at his court were shocked that he would refuse such an honour. Henry had never been interested in extending his rights beyond what he had inherited or acquired by marriage. He was not a conqueror, nor was he greedy or willing to overreach himself. An escape to the Holy Land offered release from his present problems, though it must have looked like a move out of the frying pan and into the fire. At least where he was, he knew the lay of the land, and he knew his opponents, even if they were his sons. Leaving his legacy unsettled must have felt like too much unfinished business for Henry to be lured by the eternal glory of the Holy Land.

Henry was becoming an invaluable prop to the young king of France too. Philip, who was 20 in 1186, frequently hit problems with his senior advisors, most notably Philip, Count of Flanders. Whenever he got into trouble, Philip ran to the 53-year-old Henry for help, and Henry always resolved disputes in Philip's favour. The confidence this gave Henry in their relationship caused him to take young Philip somewhat for granted. When the king of France asked that the marriage between his half-sister Alice and Henry's son Richard be concluded, Henry offered vague assurances that it would happen soon. The pair had been betrothed for more than twenty years, and Henry had no intention of causing the union to go ahead. There were rumours that Henry had taken Alice as his mistress and some speculation that she had borne the king a son. Allowing Philip to believe the marriage was still part of Henry's plans prevented the relationship souring while leaving Henry free from real commitment. He knew that Philip needed him more than he needed Philip, but revelling in his new ascendancy over the French Crown caused Henry to lose sight of the fact that making his overlord in much of his territory nervous was not a good move. He would never have done it to Louis, but Philip's youth blinded Henry to the care he used to take.

In the wake of Henry's vague reassurances, Philip focused his attention onto Geoffrey. Still in Normandy, it may have become clear what Henry's plan for the succession might be. Geoffrey was already married, but Philip hoped to both build a bond with him and perhaps sow fresh seeds of discord among Henry's family. It was fertile land for the Capetian kings by now. Despite Henry's protestations to his son, Geoffrey was lured to Philip's court and lavishly entertained. On 19 August 1186, Geoffrey was in Paris competing in a tournament when he was thrown from his horse and trampled to death. At 27, he was the second of Henry's sons to die in opposition to their father in just three years. Philip, perhaps in genuine grief and guilt, or possibly to slight Henry, had Geoffrey buried at Notre Dame de Paris. Philip, who was 21 two days after the accident, was said to be distraught at the death. His advisors had to physically restrain him at the graveside as the king threatened to throw himself into the hole to join Geoffrey.[9] Philip now had a political problem to face. He had exposed his opposition to Henry only to lose his trump card instantly.

Aside from fresh personal grief at the loss of another son, Henry faced dynastic turmoil again. The tentative trial settlement was blown out of the water. Some cynical commentators believed Henry did not mourn for Geoffrey, and that if the king was sad, it was because the loss reminded him of Henry the Young King. That is unfair. Henry had proven a doting and indulgent father, perhaps to an extent that created many of his problems. However much his sons rebelled, he forgave them. He mourned their passing with a heavy heart, even when it happened at the peak of their opposition to him.[10] Hindsight has seen the division between Henry and Eleanor played out by their respective favourite sons, John and Richard. Henry would seek to insert John into the top of the line of succession as Eleanor fought for Richard's rights. It was never that simple. Richard had demonstrated his lack of interest in anything beyond Aquitaine's borders. For the remainder of the vast Angevin territories, there was now no choice available other than John. Henry still refused to make any firm acknowledgement of the plans for his legacy though.

In the immediate aftermath of Geoffrey's death, Henry's relationship with Philip became strained. Philip demanded that Geoffrey's pregnant widow Constance and their daughter Eleanor be placed in the care of the French Crown, along with control of Brittany. Henry utterly refused on all counts. Brittany was subservient to Normandy and effectively out of Philip's reach as far as Henry was concerned. Constance might (and did, in March 1187) give birth to a male heir to Geoffrey, Henry's grandson with a rightful claim to Brittany. Keeping them out of Philip's control was a high priority for Henry. Philip then added an insistence that Richard withdraw from Toulouse, which had been recognised as part of Aquitaine, but which Philip now accused Richard of invading. Philip threatened to assault Normandy if Henry refused to do as instructed, and although Henry managed to negotiate a tense truce, it was short-lived.

A local spat between Gisor and Trie saw hostilities escalate. Richard de Vals fortified his castle, and when the local constable, one of Henry's men, went to confront the knight, a skirmish broke out. Several men were injured, and Richard de Vals's son was killed in the fighting. The constable, too afraid to face the consequences of what had happened, ran to Richard in Poitou. Philip ordered the arrest of all English subjects in France. Henry retaliated by having all French subjects in England seized. As Richard pressed further into Toulouse, Count Raymond appealed to Philip for help and, as Louis had done when Henry invaded Toulouse, Philip decided that it was his duty to protect his vassal. In truth, his political aims happened to align with Raymond's plight briefly. Philip began harrying the borders of Normandy as a punishment for an unruly vassal. By the end of the year, both kings had released their prisoners, but tensions were high.

In February 1187, Henry met Philip, but the French king made so many demands that Henry found impossible to accept that the talks broke down. As he left, Philip lay siege to Chateaux Raoul on the disputed border between Philip's land and Aquitaine. Both Richard and John were inside, and Henry rushed to his sons' aid with an army. The two sides were arrayed ready to fight when Pope Urban intervened to encourage them to find peace. A two-year truce was agreed. Although neither really wanted it, Philip knew he risked being beaten by the more experienced and better equipped Henry, and Henry retained his reluctance to attack his liege lord in France. The same concern, both for the risk of seizure of his lands as a traitor and setting a precedent for a subject militarily assaulting their king, had always restrained Henry.

To Henry's horror, Richard left the negotiations for the treaty in Philip's company. He had watched two sons die in the jaws of the French court and now saw a third falling into the same trap. Richard, almost certainly at Philip's prompting, was suddenly outraged that his father was failing to recognise his oldest remaining son as heir to all his lands and titles. Henry was shocked. Richard had made it clear he cared only for Aquitaine but was now demanding England and all his father's French lands too. Henry asked Richard to leave Paris. Then he pleaded. Finally, the king ordered his son to come home. Richard refused to listen to anything his father had to say, though he stopped short of matching Henry the Young King and Geoffrey by renouncing his fealty to Henry. As he had done with Geoffrey, Philip showered attention on Richard so that 'every day they ate at the same table and from the same dish, and at night had not separate chambers'.[11] Terrified that he was watching history repeat itself, Henry made another plea to his son to leave Paris. Suddenly, Richard agreed and made his way to Chinon, only to loot the castle and use what he stole to pay for the fortification of castles in Poitou against his father.

As quickly and inexplicably as Richard had joined Philip, he appeared before Henry pleading for forgiveness and poured out oaths that he would never again disobey his father.[12] It is possible that Eleanor had reminded her son both that Aquitaine was enough for him, and that dalliances with the French court had killed two of his brothers. If the queen became involved to bring about the dramatic change in Richard, then it demonstrates that the royal couple was once more working as a team, even if Eleanor was still not at liberty. Henry and Philip agreed a truce, but tensions remained high. Henry married his widowed daughter-in-law, Constance, now with a son and a daughter, to Ranulph, Earl of Chester. The north-west of England kept her far from Brittany and even farther from Philip.

Worsening news from the Holy Land culminated in the fall of Jerusalem on 2 October 1187. Richard took the cross immediately on hearing the news. As Henry and Philip edged toward fresh aggression over Richard's proposed marriage to Alice, the archbishop of Trie admonished them for petty squabbling as Jerusalem suffered so that both kings took the cross on 21 January 1188. Henry had sworn to travel to the Holy Land ten years earlier, having pledged to go on crusade in the wake of Becket's murder, and having turned down the throne there. Both kings agreed to maintain peace until they had returned from the Holy Land, but as Henry made preparations in England, Philip invaded Berry. The French king blamed Richard's continued efforts against the count of Toulouse, but Henry insisted he had not instructed Richard to act and demanded that Philip leave his lands. Henry was forced to return to France, and peace talks faltered, with Philip ordering the destruction of the tree between Gisor and Trie under which kings of France and dukes of Normandy had traditionally met. Eventually, an agreement was reached the Philip would hand back what he had taken in Berry and Richard would give back what he had seized from the count of Toulouse. Then came another shock for the king of England.

Richard publicly submitted the dispute over Toulouse to Philip for judgement. On the surface, there was little to cause concern. Henry had never denied the overlordship of Philip or his father for his Continental holdings. Henry had given homage when required. Richard himself had already offered fealty to Philip as Count of Poitou. What the young man overlooked in his drive to resolve the matter and refocus minds on preparations for the crusade was his father's careful avoidance of precisely this. Henry had always insisted on his right to maintain order within his own lands and never referred disputes to Paris. Although he conceded ultimate lordship to the king of France, Henry had denied Paris any hand in what happened within his borders. In a moment of what may have been well-intentioned impulsiveness, Richard had shredded decades of careful policy.

Philip jumped at the opportunity and negotiations were arranged at Bonmoulins on 18 November. To Henry's horror, but perhaps no longer to his surprise, Richard arrived in Philip's party. The king of France had spotted an opportunity to achieve by diplomatic means what he was unable to attain by military effort. Philip's desire for certainty about what would happen after Henry's death seemed to have rubbed off on Richard. The conditions for peace were simple. Philip would hand back all he had taken since the outbreak of hostilities if Henry would cause all of his vassals in England, Normandy, Anjou, and Aquitaine to give their homage to Richard as Henry's heir. Infuriated at having the terms of his own dynastic settlement dictated to him – particularly in England, which was none of Philip's business – Henry refused. Richard immediately took a knee, placed his hands between Philip's, and gave homage to the French king for all his father's Continental possessions before swearing fealty to Philip above all men. The papal legate who had been sent to ensure peace was reached and the crusade became the primary focus excommunicated Richard for destroying any hope of a settlement.[13]

Henry spent Christmas at Saumer in Anjou but fell ill. He sent word that he was unable to attend the next round of peace talks on 13 January 1189. Philip was sure Henry was lying to stall for time. It was May before they finally met at La Ferté-Bernard in Maine. Henry was still unwell, but the first ships packed with crusaders had left England earlier in the month, and Henry had no desire to put things off any longer. Philip not only restated his demands but added to them. Richard was to receive the fealty of all Henry's subjects as his heir once the marriage to Alice had been completed. Then, when they left on crusade, John was to be required to go with them too. Richard petulantly told his father that unless John went also, he would no longer go on crusade. Clearly, there was a concern, perhaps fostered by Philip, that John would swoop in and take what was rightfully Richard's as soon as his back was turned. If the king of France sowed that particular seed, it was to provide a rich harvest for him.

Henry was now placed in an impossible position. If he and both his remaining male heirs left on crusade, his lands would be unprotected and his dynasty in mortal peril. Henry countered with an offer that Alice should marry John instead. He was probing to see if Philip would give up Richard in favour of the political union he really wanted. Henry needed Richard to know that he, like his brothers, was being played by the king of France, and it could cost him his life. Philip stormed out, only for the dismayed papal legate to threaten France with an interdict if Philip failed to return. Henry withdrew to Le Mans to give some space, but Richard and Philip went on the offensive. They took Henry's castle at La Ferté-Bernard before moving on to seize Montfort, Malestroit, Beaumont, and Balim with ease. There was little resistance across Maine from bemused castellans who could no longer fathom whose orders they should obey. The crisis reached a shocking level when Richard, Philip, and an army appeared outside the walls of Le Mans.

The seneschal of Anjou ordered the suburbs fired, a traditional tactic to deny the French cover and comfort. As the wind changed, red hot embers were blown into the city, and buildings burst into flames. Still unrecovered from the illness that had dogged him all year, Henry's composure abandoned him, and he panicked. Le Mans was the place of his birth, the city he had grown up in, and the walls within which he had chosen to bury his father. He took 700 knights and rode away as fast as he could. Richard and Philip pursued him until they reached a river Henry had managed to cross but which they could see no way over. When he finally stopped galloping, Henry sat in his saddle, perched on a hilltop, and watched the plumes of smoke rise from the city he described as his favourite in all the world.[14] If ever there was a sight Henry could reflect summed up the point his life had reached, watching the city he loved most burned to the ground by his son came painfully close.

During the effort to catch his father, Richard is reported as coming into contact with Sir William Marshal, whose rear guard was protecting the king's withdrawal. Marshal drove his horse, lance couched, directly at Richard. When the king's son pleaded with Marshal not to kill him as he was unarmed, Sir William lowered his lance and ran Richard's horse through instead, replying, 'Let the Devil kill you! I shall not be the one to do it.'[15] Few men could ever claim to have bested Richard, and fewer to have spared his life. Marshal's engagement bought Henry enough time to reach the safety of Chinon.

Henry agreed to a meeting at Ballan, north-east of Chinon. When he arrived on 4 July, he was so obviously ill that Philip, in apparently genuine concern, offered his cloak for Henry to sit on more comfortably on the ground. Gruffly refusing the French king's sympathy, Henry insisted on remaining on his horse throughout the negotiations. His attendants on either side kept steadying hands on the king as he swayed precariously in his saddle. What, Henry demanded, were Philip's terms? Henry was to personally do homage to Philip for all his Continental holdings. He was then required to cause all his vassals on both sides of the Channel to swear fealty to Richard as his father's heir. Philip demanded a surety of 20,000 marks and three castles, and a promise that Alice and Richard would be married as soon as Richard returned from the crusade. Finally, he was not to demand oaths of loyalty from those who had joined Richard's uprising until one month before the crusading army left to prevent reprisals.

Henry listened to all of the things he had resisted for so long, which he had constructed policies of mirrors angled perfectly to avoid addressing directly. He had no anger left to offer. The king agreed to everything that was demanded of him. He gave his son the kiss of peace, though reportedly growled in his ear 'May the Lord never permit me to die until I have taken due vengeance upon you.' Then, he rode away. Feeling every one of his 56 years, Henry had to be carried back to Chinon on a litter. Once in bed within the castle, the king asked for the list of those he was unable to extract oaths from because they had joined Richard. He was, his advisors protested, too ill to concern himself with such things. Henry bellowed his demand to be obeyed and was sheepishly handed the list. The first name, at the very top of the list, was John. His youngest son; the only one who had not, until now, betrayed him. Henry slipped into delirium. In a lucid moment, he asked to be carried to the chapel where he made a final confession and received Holy Communion. Then, on 6 July 1189, he released his grip on a life that no longer offered much to cling too. His last words were a lament: 'Alas, the shame for a king to be thus overcome! alas, the shame!'[16]

Henry's body was prepared for burial. His coffin was carried along the banks of the River Vienne to Fontevrault Abbey. Henry had once heard a prophecy from a monk, who had received a vision of a man in white robes. The figure had told the monk 'Observe and read these things about the king: "I have set my seal upon him; the womb of his wife shall swell against him, and in torments he shall suffer torments, and among the veiled women he shall be as one wearing the veil."'[17] His sons had indeed risen against him. By the end, all four had caused him grief, two of them dying in the effort, the third and fourth coming together to all but cause his death. Now, as his body rested at Fontevrault, he was finally ready to take his place amongst the nuns there, the veiled women. Richard arrived to pay his respects, or to check his father was really dead. He had been sure that stories of his worsening illness and death had been lies. As he approached the body, fresh blood ran from his father's nose, a sure sign that the corpse's murderer was nearby.[18] Kneeling at his father's side for a while, Richard offered silent prayers, and perhaps reflected on what he had done to bring this about. They had never been particularly close, but had he really wanted his father dead? As quietly as he had entered, Richard rose and left Fontevraud to take possession of everything that had been his father's.

Henry II had endured almost endless rebellions against his rule. The sheer breadth of his possessions, spanning Europe from north to south, made keeping them in line under one ruler, who was to many of them a foreigner, all but impossible. Henry had displayed a knack for taking castles that astounded his contemporaries. Aquitaine in particular was a fractious place that defied strong governance, but Henry found ways to establish and enforce his authority through his wife and Richard. During the last decade of his life, his imminent arrival with an army of mercenaries was more often than not enough to cause opposition to evaporate. The one source of rebellion he never managed to get to grips with was his sons. Henry the Young King had set a precedent as the first junior king in English history but had never been able to come to terms with the role and the lack of immediate authority. He felt himself squeezed between the power of his father and the increasing freedom and prestige being given to his younger brothers. He took to the tournament circuit to vent his frustration and find a niche for himself, but always returned to the question of what he ought to have right now.

Many contemporary commentators viewed Geoffrey as a troublemaker. One dubbed him 'that son of perdition'.[19] He seemed keen to join in his brother's rebellion, though his reasons remain unclear; did he dislike his father, have selfish motives, or support his sibling in a manner he might have considered loyal? After the death of Henry the Young King, Geoffrey leapfrogged Richard in his father's planning. Henry's caution in explicitly laying out his plans was understandable but left room for Geoffrey to be seduced by the king of France. Philip played the game he had watched his father perfect. A second son died in a revolt against his father to which Henry was utterly unable to bring an end.

Neither Henry nor Richard seem to have been able to get at the other's intentions. If Henry considered making Richard heir to England, Normandy, and Anjou, then Richard would appear focussed entirely and exclusively on Aquitaine. Yet whenever there was a suggestion of John getting everything but Aquitaine, Richard would fly into a fury and run into the arms of the French king. Henry must have been terrified that he would lose a third son to the games Philip played. It was perhaps this exhausting fear that mired his health. If Henry the Young King had been unsuited to the power he demanded, and Geoffrey had been an impetuous nuisance, Richard was a very different animal. Militarily he was one of the few men who could match his father's talents. He would not give up a right he considered his, even if he was uncertain whether he actually wanted it. In attitude, he had too much of the Aquitanian independence that had been designed to protect his mother's homeland. Eleanor's favourite, Richard turned out to be a lot like his father.

At the peace talks two days before his death, Henry perhaps saw clearly for the first time through the fug of his illness. Could it be that he was the problem? Had he driven two of his sons to their deaths by pushing them into the French king's influence? The sight of Richard embarking on the same road might have been the tipping point for Henry, rather than his poor health. When he gave in to demands that he had resisted for thirty-five years, it may well have been to save his son at his own expense. Finally, aged 56, Henry had learned to bend. News that John had betrayed him might have caused Henry to release his grip on life, or confirmed that he was making the correct decision to let go. He could reflect in those final days on whether he had made the right choice not to go away and become king of Jerusalem, or whether leaving had always been the only way to end the rebellions of his sons.

Uprisings by the monarch's children had proven incredibly difficult to deal with. In Henry's reign, the execution of rebels among the nobility was still a rare occurrence. Robert, Earl of Leicester, and others who had openly fought against Henry in his sons' names were usually pardoned after a time. Eleanor was unusual in the length of her penance for a part in her sons' actions that is still unclear. Nevertheless, dispossession and ultimately a death sentence were weapons a king could deploy against recalcitrant rebels. It was the end of the road of which all parties were aware, and which the desire to avoid would generally lead instead to reconciliation. What final sanction could the king have against his son?

Kingship set a man apart as divinely appointed. His son and heir would one day acquire the same protection, but while the king lived, he needed the perception of God's approval to extend to his son to safeguard his dynasty. When that heir entered open revolt against the king and refused to be brought to terms, the king had little in his arsenal to force an end. If a king and his son were diametrically opposed, surely only one could be enjoying God's favour. No king would wish to disinherit an heir in favour of another son, knowing that it would leave bitterness to resurface at some point. The sons of William the Conqueror had ably displayed how that might play out. Execution was never an option, not least dynastically, but more importantly, because no father would wish to kill his own son, and Henry II seems to have been a doting father to his wayward brood. Rebellion, then, was possible for those in the direct line of succession because the accident of their birth provided some immunity from the measures used to keep other nobles in line.

In truth, though, it is hard to say that anyone really won from all of the revolts against Henry. Two of his sons, and ultimately Henry himself, paid with their lives. Richard got more than he wanted. John was left under a cloud of suspicion and rivalry that would lead to the next great round of rebellion. Only Philip, from his throne in Paris, could reflect that he had gained something. Henry had been the most powerful vassal of Louis and then his son. Philip would be remembered as Philip Augustus for his assertion of the dominance of the French Crown, and Henry had provided the blueprint for achieving what successive Capetian monarchs had coveted. In England, Henry had centralised authority, and he had managed his relationship with an overlord in France delicately to extract maximum prestige for himself. Philip would do the same, and it was under his rule that a more cohesive idea of a nation developed. Where his predecessors had used the title King of the Franks and exercised influence from a small spit of land around Paris, Philip adopted the title King of France and transformed influence into authority. In an odd way, Henry II was responsible for the emergence of France as a superpower.

Henry had a mural painted at Winchester, according to Gerald of Wales, that summed up the king's predicament. The image was of an eagle being attacked by four of its young. Two pinned down the eagle's wings, a third beat its body, and the fourth sat on its neck, about to peck out the eagle's eyes. Henry explained the painting to an enquirer. 'The four young ones of the eagle are my four sons, who will not cease to persecute me even unto death. The younger of them, whom I even now embrace with such tender affection, will sometime at the last insult me more grievously and more dangerously than all the others.'[20] If the story is not apocryphal, it is chillingly prophetic. What Gerald fails to tell his readers is what the eagle is doing. By 1189, the mighty Henry II might well have been taking the blows, with the knowing smile of a parent. They are, he might have said, my sons. What else can I do?

Chapter 5

The First Barons' War

The surest way to encourage rebellion toward success is
to unite enemies against you behind a common cause.
The leader who manages this will manage little else for long.

King Richard I showed little interest in England. His heart had always been in Aquitaine. Wanting everything else was more about preventing John from getting it than Richard having a real interest in ruling England, Normandy, Maine, Anjou, and the rest. Richard was gripped by crusading fervour, believing he could follow in the footsteps of his mother's Aquitanian uncle Raymond, Prince of Antioch, or his paternal great-grandfather Baldwin, King of Jerusalem. He undoubtedly possessed the military experience and natural ability that would serve the church well in the Holy Land. Despite heavy taxation and a fire sale of land and offices to raise funds, it proved difficult to rebel against Richard because he was never around. Although he ruled from his coronation on 3 September 1189 until his death a decade later, Richard spent only a handful of months in England.

In the summer of 1190, Richard set off for the crusade. Along the way, he occupied Sicily, conquered Cyprus, got married, and tried to convince his widowed sister Joan to marry Saladin's brother to end the war in the Holy Land. Joan flatly refused, and Richard continued his journey. He arrived in the Holy Land in June 1191 and although he was only there for just over a year, by the time he left in October 1192, Richard had secured peace and his military reputation. Captured on the way back, his territories were taxed to the hilt to raise a ransom to free him. Whilst payment was painful, having a king in captivity was an embarrassment the English were willing to pay to correct. His freedom had been secured largely by the efforts of his mother Eleanor of Aquitaine. Once released, Richard was forced to deal with King Philip of France, who snatched his Continental lands in his absence, and John, who had his eye on the rest. In March 1199, Richard was besieging the castle of Châlus-Chabrol in Limousin when a crossbow bolt fired from the walls struck him. The wound became gangrenous and took his life, aged 41 and childless.

There was some dispute over who should succeed Richard. John was in a strong position, though he had proven himself treacherous during his brother's absence. The alternative candidate was Arthur, Duke of Brittany, the son of John's older brother Geoffrey. It is a demonstration of the uncertainty around succession that lingered that no one was certain who possessed the best claim. At least one person, though, was certain who would be king. Eleanor pushed John to the fore. Arthur was too far removed from her influence to be acceptable to the redoubtable lady. The duke was only 12 and was immured in the influence of his mother and of Philip, neither of whom Eleanor was willing to have controlling the heir to the Angevin empire, or at least what remained of it. So it was that John became king of England. Arthur would vanish after being taken prisoner by John, and it seems likely that his uncle murdered the young man in his mid-teens.

Eleanor of Aquitaine lived until 1204, reaching the age of 80. She may well have survived long enough to regret her decision to champion her youngest son. John proved an unsuitable and dangerously unpopular king. Circumstance also worked against John. He inherited claims to a sprawling portfolio of lands that had been forgotten by the previous ruler and subject to scheming by both Philip and John himself. Much of the Continental holdings was slipping into France's hands. Philip had continued the Capetian trick of dividing the overmighty Angevin rulers by using John against Richard, but that left John the victim of his own schemes once those titles fell to him. He acquired a ramshackle collection of neglected lands with no control over some and a slipping grasp on others. Within a brief time, he had been pushed out of virtually all the Angevin Continental lands, including Normandy. For the first time in almost a century and a half, the king of England would be forced to live from his realm only. That meant an increased focus on England, and a drive to increase revenue to fund an attempt to recover what was lost, that become uncomfortable.

John's methods made matters worse. He was high-handed, cruel, and lacked sympathy. John exploited every potential avenue to raise money. When Hugh of Avalon, Bishop of Lincoln died in 1200, John kept the see vacant until 1203, allowing him to draw around £2,000 in income before filling the post. When the archbishop of Canterbury died in July 1205, John spotted another opportunity to replenish the royal coffers. The monks at Canterbury had other ideas and promptly elected their sub-prior. Enraged, John forced them to annul the appointment. Realising he would struggle to keep the see vacant, John ordered the monks to select his choice, John de Gray, Bishop of Norwich. Pope Innocent III spied a chance to flex papal muscles against secular rulers interfering in church elections. He set aside John de Gray and appointed Stephen Langton. Langton, who was in Rome, was prevented from entering England and John seized all of Canterbury's lands and incomes. This kind of friction between the papacy and secular rulers was not new. John, though, was becoming so unpopular with his barons and subjects, who squirmed under his focused gaze and were left embarrassed at his losses across the Channel, that he had no support from any quarter.

On 23 March 1208, Pope Innocent placed England under interdict. All religious activity within the kingdom was to cease. Church bells fell quiet. The routine of pastoral services that helped shape and define life in England was withdrawn. With the exception of care for the dying, the church shut its doors to John and his people. The purpose of an interdict was to frighten those placed under it into obedience. The problem in this instance was that it was not the people of England who were at odds with the pope, and John found himself enjoying all of the income of the church in England. The interdict had no sting. In October 1209, Archbishop Langton excommunicated John so that the king was personally removed from the community of the Holy Church. Pope Innocent ordered every bishop in England to leave immediately. All but one, the worldly Peter des Roches, Bishop of Winchester, obeyed. Alienated from the church, John set about disaffecting his barons.

The first target was William de Braose, a man who had been loyal to John and whose holdings on the Welsh borders made him wealthy and influential. William had been the custodian of John's nephew, Arthur, and perhaps a desire to tie up loose ends around Arthur's fate drove John to persecute William. The king suddenly demanded settlement of a raft of debts he claimed William owed him. Under the weight of John's pressure, William fled to Ireland. In 1210, he tried to return in alliance with Llywelyn the Great, a powerful Welsh prince, but they made little headway, and William was forced to escape to France where he died the following year. William's wife Maud and oldest son William were taken into custody, and John demanded the extortionate sum of £40,000 for their release.[1] Unwilling, or unable, to pay, Maud and young William were locked away and left to starve. When their cell door was eventually opened, both were dead. Maud, who cradled the wasted body of her son in her arms, had been driven by the primal human urge to survive to try to eat her son. Teeth marks in William's cheek were testament to the lonely desperation in which she died. The fate of the de Braose family laid bare John's petty cruelty in persecuting William Snr and leaving Maud and William Jnr to starve to death.

Church funds swelled John's coffers as he turned his attention to the retaking of his lost lands across the Channel. Many of his barons still considered themselves Norman and had lost lands to Philip's expansionism.

Getting them back might settle some of the discontent in England and make John even richer and more powerful into the bargain. As John began to lay the groundwork in 1212, Pope Innocent moved to block his efforts. Allowing the English king to prosper as a direct result of his alienation from the church would set a dangerous precedent. John was formally excommunicated by the pope and was furthermore declared dethroned. The drastic step meant that all those who had given homage to John were absolved of their fealty and were free to select a new ruler. In the early months of 1212, John uncovered a plot to assassinate him and exile his children. The leaders of the scheme, Eustace de Vesci and Robert Fitzwalter, were barons who had worked for John and when the plan failed, they fled to Scotland and France respectively. John's young children were placed under close watch. His oldest son, Henry, was just 4 years old and was already feeling the warmth of the burning hatred his father attracted. This attempted revolt was enough to cause one ageing servant of the Angevin throne to emerge from a self-imposed retirement to offer his service once more.

William Marshal is frequently remembered by the epithet given him by his contemporary biographer: The Greatest Knight. This is the knight who had charged at Richard the Lionheart when he had pursued Henry II across the French countryside and had, at the last moment, dipped his lance to kill the prince's horse. Stories of Marshal's life swirl together legend, myth, and fact to create one of the most exciting life stories of the age. He first appears as a small boy, a hostage at the court of King Stephen for his father's good behaviour. When John Fitz Gilbert, known as the Marshal, rebelled, Stephen descended on his castle at Newbury to bring him to heel. He took little William with him and supposedly threatened to catapult the lad over the walls, his life forfeited by his father's treachery. John's reported response to the warning was cold. He shrugged his shoulders and told Stephen he was not worried about the loss of a son, for 'he still had the anvils and hammers to produce even finer ones'. Although the story probably grew in its retelling over the years that followed, and Stephen was unlikely to have done anything so vicious even if he threatened it, the course of English history might have been very different had William Marshal, who was in his mid-sixties by 1212, not survived. He had served Henry II, Richard I, and John before the two had fallen out. Marshal had retired to his lands in Ireland to keep out of the king's way, but this new development drew him back to the frontline. William's loyalty was to the crown, however he felt about the head upon which it sat.

Some of the barons must have contemplated making a bid for John's throne. What Eustace de Vesci and Robert Fitzwalter had planned if they succeeded in killing John is unclear. The tense inertia that followed the pope's latest measures betrayed a fundamental problem with an attempt to rebel that encompassed something closer to revolution by removing the reigning monarch: What next? The Crown remained something utterly apart from the nobility. God selected kings, and they were anointed in His name with holy oil in an act that transformed them from mere men into kings approved by God. Killing or removing them risked acting against God's will since the Lord would not have made a mistake. Even if that hurdle could be overcome, the next was harder to work around. A feudal society required a king at the top to function, and none, at least in England in the Middle Ages, were thinking outside that particular box. Who wore the crown might be open to question. It had been after the death of William II, Henry I, and Henry II, but there had to be a king.

The problem with a baron attempting to fill a vacancy, if one could be created, lay in the distance between nobility and royalty. It was not a social, political, and religious leap that could be made easily. England had been conquered in 1066 by a duke, but he had blood links to the English royal family as a distant cousin to Edward the Confessor. Since then, even where there had been contested successions, it was contested between close blood relatives, all of whom were William's descendants. The last precedent for a nobleman making himself king was Harold II in 1066, and that was a template few would be willing to follow. Promoting a member of the English aristocracy also created the tangled problem of a group of peers setting one of their number above the rest of them. It risked resentment, difficulty in controlling fractious nobles, later challenges to the validity of kingship. Even before that, it relied on noblemen unanimously selecting one of their number as the best among them. It was safer all round to stick to royal blood. The problem was that John really was it by 1212. All his brothers were long dead. Only one of them had a son, and John had seen to it that he would be no threat. John's children were too young, and any other grandsons of Henry II and Eleanor of Aquitaine were in Germany or Castile. Perhaps the natural place to look was much closer to home. The French Crown was growing richer and increasingly powerful. The Capetian monarchs could reunite the English nobles with the Continental lands they had lost. There may have been the seed of an idea, but no one moved just yet.

The force John assembled for an invasion of Poitou in 1212 had to be diverted at the last moment to deal with an uprising in Wales led by Llywelyn the Great. King Philip began his own preparations at the beginning of the campaigning season in 1213 to take the initiative. He had no intention of waiting for John to bring an army to France. With papal approval and John considered dethroned, Philip prepared to invade England to take John's crown. John was thrown into a desperate panic. It had proven embarrassing and divisive enough that he had lost all his father's Continental holdings. He still held the most prestigious prize, but for how long? Philip had proven himself more than a match for John militarily, and the thought of the Capetian king crossing the Channel to take away the last vestige of his power threw John into a spiral of fear. His response was unexpected and drastic.

On 15 May 1213, John met with Pandulf, a papal legate who had arrived in England to discover the truth of the shocking new development. He was greeted by a king eager to get on with it. Pandulf listened in amazement as John, whose kingdom had been under interdict for five years and who had been personally excommunicated by the pope, gave his kingdom to the church. To prove he was serious, John gave Pandulf a letter to be taken to Rome in which he confessed 'we have grieved and offended God and our mother church of Rome' before admitting 'we have need to the mercy of our lord Jesus Christ'. John then laid out his astounding proposition: 'We offer and freely grant to God, and to the apostles Saint Peter and Saint Paul, and to our mother church of Rome, and to our Holy father the pope, Innocent the third, and to all the popes that cometh after him, all the realm and patronages of churches of England and of Ireland.' England would become a papal vassal if Pope Innocent would restore John to favour. Kings of England would do fealty to popes from this moment on for the right to rule.[2]

This submission was John's desperate move to prevent an invasion from France. As an excommunicated, deposed ruler whose kingdom languished beyond the embrace of the church, he was fair game for Philip. Attacking England took on the air of a crusade. Unwilling to risk the delays he might experience in negotiating a return to the fold and lacking the subtle grasp of such relationships his father had honed, John threw his crown at Pope Innocent III. At the same time, the tactic was not without merit. If Innocent accepted, England would enjoy unique protections in Europe as a papal fiefdom. John was frightened by Philip's aggression and the French king's ability to portray a campaign against England as a crusade. This was as likely to be the breaking point for his subjects as see a successful French invasion. There was no winning, except by taking the crown of England out of the game. John had witnessed first-hand that papal protection alone offered little security. Richard's lands were assaulted, by John as well as Philip, despite the prohibition on attacking the territories of anyone on crusade. Yet if England were a vassal state of the papacy, an attack on its shores would be an act of aggression against Rome and the pope himself as England's overlord. John would be protected within his kingdom from assault by his barons too. The only catch was that it would not really be his kingdom any longer. He must have felt he could rely on the distance to Rome to keep any interference light and easy to deflect, but he was clear in his letter that his submission would 'bind us, and all that cometh after us, and our heirs forevermore, without any gainsaying, to the pope'.[3]

England was transformed at a stroke from international pariah state and legitimate target to Rome's favourite kingdom, with John as the pope's fêted son. Innocent was quick to accept the offer. England was perceived as rich beyond belief, and Rome saw a chance to open a bottomless purse to fund its crusading desire. John had to swallow some conditions. All clerics were to be allowed to return to England unmolested. Stephen Langton, the archbishop of Canterbury in exile, was to be recognised and welcomed into the kingdom. Those like Eustace de Vesci and Robert Fitzgerald who had rebelled against John on the pope's instructions were to be pardoned and permitted to come home. All of this might have been hard to swallow but was a price worth paying to secure a papal prohibition on Philip's planned invasion of England. With his throne protected, John began again to prepare for an offensive against Philip.

In early 1214, John managed to create a powerful alliance against the French king. Emperor Otto IV was John's nephew, the son of his sister Matilda, and had become Holy Roman Emperor in 1209 after more than a decade as King of the Romans, and also held the title King of Burgundy. They were joined by the dukes of Brabant and Lorraine as well as the counts of Flanders and Boulogne. When the armies met on 27 July 1214, the English contingent was led by William Longspée, Earl of Salisbury, one of Henry II's illegitimate sons and so a half-brother to John. The Battle of Bouvines was a disaster for John's coalition. William Longespée, along with the Duke of Lorraine, and the counts of Flanders and Boulogne were captured. Otto escaped the battlefield but was soon deposed as Holy Roman Emperor by his rival Frederick. The Battle of Bouvines became a defining moment in the emergence of the nation of France, but it also forced John to agree to a five-year truce and abandon his plans, embarrassed and having lost all the money he had raised.

By January 1215, the barons of England were at breaking point with John, papal vassal or not. The king was confronted by armed representatives of the nobility who demanded a Charter of Liberties based on the coronation charter of Henry I. As the barons reached back for some precedent to build their demands on, Henry was the best fit they could find. He had come to the throne unexpectedly, and by taking a bride from the House of Wessex and pledging to restore many of the laws of pre-Conquest England, he had offered conciliation to bolster his own position. The suggestion to John was not subtle. Henry had promised not to extract fines from barons for inheriting their lands, to refrain from demanding payment for a lady to be married, and to correct several other wrongs in the kingdom.[4] The barons offered John the opportunity to correct his bad behaviour by reverting to this set of rules. Rather than a voluntary offer from a new king, this was a set of restrictions to be imposed on a reigning monarch because he was ruling badly. Henry I had promised not to do many of the things John was guilty of in the barons' eyes, and they offered John the chance to correct his wrongs. One chronicler complained that John 'did so much shame and villainy to God and Holy Church, and also he held and haunted his own brother's wife, and lay also by many other women, great lords' daughters, for he spared no woman that he liked forto have'.[5]

The barons were at the end of their tether with John. His incompetence in losing all of his Continental lands was one thing, but his tyranny that increasingly focussed on what remained, England, was too uncomfortable to bear. What caused even more outrage and tipped many over the edge was his wanton pleasure-seeking. He forced himself on any woman he set his eye on, including the wives and daughters of his noblemen, leaving them seething, embarrassed and dishonoured. John was outraged at the demands placed before him, not least by the nerve of those insisting he curtail his own power over them. His response was to take the cross on 4 March 1215 and to pledge to go on crusade. He effectively dodged the issue by tying his cause even more tightly to Rome. In April, Pope Innocent wrote to give his support to John's position. The barons refused to accept the situation, and in May they gathered at Northampton, where they renounced their fealty to John. As the armed barons moved towards London, John, seemingly frightened again, offered to submit to the judgement of a panel headed by the pope. The barons, unsatisfied that the sympathetic Innocent would surely find in John's favour, refused. Next, John turned to the archbishop of Canterbury, who was in communication with the barons, to find a route to peace.

It was these negotiations that led to a meeting at Runnymede on the banks of the River Thames. On 10 June 1215, the barons presented their list of demands in what is known as the Articles of the Barons. The archbishop worked between the two sides to find agreement and the terms of a charter were settled and sealed on 15 June. The document would become known as Magna Carta and its fundamental principle that the king was not above the law, and that justice should not be denied or sold to any man, formed a foundation for England's legal development from the thirteenth century onwards. In 1215, it was essentially a list of demands for reform that would benefit the narrow class of the nobility who were trying to impose themselves on the king. There was no real intention to redefine English society to the benefit of all, and much of the lasting legacy of Magna Carta would be an unintended side effect of the more selfish motivations of the barony as well as the fallout of the tensions that were beginning to build.

On 19 June, the barons renewed their fealty to John, and the charter was copied for distribution. As soon as the threat of armed confrontation was withdrawn, John tore up the charter and applied to Pope Innocent III to be released from the oath he had been forced to swear. The pope, who saw a challenge to his new control of his fiefdom, readily agreed. John was excused from the promises he had made, and Innocent condemned the barons who had sought to shackle their king. A papal bull issued on 24 August 1215 insisted that John had been forced to seal a document described as 'illegal, unjust, harmful to royal rights and shameful to the English people'. Magna Carta was, Innocent declared, to be considered 'null, and void of all validity for ever'.[6] If John thought he had won, the illusion was to prove short-lived.

The baron's response was drastic and dramatic. Appointing their finest orators, the disgruntled nobility despatched a delegation across the Channel to Paris. Once before King Philip, the men 'prayed him that he would send Louis his son to England, to be King of England and have the crown'.[7] The barons returned to the idea of deposing John if he was to prove impossible to restrain or control. John's heir was still just 8 and likely to be under his father's influence or less than grateful to the men who drove him from the throne. Prince Louis was married to Blanche of Castile, a granddaughter of Henry II and niece of John, so the focus on Philip's heir was a way to keep the Angevin blood of Henry II on the throne while keeping England under a control that was familiar to the Anglo-Norman barony. French rule was not alien to most of them, and it turned the key that might unlock the door to recovering their own Norman and French lands. Armed with a viable, even attractive, alternative, the barons went on the offensive against John.

On 22 May 1216, a fleet drove onto the shore at Sandwich in Kent. As the ships disgorged an army onto the beaches, the weight of opposition to John became increasingly apparent. Prince Louis had brought an army, his numbers swollen by rebel barons to such an extent that John's half-brother William Longespée, briefly a French captive after the Battle of Bouvines, joined the rebellion. John was at Corfe Castle, west of the landing point, and made frantic preparations as ever-worsening news poured into his court. Louis had entered London unopposed. The kingdom was on the brink of falling. For all his manifold faults, John could never be accused of being idle. With his usual energy and speed, he marched north along the Welsh marches before turning east to try and confront the threat. London was already out of his grasp and too tough a nut to crack once it was defended. Instead, John thundered around the Midlands and East Anglia, putting out fires wherever he spotted smoke. For every one he managed to extinguish, two more sprung up to demand his attention. Pope Innocent III passed away and was replaced by Pope Honorius III, who was preoccupied with the efforts to resurrect the crusade and offered no support.

It was during this frantic period of activity that John made a risky crossing of the Wash on the east coast. When the tide rushed in, he lost carts that were rumoured to contain most of his treasure, an array of holy relics, and most worryingly of all, his crown. It was a bad omen. Combined with the stress of recent months, John's usually robust health faltered. He probably contracted dysentery, the scourge of all medieval campaigns that was essentially a deadly form of diarrhoea. The king struggled on to Newark, carried in a litter for the final miles, too ill to ride. John wrote his will, aware that he had barely any hope of handing a kingdom to his 9-year-old son Henry. What would become of his young children in an England ruled by a French prince he could only dare to imagine as he slipped from consciousness during the night of 18 October 1216. John was dead, but the problems facing England remained very much alive.

As the king was buried within Worcester Cathedral, the most suitable place still in royal hands, those named as executors of his will pondered what to do next. Large numbers of barons, including dissatisfied northern lords, had swung to Louis's cause, but the thirteen men named by John represented some of the most powerful forces in England. Guala, the papal legate headed the list. Rome had good reason to keep John and his heirs, who were bound by the pledge to hold England from the pope, on the throne. Louis and Philip would not feel themselves bound by the promises of a vanquished dead man. Peter des Roches, the wealthy, worldly, and influential Bishop of Winchester was also on the list, as was Aimery de Saint-Maur, the Master of the Knights Templar in England. The list of secular lords was led by William Marshal, Earl of Pembroke, that greatest of knights. Ranulf, Earl of Chester was a powerful figure who had remained at John's side, as was the earl of Derby. Also on the list were Savaric de Mauléon and Falkes de Bréauté, mercenary captains central to John's military efforts. It was a roll call of those loyal to the Angevin cause, bequeathed by John to his

William the Conqueror lands in England, changing the kingdom forever in the wake of the Norman Conquest. (Royal 19 E VI f.403 c5575–07 via British Library Digital Catalogue of Illuminated Manuscripts)

Hereward the Exile fighting Normans in a drawing by John Cassell, 1865. (Public domain via Wikimedia Commons)

Left: Henry I mourning the sinking of the White Ship, which caused the death of his only legitimate son and heir as well as two of his illegitimate children and decimated generations of Anglo-Norman aristocracy. (Royal 20 A II f.6v via British Library Digital Catalogue of Illuminated Manuscripts)

Below: King Stephen, who rushed to the throne on the death of his uncle Henry I before his cousin Empress Matilda could press her claim. (Royal 20 A II f.7 E087488 via British Library Digital Catalogue of Illuminated Manuscripts)

HNO dm ō. ē. xiiii. Impr᷑ henric᷑ natalē
dm̄. babenb᷑. celebrauit. dispositis nuptiis suis

Above: Contemporary image of Empress Matilda seated at a feast beside her first husband, Holy Roman Emperor Henry V. (via Wikimedia Commons)

Right: Henry II and Thomas Becket, Archbishop of Canterbury, quarrel. Their dispute would cost Becket his life and damage Henry's kingship. (Royal 20 A II f.7v via British Library Digital Catalogue of Illuminated Manuscripts)

Left: An early manuscript image of the Murder of Thomas Becket in Canterbury Cathedral. Thomas became a saint, and it is possible he planned to be martyred to secure a victory over Henry II. (Harley 5312 f28v via British Library Digital Catalogue of Illuminated Manuscripts)

Below: Henry II and Eleanor of Aquitaine visiting the King of France. (via British Library Digital Catalogue of Illuminated Manuscripts)

Right: The Coronation of Henry the Young King, the only king crowned in his father's lifetime in English or British history. The experiment to mirror the French crown's method of protecting the succession caused problems and was never repeated. (Becket Leaves (c.1220–1240), f.3r BL Loan MS 88-2 via British Library Digital Catalogue of Illuminated Manuscripts)

Below: The children of Henry II and Eleanor of Aquitaine. In turn, each of their sons would cause problems and rebel against their father. (Royal 14 B VI Membrane 6 via British Library Digital Catalogue of Illuminated Manuscripts)

Statue of Richard I, the Lionheart, outside the Houses of Parliament in London. Richard hounded his father to death in 1199. (Author's collection)

Manuscript image of King John hunting. His personality and style of rule dragged England into crisis and caused the barons to impose Magna Carta, then invite Prince Louis of France to invade. (Cotton Claudius D II f.116 via British Library Digital Catalogue of Illuminated Manuscripts)

Magna Carta, the document John's barons tried to force him to abide by to restrain royal authority in England. John's immediate revocation of the document led to civil war. (British Library Cotton MS Augustus II.106 via British Library Digital Catalogue of Illuminated Manuscripts)

The tomb of King John at Worcester Cathedral. John had wished to be buried at Beulieu Abbey but so much of the country was in French and rebel hands when he died that Worcester was the best place available. (Author's collection)

John's effigy atop his tomb in Worcester Cathedral. He is flanked by two of his favourite saints, St Oswald and St Wulfstan. (Author's collection)

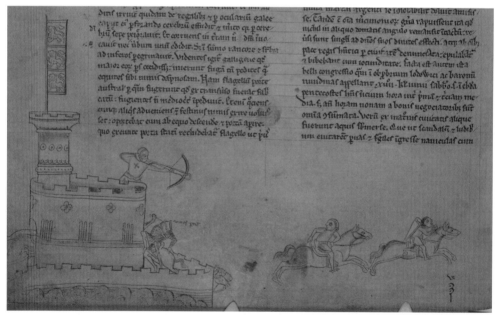

Manuscript marginal drawing of the Battle of Lincoln in 1217, where William Marshall defeated the French and rebel baron force to save Henry III's throne. (Matthew Paris's Chronica Maiora)

Henry III with his wife Eleanor of Provence in a marginal drawing. Henry's reign was long and saw the Second Barons' War erupt. (BL Manuscripts Royal 14 c VII f.124v via British Library Digital Catalogue of Illuminated Manuscripts)

Simon de Montfort, Earl of Leicester. A charming and driven man, who married Henry III's sister and rebelled, capturing the king and holding a parliament that has gone down in history as revolutionary. (Unknown author; Public domain via Wikimedia Commons)

HERE WERE BURIED THE REMAINS OF
SIMON DE MONTFORT, EARL OF LEICESTER
PIONEER OF REPRESENTATIVE GOVERNMENT WHO WAS
KILLED IN THE BATTLE OF EVESHAM ON AUGUST 4th 1265.

THIS STONE BROUGHT FROM HIS BIRTHPLACE THE
CASTLE OF MONTFORT-L'AMAURY IN FRANCE WAS
ERECTED TO COMMEMORATE THE SEVEN HUNDREDTH
ANNIVERSARY OF HIS DEATH.

UNVEILED BY THE SPEAKER OF THE HOUSE OF COMMONS
AND DEDICATED BY
HIS GRACE THE ARCHBISHOP OF CANTERBURY
ON THE 18th DAY OF JULY 1965.

Above: The stone that marks the spot where Simon de Montfort is believed to have been buried. He was killed and dismembered at the Battle of Evesham. The monument was erected in 1965, on the 700th anniversary of the battle using stone imported from Simon's birthplace at Montfort-l'Amaury. (Author's collection)

Left: Queen Isabella, wife of Edward II, and Roger Mortimer, a rebel baron. Together they landed in England and ultimately forced Edward to abdicate in favour of his son, though Isabella may not have meant matters to go so far. (Jean de Wavrin, Public domain via Wikimedia Commons)

The tomb of Hugh Despenser the Younger, the last and most objectionable favourite of King Edward II. Hugh used his connections to profit and accrue power but was ultimately subjected to a gruesome execution by his enemies. (Author's collection)

The tomb of Edward II at Gloucester Cathedral. Edward was reportedly killed in 1327, but suspicion has lingered that he lived on, perhaps buried in this tomb much later. (Author's collection)

The effigy of Edward II, the first King of England to be deposed by parliament. From his tomb at Gloucester Cathedral. (Author's collection)

A young Richard II. He succeeded his grandfather aged ten in 1377 and was soon confronted by the Peasants' Revolt in 1381. (Royal 14 E IV f.10 via British Library Digital Catalogue of Illuminated Manuscripts)

Right: Richard II gives the duchy of Aquitaine to his uncle John of Gaunt, Duke of Lancaster. Gaunt was an unpopular figurehead for Richard's minority government and a target of the Peasants' Revolt. (Harley 4380 f.21 via British Library Digital Catalogue of Illuminated Manuscripts)

Below: Richard II addresses the crowds after the death of Wat Tyler. (Chroniques Jean Froissart, Public domain via Wikimedia Commons)

Henry IV, the first Lancastrian King of England. He replaced Richard II but sat uneasily on his throne. (Yates Thompson 48 f.147 via British Library Digital Catalogue of Illuminated Manuscripts)

Henry VI, grandson of Henry IV. He became King of England aged nine months on the death of his father Henry V. He would prove unsuited to life as a medieval king. (Yates Thompson 48 f.190 via British Library Digital Catalogue of Illuminated Manuscripts)

Above left: Humphrey, Duke of Gloucester, youngest son of Henry IV, brother to Henry V and last surviving uncle of Henry VI. He championed the prosecution of war with France against his nephew's desire for peace and died in 1447 after being arrested. (British Library, Royal 15 E VI f.2v via Wikimedia Commons)

Above right: Richard, 3rd Duke of York, heir to the House of Mortimer and claimant to the throne of England. He was allied to Humphrey, Duke of Gloucester. Both men are supporting the English claim to the throne of France in this image from the Talbot Book of Hours. (British Library, Royal 15 E VI f.2v via Wikimedia Commons)

Ludlow Castle, the Mortimer fortress on the Welsh Marches used by Richard, Duke of York to gather support to oppose Henry VI's government. The Battle of Ludford Bridge in 1459 saw York flee from Ludlow and the town ransacked by a royal army. (Author's collection)

Left: Micklegate Bar, York, one of the city's medieval gates. After the Battle of Wakefield, the heads of York, his son Edmund, Earl of Rutland, and Richard Neville, Earl of Salisbury were fixed to the gate. (Author's collection)

Below: Richard, Duke of York and his oldest son King Edward IV in a stained-glass window at St Laurence's Church, Ludlow. After York's death, Edward claimed the throne as the first monarch of the House of York. (Author's collection)

young son and charged with protecting his inheritance from the ruin John had called down upon it.

Louis had a firm hold on London and the south-east. The northern barons were inclined to support the invasion, and to the west, Llywelyn the Great was using the fresh disruption in England to make gains of his own in Wales. The cause for these thirteen men must have looked bleak, almost pointless. Trying to champion the claim of a 9-year-old child only made the matter harder. Yet, this final dilemma also presented a unique opportunity. For someone like William Marshal, now 70, the prospect of shunning a life of chivalry and abandoning a small boy to the ravages of fate must have seemed unthinkable. Alongside such considerations sat the knowledge that if Louis were successful, he would be looking to give his supporters lands and titles taken from those loyal to John, or at least to his crown. That meant Marshal, Chester, and the others turning their back on all they owned as well as a helpless child.

William was appointed to lead little Henry's cause, and as he pledged himself to his new king, the Marshal saw in his innocent face a possible solution. The first step to be taken was a coronation. Previous experience had demonstrated the high level of protection the ceremony could provide to even the most unpopular king. Louis had not made any move to have himself crowned in London, and William saw a chance to steal a march on his enemies. The papal legate Guala excommunicated Prince Louis so that no member of the clergy would be permitted to crown him. At Gloucester Cathedral on 28 October 1216, King Henry III was crowned in a ceremony overseen by Guala. A gold circlet had to be borrowed from Henry's mother in the absence of a crown, and his heavy robes had to be hastily shortened and taken in to make them fit his small frame. During the coronation feast, word arrived that Goodrich Castle, only a dozen miles from Gloucester, had been placed under siege by Louis's forces. Peter des Roches, who had already served as Henry's tutor, was given control of the person of the new king and Marshal, though he appeared reluctant until offered remission of his sins by Guala, agreed to lead the military effort.

Guala placed Wales under interdict for challenging the authority of the king, whose overlord was the pope. Louis's allies were also excommunicated so that the royalist cause took on the glittering sheen of a crusade. What William Marshal and those around him realised was that in Henry's youth, they had the perfect opportunity to take all of the sting out of Louis's invasion. The issues that had led the barons to rebel had all revolved around a personal conflict with John. It was John's attitude and his personality that had driven them to seek to depose him. With John dead and gone, they were faced with the reality that their new opponent was a small boy who had done nothing wrong. All of a sudden, their rebellion looked unappealingly like a military assault on a 9-year-old innocent.

The royalist council sought to exploit the space created by the sudden uncertainty by reaching out an olive branch to the rebel barons. On 12 November 1216, Magna Carta was reissued in King Henry's name. The spark for calling Prince Louis to England had been the tearing up of the Great Charter in 1215. By offering to be bound by it, Henry and his government could suck all the oxygen out of the revolt. There were a few alterations to the document the barons had presented in 1215. The critical change was the removal of the security clause that provided for a panel of barons to restrain and, if necessary, punish the king. Given that Henry had a minority regency council, this most offensive of provisions was not required, and the issue could be kicked into the long grass until Henry was an adult. The new document was issued in Henry's name by William Marshal as head of his government and with the approval of Guala. This last measure offered some assurance that Rome would not revoke the offer as it had overturned the Charter in 1215. The reissue of Magna Carta was simultaneously an acknowledgement of the weakness of Henry's position and a stroke of political genius that offered an end to the rebellion.

Initially, it appeared to have only limited success. A few of the *reversi*, as the royal records dub those who returned to Henry's cause, appeared at the court, but not enough to turn the tide. They were treated leniently, an encouragement to others considering leaving Louis's side, but it was a slower burn than Marshal may have hoped for. The cold, hard fact was that Louis still held the capital and the south-east, and many had given oaths to him and had been promised rewards in return. Henry's cause did not yet look enticing enough for most to make the leap to his side. Something dramatic was needed. William Marshal gave up some castles held in Henry's name to Louis's men. Feeling things were progressing well, but not quickly enough, Louis went back to France to gather more men and money for a final push. If he saw in Marshal's abandonment of royal fortresses an indication of weakness, Louis had fallen into a trap. The castles that were surrendered were a few outposts, cut off from the royal cause by lands controlled by Louis. Marshal was neither retreating nor giving up. He was consolidating.

In March 1217, two high profile rebels defected from Louis's cause. One was Marshal's son, and the other was William Longespée, Earl of Salisbury, John's half-brother. It kick-started the campaigning season and saw the royalists take Farnham, Winchester, Southampton, Odiham, and Marlborough castles. Porchester, Chichester, and the Isle of Ely soon followed suit. These targets were selected to extend the boundaries of Henry's influence while maintaining a solid, coherent block that was easier to manage. Marshal was making significant gains and exploiting Louis's continued absence. It was late April before Louis managed to sail from French shores with reinforcements. He made for Dover, where he had left the castle under siege, to find his forces had vanished. He watched from his ship as men led by Oliver, one of John's illegitimate sons, and William of Cassingham, leader of a guerrilla force, ran into the town and set fire to the huts. Turning away from the plumes of smoke, Louis made for the port at Sandwich.

As soon as Marshal heard of Louis's return, he ordered all of those castles the royalist cause had won to be abandoned and destroyed, with the exception of Farnham, which was retained as a distraction. However much he had gained, Marshal was all too aware that the royalists lacked the resources and time to indulge in protracted castle warfare. The earl of Winchester urgently appealed to Louis for help before his castle at Mountsorrel fell. He was so impassioned that Louis sent him to London with a commission to raise men. As this army approached Mountsorrel, the royalists withdrew all the way to Nottingham, continuing the policy of avoiding prolonged confrontation. The army was diverted to support Hugh of Arras at the siege of Lincoln, the last bastion of royalist resistance in the region. Louis rolled his siege machinery back to Dover Castle as the other portion of his forces arrived at Lincoln. Marshal was at Northampton with Henry, and his experienced ears pricked up at the news. Louis's forces were divided into two. Now, Marshal urged the royalists, was the time to strike. They stood a chance against half Louis's army that they did not against the whole, and they may never get another opportunity like this.

Marshal's plan was daring to the point of recklessness. The one thing all medieval commanders sought to avoid was the unpredictability of a pitched battle. Time and resources favoured Louis. Marshal wanted to role the die in a fight against half of his enemy's host because it was their best, and perhaps only, hope. With the grudging, uncertain consent of the rest of the royalist noblemen, Marshal set a muster at Newark for 15 May. Four days later, the army, all that could be raised in Henry's name, marched out. Guala repeated the excommunication of Louis and his allies, reinforcing the crusading element of the fight to come that would encourage the unwilling participants. Henry was placed behind the stout walls of Nottingham Castle to await what might be the final outcome of his cause.

The approach to Lincoln was carefully planned using all of the military expertise available. Peter des Roches, the warrior-bishop of Winchester, had once been attached to Lincoln Cathedral so brought with him a good knowledge of the city and its surroundings. The Fosse Way, an old Roman road, cut a straight line from Newark to Lincoln's south gate, but it also meant crossing a narrow bridge over the River Witham just outside the walls and then fighting uphill through the town towards the castle. Tactically, it was a recipe for disaster. The royalist army instead took a longer route that would bring them to the north-western corner of the city where the castle butted against the walls. They arrived on 20 May.

Lincoln had withstood the attentions of Louis's forces for three months and was in a desperate condition. The castle remained an outpost of royalist loyalty at a time when Marshal had been divesting himself of such untenable holdings through the sheer determination of Lady Nicola de la Haye, castellan of Lincoln. Nicola had resisted a siege before, in 1191, when her husband had been away. One of John's final acts before his death in 1216 had been to refuse to accept the keys to Lincoln from Nicola. She was in her mid-sixties and wanted to retire, fearing she was too old to do the job properly any more. John pleaded with her to remain in post and made her Sheriff of Lincolnshire in acknowledgement of her steadfast loyalty and evident ability. When the royal army arrived outside the city walls, the castle was in a desperate state. Nicola sent her constable, Geoffrey de Serland, out to report on the condition of the siege and the city.

Peter des Roches, Bishop of Winchester, entered the castle through a postern gate, possibly the same one Geoffrey had used to get out, or one he knew of from his time in Lincoln. Returning to Marshal, the bishop reported that the gate at the north-west corner had been roughly blocked up from the inside, but might be breached if they were careful. The mercenary captain Falkes de Bréauté snuck into the castle through the postern gate with a detachment of crossbowmen. They took up positions on the walls overlooking the narrow space between the fortress and the cathedral and waited. Ranulf, Earl of Chester, demanded the honour of the first charge and was tasked with leading an attack on the north gate further along the walls. The distraction it provided worked. As the French force packed between the city's monolithic buildings jostled to confront the assault, Falkes's men sprang up from behind the ramparts and opened fire into the throng. It went so well, panic spreading throughout the courtyard below, that Falkes led a small band of his men out to attack the French. He was quickly captured, and more of his men were forced to venture out to free him.

Even if they were overenthusiastic, the diversion worked perfectly. In the confusion, Marshal had taken most of the army to the north-west gate and quietly set about breaking the gates open and dismantling the barricade.

Once the way was cleared, Marshal dug his heels into his warhorse to lead the charge into the city. One of his squires caught his reins and reminded his master that he had neglected to put his helmet on. Once properly dressed, Marshal spurred his horse into a gallop through the gate, his bravery and enthusiasm undiminished by his 70 years. Marshal's biographer gleefully wrote that 'hungry lion never rushed on its prey so hotly as the Marshal on his foes' as Peter des Roches urged those behind to follow, calling out 'God help the Marshal!'[8] The French force was entirely caught by surprise. One man, who was operating a stone-throwing siege machine, looked up from his work to see what the commotion was only for a passing royalist knight to cut off his head. When one of the rebel barons, Robert of Ropsley, shattered his lance on William Longespée, Earl of Salisbury, Marshal retaliated by delivering such a shuddering blow that Ropsley was sent crashing from his horse.

Chaos filled the space as the noise of battle rang around the walls of the castle and cathedral. 'Then sparks of fire were seen to dart, and sounds as of dreadful thunder were heard to burst forth from the blows of swords against helmeted heads'. The crossbowmen on the walls brought down the horses of the French army so that their pinned riders were taken hostage. Surrounded, the French commander, the count of Perche, refused to surrender to men 'who were traitors to their lawful king'. At that, one knight rushed forward and drove his sword through the count's visor and into his eye, killing him instantly.[9] Horrified, for the loss of a noble life in battle was almost unheard of, the French force panicked and began to flee. Pursued down the slope and bottlenecked at the gate and bridge, they were picked off by the royalists. Without waiting to eat or refresh himself, Marshal galloped to Nottingham to relay the news of their victory to the young king. The army was sent home for a few days to rest and secure their hostages while the king's advisors decided how best to capitalise on their crushing triumph at Lincoln.

In the flush of their success, the royalist cause found more notable men, around 150, returned to the service of the crown. When Louis heard the news of the battle's outcome, he packed up his siege machinery at Dover and returned to London. Realising his cause was faltering, Louis wrote to his father pleading for help. He complained that Henry's forces were parading around outside London so that he was effectively trapped. 'Moreover,' Louis added, 'all kinds of provisions are failing us and our followers in the city, and even if they abounded there, we have no means of buying them; therefore I inform you that I have no means of resistance, or of leaving England, unless you supply me with strong military aid.'[10] Louis knew what Marshal was daring to hope. The tide of the war was turning. Philip was stuck between the desire to give his son assistance and the prohibition of the pope, who pointed out that Louis remained excommunicated. The French king sidestepped the problem by suggesting that his daughter-in-law Blanche support her husband.

In a signal of their growing strength and confidence, the royal forces divided into two. Louis was penned in at London, his forces resorting to raiding into East Anglia in search of food. Henry and Guala moved closer to the capital as Marshal and other military leaders made for the south coast to confront the fleet Blanche had assembled at Calais. At Dover, Marshal called out all the ships of the Cinque Ports to muster at Sandwich. The 70-year-old William wanted to hop onto a boat, but all those around him advised against risking himself again. The justiciar Hubert de Burgh was given command of the fleet instead. Louis and Blanche made a desperate last-ditch bid to revitalise their cause. At the beginning of the barons' rebellion, John had employed a pirate, Eustace the Monk, but in true pirate style, Eustace instead invaded the Channel Islands and took control of them.

On 24 August 1217, Eustace joined with the fleet from Calais to try and relieve Louis. When Marshal and his allies awoke on a clear summer morning, they could clearly see the French fleet. At least ten were large warships bristling with soldiers, and Eustace was in the lead. As they sailed towards the Thames Estuary, the royal fleet left port aiming directly at the French. Suddenly, Hubert's flagship veered off course and picked up speed. Those behind him followed suit. On the shore, the watching royal forces were thrown into uncertainty. Was Hubert fleeing without even trying to engage? The French sailors hurled abuse at the cowardly English as they skidded across the sea behind them. A moment later, it became clear what was happening. Hubert had altered his course to get the wind behind his sails. As they moved closer to the French fleet, the English sailors threw plumes of powdered lime into the air, and the blinding, stinging cloud engulfed the French fleet. Powdered lime becomes caustic on contact with liquid, so when it blew into eyes, mouths, and hit sweating brows, the French sailors were blinded and in agony. Drawing alongside the French ships, the English crews fired crossbows into the fog of confusion and rammed the sides of the French ships with their iron-clad prows. Many ships were captured, including the flagship. Eustace the Monk was found hiding below decks and dragged up to be executed. What remained of the French fleet limped back to Calais.

When Marshal, Hubert, and the victorious force returned to London to re-join the other half of their army, they also sent the fleet to blockade the Thames Estuary. Louis knew his cause was lost and sought terms. Many on the royal side wanted to besiege London and crush the French, but Marshal saw things differently. He had avoided costly and time-consuming siege warfare throughout the effort to restore royal authority, and he had no intention of changing a winning tactic. William decided that the best route to peace was to encourage Louis out of England. That meant finding terms that Louis could swallow easily and quickly. For his part, Louis made it known that if the royalists sent their demands, he would accept them provided they refrained from trying to impose anything that would dishonour him or his companions. When the terms arrived, they were temptingly reasonable.

Lands were to be restored to those who held them prior to Louis's invasion. All prisoners on both sides would be freed without further ransom, and Louis was to release any English barons in his party from their oaths of fealty to him. As soon as that was done, the barons were to give homage to Henry. Louis was required to write to the brothers of Eustace the Monk and order them to hand back to Henry the Channel Islands or stand outside the agreed peace. To encourage Louis further, all debts owed to him were to be paid in full, and there was even the offer of a cash incentive to leave. Louis tripped over himself to accept the terms, perfectly aware that they could have been much harsher. The treaty was formally agreed on 12 September 1217 on an island in the middle of the Thames near Kingston. Louis met with King Henry, William Marshal, Guala, and others to swear to uphold the terms. Louis even added a voluntary offer to try and convince his father to return all of Henry's lost Continental lands once he was back in France. On 28 September, Marshal watched from the shore as Louis's ships sailed away from England, promising never to return again in anger. [11]

On Sunday 29 October 1217, a year and a day after the first desperate ceremony at Gloucester Cathedral, Henry was crowned at Westminster Abbey. The rebellion against the crown was over, though it remained to be seen whether peace would stand the test of contact with reality. William Marshal, Earl of Pembroke, as regent and military leader of the effort in King Henry's name, had pulled victory from the snapping jaws of defeat. With the reissues of Magna Carta and the Charter of the Forest, during and in the years following the war, the rebellion was more successful than most before it. The barons had been pressed into opposition by John's contempt for the law and good rule. Starvation was used as a terror tactic to bring enemies to heel in a totally unacceptable way.[12] John combined cruelty with a slippery refusal to be pinned down. When the barons were driven to take up arms, John handed his crown to the pope to prevent them from imposing restrictions on him. When forced to agree to Magna Carta, he sealed it with no intention of keeping his word. John immediately used his connection to Rome to burn down the peace Magna Carta had sought to secure.

The rebel barons achieved a level of success against John by recognising the critical distinction between other revolts and the Anarchy. They maintained unity but created a viable alternative to John by offering the crown to Prince Louis. Attempting to promote one of their number risked division, and without an option, they remained rebels subject to John's vicious justice and his unpredictable whim. The Anarchy had endured and resulted in a dynastic change because there had been two viable claimants to the throne. When they invited Prince Louis to invade, the barons recreated that dangerous position. What might have happened if John's health had not failed can only ever be a matter of speculation, but things were going incredibly badly in the weeks before his death. The cold, hard fact is that John's death probably prevented the success of the barons' rebellion. It did not quite guarantee its failure, though.

The small group gathered around the 9-year-old Henry might have given up on what looked like a lost cause. A degree of self-interest may have encouraged them to continue resisting Prince Louis. The confidence to attempt a revitalisation of the royalist cause came from a convergence of promising elements. Henry's youth, which in so many ways was a dangerous bar to success, was also a strength in that climate. Henry had caused no offence. The barons' issues had all been with John personally. With John gone, many of their complaints evaporated. In Henry, there was the promise of a different future. He could be taught to rule in a way acceptable to his barons and was young enough not to have learned from his father. It is hard not to place a significant amount of the credit for the success of the royalist cause on the broad shoulders of William Marshal. His political experience allowed him to understand what the rebel barons had been upset about and how Henry could present a solution that would negate their motivation for rebellion. Militarily, he saw clearly that there was one way, and one chance, to win. He avoided the traditional methods of castle warfare that drained funds and time that Henry lacked. Marshal's long experience on the tournament circuit meant he was unafraid of armed confrontation and could see the benefit of it in the current situation.

Marshal manoeuvred to perfection. He consolidated Henry's holdings to avoid overreaching in attempts to protect outposts. During the Anarchy, it was a few key impenetrable fortresses that had contributed to the persistence of civil war. Marshal used Louis's absence from England to strike out in a way that would tempt, or perhaps demand, a response on Louis's return. Rather than try to keep a grip on the gains he made, Marshal destroyed the castles and withdrew. As soon as he saw Louis's forces divided in half, Marshal knew that the moment of truth had arrived. Lincoln had seen the crushing of one king's prospects when Stephen had been captured, but Marshal saw that a gamble was the only chance. A surprise victory on land and another at sea gave the royalist cause an unexpected ascendancy. In proposing terms for peace that were punitive neither to Louis nor to the rebel English barons, Marshal allowed a settlement against which none had cause to buck. John's grant of overlordship to Rome had also allowed the royalist cause, supported by the legate Guala, to cast their efforts as something of a crusade, adding a potent edge to their actions.

The one thing that William Marshal did that created the space in which the royalist cause could succeed was to reissue Magna Carta. Although changes were made to the barons' original document sealed by John at Runnymede, it was an indication of a willingness to compromise that had been utterly absent from John's administration. As a baron himself, Marshal was able to sympathise with the perspectives and complaints of his peers. The reissue of the Great Charter, even with some articles removed, demonstrated a flexibility with which the barons could work. The reason and excuse for their revolt were whipped away. Many returned to the royal fold as soon as the cause appeared to have hope, demonstrating a predisposition towards feudal obedience and operating within a defined and recognisable framework that was often the cause of the failure of rebellions. What Marshal forged was a feeling that no one had lost the conflict, with the possible exception of Louis and Philip. The barons had rebelled because they wanted Magna Carta. Now, with Henry as their king, they had it.

The First Barons' War, as this moment of rebellion and potential revolution became known, was, in many ways, more of a success than any other uprising. The barons had learned what worked: unity among themselves, commitment to clear objectives, and the threat of a replacement monarch if they were denied. Although Marshal led a successful campaign to restore royal influence and control in England, he only achieved it by giving the rebels what they had demanded. From those early days of Henry III's reign to this, the English crown has been subject to the rule of law, and every English subject has had the right to justice without paying to obtain it. Many of the articles of Magna Carta were explicitly concerned with the particular complaints of a group of thirteenth-century English noblemen and reached no further. That it provided any broader impact was its greatest, most glorious accident.

In 1217, the rebel barons both lost and won. Had John remained on the throne, the uprising may have played out very differently, but it was clear that more than dynastic upheaval, what the barons wanted was to be heard. Throughout Henry III's long reign, Magna Carta became the basis of a compact between the king and his barons that aided the development of parliament. A relationship was created between the crown and the barony, who retained their unity by acting as a House of Lords. The king was to correct what was deemed unacceptable behaviour in return for grants of taxation to fund any large projects. This offered the opportunity for balance. Henry would be required to accept restrictions on his authority that no other king of England had operated within. That would undoubtedly mean friction as boundaries were more clearly defined, but in all of the ways that mattered to them, the barons had gained a victory over the crown and bent it to their will.

Chapter 6

The Second Barons' War

Rebellion is just when it is required to maintain obedience to oneself.

Henry III would be the longest-reigning monarch in English or British history until George III overtook him in the nineteenth century. Despite fifty-six years as king, he is largely forgotten amongst the ranks of his predecessors and successors. His regency government had managed to bring about an end to the First Barons' War and ensure his security. As he emerged into adulthood, Henry had many qualities to recommend him to his subjects. Although he tried to regain the lands in France his father had lost, he managed to face up to the political reality that they were beyond his reach and find peace with the son of the man who had invaded his kingdom. Philip was succeeded by Louis VIII in 1423, but only for three years. On his death, Louis was followed by his son as Louis IX, who would go to be canonised as Saint Louis. He and Henry shared many traits in common, and Henry would have been incredibly jealous that his contemporary made it into the panoply of saints. Henry III favoured peace and made it where it could. He was pious, developing a devotion to Saint Edward the Confessor that drove him to have Westminster Abbey rebuilt and Saint Edward's remains translated to the centre of his new gothic masterpiece.

Alongside his positive points, Henry was considered to have displayed troubling weaknesses. Some contemporaries describe him as *simplex* – a Latin word with a frustrating array of meanings. Although it can mean stupid or suggest an issue with his mental health, it was also a word frequently applied to saints who were considered unworldly, lacking in guile or cunning. Henry might have thought it a compliment, in his *simplex* way. As well as learning to live within the bounds set by Magna Carta, Henry had to deal with the reality of his father's desperate decision to submit the English crown to Rome as a vassal. England was, for reasons that remain unclear, viewed as rich beyond measure, and the papacy saw it as a deep well of funds for the crusading effort in the Holy Land. Representatives of the pope arrived with startling frequency to try to wring cash from a population that resented the attempts to squeeze them for money they insisted they simply did not have.

More than half a century on the throne left Henry well within the swing of the pendulum of time towards another period of rebellion. This time, an enigmatic figure who in many ways represented the antithesis of Henry in personality, yet who shared many of his values, would lead the opposition to the king's rule. Henry, to the concern of his influential subjects, was always keen to promote those from outside England who could claim some relationship to him. His wife, Eleanor of Provence, had brought many of her Savoyard relatives to England and Henry had striven to find them incomes and jobs in his government. When the king's mother Isabella of Angoulême died on 4 June 1246, Henry was bombarded by petitions from his half-siblings. Isabella had married Hugh de Lusignan after John's death, and the couple had raised nine children to adulthood. In the wake of their mother's death, four made straight for Henry's court in England. The nobility rolled their eyes at the arrival of more leeches seeking to latch on to the open-handed Henry.

On 1 May 1247, Simon de Montfort was appointed Seneschal of Gascony for a seven-year term. The protections against dismissal meant that only his own decision to resign could bring an end to his time in post. Simon had arrived in England in 1229 in his mid-twenties to seek his fortune. As a second son, he saw scant opportunity to build a future on his family's lands at Montfort, twenty-five miles west of Paris. His father, also named Simon, was one of the most famous and experienced military commanders of his day. He had participated in the Fourth Crusade of 1202–04 but gained even more fame as a leader of the Albigensian Crusade. This twenty-year episode saw crusading zeal put to work on French soil as the Cathars were persecuted relentlessly. Pope Innocent III had initiated the crusade against the variation of Catholicism, but King Philip of France prosecuted it and sought to make political and territorial gains from it. Cathars believed that there were two Gods – the good God was the source of the New Testament and the creator of the spiritual world, and the evil God, Satan, was the God of the Old Testament and had created the physical world.

Simon's father sits in a place made foggy by the mists of time. He was utterly ruthless during the Albigensian Crusade, joining it in 1209 and quickly being appointed its leader. He was given lands taken from the count of Toulouse, who was a supporter of the Cathars, making him a significant landholder in Aquitaine in the south of France. Simon hosted Dominic Guzman during the campaign, a man who would found the Dominican Order and later become Saint Dominic. This connection helped fuel his religious zeal and burning desire to tear down heresy. By ignoring the Roman monotheistic doctrine, the Cathars fell squarely within his sights. Early in the crusade in 1210, Simon had burned 140 Cathars who refused to recant their beliefs, though he spared any who did. To a modern ear, he was a cruel and vicious monster who persecuted what were essentially fellow Christians for a slight variation in their understanding of the religion. To his contemporaries, he was nothing short of a hero, rooting out heresies that threatened the church, acting as the pope's enforcer of doctrine, and punishing those who required correction, or death. The distinction is vital, because to Simon de Montfort Junior, his father was at the pinnacle of what a Christian knight might aim for and was an exemplar to be emulated and, if possible, lived up to. Simon's father was killed on 25 June 1218 during a siege at Toulouse. In his early forties, he had been at the peak of his reputation. Two years later, Simon's younger brother Guy was killed fighting at Castelnaudary as Aquitanian lords rebelled against their father's heir Amaury. Simon came from a family of orthodox, devout crusaders, and that coloured his image of the world around him.

England offered opportunity to this charismatic, magnetic young man. His paternal grandmother was Amicia de Beaumont, daughter and eventual co-heiress to Robert de Beaumont, Earl of Leicester. Robert had been close to Henry the Young King and had joined his rebellion against Henry II. When his male line failed, Simon's father had laid claim to the earldom of Leicester in his mother's right. As a second son, Simon now sought out this maternal patronage as a fitting doorway into English nobility. The initial problem was that King John had denied Simon's father possession of the earldom and given it to Ranulf, Earl of Chester, as Simon Senior's cousin. As soon as he landed on English shores, Simon staked his claim to the earldom. Henry III refused to order Ranulph to give it up, fearful of upsetting one of his most powerful nobles. Mustering all of his charm and persuasiveness, Simon somehow talked Ranulf into ceding his rights in the earldom and its lands to Simon. At the coronation of Henry's young queen Eleanor in 1236, Simon vehemently defended his right to act as hereditary steward against Roger Bigod, Earl of Norfolk, and won. Simon had talked his way into the English nobility and was now elbowing his way up their ranks. It was remarkable but should have offered a warning too.

Simon's social climbing reached a new peak just two years later on 7 January 1238. King Henry himself organised and presided over Simon's marriage, conducted in secret in a royal chapel.[1] The king gave away the bride because she was his sister, Eleanor. At 23, Eleanor was the widow of William Marshal, 2nd Earl of Pembroke, the son of that most famous of knights. On her husband's death when she was just 16, Eleanor had taken a vow of chastity which she now set aside to marry the charming earl who was ten years her senior. The couple were said to have been in love, and the marriage may have been conducted so swiftly and secretly because they were already lovers and Henry disapproved of extra-marital physical relationships. There was another reason for the clandestine ceremony. Henry, perhaps owing to his *simplex* nature, had promised the nobility that he would not make decisions about significant matters of state without first consulting them. The marriage of one of the king's sisters was a substantial issue that ought to have fallen into this arrangement.

Eleanor was the daughter and sister of a king. Her two older sisters were Queen of Scotland and Holy Roman Empress. Her marriage to the Marshal's son had been recognition of William's central role in preserving the English crown and Eleanor's subsequent vow of celibacy had removed her from the marriage market. If she were to re-enter that arena, she would provide the opportunity for a new foreign alliance over which the barons ought to have input. Instead, she was married to the second son of a minor French noble who had inserted himself into English society and jostled his way up the ladder. It is hard to discern whether the nobility were more upset that Henry had failed to consult them or that Simon had transformed himself further into the king's brother-in-law, whose children would have royal blood in their veins. The influence Simon, clearly a charismatic and persuasive man, might have over the unworldly king now that he was part of the family was also an unnerving thought. Henry's brother Richard, Earl of Cornwall led the chorus of complaints. The king found the nobility united against him to protest at his actions. A council was called to meet in London to resolve the matter and, perhaps unsurprisingly by now, Simon emerged having received the kiss of peace from Richard, Earl of Cornwall 'by means of many intercessors and some presents'. The rest of the barons were less pleased but saw that they could do nothing to stop Simon's rise.[2]

On 17 June 1239, Queen Eleanor was delivered of the royal couple's first son, named Edward after Henry's favourite saint, Edward the Confessor. Earlier in the year, Henry had formally invested Simon with the earldom of Leicester he had been in effective possession of for a decade, having first called Simon's older brother Amaury to England to confirm he had no wish to claim it.[3] Simon acted as godfather to the new heir to the throne alongside Richard, Earl of Cornwall, yet trouble was brewing on the horizon. On 9 August, Queen Eleanor left the birthing chamber where she had remained, as was traditional, for some weeks after delivering her son to be churched. The ceremony removed the spiritual uncleanness associated with childbirth and prepared a woman to re-enter society. Simon and his wife arrived at the church door to attend the ceremony, only to find King Henry himself physically blocking their entry.

Henry railed against Simon, calling him an excommunicated man who was not fit to be present in the church for such a ceremony. Bemused, Simon and Eleanor tried to discover what was wrong and pleaded with Henry to let them in. The king would not be moved from the doorway, and eventually, Simon and his wife withdrew in confusion. They took a boat along the river back to the bishop of Winchester's palace, loaned to them by Henry, desperately trying to work out what had gone wrong. When they got to their lavish lodgings, they found the king's men there to throw them out. In dismay, they returned to Henry full of 'tears and lamentations', demanding to know what they had done wrong. Finally, Henry uncharacteristically lost his temper. He shouted, 'you seduced my sister before marriage, and when I found it out, I gave her to you to avoid scandal'. Furthermore, Simon had gone to Rome to ensure Eleanor's vow of chastity would not prevent the union only to bribe his way to the answer he wanted. The direct cause of Henry's rage now was that he had named the king as security for the bribes without Henry's knowledge and then failed to pay them. Simon had, as a result, been excommunicated and had embarrassed Henry. Simon, 'overcome with shame', took his wife to the coast and sailed out of England in disgrace.[4]

Simon briefly returned to England in 1240 to sell off some of his lands. He informed Henry that he was going on crusade to the Holy Land, which pleased the king. Although Simon was able to secure the release of his brother Amaury from captivity, he does not appear to have fought in any battles. It would serve both to remove the stain of his excommunication and re-root him in the family's crusading tradition. Simon was back in Europe to take part in Henry's disastrous campaign into France in 1242. Henry was unwilling to address a widening gap in England between the barons and those they felt the king lavished his favour on too freely, predominantly his wife's Poitevin relatives and his own Lusignan half-siblings. Simon emerged as a leading voice but found he was also ignored. It was amid these growing problems that Simon was handed a commission as Seneschal of Gascony in May 1247. His reputation as a military leader and crusader was high, while Henry's was low, but as a man willing to speak his mind to the king on uncomfortable subjects, it suited Henry to turn Simon's attentions elsewhere. When de Montfort travelled back to England in January 1249 to report on his successes, he was shocked to be confronted by Henry's complaints that the barons of Gascony felt Simon had been too heavy-handed. Was that not, Simon frowned, why he had been sent there, because a firm hand was required? In November, 10-year-old Prince Edward was given Gascony, though Simon could not be removed as Seneschal due to the terms of his appointment.

In January 1251, Simon came to Henry again to ask for money and men to subdue the rebellious Gascon barons. Henry once more voiced his concern that he was hearing terrible things about Simon's cruel style of government, but Simon stood fast. The Gascon lords, Simon insisted, were 'unworthy of belief'. Given what he asked for, Simon returned to Gascony, but in November he was back in England having been driven out altogether. Simon was Henry's most capable general and was not lacking in personal charisma. If de Montfort could not hold Gascony, the last English possession on the Continent, no one could. Lacking options, Henry turned Simon around and sent him back to Gascony to fix the problem. In May 1252, Henry summoned Simon back to England again to answer another stream of complaints. The earl was enraged when Henry accused him of being a traitor and threatened to remove his commission in Gascony. Simon even told Henry that if he were not the king, Simon would have killed him for his remarks. Henry eventually told Simon 'Return to Gascony, that thou, who art so fond and such a fomenter of wars, mayst there find enough of them, and bring back with thee therefrom thy merited reward, as did thy father.'[6] Given that Simon's father had died during the Albigensian Crusade, it seemed like an invitation for Simon to meet a similar end. By September, Henry was paying Simon to quit his office in Gascony, and de Montfort skulked away into France.

Simon next found himself at the centre of English politics in 1258. Henry was pursuing an impossible task to secure the kingdom of Sicily for his second son. The pope had encouraged the enterprise but demanded an extortionate fee for the privilege. Henry had been desperately trying to meet the cost from his subjects' purses. Unsurprisingly, no one was pleased. In April a group of barons clattered into Henry's chambers in full armour, though they had left their weapons outside. Shocked, Henry asked if he was their prisoner, but was assured that was not the case. There was, though, the air of a threat that drew Henry to negotiate. In June, parliament met at Oxford to compile the Provisions of Oxford. Magna Carta was confirmed, and Henry was required to appoint a justiciar to head his government, the king selecting Hugh Bigod.

The Provisions also created a twenty-four-man panel, half selected by the king and half by the barons, that could act as a check on the king. It was the re-emergence of the most controversial element of the 1215 Charter, though this time there was no provision to make war on the king. Henry was, after all, a very different man from his father. Simon de Montfort was amongst those chosen by the barons to sit on this new committee. A few weeks later in the summer, a terrible storm burst over London as Henry was being rowed along the Thames. He rushed to the nearby bishop of Durham's palace to get out of the tempest. Simon happened to be staying here, and welcomed the king inside, asking why he was so frightened. Henry replied 'I fear thunder and lightning greatly, but by God's head I fear you more than all the thunder and lightning in the world.'[7] Simon protested that he was the king's faithful servant, but Henry betrayed a growing shadow of fear gathering around Simon de Montfort.

When Henry returned from a visit to France in 1260, he was dismayed to find that Simon was stirring up the barons against the king. Even more shocking was the news that Henry's oldest son and heir, Edward, had joined his godfather Simon's cause. A cold war ensued for a year until Henry made a move. At a session of parliament in June 1261, the king produced letters from Rome that absolved him from his oath to abide by the Provisions of Oxford. When push came to shove, Prince Edward returned to his father's side, and even the king of France was offering Henry troops against the threat of the barons, who Henry accused of failing to hold up their side of the agreement. The barons begged the king to maintain the Provisions, and Prince Edward refused to be absolved of his oath to be bound by them. There was a tense standoff until January 1263 when Henry was persuaded to renew his recognition of the Provisions of Oxford.

Simon de Montfort was unimpressed. He had emerged as a figurehead for the rebel barons, a mixture of his charisma, crusading reputation, and ability to speak directly to Henry causing his peers to look to him for a lead. Whether this attention had gone to Simon's head or he no longer felt he could rely on Henry's fickle and changeable word is uncertain, but he made his move in the summer as rebellion finally erupted. Simon led an army into London and took control of the city. He was welcomed by a populace fed up with the king's constant financial demands on them. Henry and Queen Eleanor were at the Tower, and when the queen tried to escape the growing threat by river to Windsor, she was driven back. A mob 'gathered at the bridge under which she had to pass, loaded her with abuse and execrations, and, by throwing stones and mud, compelled her to return to the Tower'.[8] Prince Edward was mortified, and as king, he would have a tense relationship with London that possibly resulted from the city's treatment of his mother.

In July a truce was agreed between Henry and Simon, and in September, amid unabating tensions, they travelled to France to submit their quarrel to the arbitration of Louis IX. Simon might have tried to rely on his charm, but he must have seen that no king would agree to the curtailing of another king's authority at the whim of his barons. Unsurprisingly, Louis found in Henry's favour. When they returned to London for parliament in October, the session immediately broke up in disarray, caused by a squabble over appointments to Henry's household. Henry and Prince Edward left for Windsor as Simon brooded in the capital. Neither side seemed quite ready for a fight. Simon and the barons wanted reform but had not yet been pushed into armed revolt and had no desire to dislodge Henry. The king's brother, Richard, Earl of Cornwall, agreed to mediate between Henry and the barons. Simon left London and withdrew to his fortress at Kenilworth, waiting to see what the outcome might be.

With Simon gone for the moment, Henry unsettled nerves again by demanding that the keys to royal castles be handed over. He sped to Dover in early December, where he found he was unable to gain control of the fortress. A rumour flew through the south that the king meant to bring over an army of mercenaries from France and tensions soared. As the king turned back to London, he received news that Simon, along with the earl of Derby, had appeared at Southwark, south of London. The king sent orders that the bridge was to be closed to Simon to prevent him re-entering the capital he had breezed through, and although it was done, on 11 December the city's gates were thrown open to the earl. The two men finally agreed terms on 16 December. Confrontation was averted once more, but when Henry set out for France to hear Louis's final judgement, Simon was unable to travel. On his way to Southwark, he had been thrown from his horse and broken his leg. Henry might have been quietly pleased.

Eleven days after Henry reached Louis's court, on 23 January 1264, the French king's adjudication was delivered in a document known as the Mise of Amiens. Unsurprisingly, Louis found the Provisions of Oxford to be null and void. They had, Louis claimed, 'been of exceeding great hurt to the king's rights and honour, and have occasioned disturbances in the kingdom, depression and damage to the church, and much loss to other persons'. Louis was also mindful not only of the continuing problems the Provisions of Oxford might result in but that the pope had already ruled them to be of no effect and proscribed adherence to them. The barons were instructed to return all royal castles to Henry along with any letters or grants obtained under the Provisions. He further set out that Henry should be allowed to appoint his own ministers and household staff as he had previously done.[9] The presence of foreign favourites about the king had been a key complaint, and even their removal was undone.

The barons must have known Louis was never likely to uphold their grievances against the king. The Provisions sought to restrict the power of the monarch and Louis could not endorse something that his own barons might begin to eye with interest. Simon's smooth charm might have been their only hope, but Simon was not there. What Henry saw as a victory merely reopened the wound of disaffection. His submission of a purely internal, English matter to the arbitration of the king of France was something his predecessors would never have countenanced and risked diminishing the prestige of the crown of England. Ultimately, the Mise of Amiens was not a helpful episode.

When Henry returned to England on 8 February, his son Edward immediately left his company to dart west. Although Simon de Montfort was still nursing the injury some feared would kill him, he had not been idle. Two of his sons, Simon the Younger and Henry de Montfort, had formed an alliance with Llywelyn ap Gruffudd in Wales and the earl of Derby. As they pressed out of Wales, the Marcher lords prepared for war. King Henry's brother Richard, Earl of Cornwall rushed to the region and ordered the destruction of all bridges over the River Severn except the one at Gloucester. Already on the eastern banks, the rebels took the town of Gloucester, though the castle held out, and Worcester just before Prince Edward arrived. He was incensed that his lands were being used to threaten his father. Displaying military and political adeptness that eluded his father, Edward set about pressing the rebels back against the River Severn before offering an olive branch. The 24-year-old prince used the bishop of Worcester to negotiate a truce with the de Montfort brothers. This drove a wedge into the rebel's alliance, frustrating Llywelyn and the earl of Derby, who had exposed themselves to risk and now been abandoned.

Henry called a parliament at Oxford, where he courted those bishops who had been sympathetic to the Provisions of Oxford. He brought them back on side with assurances that he would not reintroduce his despised foreign favourites even though he was now permitted to do so. Alongside this political effort was a muster. Once the royal forces were arrayed, Prince Edward led them to Northampton, where those coalescing around de Montfort were gathered. The town was attacked and amongst those seized and packed off to fortresses on the Welsh border was Simon the Younger. His father had been in London, still convalescing and trying to keep a hold on the capital. He rode out to help his allies but was too late and turned back. Henry moved on to Nottingham and Edward ravaged some of the earl of Derby's lands in Staffordshire to the west when they would have been better served by focusing on London and Simon.

In the unexpected space he was gifted, Simon worked hard. He gathered men to him, including Robert de Vere, Earl of Oxford, and Gilbert de Clare, Earl of Gloucester. Leaving London, this force set out east and laid siege to Rochester Castle, the site of King John's fierce siege in 1215 that had left the castle a smouldering wreck. Henry had rebuilt it and used it regularly. Now, Simon and his allies took the outer bailey, burned the refurbished hall set about reducing the keep. Whether this was part of a more sweeping plan or meant only to lure the king south remains unclear, because it got Henry's attention. As the king drove south, the rebels moved back into London to wait for him. The royal army skirted the capital, though, and pressed on to the south coast. Henry and Edward set about securing the Cinque Ports (Hastings, Romney, Hythe, Dover, and Sandwich, with other ports seen as a critical set for access across the Channel). There was some fear of being cut off from support that might come from Queen Eleanor and King Louis on the Continent, which suggests that fear of Simon was intensifying.

No doubt because it played to his strengths and experiences, Simon began to add a crusading flavour to his opposition to Henry. Anti-Semitic violence in London erupted as Simon's force swelled.[10] When they marched south, the earl sent the bishop of Chichester ahead to ask Henry whether he would accept the Provisions of Oxford again if they were modified by a panel of theologians, layering on a religious aspect to his rebellion. Henry refused, and both Prince Edward and Richard, Earl of Cornwall, issued personal challenges to Simon. Simon wrote to the king on behalf of the barons, assuring Henry that 'we shall always be found faithful subjects of yours', but complaining that 'some people who are about you have heaped lies upon lies concerning us'.[11] Henry's reply was to refute the professions of loyalty utterly. 'It is clearly evident,' the king replied, 'by the warlike proceedings and general commotion excited in our kingdom by you, as also by acts of incendiarism, that you do not observe towards us the fealty due to us.' Henry insisted that most of his nobility remained loyal and that Simon's attack on the king was also an attack on his peers. 'Now we consider their injuries to be injuries done to us, and their enemies to be our enemies.'[12]

Prince Edward may have been behind this careful positioning of the king as the defender of the barons as some of their number approached with an army. It contains a degree of guile usually missing from Henry III but already displayed by Edward. When the king's brother Richard, Earl of Cornwall, wrote back to the barons, Edward and others put their names to the letter too, condemning Simon and Gilbert de Clare as 'perfidious traitors'. They offered a safe-conduct for both men to come to the king's court and lay out their accusations of evil counsel so they might 'prove our innocence, and the falsehood of both of you'. Otherwise, the barons were ready to fight Simon and Gilbert wherever they could catch them.[13] Simon sent the bishops of London and Worcester to try and mediate, but they were sent packing by Earl Richard, who remained incensed at the afront Simon offered. When he understood that war was inevitable, Simon stepped up his efforts to portray his rebellion as a crusade for truth and justice. The earl spent the night in prayer while the bishop of Worcester absolved his entire army of all sin and promised any who died in the conflict to come entry into Heaven. This was now a fight Simon could understand, a war for which his family was made.

Henry and his brother Richard had lodged at the priory of St Pancras just outside Lewes, with Prince Edward staying at Lewes Castle. On the morning of 13 May 1264, Simon approached Lewes with an army almost as large as the royal force. As the king's army arrayed at the top of a slope on the edge of the town, Henry took the centre, his son Edward led the vanguard to the right, and his brother Richard held the rear on the left flank.[14] Simon, still incapacitated by his broken leg, was forced to travel in a covered carriage which was positioned to watch the battle behind the London contingent. Word reached the royal army that Simon's troops were unhappy the earl had chosen not to fight with them but watch on from the rear instead. The Battle of Lewes began with Prince Edward charging into the Londoners, with whom he was still unhappy after his mother's shoddy treatment at their hands. His real target was the iron-clad carriage containing his uncle and godfather Simon de Montfort. When he reached it, his fury erupted afresh.

Inside the carriage were two elderly citizens of London, placed there to punish their resistance to Simon and the rest of the city.[15] The earl had mounted his warhorse and hidden himself amongst his knights on the right flank, from which position he was orchestrating his army's efforts. Edward returned his furious attention to the Londoners and assaulted them with savage energy. The citizens were not a fighting force and quickly broke and scattered. Edward, perhaps driven by his grudge against the city, pursued the Londoners for miles from the field. If he drew any satisfaction from the chase, it was short-lived. When he returned to the battle, he was confronted with a shocking scene. King Henry had been forced back to the priory, and Earl Richard was sheltering in a windmill with his son Henry of Almain. In short order, Henry was forced to surrender, handing his sword to Gilbert de Clare, Earl of Gloucester. Earl Richard, who was also King of the Germans and Holy Roman Emperor, found himself taunted by the rebel army. 'Come down, come down, you wretched miller! Come out unlucky master of the mill, come out!' they called up. 'It is a great pity for you', the rebels added, 'that you must be made a miller – you who so lately defied us poor barons to battle; and when you defied us no less glorious title would serve you than king of the Romans and ever Augustus.'[16]

Simon almost immediately publicised the Mise of Lewes, his peace settlement produced in King Henry's name.[17] The Scots barons, including John Baliol and John Comyn, and Marcher lords such as Roger Mortimer and Roger Clifford who had been taken at Henry's side were released to return to their lands. This was an admission by Simon that he needed them in place to help govern England, and perhaps also that he could not take a large portion of the nobility hostage indefinitely. Prince Edward and his cousin Henry of Almain were to remain hostages for the good behaviour of those set free. Earl Simon secured the release of his son Simon the Younger and asserted that Henry would now uphold Magna Carta, the Charter of the Forests, and the Provisions of Oxford. A copy of the Mise of Lewes was despatched to King Louis in an effort to secure his support, or at least prevent him from coming to Henry's aid. It may have been Simon's riposte to Louis's issue of the Mise of Amiens that the French king insisted should be observed in England.

The Song of Lewes, produced anonymously in Latin shortly after the battle, explained at length the events of the day, but also offered Simon de Montfort's vision of a reformed government.[18] The Song continued the crusading language of Simon's campaign in asserting that the king was subject to the law. 'Soloman was unwilling to crush Israel, nor did he compel any of the race to be a slave; because he knew that it was God's people whom he ruled.'[19] It is not hard to discern the person being compared to the wise King Soloman. The Song explains that only God is an incorruptible, infallible ruler who needs no assistance, and that Henry is wrong to think those who aid him are his inferiors. Earthly rulers, though chosen by God, 'are able to fail and able to err', and 'cannot stand by their own strength'. Without using the assistance provided them by God, they 'go badly astray in the pathlessness of error'.[20] Simon was here to keep the king on the right path. The flaw in that logic is that if kings can be wrong, so, surely, can the nobles who seek to depose them. Simon, like Henry, was one man. If he was to make a lasting difference, he needed to build this consensus and conciliar rule that sat beside the king, equal as a body to his royal authority.

This experiment, which sounded an awful lot like restoring the council of barons set out in article 61 of the 1215 version of Magna Carta which had been so offensive to John, began on a narrow platform. William de Nangis explained that Simon and his ally Gilbert de Clare, Earl of Gloucester, 'entered upon a mutual agreement and covenant that they would both handle the business of government on an equal basis and would guard the people by faithfully ruling in the manner of a republic to the advantage of the king and kingdom'.[21] The idea of a republic with two joint rulers harked back to a Roman model, and there was little sense of a partnership with the king, but rather of ruling instead of him. There was anger at the papal curia when news reached there. Pope Urban was Henry's overlord, and England was, in effect, his. Despite the crusading spin employed by Simon, his rebellion was ultimately against the pope. Urban tried to send a legate into England but found a fleet from the Cinque Ports blockading the Channel. When he summoned the English bishops to appear before him at Amiens, the pope was forced to repeat the demand, moving to Boulogne. When they finally obeyed, the bishops were instructed to return to England and excommunicate the city of London, the Cinque Ports, and 'all disturbers of the peace of the king of England'.[22] The bishops listened but did nothing.

In June, a charter was issued from London formalising the structure of the government now that Henry, his heir Edward, Earl Richard, and his son Henry were in custody.[23] Stephen Bersted, Bishop of Chichester, was added to the earls of Leicester and Gloucester to form a triumvirate of electors on a panel of nine councillors. The three electors could select and change the other six members if required for the benefit of the realm, and at least three of the nine were to be in attendance on the king at all times. As Simon moved around the country trying to embed this new system, he took his royal hostages everywhere with him. As he gained control over royal castles, Simon relaxed a little. Richard, Earl of Cornwall was placed within the Tower of London and his son, along with Prince Edward, were sent to Dover Castle so that only the king continued to accompany Simon.[24] When there was trouble on the Welsh borders, originating with men loyal to Henry including Roger Mortimer, Simon collected Prince Edward and went to subdue the region. The earl forged an alliance with Llywelyn and pressed into Edward's lands. The prince's presence seems to have been enough, because the Marcher lords came to Simon in Montgomery and made their peace, providing hostages for their good behaviour.[25]

When Simon caused parliament to gather at Westminster on 20 January 1265, it was to prove a defining moment for his reputation over the centuries that followed. Simon de Montfort has entered a hallowed space in the history of democracy because of the makeup and elected nature of the parliament he summoned, a meeting vaunted as the first parliament in English history. The one certain thing is this was the first time such a meeting had been convened by someone other than the king. Beyond that fact, it is less clear that Simon's parliament was as novel or well-intentioned as has been claimed. Kings had gathered councils of their senior nobility and clergy since before the Norman Conquest, known until 1066 as the Witenagemot, or Witan. The word *parliament* to describe such a meeting first appeared in 1236. Summoning knights to attend was not new in 1265 either and had happened for several decades. The first mention of elected knights attending originated in 1254 when Henry was looking for taxation to fund a military effort in Gascony.

On the issue of representation, Simon did summon representatives of boroughs, but there is some evidence this was not the first time this group had been represented either. If Simon embraced this section of society, it was to add a populist flavour to his efforts to impose himself on England. This is supported by the summoning of just twenty-three barons, exclusively those who had supported Simon against Henry. The rest were not permitted to take up a seat in parliament. In comparison, there were more than 100 bishops and clergymen, who were more sympathetic to Simon's aims than the nobility. Even within the elected element of parliament's composition, there are visible efforts to sure up support for Simon. York, Lincoln and many other towns were asked to send two representatives each. The Cinque Ports, which favoured Simon's rebellion, were permitted to elect four delegates each. Rather than demonstrating a commitment to democratic representation that was ahead of his time, Simon de Montfort did little more than use whatever tactics he could to pack parliament in his favour.[26] One other aspect in which Simon's parliament is distinctive is that it sought the political opinion of those summoned. Usually restricted to granting taxation, this was an extension of the purpose, if not the authority, of parliament.

The primary legislative efforts of the parliament Simon held focussed, unsurprisingly, on enshrining the Provisions of Oxford. As the basis for his opposition to Henry, it was the one thing he had to achieve and was the main reason he packed parliament with those on whose support he could rely. Queen Eleanor was still on the Continent and rumours flooded into England that she was assembling an army with the help of her brother-in-law King Louis IX to rescue her husband and son. Chroniclers believed Simon's victory and his partisan efforts to shore up his position did nothing to bring peace. England 'trembled with the horror of war'[27] and piracy in the Channel was rampant. The sailors of the Cinque Ports 'became crueller, in their destruction, than the whirlpool of Scylla or Charybdis' as they attacked merchant shipping.[28] Against all of this, Simon needed to steady the ship and strengthen his hold on the reins of power.

The partnership between Simon and Gilbert de Clare, Earl of Gloucester, that was central to the vision of government in the wake of the Battle of

Lewes soon began to unravel. Simon was treating Henry with respect while carting him around England to add royal weight to the earl's actions.[29] Gilbert began to feel increasingly that Simon's profession of a belief in some sort of republic with conciliar rule was melting on contact with reality. Simon kept Henry close, Gilbert grumbled, so that he could keep power in his own hands. Royal castles were being handed over to Simon personally rather than any council or panel of barons. Beyond this, 'a principal ground of offence'[30] was Simon's pocketing all of the kingdom's incomes, and the ransoms from prisoners that had been taken. He was accused too of giving castles to his sons, but no one else. When Gilbert asked for the handover of those he had captured at Lewes for ransom, Simon flatly refused. The very complaints about unaccountable, authoritarian rule and favouritism that had led to the baron's opposition to Henry were transferring to Simon, who did nothing to correct his policies.

Gilbert had remained close to the Marcher lords excluded from power by Simon, and the dissection of de Montfort's greatest ally from his cause proved easy as Gilbert began to feel disgruntled too. An opportunity was presented to those opposed to Simon by the continued presence of Prince Edward at Hereford Castle, left in place after Simon had subdued the barons of the border. On 28 May 1265, Edward managed to get permission to take some exercise outside the castle. He was a soldier, and those around him understood his need to keep up his martial training. Accompanied by a handful of his guards and Thomas de Clare, Gilbert's brother, they went into the open space beyond the walls to go through their drills. Edward showed great interest in the horses stocked by the castle, and enthusiastically practised his horsemanship, riding successive mounts to exhaustion. When he got on the last fresh horse, Edward made his move. '"Lordings," he said, "have now good day, And greet well my father the king; and I shall, if I may, Both see him well betime and out of ward him do."'[31]

With that, Edward turned the steed and spurred it into a gallop. His bemused guards took a moment to catch on to what was happening. They were surrounded by exhausted horses unable to keep up with their prisoner. By the time they had found fresh ones and given chase, Edward was far ahead of them and had made a rendezvous with Roger Mortimer and Roger de Clifford. The guards were now outmanned and turned back to Hereford to explain to their master what had happened. Edward made it to Roger Mortimer's castle at Wigmore and immediately set about making the most of his freedom. Men flocked to the prince's side from Hereford and Worcester to the south and across Shropshire and Cheshire to the north. Edward laid siege to Gloucester and quickly took the town and castle. Simon responded by assaulting Gilbert's castle at Monmouth in alliance with Llywelyn, pushing into Glamorganshire and more of Gilbert's properties. As Simon busied himself in Wales, Edward ordered the destruction of bridges over the Severn, joined with Gilbert, and led an army to the base of de Montfort's operations at Kenilworth Castle.[32]

Kenilworth had been extensively refurbished by Henry III before he had, in a time of closer friendship, gifted it to Simon. With a manmade lake adding to its defences, the castle was a powerful fortress as well as a comfortable one. Edward made the fifty-mile march in short order and caught the forces mustering there under the banner of Simon the Younger by surprise. Although de Montfort's son made it inside Kenilworth's walls, the rest of the barons and the men-at-arms there were captured. Edward's military abilities were becoming increasingly honed, and he recognised both the need to maintain the momentum he had created and the presentation of an opportunity. His father was still with Simon de Montfort in the west, and Edward turned around as soon as he had dealt with the muster at Kenilworth to set about freeing the king.

On Sunday 2 August, Simon managed to force a dangerous crossing at a ford near Worcester and made for Kempsey. He seems to have believed Edward was still in the region and on 3 August, they arrived at Evesham. Simon and Henry lodged at the abbey. The king, now 57, must have been exhausted from being trailed around what felt less and less like his own kingdom. When Simon rose on the morning of 4 August, he was cheered to see the banners of his son approaching at the head of a large army. By the time they were close enough to see Prince Edward at the front of the force, beneath the banners of Simon the Younger, it was too late. Even as they scrambled to prepare for a fight they had not expected, Edward was outmanoeuvring the earl's men. Part of his force split off under the command of Roger Mortimer to block one of the exits from Evesham as the main body straddled the only other behind the prince. As Edward advanced in preparation for a fight, Simon could spot an unfamiliar badge adorning the surcoats of the prince and his men. The red cross on a white background, the badge of St George, appeared with an English army for the first time.

Simon's oldest son Henry de Montfort pleaded with his father to find a way to flee. Simon knew Edward had them trapped by a bend in the River Avon at their back. To Simon, this was a crusade. He had built it into a holy mission to correct the government of England, encouraged by the backing of the English clergy and his victory on the field at Lewes. His father and brothers had forged a fearsome reputation as crusading warriors, and Simon felt the weight of expectation as heavily as the fear of disappointing or paling in comparison. To his son's appeals, he replied:

> Far be this from me, who in my days am already an old man, whose journey through life is hastening to its end, whose parental bloodline is known to be so illustrious as one who was never wont to flee from battle; but you, preferably ought to turn aside from such a dangerous conflict so that you do not perish in the flower and time of your youth but live to be a successor to your father and his famous ancestors in feats of arms, which God grant.[33]

As they rode out of Evesham Abbey, Simon's standard-bearer Sir Guy de Balliol misjudged the height of the gate and shattered the lance that displayed Simon's standard against the stone. As it fell to the ground, Simon grumbled 'Now God help us – now!' As they reached the town's conduit in Market Square, Simon offered any who wished to leave the chance to do so, particularly the younger knights amongst his company. He also told Sir Hugh Despenser to 'consider your great age and look to saving yourself', believing the ageing warrior had much wisdom that would benefit the kingdom. Sir Hugh refused, telling Simon 'My lord, my lord, let it be. Today we shall all drink from one cup, just as we have in the past.'[34] The chivalric code did not allow for the abandonment of brothers when times got hard.

Prince Edward prepared his own men for battle, knighting several in a meadow named Mosham before appointing a hit squad of twelve of his finest fighting men. This small group had one very specific task: to kill Simon de Montfort. Their orders were to 'look at no one nor let anyone come between them until they reached the person of the earl'.[35] It was a startling tactic. At a time when noblemen on the battlefield could expect to be spared and taken into captivity for the ransom that could be extracted, it was shocking to mark an earl for death. Edward was a far more ruthless man than his father and clearly believed there could be no resolution and no peace while Simon lived.

The clash was short and sharp. Sir Roger Mortimer, who may well have been one of Edward's twelve-man death squad, managed to reach Simon's position and charged, driving his lance into Simon's neck. This shock had the desired effect of throwing the rest of de Montfort's army into panic and disarray. They broke and fled, many falling into the river at their back, drowning under the weight of their armour. The rest were chased down in the surrounding fields, and many were slaughtered. Simon's body was decapitated, his hands and feet cut off and his genitals hacked off.[36] It was a shocking example of post-mortem humiliation of a defeated enemy. It was claimed that however the royalists hacked at Simon's body, it did not bleed.[37] Taken as a miracle, the monks of Evesham Abbey were quick to retrieve Simon's corpse and bury it within. The tomb would become a pilgrimage site, and Simon took on the air of a martyr, which may well have been precisely what he wanted from his crusading opposition to Henry's government. Roger Mortimer claimed Simon's head as his prize for striking the killing blow. He sent it home to Wigmore Castle as a present for his wife Maud, who kept it as a focus for abuse for a time.[38] What finally became of this grizzly trophy is not known.

Simon had ordered King Henry to be dressed in armour but denied him any way of identifying himself. The plan may have been to force the royalist army to inadvertently kill the king, damaging their cause. Jostled around in the press, as men began to lay clanging blows on him, Henry cried out 'I am Henry, the old king of England,' cursing 'By God's head' and 'By the love of God' as he was shoved and battered. Those attacking Henry suddenly heard some of the old king's favourite curses and stopped their assault, pulling him aside and removing his helm to confirm that it truly was King Henry before escorting him to safety.[39] Henry de Montfort, Simon's oldest son, and Hugh Despenser were among those slain. Humphrey de Bohun would die of his wounds a week later, and Simon's youngest son Guy was wounded and captured.

King Henry was restored, owing much of his newly won security to his son Edward, on whom he would lean heavily in the years that followed. Three days after the Battle of Evesham, Henry issued proclamations publicising his full resumption of authority in England. Simon's rebellion had been ended by the certainty that its charismatic and driven leader was dead. Some opposition lingered, not least in the form of Simon the Younger, who was still ensconced within Kenilworth Castle. Eventually, Simon's surrender was negotiated peacefully, and he was paid off to leave England, though the garrison at Kenilworth refused to back down so easily. Insisting their commission came from Earl Simon's widow, not his son, they refused to surrender until a siege overseen by Henry reduced them to terms.

Simon de Montfort settled into a venerated place in English history. For centuries he was viewed as a father of parliamentary democracy, but few of the aspects of his parliament were novel. Knights had attended before, and there is evidence that elected representatives of the towns had too. Perhaps his real innovation was in placing questions of policy before parliament for a political opinion. Much of what he did was aimed at broadening his narrow support base. He deliberately excluded those he knew opposed him and replaced them with men on whose support he could rely. If anything, it was almost the opposite of democracy. Simon became viewed as a radical forerunner of a parliamentary system Britain came to cherish, but his vaunted position is neither reflective of his intentions nor of his policies.

Simon de Montfort was not a radical. He rebelled against the crown of England as the result of a long period of declining relations with Henry. Simon had been a favourite of the king when he arrived to seek his fortune. His charm, charisma, and persuasiveness were plain to see from the beginning when he secured the earldom of Leicester. When he served Henry in Gascony, he developed a reputation, rightly or wrongly, as a harsh and unfair governor. Simon managed to marry one of the king's sisters, though Henry would later rage against the earl's seduction of a lady who had taken a vow of chastity, and as Simon took liberties with Henry's name in Rome, their friendship was torn apart. In championing the Provisions of Oxford and the restricting of royal authority, Simon crafted for himself a crusade, albeit political rather than religious. Coming from a family with a powerful reputation for crusading success, this both played to Simon's strengths and transformed his opposition to Henry into something more meaningful that Simon and his allies could get behind.

As a rebel, Simon achieved something in England few others ever had, or would in the future. He took custody of the reigning monarch and began to govern the country. The Provisions of Oxford, the core of the dispute, were enshrined in law at a parliament summoned at Simon's behest, not the king's. The manner in which Simon de Montfort went about his rebellion demonstrates that beyond his charm and passionate zeal, he understood how to rebel successfully. There was no effort to depose Henry, to bring about a new form of government that entirely replaced the monarch. In the Provisions of Oxford, Simon saw the same benefits to his own class as the barons who had forced Magna Carta on John in 1215 saw in the security clause that allowed them to restrain the worst excesses of a king. It was an idea that had not quite died away half a century later, and Simon sought to reinvigorate it, ignoring the fact that more than anything else, this element of Magna Carta had brought the whole document tumbling down.

The ultimate problem for Simon lay in the narrow support he garnered from the nobility. It is unclear whether this is despite trying to reimpose controls on the crown and its wearer, or because he took a step his contemporaries knew was one too far. Henry's reign saw the royal council evolve into parliament, and this body took on the power to negotiate with the king. Parliament granted taxation for the crown's projects, but only in return for the observance of the terms of the reissued Magna Carta. It was a careful balance, an agreed diplomatic relationship. Simon sought to stretch it back to the point at which it had snapped in 1215, almost causing a French prince to replace the English king. For some in 1215, that had been not only acceptable but desirable. John was despised, but his son had shown himself a very different man. The nobles may have disapproved of some of what Henry did and the favour he showed to foreign relatives and in-laws, but that was different to a king who tortured his subjects, extorted money, and defiled their wives and daughters. There was simply no appetite to remove from Henry the authority God had granted him. Not for the last time, he was considered too personally inoffensive, and indeed likeable, to merit harsh treatment.

If Simon misjudged how far his fellow barons were willing to go, he understood that Henry could not merely be deposed in favour of some model of republicanism. He kept Henry at his side but showed him the respect due to a king. Society relied on the deeply embedded structures that placed a king at the pinnacle, appointed by God to rule those below him. Simon never sought to redefine that monolith. There was danger in doing so; if the king was not needed at the top, perhaps the nobility were not required above the people. The success of the uprising that reached a peak at the Battle of Lewes in 1264 but floundered just a year later at Evesham was startling. The problem Simon created for himself was in championing conciliar rule against absolutism in opposition, yet becoming a depotistic absolutist unwilling to share power as soon as he had taken the upper hand. The earl of Gloucester was pushed back to the royalist cause by Simon's jealous guarding of authority and money. Henry's unpopular relatives were replaced with Simon's equally disliked sons. Rather than solve the problems that led to his ascendance, Simon immediately recreated them.

The Second Barons's War, as this episode became known, was the death throes of the First Barons' War. Much of what it aimed to achieve was anchored in the turmoil of 1215 and personal animosity towards John that simply did not exist in 1264. It was for this reason that Simon struggled to secure baronial support for his actions: they saw that he was taking the wrong path, even if he failed to see it. Simon emerged as a successful figure because he possessed a potent blend of charisma, character, crusading idealism, a towering legacy to try to live up to, and personality flaws to which he was blind. Ultimately, his success was in itself a trap. Rebellion could only be successful if a path were kept open to reconciliation. Simon showed no signs of seeking to correct a defined error in policy or judgement before returning to his fealty to Henry. There is a sense that the more power he gained, the more he sought, and the tighter he gripped onto it.

What Simon attempted was closer to a revolution. In 1215, the barons had been driven to notions of regime change by John's intransigence and appalling behaviour. Simon was content to keep Henry in place as a puppet. The problem came when he refused to engage in a broader coalition to rule alongside the king, instead appearing to wish to be de facto king in Henry's place. It is possible that if he had drawn more of the nobility into his plan by offering them a seat on the council he originally envisaged running parallel to the crown's authority, a longer-term transformation in government may have been possible. By stopping short of promising or achieving revolution, and stepping beyond what constituted loyal rebellion, Simon found himself furiously kicking his legs over the open void in between. In the short term, Simon de Montfort proved a dangerously effective rebel who got custody of the king. His plans unravelled quickly as a combination of a flawed personality, a system too stacked against change, and a vague vision of an end that was neither rebellion nor revolution tripped him over. In the mould of Thomas Becket, Simon was considered by some a martyr, but he would never attain sainthood as Thomas had. A match in ability and charisma for the legendary Hereward, he could never become a folk hero because his drivers were too obviously selfish and self-interested.[40]

In many ways, Simon succeeded, but only in the short term. His lasting legacy is as a proto democrat, a parliamentary reformer who sought to give voice to the common man. That perception has wobbled on a pedestal of half-truths and exaggerations for centuries. At one time it suited the aims of those who reached back into the mists of history for exemplars of English and British fairness and democracy, but there is little use in deluding a nation about its history. Simon de Montfort had no interest in elected democratic representation at the highest levels of the national government. He desperately needed support and cast about for the best place to secure it. Had he been able to embed the idea of a council to rule alongside the king, he may have invented an entirely new form of medieval government or implemented a constitutional monarchy centuries before it evolved. Even if Simon had succeeded, the cold truth is that this body would never have been elected members representative of the populace. It was to be made up of earls and barons who, as Magna Carta had demonstrated, cared little for, and knew even less of, the concerns and complaints of the common folk of England. Ultimately, Simon's success was his undoing, and he would be added to the list of distinguished figures who sacrificed their lives to the idea of rebellion against the crown.

Chapter 7

I Could Not Be Other Than I Am

*Change has something appealing in the contemplation that
can often turn bitter in the mouth.*

The remainder of King Henry III's reign was largely peaceful and settled. In 1268, Henry's two sons Edward and Edmund took the cross and swore to go on crusade, a sure sign the security of the kingdom was such that leaving it and focusing beyond England's borders was once more possible. In 1269, Henry oversaw the translation of the body of his favourite saint, Edward the Confessor, to a new tomb at the centre of Westminster Abbey. The church built by the Confessor had been torn down and rebuilt in the gothic style on a grand scale. Henry would not see the completion of his abbey, which would take another 300 years, but he left his mark with the beginnings of its rebirth, as well as his additions to the Tower of London to create the basis of the complex that we can visit today.

On the 19 August 1270, Edward left for the Holy Land. Just over two years later, on 16 November 1272, Henry III died at the age of 65. He had reigned for fifty-six years, the longest rule of any medieval King of England. He had steadied the ship after the stormy catastrophes caused by his father and passed on to his son Edward a settled, prosperous kingdom. The clearest demonstration of Henry's ultimate success lay in his son's absence from England at his father's death. Henry had altered the law to allow for his son to automatically succeed on his death, removing the dangerous uncertainty of an interregnum. Previously, the death of a king had instantly ceased all government as well as law and order; there could be no king's peace to defend without a king. There was, therefore, no assurance a king's oldest son would be the next ruler since the crown was effectively up for grabs. Henry removed this issue by creating a situation in which an heir became king at the moment his predecessor passed away. Even far away in the Holy Land, Edward succeeded to the throne of England smoothly and without challenge.

Edward did not return to England and undergo a coronation for almost two years after his father's death. On 19 August 1274, Edward was crowned in his father's monument of Westminster Abbey aged 35. Remembered as the English Justinian for his transformation of parliament into a legislative focus for codified law, Edward also redefined the British Isles. He conquered Wales, perhaps pursuing a long-held grudge to its final conclusion. The ring of castles Edward constructed strangled the finely poised notion of independent Welsh princes. Although less successful, Edward turned his fierce attention on Scotland and tried to exploit a succession crisis to bring the Scots crown more entirely under the shadow of the English one. Despite dying at the age of 68 on 7 July 1307 still embroiled in a bloody tangle, the epithet Hammer of the Scots clung to Edward. He bequeathed to his son a struggling Exchequer and an unwinnable war.

Edward II was the fourth and youngest son of Edward I and Eleanor of Castile. Born in 1284, two of his older brothers had died aged 5 or 6. For a decade, the couple's third son Alphonso had been expected to succeed his father, but he passed away four months after the birth of his youngest brother. Edward II was 26 when he became king and was forced to take over the mantle of his father's war with Scotland. Unanimously described as handsome, athletic and physically impressive, Edward was unlike his father in temperament and interests. One chronicler explained in astonishment that 'from his youth he devoted himself in private to the art of rowing and driving carts, of digging ditches and thatching houses, as was commonly said, and also with his companions at night in various works of ingenuity and skill, and to other pointless trivial occupations unsuitable for the son of a king'.[1] Enjoying indulging in such physical labour and surrounding himself with commoners was regarded as shocking and unbefitting of a king. Another writer sneered that Edward 'forsook the company of lords and drew himself to harlots, to singers and to jesters, to carters, to ditchers and to dykers, to rowers, shipmen and boatmen, and to other craftsmen, and gave himself to great drinking'.[2] Scandals would begin to swirl about Edward II almost as soon as he became king and would intensify through a challenging, disappointing, and at times disastrous reign.

One of the first acts of Edward's kingship exposed priorities that would rarely alter for the rest of his rule. Piers Gaveston, a Gascon who was a few years older than Edward, had been sent out of England by Edward I. It was effectively exile, but there was little signal that Edward I felt any hostility toward Gaveston, but rather that he grew concerned at his son's attachment to his friend. Edward I had died in Cumberland on his way north to press the war with Scotland. The obsession that consumed him until his end was not shared by his son, who abandoned the effort and whose first action was to send word to Gaveston that he should come home immediately. The king's attachment to Piers Gaveston caused disruption and disquiet from the outset. Before he finalised his marriage or underwent a coronation, Edward secured Gaveston's return and created him Earl of Cornwall on 6 August 1307. Five days after the funeral of the old king, Piers was married to the 13-year-old Margaret de Clare, a niece of Edward II.

In December 1307, Gaveston was appointed Keeper of the Realm when Edward travelled to France to meet his betrothed, Isabella, the daughter of King Philip IV of France. An anonymous chronicler wondered 'that he who had lately been an exile and outcast from England should now be made ruler and guardian of the realm'.[3] Edward and Isabella were married on 25 January 1308, and during the celebrations of their union, a group of barons drew up a document known as The Boulogne Agreement.[4] Although vague, with uncertain aims, the text essentially sought to detach loyalty to the crown from allegiance to the person of the king, rendering the institution of the monarchy separate to the incumbent of the office. It was presented to Edward on 31 January 1308, the same day that he was required to take the uncomfortable step of kneeling before his father-in-law to give homage for his French lands.

The Agreement was later produced as a Declaration in parliament in April 1308, but its extent and intent remain unclear. It may be argued that this was a similar attempt to impose magnate control on the king to that of the security clause in the 1215 issue of Magna Carta. It may have created the space for personal criticism of the monarch to be decoupled from the perils of treason, allowing for loyal opposition where it was deemed necessary. The real question was whether the magnates were hostile to Edward by this point, or were trying to protect him, or the institution of the crown, from what they feared would be the results of Edward's unusual interests. John's reign and that of Henry III had seen declines in relations until disaffected barons tried to impose themselves on the king. Edward I had been a different proposition, but in Edward II some perhaps saw the warning signs of future trouble. The provisions created at Boulogne might have been meant to avert disasters and civil war before they erupted. If so, it was another method that would prove unsuccessful.

When parliament opened on 28 February 1308, three days after the coronation, there was a signal of the troubles to come. It was reported that 'almost all of the earls and barons of England rose against Piers Gaveston, binding themselves by a mutual oath never to cease from what they had begun until Piers had left the land of England'.[5] By 18 May, the lords had achieved their aim as Gaveston was ordered into a second period of exile. Although he lost all of his lands in England, Edward insisted he should retain his title as Earl of Cornwall and replaced the lost properties and incomes with a clutch in Gascony. To further avoid divesting himself of his favourite too completely, Edward appointed Gaveston as Lord Lieutenant of Ireland during what was supposed to be his exile. Another dispute began before the end of the year when in November Thomas, Earl of Lancaster quit Edward's court. Thomas was the king's first cousin, the son of Edward's uncle Edmund, and a wealthy man who held several earldoms. It seemed that just as one problem was temporarily brushed aside, another emerged to fill the space.

In July 1309, Piers Gaveston reappeared at Edward's side to the outrage of the nobility. When parliament was called to meet at York in October 1309, and again in February 1310, most of the lords refused to attend. They would stay away, they insisted, 'as long as their chief enemy, who had set the baronage and the realm in an uproar, was lurking in the king's chamber'.[6] In March 1310, a large group of nobles confronted Edward with a long list of their complaints. Named the Lords Ordainers for the ordinances they sought to impose on the king, they complained that he wasted money, mistreated his people and, unfairly, had lost Scotland. Edward showed no interest in continuing his father's attempts to conquer Scotland, but it had never been won to then be lost. Shockingly, they also made it clear 'they would not have him for king, nor keep the fealty that they had sworn to him' if he refused to reform his ways.[7] The petition was championed by the earls of Pembroke, Lincoln, Lancaster, Hereford, Warwick, Arundel, Richmond, and Gloucester, not all of whom were hostile to Edward. The archbishop of Canterbury, six bishops and half a dozen barons added their weight to the calls too.

The Lords Ordainers presented forty-one Ordinances to Edward in August 1311. Inevitably, one of those articles required Piers Gaveston to be exiled again. Demonstrating his dangerous attachment to his friend, Edward offered to adopt the other forty if that one was dropped. The Ordainers refused, again threatening to depose Edward, and on 27 September all forty-one were accepted and published. The worrying novelties in these proceedings were how early in Edward's reign they came and that the loss of his crown was held over him from the outset. The lesson of past problems experienced by previous generations appears to have been that a monarch should not be given time to embed bad behaviour and that the ultimate sanction was the most effective threat available. They had seen something in Edward that worried them enough to take pre-emptive action to protect themselves. No King of England had ever been deposed by his subjects. There may have been an element of the empty threat to it since it meant finding a suitable alternative, as the barons had discovered in 1215. Still, it sowed enough uncertainty in the mind of one wary of losing all that he possessed to pull Edward into line, at least on the surface.

Gaveston was gone once more, and Edward was distraught. There has been much speculation over the nature of Edward's relationships with his favourites. Gaveston was the first and almost certainly the most cherished, but a pattern was being established at the outset of Edward's rule. Whether these attachments were sexual or emotional dependencies is open to debate but is almost irrelevant. What mattered was that individuals were able to nestle themselves close to the king and become so precious to him that he would do anything to protect them and keep them close and happy. Queen Isabella is frequently caricatured as disgusted by her husband, hostile to his favourites, and eager for an excuse to be rid of Edward. None of that is true. Their relationship was close and successful in many aspects, not least in dynastic terms, producing four children. Edward also had one acknowledged illegitimate son named Adam, which suggests he did not spurn the company of women entirely. Later in Edward's reign, his final favourite would turn the entire realm, including his wife, against the king, but that was to have far more to do with that individual's traits than the nature of Edward's attachment to him. In 1310–11, it was shocking enough that magnates moved to threats of deposition as a first resort.

There was little respite from Gaveston's involvement in English politics. Piers was married to the king's niece Margaret de Clare, and in January 1312 she gave birth to the couple's first child at York. On the following day, 13 January, Edward met Gaveston at Knaresborough and accompanied him to York to see his wife and child. On 18 January, Edward revoked Gaveston's sentence of exile.[8] Doubtless being reunited with his friend and Gaveston's desire to be with his new family were a potent mixture working on Edward, but it should also be remembered that, like all his predecessors, he felt unable to blithely accept the impositions of his barons, his supposed inferiors. There is little doubt that Edward was obsessed, infatuated, with Gaveston, but there was more at play than merely his feelings. Edward's decision backfired quickly. Piers was trapped within Scarborough Castles and taken into custody after a short siege on 19 May. He was to be well treated but was required to appear before parliament by 1 August to answer for his crimes.

On 9 June, Piers was in the custody of the Earl of Pembroke, Aymer de Valance, when the earl left his charge at Deddington Priory to visit his wife. In the early morning of 10 June, Piers was awoken by a ruckus in the courtyard of the priory. He heard the booming voice of Guy Beauchamp,

Earl of Warwick, one of those who despised Piers, calling out 'Arise, traitor, you are taken!'[9] Gaveston was hauled outside, barefoot, and forced onto a horse. He was taken to Warwick Castle and thrown into a cell. The earls of Lancaster, Edward's powerful cousin, Hereford, and Arundel soon arrived, and on 19 June, Gaveston was told, 'Look to yourself, my lord, for today you shall die the death.'[10] Whether some of the men's resolve weakened when push came to shove is unclear, but Piers was taken to Kenilworth, two miles away, so that he was on Lancaster's lands. The Earl of Warwick remained within his castle. On Blacklow Hill, Lancaster, Hereford, and Arundel watched on as one of Lancaster's Welsh men-at-arms ran Gaveston through with a sword and another decapitated him.[11]

Piers Gaveston was dead, and it seems likely the earls present thought they had brought about an end to the matter. What they had failed to appreciate was that Gaveston was not really the problem. The success Piers had achieved, and the position to which he had risen, spoke far more to Edward's personality than the evils of Gaveston. The nobility had considered the Gascon an unwelcome parvenue. He gave them nicknames and flaunted his closeness to the king, but he had ultimately been a harmless irritation. Gaveston had understood how to exploit his relationship with the king, whatever its nature, but the nobles who despised Gaveston failed to appreciate how they might have similarly used the connection. The episode of the Ordinances had demonstrated that Edward would accept almost anything but the loss of Gaveston's company. In that fact lay an opportunity overlooked by the Lords Ordainers to exert some control over Edward by using Gaveston as leverage. Edward would never forgive or forget what had been done to his beloved friend, and the next decade would be dominated by his fraught relationship with his cousin Thomas, Earl of Lancaster, a 'mortal hatred, which endured forever'.[12] The other problem was that the space at Edward's side left by Gaveston could easily be filled by someone far worse. If the Ordainers failed to see that, others did not.

Queen Isabella was pregnant in 1312 with the royal couple's first child, and Edward saw to it that she remained safely in the north at York until July and they were apart until September. Although it is possible to see this as a distance in their relationship, it is equally likely that Edward acted out of concern for his pregnant wife. On 13 November 1312, she gave birth at Windsor Castle to their son, named for his father and grandfather. In May of the following year, Edward and Isabella travelled to France. There was much to discuss concerning Gascony, but Isabella had the chance to see her father and her brothers, who were knighted during the visit. 19 June 1313 was the first anniversary of Piers Gaveston's murder, and Edward passed it at Pontoise, entertained by Bernard the Fool and forty-four naked dancers. A week or so earlier, Edward and Isabella's tent had accidentally caught fire in the night as they slept. Waking in the flames, a nude Edward scooped up his wife and carried her outside to safety, suggesting once more that there was love and affection still very much alive in their relationship.

In 1314, the war with Scotland that had never gone away was reignited. Edward had organised and cancelled numerous offensives, leading one writer to complain that 'The king of England undertook scarcely anything against Scotland, and thus lost as much by indolence as his father had conqured.'[13] When Edward was finally moved to action, it proved disastrous. On Sunday 23 June 1314, the first day of the Battle of Bannockburn went badly. Edward donned his armour on the next morning to join the assault. When the earl of Gloucester enthusiastically charged without orders, he and most of his men were killed. Edward was forced to flee from the battlefield, reaching Dunbar before taking a fishing boat to Berwick. In the wake of the embarrassing disaster, parliament in September 1314 compelled Edward to accept his cousin Thomas, Earl of Lancaster as the head of his government. During the years that followed, Edward became little more than a puppet, but Lancaster proved to be his cousin's equal in unsuitability to govern.

Throughout this period, Edward grew close to Roger Damory and Hugh Audley, both knights, and William Montacute, whose father had served the king's father. These men encouraged Edward to despise his cousin with ever-greater intensity until the earl took to staying away from the government he was meant to be running. In April 1317, and again in July, Lancaster was summoned to council meetings but refused to attend out of fear for his person. He was uncertain of his own position but too strong to be dislodged by Edward and his new favourites. Still, there was enough room to begin to manoeuvre. Antonio di Pessagno, who had been considered almost on a par with Gaveston in the king's affections years earlier, was appointed Steward of Gascony. In July 1317, Edward gave Isabella the county of Cornwall, which had been Gaveston's. In February 1318, Edward's stepmother Queen Margaret died, and her dower portion passed to Isabella. The following month Edward gifted the queen his French county of Ponthieu, reinforcing the idea that there was no rift between the royal couple and that Edward felt making her stronger benefitted him. It may also have represented a recognition of Edward's own failings and weaknesses that made him unable to rule effectively on his own.

The stalemate was broken when Edward and Lancaster finally met on 7 August 1318. They exchanged the kiss of peace and agreed the Treaty of Leake two days later. Led by the earls of Pembroke and Hereford, the nobility mediated between the king and his cousin. The Ordinances were reaffirmed, and Edward agreed to send away Roger Damory, Hugh Audley, and William Montacute. This was less a signal that Edward had learned any lessons than that these three had failed to capitalise on their closeness to the king. Edward would never have sent Gaveston away, at least not for long, and would soon prove himself willing to protect another beyond all reason. In October 1318, parliament confirmed the appointment of a new chamberlain to the king. Hugh Despenser the Younger, so called to differentiate him from his father, the Elder Hugh, was put in place by the lords with no complaint from the earl of Lancaster. Although Lancaster seems to have disliked the Elder Hugh, his son was obviously viewed as inoffensive and not too close to Edward. It was to prove the worst misjudgement in living memory, leading to a catastrophe only previously imagined.

By late 1320, the problems were becoming plain for all to see. Hugh had succeeded in casting a spell on the king that rivalled that Gaveston had spun. One chronicler complained that 'no man could approach the king without the consent of the said Sir Hugh',[14] and the system of control seemed to be seeping into the relationship between Edward and Isabella too. The queen had never shown much personal hostility towards Edward's other favourites. Whatever the truth of his relationships with them, they never seemed to encroach on the apparently happy and effective one with his wife. Hugh Despenser was proving a very different man from Gaveston, driven only by an all-consuming lust for money and power. When Hugh tried to use his position at the king's side to resolve a disputed inheritance in his favour, in caused outrage. Despenser claimed possession of the Gower Peninsula in south-west Wales and the other nobles with an interest, joined by Hugh's rivals along the Welsh Marches, rebelled. The group included some who had previously been steadfastly loyal to Edward but now felt driven into opposition. Perhaps the most significant of these men in the long run was Roger Mortimer of Wigmore, a former ally who had previously served as Lieutenant of Ireland.

Edward ordered this coalition of dangerous men to appear before him on 28 March 1321. They refused. The Marcher lords were used to operating under only the lightest touch from the crown on what had been a front line with Wales before Edward's father had all but erased the frontier. This new interference in their business was unwelcome and uncomfortable. They lurched for a threat that had shocked Edward into acquiescence before, demanding Despenser be arrested and put on trial, or they would seek to depose Edward.[15] What followed was short, sharp and created more problems than it solved. The Despenser Wars began in early May 1321 when the Marcher coalition attacked Hugh's castle at Newport, moving on to plough through his other Welsh lands after it fell quickly. The rebels adopted a uniform of green tunics with yellow and white bands to proudly broadcast their opposition to Edward and Despenser. Once they had finished working their way through Hugh's Welsh lands, they turned their attention to devastating his father's English properties.

Relying on the earl of Lancaster's hatred of Hugh Despenser the Elder to keep him from interfering, the Marcher lords met little resistance as they robbed manors and killed tenants whose only crime was having the wrong landlord. In late July, they appeared outside London, and although the city's gates were locked against them, they negotiated, or threatened, their way in on 1 August 1321. Edward appeared at Westminster Hall on 14 August to agree to the exile of his favourite and Hugh the Elder. Unlike Damory, Audley, and Montacute, Edward had no intention of letting go of Hugh for long. He had taken the place in the king's affections long vacant since Gaveston's death. Hugh the Elder immediately took ship from Dover, but his son went into hiding amongst the Cinque Ports and indulged in piracy. It seems unlikely that Hugh the Younger ever left England, or ever had any intention of doing so. Just two months later, the plan had been set for revenge.

Queen Isabella, who was still willing to help her husband against the enemies of Hugh Despenser the Younger, went on a pilgrimage and on her way back, taking a circuitous route, reached Leeds Castle in Kent one evening. It had been very carefully selected for the laying of a trap. The castle was held by Bartholemew of Baddlesmere, a former steward of Edward's household who had joined the Marcher lords' rebellion. His treachery therefore took on a personal edge that appealed to Edward in making him the target of the plan. Bartholemew was not at Leeds Castle because he was with his co-conspirators, but his wife was in residence. Queen Isabella requested entry to the castle to rest for the night. Lady Baddlesmere refused, believing she did as her husband would wish, but offering a grave insult to the queen's person. When Isabella adjusted her tone and demanded entry, the garrison opened fire, and several of the queen's men were killed. Lady Baddlesmere had handed the king the excuse he had sought to act.

In December 1321, Edward issued safe-conducts to both Despenser men to return to England and his presence. In early 1322, a flurry of writs was sent out ordering the arrest of anyone involved in the Marchers' revolt. As the pressure increased and their own lands were threatened, the coalition began to crumble. Roger Mortimer and his uncle of the same name, Roger Mortimer of Chirk, both surrendered to Edward's men and were sent to the Tower. Others gave themselves up, but a clutch of the rebels dashed north to seek safety with the earl of Lancaster. Their way was blocked at Boroughbridge on 16 March 1322 by Andrew Harclay, Sheriff of Cumberland, though Lancaster was with the rebels by this point. Harclay held the only bridge for miles and refused to let them pass. With a royal army hot on their heels, the smaller force saw little option but to force a crossing.

Harclay's men employed the same schiltron tactic that had been used by the Scots at Bannockburn almost a decade earlier to devastating effect against cavalry. Humphrey de Bohun, Earl of Hereford was killed during the fighting as he tried to hold the bridge. One of Harclay's men snuck beneath him and thrust a spear up into the earl's backside 'so that his bowels came out'. It was not to be the last mention of death brought about by an injury caused 'into the fundament'.[16] Andrew Harclay was created Earl of Carlisle for his valuable service. The earl of Lancaster was captured and led to his favourite castle at Pontefract, where he had sat out most of the last decade hating his cousin the king from afar. When the earl was taken before Edward, he was dressed in the tunic of his servants to humiliate him. The king put his cousin on trial for a list of crimes that dated back to 1312, and there can be little doubt that primary amongst them for Edward was Thomas's part in Gaveston's murder. What followed, by recreating the incident, drove that home. Edward did not forgive or forget.

His trial a foregone conclusion, Thomas, Earl of Lancaster was sentenced to be hung, drawn and quartered. Just as Gaveston had been denied the right to speak in his own defence, so Lancaster was kept silent throughout the show trial. The king commuted the gruesome punishment to beheading. Though it was usually done out of respect for a nobleman's position, the reason in this case was far more vindictive and allowed Lancaster's treatment to mirror Gaveston's. On 22 March 1322, the earl of Lancaster was placed onto a mule and ridden to a nearby hilltop, just as Piers had been in 1312. According to one account, the earl knelt facing east, towards the Holy Land, but he was forced to turn north, looking towards a Scotland he had been accused of conspiring with against Edward. Then, a man-at-arms cut off Lancaster's head.[17] A cult would soon spring up around Thomas, Earl of Lancaster, and there would be efforts to canonise him that Edward did all he could to resist.

Other rebels were tried, made to wear their green tunics that had been the uniform of their uprising. Bartholomew of Baddlesmere was executed, his betrayal deemed more personal than the others and his wife's insult and attack on the queen sealing his fate. The rest were imprisoned, many later released on paying fines. Some of their wives and children were also incarcerated as part of the punishment. On 14 July 1322, both Roger Mortimers were condemned to death but had their sentences commuted to life imprisonment by the king. The clemency may have been due to Roger Mortimer of Wigmore's previous good service, or because both men had been quick to surrender to Edward. Roger's wife Joan would spend the rest of Edward's reign his prisoner, but this decision was to have consequences for Edward he could not reasonably have foreseen in 1322. As Edward jubilantly took back control of his kingdom again, he formally cancelled the exiles of the Despenser men, revoked permanently the Ordinances of 1311 that had restricted his authority for more than a decade, and created Hugh Despenser the Elder as Earl of Winchester. Hugh the Younger did not receive an earldom but seemed more concerned with accruing wealth and power than titles. Besides, he would be an earl when his father died now. Before the end of the year, the king would try another assault on Scotland. Feeling buoyed by his recent successes, acts of revenge, and renewed freedoms, he nevertheless failed even more thoroughly than at Bannockburn.

Things grew worse for Edward on 1 August 1323. It was the Feast of St Peter ad Vincula, the patron of the Tower of London, and Roger Mortimer organised a party to celebrate. The guards were encouraged to indulge in the free-flowing wine provided. Possibly Mortimer slipped them some drugs he had procured that left them unconscious for two days. Gerald D'Alspaye, the sub-lieutenant of the Tower, broke Roger out along with a fellow prisoner, Richard de Monmouth. The three men climbed up a chimney in the kitchen, which suggests a cook was in on the plan and left a fire unlit, and scaled the outer walls with a rope ladder Gerald had brought. They were rowed along the Thames to Greenwich where they met horses to make their escape.[18] Roger reached the coast and got across the Channel to France. What began as an irritation to Edward would soon become much, much more.

In 1324, relations with France went downhill again. Charles IV was now King of France, the third of Isabella's brothers to follow their father onto the throne. With each new accession, Edward was required to travel to France and give homage for Gascony, an embarrassment English kings always avoided. When Edward delayed beyond what Charles deemed reasonable, Gascony was seized, and an army sent to take control of it, effectively marking the outbreak of war between England and France. For reasons that are unclear, Edward selected this moment to take his wife's estates in Cornwall from her without explanation. Although he replaced them with an income from the Exchequer, it reduced Isabella's independence. Whether Edward was planning to make Hugh Despenser the Younger the new Earl of

Cornwall in Gaveston's likeness is little more than speculation, but it seems possible that Edward would make such a move at such an inappropriate moment.

If he had caused any heartache to his wife, Edward seemed oblivious, though his options began to shrink around him. The solution that offered the most likely path to a resolution with France was to send Isabella to negotiate with her brother. In March 1325, she travelled to France to try to find peace, leaving with Edward's blessing and plenty of his cash suggesting that there was no open rift between the couple even now. Edward's primary concern seemed to be that his wife might be at physical risk from Mortimer and other rebels now at the French court. In April, Edward sent an army to Gascony under the earls of Surrey and Athol to defend his lands there until matters with Charles could be settled. There was progress when Isabella sent a draft treaty to her husband at the end of May, and on 13 June, Edward ratified it. Under the terms agreed, Edward was to give homage to Charles for Gascony by 29 August 1325 or lose it forever.

Edward was now presented with an impossible dilemma. Going to France himself was an even greater risk than allowing Isabella to travel. A court packed with his rebels might prove dangerously hostile and leaving England opened the door to rebellion. Taking Hugh Despenser to France would be a comfort to Edward, but risked antagonising Isabella and Charles as well as the English exiles. Leaving Despenser behind in England left him at the mercy of his enemies. If Edward remained oblivious to his favourite's lack of popularity, Hugh himself saw it. Hugh warned Edward that 'if he passed beyond the sea, he [Hugh] would be put to death in his absence'.[19] Despenser played on the memory of Gaveston's fate, aware of the guilt Edward must have felt at leaving his friend to be captured. Charles had made it known he was willing to accept the homage from Edward's son, but that meant sending his heir into hostile territory, to the court of a man he was at war with, and risk him being abducted or assassinated. The weight of the problem and Edward's indecisiveness in the face of it is demonstrated by his vacillations as Charles's deadline approached.

The king began preparations to travel to France himself, but on 24 August, five days before the deadline to give his homage, he wrote to Charles that he was too ill to make the journey. It was almost certainly a lie to buy time. On 30 August, Edward changed his mind and recommenced the arrangements to go to France, appointing his 12-year-old son Edward of Windsor as regent while he was out of England. Three days later, Edward changed his plans again. On 2 September, Edward of Windsor was created Count of Ponthieu so that he could give homage to Charles. It meant giving up the incomes of the county, but Edward was clearly flapping by this point. Finally settled on a course of action, Edward also made his son Duke of Aquitaine on 10 September and accompanied him to the south coast. One of the things the king impressed upon his son was that he was not to allow himself to be married without his father's permission, demonstrating that Edward understood the dangers of his heir being influenced by his enemies once beyond his control.

It was from this point that things really began to fall apart for Edward. He had little choice but to make a tough decision by the autumn of 1325, and none of his options was a good one. The situation was the culmination of years of flawed rule and alienation of sections of his nobility for the promotion of successive favourites. Other kings had unpopular close advisors, but Edward had drawn this problem out to a new extreme by his complete emotional as well as political reliance on such figures. Queen Isabella had seemed unperturbed by Gaveston and others, but Hugh Despenser added a dimension of cruelty and avarice to his tightening grip on the king that was different. Despenser was the first to try and drive a wedge between the king and queen, and Isabella would not tolerate it. It seems entirely possible that Isabella was behind her brother's demand that Edward travel to France to do homage for Gascony as a way to separate her husband from Despenser and hope to talk some sense into him. The provision for their son to represent his father might have been Isabella's acknowledgement that Despenser would prove challenging for Edward to wriggle free from and that the heir to the crown would provide a significant bargaining chip. In this instance, Isabella must have been disappointed to be proven right.

Prince Edward performed homage to his uncle King Charles IV of France for Gascony on 24 September 1325 at Vincennes. Shortly afterwards, another uncle appeared at the French court. Edmund of Woodstock, Earl of Kent, was Edward II's younger half-brother, the second son of his father's second marriage to Margaret of France. Edmund arrived in France to join those increasingly disaffected with his half-brother and, more particularly, Hugh Despenser. Isabella now made plain what must have been her plan from the moment she departed for France. 'I protest that I will not return,' she insisted, 'until this intruder is removed, but discarding my marriage garment, shall assume the robes of widowhood and mourning.'[20] It could hardly be more clear that Isabella's real grievance was with Despenser rather than Edward, whom she knew well enough by now to understand that he lacked the ability to control such relationships.

Queen Isabella goaded her husband, no doubt praying he would leap to choose her and their family over Hugh Despenser. Edward had previously discussed marrying their son to a daughter of the count of Hainault. Although not originally Philippa, his eventual bride, Isabella resurrected the idea publicly. Edward was sent into a tailspin of fury and panic. He had altered his plans to consider a marriage into the Castillian royal family of his mother to strengthen bonds between England and the Iberian Peninsula. Isabella's actions threatened to undermine that work and embarrass the king, who, the world would see, had lost command of his policy to his wife. Doubtless, Isabella considered it worse that her husband had handed control of such matters to someone as unsuitable and objectionable as Despenser, but her lure worked. The king frantically tried to remind his son of his promise not to marry and attempted to convince him to return home. In early February 1326, Edward issued a proclamation to be read out by all of the sheriffs of England. The king ordered preparations to be made against a possible invasion, admitting that he feared his wife would attack the kingdom. It must not have sat well to confess that 'the queen will not come to the king nor permit his son to return'.

Furthermore, the proclamation asserted that Edward 'understands that the queen is adopting the counsel of the Mortimer, the king's notorious enemy and rebel, and of other rebels' before adding that she was making alliances with the French and the king's enemies. Edward insisted that if the queen and prince return peacefully, they should be well treated. If they come with an invading army, the sheriffs were ordered 'to save the bodies of the queen and Edward only and to treat the aliens as the king's enemies'.[21] The king was not yet certain of his wife's intentions but appeared to want to believe she was acting against her will and might come back to him at any moment. It was a startling admission of just how far beyond Edward's control matters had got. It is also the first reference to Isabella working with Roger Mortimer. There is no hint in any of the king's desperate preparations, his diplomatic efforts, or the contemporary chronicles of an affair at this point. If there were such rumours, it would have been an additional shame for Edward, but could also have worked in his favour. He could expose Isabella as a cheat and hold over her the threat of ending their marriage and leaving her in disgrace. The most likely explanation at this point is that Edward identified the man he considered the most significant threat, the capable Mortimer, who was already an escaped traitor in exile. Placing the blame at someone else's feet made space for Isabella to return and be forgiven. Edward, it seemed, had no intention of discarding his wife. Isabella and Mortimer shared a common goal, to be rid of Despenser rather than, for now at least, a bed.

In March, Edward wrote from Lichfield to his son and to Charles. He reminded Edward that he was not to marry 'or suffer himself to be married' without his father's permission. Complaining of Isabella's refusal to return home, the king wrote that he understood the queen kept Mortimer's company 'within and without house'. The phrase may be meant to convey the king's fears of an affair between the two, or simply that Isabella was spending all of her time plotting in private with Mortimer. The prince was instructed to return to his father 'as speedily as possible, notwithstanding the above or any other excuses'.[22] The letter to Charles expressed Edward's disbelief that his wife cited Hugh Despenser as the cause of their falling out, particularly since she 'sent to le Despenser letters of as great and especial friendship as she might from time to time'. Edward then all but pleaded with Charles to send his son home.[23]

The letters did not have the desired effect. On 27 August 1326, Prince Edward was formally betrothed to Philippa of Hainault. Within a matter of days, Edward sent some of the men standing ready for an invasion across the Channel to enter Normandy. Whether he meant to disrupt French plans for an attack or was trying to snatch back his son is unclear, but the hurried assault was a dismal failure. The moment Edward had been preparing for came on 24 September. Isabella, Mortimer, Prince Edward, the earl of Kent, and other exiles landed at Orwell in Suffolk with around 1,000 men. As soon as they disembarked, they were joined by Thomas, Earl of Norfolk, Edward's other half-brother. The small force marched west and found surprisingly little opposition. When news reached Edward at the Tower of London on 27 September, things were already looking bad. Several bishops, including those of Hereford, Lincoln, and Ely had already joined the rebels too. Henry, Earl of Lancaster, the brother of the executed Thomas, was also quick to join those opposing Edward. The following day, 28 September, Edward placed a bounty of £1,000 on the head of Roger Mortimer.[24] In retaliation, Isabella set a price of £2,000 on Hugh Despenser's head.

By 2 October, Edward realised he was in dire straits. He packed what he could take quickly and left London. Most telling of all was the fact the Hugh Despenser remained at Edward's side as they rushed west towards Wales. Even now, it seems likely that abandoning Hugh would have saved Edward's position. He was the focus of the ire that poured into the country, but it was a symptom of the situation created by Edward that he was utterly incapable of giving up his favourite even in the face of the loss of everything else. The king had a narrow escape. As the rebels took control, Walter Stapeldon, Bishop of Exeter, an ally of Edward's, was pursued by an angry mob as he tried to reach St Paul's to take sanctuary. Although he got into the church, he was dragged out and hacked to death 'with more than pagan cruelty'. The bishop was beheaded and his body thrown to the city's hungry dogs.[25]

In the meantime, Edward and Hugh made it to Chepstow Castle as Hugh the Elder headed to Bristol. The king and his favourite tried to sail into the Bristol Channel to Lundy Island, but adverse winds kept them pinned in port. On 25 October, they were ensconced within Cardiff Castle.

The queen oversaw the issue of a memorandum on 26 October that condemned the king for 'going away from his realm of England with Hugh le Despenser'. Even though he was still in Wales, but perhaps in response to his efforts to sail away from English shores, the kingdom was deemed to be 'left without rule'. The gathered nobles and prelates agreed that the prince, referred to as the Duke of Aquitaine, should take the role of keeper of England as was required any time the monarch was out of the realm. They were careful to describe the prince as taking the position 'to rule and govern the realm in the name and right of the king his father, who was thus absent'.[26] Prince Edward was effectively appointed regent, but it is striking that he was to hold the power to govern only on behalf of his father. It remained clear even to this point that there was no intention to depose the king yet.

A week earlier, on 18 October, Isabella and her army had arrived at Bristol to lay siege to Hugh the Elder's castle. It fell quickly, and on the same day as the memorandum decrying Edward's abandonment of his kingdom, Hugh the Elder was subjected to a recreation of the earl of Lancaster's fate, which had itself been a repeat of Gaveston's. Hugh was denied the right to speak in his own defence, though he was not beheaded as Lancaster and Gaveston had been. Despite his position as Earl of Winchester, a rank that would usually cause a sentence of death to result in a beheading, Hugh the Elder, aged 56, was hanged. He was dragged to the public gallows in Bristol wearing his full armour and strung up for the crowd to jeer at. Only once he was dead was his corpse decapitated. The body was fed to the dogs, and his head carried on the end of a spear to Winchester and displayed.[27]

Edward and Hugh the Younger had left Cardiff for Caerphilly Castle, where they remained for a couple of weeks before deciding to give up the safety of the fortress for Margam Abbey on 2 November. A fortnight later, on 16 November, the king of England was apprehended with no more than a handful of followers wandering, apparently aimlessly, around the countryside of Wales near Llantrisant. The king was taken to Kenilworth Castle in the custody of his cousin Henry, Earl of Lancaster. Forced to hand over his Great Seal to allow his son to govern, Edward was otherwise treated with respect. Others were less fortunate. On 17 November, Edmund Fitzalan, Earl of Arundel, was executed on Mortimer's orders. The two were cousins, and this may have been the resolution of a personal dispute dating back to the Marcher revolt of 1322. The full wrath of the swiftly victorious queen was saved for one man.

Hugh Despenser the Younger was apprehended with the king and taken to Hereford. The queen wanted Hugh taken to London so that his trial could be a large and public spectacle. Aware of the plan, Hugh went on hunger strike. There were fears that he was growing so weak he would not survive the journey to London and might thereby avoid the queen's vengeance. On 24 November 1326, Hugh was put on trial at Hereford. His conviction a foregone conclusion, Hugh was ridden through the city with his coat of arms reversed to display his perpetual shame and a crown of nettles jammed onto his head, a stinging reminder of his crimes. At either side, a trumpeter loudly proclaimed his guilt into his ears throughout the short journey. A fifty-foot-high set of gallows had been specially constructed in Hereford so that all would have a good view of the spectacle.

Hugh was subjected to the most gruesome form of execution; hanging, drawing, and quartering. Raised in a noose until he was on the very brink of death, he was then cut down. His stomach was sliced open, his intestines pulled out and thrown onto a brazier so he could watch them burn as he clung to life. With the scent of his own burning insides filling his nostrils, Hugh's genitals were cut off and thrown into the fire too. Finally, he was beheaded, and his body cleaved into four parts. His head was sent to the capital to be mounted on London Bridge. The quarters of his corpse were sent to Carlisle, York, Bristol, and Dover to be exhibited at the corners of the realm. It was four years before these parts of his body were reunited to be buried at Tewkesbury Abbey. Hugh Despenser the Younger's time in power had been brief but destructive. His problems were now over, but some awkward issues remained to be resolved.

Isabella's aim had been to rid herself of Hugh, and she had succeeded. It seems unlikely that any malice extended to her husband, but he had shown himself to be a disastrous ruler who might take another favourite at any moment. Gaveston had seemed terrible until Despenser had arrived. Whoever came next could prove worse still. Prince Edward held no known grudge against his father. The earls of Norfolk and Kent, the king's half-brothers, hated Despenser but seemed to bear Edward himself no real ill will. They may have been working out a way to step down Edward's incarceration, to return his power to him. At the extreme, they perhaps thought of finding a way to keep Prince Edward involved to retain a handle on government. One person, though, knew something more was required. Sir Roger Mortimer had already been excluded from the king's mercy, marked as a traitor, and had a bounty placed on his head. If the king's wife, son and two brothers could be confident of finding a path to peace with Edward, Mortimer must have known that Edward would come after him. It had taken years, but Edward had got his revenge on those responsible for Gaveston's death. Mortimer knew that to free Edward was to sign his own death warrant.

A council meeting decided that Edward should be deposed, and the nobles and barons who feared his retribution were almost certainly the driving forces behind the conclusion. Their solution was that Edward should abdicate the throne to his son but be permitted to live out his life in peace. On 7 January 1327, parliament met to discuss this novel duty. No king had been compelled to abdicate before. How it should be done to make it a legally binding arrangement was unclear, unknown. Even as parliament assembled, no one knew whether the session was legal, having been summoned without the king's consent or involvement. Lacking options, they continued anyway. Edward was informed at Kenilworth on 20 January 1327 that he was no longer King of England. Touchingly, he was reported as reflecting, 'I greatly lament that I have so utterly failed my people, but I could not be other than I am.'[29] Edward knew a ditching, swimming thatcher unable to control his attachments to friends was not what England needed, but that was who he had always been. His reliance on favourites was perhaps an effort to make up for the shortcomings he saw in himself, but poor judgement of character was a flaw for which he failed to compensate.

The reign of King Edward III officially began on 25 January 1327, and his coronation took place a week later on 2 February at Westminster Abbey. Now known as Sir Edward of Caernarfon, the former king was initially left in the custody of his cousin Henry, Earl of Lancaster. By early April there was some unease about the arrangement. It was perhaps felt that Henry was too close to Edward and may become sympathetic to his cause, or that he was too powerful for the regency council to be sure of controlling. Although Isabella and her son now had an interest in keeping Edward safe and at a distance, it was perhaps Roger Mortimer who still had the most to lose from the threat of a reversal of Edward's deposition. Sir Edward was transferred into the joint custody of Thomas, Lord Berkeley, Mortimer's son-in-law and one of the Marcher lords imprisoned in 1322, and Sir John Maltravers. The latter had been in exile with Mortimer after escaping from the Battle of Boroughbridge. These men were charged with keeping the former king safe, but it marked a change in his circumstances that cannot have been entirely welcome.

It would not be unreasonable to expect Edward's story to end there, or at least very soon afterwards. Beyond the predictable moment that followed his transfer into less sympathetic hands, the saga is far from simple. In late June 1327, Robert Bruce invaded northern England again. Roger Mortimer took an army north, and in the space this created, two brothers, Thomas and Stephen Dunheved, attacked Berkeley Castle. The aim of the assault was to free Edward, but the outcome is far from clear. The brothers and their allies may have got the former king away from Berkeley or could have fled without him after failing to secure his person.[30] In October of the same year, Mortimer ordered the detention of twenty-six people at Caernarfon Castle, Edward's birthplace, for involvement in a Welsh plot to free the old king. By then, officially at least, it was too late. The traditional date given for Edward II's death is 21 September 1327, when Lord Berkeley wrote to King Edward III to relay the sad news that his father had died. The report was broadcast by the king a few days later; Edward II had died of natural causes.

From 21 September until 20 October, Edward's body lay in state at Berkeley Castle, guarded at all times by just one man, William Beaukaire, who had been in the service of Edward and Hugh Despenser, and who appears to have arrived at Berkeley just a few days before the death. In early October, a group of local ecclesiastical notables visited the body. The cost of embalming the corpse appears in Lord Berkeley's accounts and raises the question of whether the king's body and indeed his face were visible, or were already wrapped in waxed cloth. Were they looking at a bound-up shape that roughly resembled the height and build of the former king? On 21 October, the body was moved to Gloucester Cathedral but rested there for a further two months before it was buried. A funeral was finally held on 20 December 1327, attended by the new king, Queen Isabella and a clutch of dignitaries.

Even that was not the end of the tale. In late 1329, Donald, Earl of Mar, a Scots nobleman who had been at Edward's court and had been close to the king, promised to raise an army and head south to free Edward. This, despite his funeral having taken place two years earlier. In January 1330, William Melton, Archbishop of York wrote to Simon Swanland, Mayor of London asking him to procure supplies and £200 in gold. Edward's biographer, Kathryn Warner, has pointed out that gold was rarely used as currency in England but was common on the Continent. The shocking part of the letter was Melton's claim that 'We have certain news of our liege lord Edward of Caernarfon, that he is alive and in good health of body, in a safe place.'[31] The archbishop was not the only significant figure who became entangled in this murky pool of rumour. Edmund, Earl of Kent, Edward's half-brother, was tried in parliament in March 1330 for attempting to get into Corfe Castle to see if his brother was still alive and being held there.[32] Usually understood to have been set up by Roger Mortimer as a pretence for killing the earl, Edmund was unsure enough of the tale of his brother's death to die trying to find the truth three years later.

The scheming even took on an international dimension when some rebels fled to the court of the duke of Brabant, Edward's nephew, to continue their plans. The situation in England changed dramatically on 19 October 1330 when the 17-year-old Edward III sprung a coup at Nottingham Castle that dislodged his mother and Mortimer from the regency authority they had exercised. Believed by many to have been lovers by this point, the truth remains obscure and irrelevant. Mortimer had created himself Earl of March to establish his family's dominance in the Welsh border region and had ruled in a high-handed, corrupt fashion that endeared him to no one. Few mourned him when he was hanged without a trial at Tyburn on 29 November 1330, closing a cycle that had seen Gaveston killed for his influence over the king, Thomas, Earl of Lancaster, murdered in revenge, and Hugh Despenser, Senior and Junior executed in turn.

During the first parliament after Isabella and Mortimer's fall, the issue of the old king's death, or murder, was examined. Thomas Gurney and William Ockley were convicted in their absence of the murder but never apprehended. Lord Berkeley made an odd speech in defence of himself during which he claimed 'he was never an accomplice, a helper or a procurer in his death, nor did he ever know of his death until this present parliament'.[33] This may have been a desperate bid to avoid the whiff of culpability that might cost him his head, but Lord Berkeley had been one of Edward's joint custodians, and the supposed murder had taken place at his castle. To brazenly state three years later that this was the first he had heard of it was brave, foolish, or the truth. Had those responsible for the king been aware of the plan to fake his death, bury an embalmed effigy of Edward, or some poor substitute, and hide him from further attempts to release him, perhaps at Corfe Castle? That would fit with later stories such as the Fieschi letter, written to Edward III in the 1330s to explain to him that his father was alive and well and living in Italy.[34] In September 1338, a man named as William le Galeys – William the Welshman – was given money during a visit to Edward III in Koblenz, Germany. The payment remarks that the man 'says he is the king's father', brought to see his son by an Italian merchant. This William also spent a further three weeks with Edward III in Antwerp. It was odd for a monarch to entertain a royal imposter, and none of the times that he is mentioned accuse him of lying. Was Edward II living a quiet, rustic life on the land in Italy, visiting his son when he was out of England, and he was able to go to him safely, and, perhaps more importantly, without posing a threat? That would sound like a dream life for a man who never enjoyed being king, who preferred the company of the common folk, and loved working with his hands. The truth remains tantalisingly elusive for now.

Chapter 8

The Peasants' Revolt

Rebellion is the final right of the people, to be exercised when all others have been withheld.

England had seen the first deposition of an anointed king in favour of his son. The male line of kings had been preserved, but there was now the political suggestion that abdication was a legitimate tool and aim of rebellion. Precedents, once set, can never be undone. Edward II's reign had been one long act of rebellion that had started with arrangements to compensate for weak government and warnings of deposition and ended with the fulfilment of what were probably idle threats. Mortimer had proved himself no better, grabbing what he could before he fell fast and hard at the young hands of a man destined to become one of the most famous and successful English monarchs.

Edward III grew to be a man with the kind of magnetic personality that attracted people to him and a knack for winning that bound them to his cause. In 1333, Edward defeated a Scots army at the Battle of Halidon Hill, offering a sharp contrast to his father before agreeing a peace treaty to avoid a prolonged, and demonstrably unwinnable, war. In 1337, Philip VI of France seized the duchy of Aquitaine from Edward. It had happened before, either to force English kings to perform homage to their French counterpart or to initiate peace talks that might offer the French crown better terms. Philip must have been startled by Edward III's response. The 24-year-old laid claim to Philip's crown, and to the whole kingdom of France.

The Capetian kings of France had ruled in a direct male line, from father to son, since 987, making them one of the most successful medieval dynasties. Edward's grandfather, Philip IV, had produced three sons, and each had ruled in turn as Louis X, Philip V, and Charles IV, but all had died without sons. The crown had passed into the cadet line of the House of Valois on the death of Charles IV. Philip VI was a grandson of Philip III; his father Charles, Count of Valois, was the younger brother of Philip IV. Rather than scurry to his French rival and plead for his duchy back, Edward pointed out that as a grandson of Philip IV, his claim to the French throne was better than that of Philip VI. His mother was the sister of the last three Capetian kings, and so he had a rightful claim to the throne. French rules of inheritance tended to prefer the male line and consider the female line barred, and Queen Isabella's brothers had enshrined a law that female succession was not possible. Given that Edward's kingdom in England recognised no such legal impediment, he felt justified in pressing his own claim. The Hundred Years' War was birthed.

Edward III's reign marked a settled period for England in terms of rebellion driven in part by military successes abroad, including Sluys, Crecy, and Poitiers, along with the capture of the French king John II at the Battle of Poitiers in 1356. The other significant factor of Edward's reign was the devastation of the plague remembered as the Black Death, which killed between one third and half of the population of Europe, wiping some small towns and villages entirely from the map. Arriving on ships making port on the south coast in the summer of 1348, the contagion spread with terrifying speed and an unstoppable death toll. Within a year, it had reached its cold fingers into every corner of the kingdom, taking rich and poor, young and old, men and women, churchmen, and secular folk with utter indifference. Neither wealth nor service to God protected those who suffered briefly and died quickly. Perversely, those who survived the initial outbreak and the recurrences in 1361–62, 1369, and in 1374–75 found themselves significantly better off as a shortage of labour drove up wages, a surplus of food pushed down prices, and there was more opportunity to move in search of a better life.

Edward III died on 21 June 1377, aged 64 and having been king for half a century. He had struggled with his health in his final years, strokes taking away the vigour and affability that had defined his kingship and prosecution of the war with France. Edward had been blessed with five sons, and as he declined, he looked to them to represent and pursue his policies. His oldest son and heir Edward, Prince of Wales, remembered now as the Black Prince, had proven himself a mighty warrior, though he seemed to lack some of his father's diplomatic subtlety. A life of campaigning had taken a severe toll on the prince, who was no less hampered than his father. He would die on 8 June 1376, a year before the king, aged 45. Lionel, Duke of Clarence, had passed away in 1368, just before his thirtieth birthday. Three sons remained. The oldest was John of Gaunt, born in Ghent, which had been Anglicised to Gaunt. He was by far the wealthiest man in the kingdom after his father, having acquired the rich duchy of Lancaster in right of his wife, and the earldoms of Leicester, Lincoln, and Derby. The fourth son, Edmund of Langley, had been created Earl of Cambridge, but left little impact on the government of the realm, as did his younger Thomas of Woodstock, who had been given the earldom of Buckingham by his father.

The death of the king, coming as it did after that of the Prince of Wales, posed a problem. Worryingly, it was the same question faced in 1199 when Richard I died. Then, King John had taken the throne from his nephew Arthur of Brittany, and people began to murmur that they may soon see King John II. For some, there was plenty of appeal in the thought. The other option, the one Edward III had preferred before his death, was for his grandson to succeed him, but Richard of Bordeaux, only surviving son of the Black Prince, was just 10 years old. A child king was never a welcome prospect, and to add to the problems it would cause, France, ruled now by Charles V, was growing increasingly confident and aggressive, raiding the south coast of England in the wake of the old king's death. John of Gaunt was obscenely rich, 37, and had several children, including an illegitimate family with his mistress Katherine Swynford known as the Beaufort family. Against this, he lacked any of the military prowess or political skill of his father and could not even boast much success as a soldier as his brother had done. Richard was only ten, but that meant he came with none of the baggage John carried about with him. He may yet grow up to be like his father and grandfather if the kingdom could wait. And he was the old king's selection. In a choice between two far from ideal candidates, the boy-king seemed the lesser evil, but John of Gaunt remained his heir presumptive for the foreseeable future.

A perpetual council was established to govern the kingdom during Richard's minority. Two earls, two barons, two bishops, two knights banneret, and four other knights were to decide and enact policy on the king's behalf. It is striking that none of the king's uncles was appointed to this council, though their connection ensured them influence, and John of Gaunt's position both as heir and wealthiest subject gave him a status that guaranteed him a voice. Unfortunately for England, Gaunt was obsessed with trying to press his own claim to the crown of Castile through his second wife, Constance. He arranged a marriage for his acquiescent younger brother Edmund of Langley to Constance's sister, Isabella, to strengthen his cause, and John would try to divert money and focus to his pet project rather than concentrating on England's problems.

In 1381, just four years into Richard II's rule, the country would erupt in a series of violent risings that shocked the government because the trouble came not from disgruntled nobles or barons, but from a coherent, organised group of ordinary folk, who not only coordinated efforts across England to great effect but had a defined agenda. Remembered as the Peasants'

Revolt, it was familiar to contemporaries as 'the great insurrection', or even 'hurling time'. The name Peasants' Revolt appeared centuries later and was based on the description of many involved as 'rustics'. Taken to mean exclusively poor rural people – peasants – it was both misunderstood and misleading. Rustics referred to anyone living in the countryside, including the wealthier tradesmen and even land-owning gentry. Some of those most involved in events were the most affluent in their region. Not only that, but towns played a central role in the revolt too, with London at the forefront. The rebellion of 1381 very nearly changed the face of medieval England forever, but eventually served to demonstrate how concentrated true power was in the tight grip of the few.

It is difficult to characterise the great insurrection as a rebellion against the crown too. From the outset, the rebels made it clear that they laid no blame for their grievances at the feet of their 14-year-old king. Their stated aim was to remove the layers between them and the king, which they felt bred the corruption and unreasonable exactions to which they were subjected. Throughout, they were to insist that 'they hold and will hold you for their king'. As the traditional refrain of rebels wishing to avoid a charge of treason, aiming criticism at the king's chief ministers was nothing new. In this case, however, it was probably more genuine than at other times. The new king was young, may still be idealistic and open to persuasion of the merits of the insurgents' cause. It was this promise of a new dawn, and its failure to arrive, that led to problems in 1381. The outbreak of both heartfelt and organised rebellion was also the culmination of many long-standing issues that created a perfect storm in that year.

The most well-known of the concerns that fed displeasure was the Statute of Labourers. The Black Death, the combination of the bubonic and pneumonic plague known to contemporaries as the Great Mortality, had rushed across Europe and reached England's shores in the early summer of 1348. Probably arriving on Gascon shipping into the south-west, it quickly gripped Bristol and by August was in the streets of London. In May 1349 cases were reported in York and the entire nation felt the fear, panic and loss that would kill between a third and a half of Europe's population. The disease had run its course by the end of 1349 but would return to haunt the survivors several times before 1381, in 1361–62, 1368, 1371, and 1373–75. The death toll devastated families and communities the length and breadth of England. It was a great leveller, claiming old and young, rich and poor, laity and clergy alike. The indiscriminate nature may have played a part in creating a sense of greater equality deserved by and kept from the poorer in society.

For those who emerged from the dark days of the pestilence, there was a surprising positive to be found. Fewer workers meant more opportunity to demand higher wages, to break free of the bonds that had kept villeins particularly, those tied to a piece of land and a lord for life, all but enslaved. As power shifted into the hands of those able to set a price for their labour, slipping from those forced to fish in a much smaller pool, the government stepped in. Those adversely affected were necessarily the richest; noblemen and prelates who were the great landowners. In June 1349, as the plague still rampaged through England, the Ordinance of Labourers was hurriedly produced. The ordinance fixed the wages to be paid for any labour at pre-plague levels. The document complained that 'many seeing the necessity of masters, and great scarcity of servants, will not serve unless they may receive excessive wages'. Sheriffs were instructed to ensure all payments were kept no higher than those received in 1347.[2] One of the more insidious effects of the measure was to insist that it applied to free tenants as well as villeins, effectively extending the harshest form of service in England to those who had previously been free.

In the early months of 1351, parliament enshrined these regulations in the Statute of Labourers. The ordinance was confirmed, and a wage was set for a range of trades and services. Haymaking could pay no more than 1d a day. Mowing was limited to 5d per acre or per day and reaping to 2d for the first week in August and 3d for the rest of the month. Threshing a quarter of wheat or rye could pay a maximum of 2½d, with only 1½d for the same amount of barley, beans, and oats. Carpenters, masons, and tilers, including the masters of their trades, all saw the wages they could demand limited by statute. In 1361, the problem still existed, and punishments were extended to imprisonment without bail. Any labourer running away without permission to look for higher wages could be branded on the forehead with an 'F' for falsehood. The Statute may have been considered by legislators and workers alike a short-term expedient to ensure the harvest was maintained and famine avoided, but continued outbreaks of plague and the slow growth of population meant that the issues remained. They affected the wealthiest, and they were also those in the best position to resolve the problem to their own benefit. At a local level, the laws were enforced by justices of the peace. Although frequently ignored, it created a new avenue for corruption by selectively enforcing laws, and justices were not above paying over the legal limits to obtain labour for their own land while prosecuting neighbours who tried to do the same.

The church was facing serious problems during this period too. The papacy was in schism, with one pope sitting in Rome and another in

Avignon, France. Given that England was at war with France, the presence of a seat of papal authority within the kingdom was anathema and England backed the Roman pontiff. There were continuing and growing concerns about the wealth of the church too, with some clergy questioning why it held vast quantities of both money and land when Jesus had preached poverty. Such questions chimed with those who had their incomes suppressed as the church, one of the greatest landlords in England, benefitted. The other problem created within England by the prolonged war with France was the presence of an entire population trained, prepared, and equipped to fight. Amongst the provisions meant to maintain a steady supply of capable fighting men was the famous 1363 act that required all adult men to practise archery in the butts every Sunday after church. Regular arrays that checked the proper equipment was owned and maintained meant that every adult male had weapons and knew how to use them.

The spark that ignited this dry keg of powder in 1381 was taxation. Parliament had become the conduit through which monarchs levied taxation since the reign of Henry III. It had become a balancing act, with the king offering amendments and improvements in law and government in return for the grant. General taxation was usually to be used for the defence of the realm, though this was frequently stretched to include offensives on foreign soil. The usual form of a grant was a fractional tax, levied at one-tenth of the value of moveable assets for townsmen and 1/15 for those in the countryside. From 1334 onwards, this had been slightly amended so that a town or village was assessed at a fixed amount based on previous yields. The amount collected from individuals was then left to the community, meaning that wealthier, altruistic members might pay more than their poorer neighbours to even out the burden. The benefit to the government lay in the certainty this provided in the amount to be collected, usually around £37–38,000 nationally. The assessments had not been reviewed since 1334, creating a feeling there might be more wealth in the country than was being taxed.

War was expensive, and by the 1370s, the government was experimenting with ways to increase the tax yield. In 1371, a Parish Tax was imposed. This required 22s 3d from each parish in England but fell apart when it transpired the number of parishes had been incorrectly counted. The belief there were 45,000 parishes in England was wildly inaccurate, the final figure being just of 8,500. The amount imposed on each parish was accordingly drastically increased to 116s. The tax created a backlash as many saw their individual liability double. The Parish Tax was never repeated, and in January 1377 an innovation was introduced in the form of a Poll Tax. The idea was simple.

Every individual aged 14 or over, including women, were to pay 4d each. That was the equivalent of just over a day's wages for most tradespeople and between two and four day's wages for a labourer. The clergy were to pay 4d each too, though the wealthiest among them agreed to pay 12d. Genuine beggars were excluded from the lay assessment, and mendicant friars, as their ecclesiastical equivalents, from the clergy's. The tax was a success, raising over £22,000 from the laity alone, more than half a fractional tax.[4] The lack of equity meant that the richest paid the same as the poorest, and that also meant the yield was lower than it might be. The church's agreement to it's wealthiest members paying more perhaps opened the eyes of the government to a missed opportunity.

When Richard II's first parliament met in 1377, it was against the backdrop of the old king's death, a minority government, and French assaults on the south coast. The urgency caused parliament to fall back on the old system and grant a fractional tax, though they agreed to a double subsidy of $^2/_{10}$ from towns and $^2/_{15}$ from the countryside. It was collected in early 1378, coming hard on the heels of the Poll Tax. By the end of the year, the expedition led by John of Gaunt, the new king's senior uncle, against the renewed French threat had failed dismally. When parliament gathered again in November, it refused to grant further taxation. Not only was the money being squandered, but repeated rounds of impositions risked enraging those forced to pay again.

In April 1379, parliament agreed to a second Poll Tax, though secured some sureties that the money would be appropriately used by insisting on access to royal accounts. The need for such checks hints that parliament felt the money was being diverted, not least by John of Gaunt, who had his own agenda in Castile. This version of the Poll Tax was an evolution of the first that took account of lessons learned. It created thirty-three levels of taxation rather than the one flat rate previously applied. The list was headed by John of Gaunt and the duke of Brittany, who were to pay 10 marks each (£6 13s 4d). All earls and widowed countesses were assessed at £4. Barons and knights, or their widows, were to pay 40s each. The Mayor of London was to pay £4, the same amount as an earl, and the other aldermen 40s. Each innkeeper was assessed at either 2s 40d or 12d, 'according to his estate'. Anyone outside a defined category was to pay 4d. The clergy were divided into fifteen tiers, from the archbishops who were to pay £6 13s 4d, the same as the two richest lay lords, to 4d for the unendowed. The tax was to be applied to those aged 16 and over this time, and married couples in the most impoverished bracket could half their assessment so that in effect only one of them paid.

Although impressively progressive, the tax was a flop. It raised a disappointing £22,000 in total from all revenue streams, roughly the same as the first Poll Tax had raised just from the laity. Parliament met once more in January 1380 in the wake of more military failures. Angry at the continued setbacks and waste of taxpayers' money, parliament disbanded the continual council that had ruled England since Richard's accession and declared him ready to lead, aged 13. They considered that 'our lord the king was now of great discretion and handsome stature; and bearing in mind his age, which was very nearly that of his noble grandfather, whom God absolve, at the time of his coronation'. The five principal officers of state, the chancellor, treasurer, keeper of the privy seal, chief chamberlain and steward of the king's household, were to be appointed and to serve the king in place of the council. Simon Sudbury, the archbishop of Canterbury, was appointed to the senior post of chancellor. Only after this would parliament agree to another round of taxation, this time a grant of a subsidy and a half, one and a half times a fractional tax. A caveat was added that 'no parliament shall be held within the kingdom which further burdens his poor commons between now and the said feast of Michaelmas in a year's time'.[6] The measure was to prevent any further taxation until 29 September 1381, eighteen months later.

Despite this assurance, parliament gathered in November 1380 to hear of the dismal failure of the campaign to Brittany led by Thomas of Woodstock, the king's youngest uncle. The duke of Brittany had been at the English court for years, as demonstrated by his inclusion in the previous Poll Tax. Once back on the Continent to help Woodstock fight France, he sued for peace and abandoned his English allies. Thomas took his army south to Nantes and laid siege to the city. On top of this, John of Gaunt had been forced to muster an army and lead it north to confront the threat of renewed hostilities with Scotland. All of that meant only one thing: the government needed more money. The Commons were utterly disbelieving of the claim that the war chest was empty after so much had been raised in recent years. The chancellor announced the astounding figure required to meet current needs: £160,000, the equivalent of more than four subsidies.[7]

Parliament was horrified and baulked at the figure but did recognise the serious nature of the threats facing the kingdom. The assembly offered to raise £100,000, two thirds from the laity and one third from the clergy. The offer still represented an eye-watering three fractional taxes at 1334 rates. To meet this staggering requirement, parliament returned to the idea of a Poll Tax for the third time. Doing away with the fairer tiered system that had somehow led to a lower yield, they applied a flat rate again. Rejecting calls for a tax of 20d or 16d each, they settled on 12d, three times the previous lowest rate. This was the lowest assessment that would treble the income from the 1377 tax and meet the £66,000 promised. They wanted the money quickly and easily, and to know how much should arrive at the Exchequer, but in their haste to meet these requirements, parliament overlooked the disastrous inequity the regulations created. This time around, the rich would pay less than last time, and the poor would be forced to find more; three times more. There was no married couple's allowance this time, meaning that a couple who had paid 4d in 1379 because they were too poor to pay more would now be assessed at 12d each, making 24d in total, six times their previous charge. The burden was increased by the insistence that two-thirds of the tax should be delivered to the Exchequer by 27 January 1381, and the rest by 2 June. That meant collecting a crippling tax during the lean winter months when the poor in the countryside could least afford it.[8]

There was some awareness of the unfairness and weight of the burden this would impose on the kingdom. Lifting a provision from the 1334 taxation model, each town and village was to be assessed at a flat rate and collection left to local officials and the community based on ability to pay. The problem was that no rules were set beyond the limit that none should pay less than 4d or more than 20s (£1). That meant men like John of Gaunt, already widely despised, and earls and prelates everywhere would pay less than before while the poorest paid significantly more. The system was wide open to abuse, too, since the local officials responsible for assessing each individual's contribution were the wealthier men of the community. Unless they were public-spirited, as some certainly were, they held the power to impose higher assessments on others to reduce their own. When the first returns began to dribble into the Exchequer in January 1381, they were disappointing, to say the least.

The date for the delivery of the remainder was brought forward to 21 April, and the government became convinced that widespread fraud was taking place. The taxable population of Essex had apparently fallen by 17,000 since the first Poll Tax in 1377. Some 13,000 were missing from Kent, 27,000 from Suffolk and a brazen 30,000 from Norfolk.[9] The government was correct. Their unfair system had created collusion between communities and local officials to hide the most impoverished members to avoid the better off being required to pay more on their account. Another factor at play was the increasingly invasive assessments used to create centrally-held records, and a willingness to hide sections of the community to skew those records might have gone beyond financial concerns into worries about what those records might be used for. A preoccupation of the rebels would be the documentation of central government and local landlords.

The population may have felt that their resistance and laxity had born fruit. By January when the first returns were being delivered, John of Gaunt had signed a peace treaty with Scotland without the need for war. In France, Thomas of Woodstock had been forced to lift the siege of Nantes and disband his army. Many were returning home, significantly a large number to Essex, where Woodstock held lands by right of his wife, Eleanor de Bohun. These soldiers could doubtless offer stories of abject failure, but also of the end of the campaign that meant finance for war was no longer needed. The only project still alive was John of Gaunt's planned expedition to Portugal for his own end. That was strictly beyond the uses permitted for the third Poll Tax, and the determination not only to continue collecting it but to track down these missing thousands of people only added to the suspicion the money would be diverted into Gaunt's pockets.

Those hardest hit by the third Poll Tax were the broad layer of reasonably comfortable but not quite rich people in the middle of society. Plenty owned land and businesses that brought them good incomes and some local influence, but they remained far below the nobility in terms of wealth. The richest were paying far less in this Poll Tax, and the reliance on community assessment meant the poorest would pay the least, but those in the middle who made up their villages and towns were required to find the shortfall. It was, therefore, this section of society that was disproportionately hit by the third Poll Tax, and this group that would feature prominently among the rebels. Not only was this tax harsher than before, but it was also becoming the most invasive imposition in memory as re-assessors were appointed to visit door to door and double-check the assessments and counts of local officials. More than ever before, it meant strangers were intruding into private lives and spaces to make a record for the government.

The unprecedented frequency of taxation in recent years added to the disillusionment. The English might expect a fractional subsidy every few years, and between 1357 and 1371, the country had gone fourteen years with no direct taxation from parliament. The experiments of the 1370s were seen as the failures of government and Edward III's sons as their father faded from public life. Since Richard II had come to the throne and a continual council had ruled, heavily influenced by his uncles, there had been non-stop impositions. Between 1377 and 1381, there had been five rounds of taxation in four years. Parliament had granted three and a half subsidies and three Poll Taxes. And it had all been for nothing. War taxes were considered an investment and were paid to obtain the returns in plunder, ransoms, increased trade, expansion of power, and glory it could bring. Five sets of taxation had been squandered on failure after failure, and the demands continued as the fiascos mounted. All of this; a shattered church, the legacy of a pandemic, oppression of the people to deny market forces, arbitrary, ill-thought-out tax experiments, military failures, and now intrusive investigations, all came together in the summer of 1381 to ignite a tinder box of anger and resentment, but also hopes and demands for a better future.

Warnings had gone unheeded as isolated outbreaks of rioting cropped up in Winchester, Salisbury, Shrewsbury, and York before the summer. The first recorded act of violence in the build-up to broader troubles took place in Oxfordshire, away from the centre of the revolt. William Payable was working for the dean of Bicester, collecting tax monies due from the local clergy. William was beaten almost to death, and amid a growing belief those he was scheduled to visit had arranged his assault, the unknown attackers were excommunicated.[10] The revolt proper began in Brentwood in Essex in May. The royal commissioners for the re-assessment of the Poll Tax rolled into the town to explain to those representatives of local villages and hundreds what would happen. A Thomas Baker of Fobbing stopped them and informed them that since the county had already paid its dues and held receipts to that effect, they would not be paying any more. The leader of the commission, John Bampton, ordered the arrest of Baker and a hundred others for failing to do as they were instructed. The men drew bows and weapons so that the commissioners were forced to withdraw.

They must have known both that they would get short shrift from the king's officers, and that what they had experienced at Brentwood would be repeated throughout England. It may have been this that caused all of their grievances to coalesce and the idea of unified resistance to this new intrusion to take on an irresistible appeal. A meeting of those willing to join an uprising was scheduled for Sunday 2 June 1381. The date was not selected by accident. It was Whitsunday, and feast days were commonly used to co-ordinate anything since the religious calendar was more widely observed than simple dates. Whitsunday was also the festival of Pentecost which marked the beginning of the Christian mission when the Holy Spirit had descended on the disciples. Given that a significant number of the grievances were against the church as a landlord and a keeper of villeins that supported the Statute of Labourers, those meeting at Bocking may have added a spiritual dimension to their cause deliberately.

On 4 June there was trouble at Dartford in Kent. Abel Kerr had led a small band from Essex to recruit and spread the word just across the Thames estuary in Kent. During the days that followed, an example of the type of person pursued by the rebels is provided by Nicholas Heryng. Heryng was a justice of the peace and steward of the king's lands in Kent. His house in Dartford was ransacked on 5 June with goods worth £100 removed. Three days later on 8 June, his homes in North Cray and Foots Cray were targeted and a further £666 worth of chattels stolen. The next day his property in Rochester was attacked. At each location, the rebels stole Heryng's property, but they also seized his paperwork, which included records of crimes, fines, debts and appearances at manorial courts. These documents were the primary focus of the rebels in the counties. They were used to keep the people oppressed by recording their status as villeins as well as the times their appeals against such things had been successful, only to be overturned by a landlord seeking to enforce non-existent rights. William Topdyne, another justice of the peace and the steward of the archbishop of Canterbury's library in Kent, was another similarly targeted. On 9 June, Trinity Sunday, a large public bonfire was held in Rochester where all these documents and records were burned, permanently erasing them from history.

Jean Froissart, a chronicler from Hainult who had connections in England, understood why these people rose up.

> There was a usage in England, and yet is in divers countries, that the noblemen hath great franchise over the commons, and keep them in servitude, that is to say, their tenants ought by custom to labour the lords' lands, to gather and bring home their corn, and some to thresh and to fan, and by servitude to make their hay and to hew their wood and bring it home. Thus the noblemen and prelates are served by them, and specially in the county of Kent, Essex, Sussex, and Bedford.[11]

The focus of their grievance was, Froissart believed, the unfairness of this system and a burning desire to break from it. 'They said they were formed to the similitude of their lords, saying why should they then be kept so under like beasts,' adding that 'if they laboured or did anything for their lords, they should have wages therefore.'[12] Several men became figureheads during these early days, including Thomas ate Raven in Kent and Robert Cave of Dartford. Cave was associated with another incident that was cited as the spark for the revolt. The *Anonimale* tells the tale of Robert Bellyng, who fled to Gravesend. Many villeins tried to escape into towns where they might gain their freedom, sometimes merely by going unchallenged for a year and day. On 3 June, Sir Simon Burley, or his representatives, rode into Gravesend and demanded Bellyng's return, since he was Burley's villein. The townspeople, who had no liking for villeinage, intervened to negotiate. £300 was the fee imposed for Bellyng's freedom, an exorbitant sum he was utterly unable to pay, and which was designed to be beyond the town's desire to help him. Bellyng was therefore arrested and thrown into prison at Rochester Castle.

Three days later on 6 June, as trouble was intensifying in Dartford, Rochester Castle was attacked, and Bellyng was set free, allegedly by Robert Cave. 'Great evil and mischief derived from this action', the *Anonimale* grumbled. Chroniclers seemed keen to find one incident that caused everything that followed. Their desire to excuse the church's involvement, since the writers were almost exclusively clerics, blinded them to the pervasive nature of discontent that meant moments like this happened simultaneously throughout the region. It also seemed beyond the chroniclers' comprehension that such people should be able to organise their efforts so effectively. It is for the purposes of neatness that three names emerged to become most closely associated with the leadership of the Great Insurrection. Two leaders were laymen appointed when 'they of Kent and of Essex made them two chieftains to rule and govern the company of Kent and of Essex'.[14] These men were Wat Tyler and Jack Straw. The former is prominent in records of the revolt, but the latter is much more elusive. Jack Straw's name appears in the list of four rebel leaders compiled two years later, but he is otherwise hard to pin down. Wat Tyler was credited with leading the Kentish rebels and Jack Straw those in Essex, and their prominence perhaps owes as much to the government's desire to narrow the apparent causes of the revolt from widespread social resentment to a few troublemakers.

The most unconvincing rebel leader associated with the events of 1381 is the third famous name: John Ball. Although he was a real person, with a long and chequered history, there is little to link Ball to the revolt, and even less to suggest he gave his famous sermon at Blackheath. As early as 1364, Ball had been noted as a heretic, wandering Essex preaching against the wealth of the church. He had been excommunicated in that year by the bishop of London, a significant property owner in Essex. The holder of that position in 1364 happened to be Simon Sudbury, who became Archbishop of Canterbury in 1375. Escalating what seems to have become a personal feud, Sudbury excommunicated Ball again at Canterbury. As late as 29 April 1381, the sentence had been repeated and a warrant issued for Ball's arrest, accusing him of preaching sermons that 'reeked of heretical depravity'.[15] Having evaded Sudbury's efforts to detain him for years, Ball was arrested quickly this time and imprisoned at Bishop's Stortford in Essex. His preaching seems to have chimed with some of the rebels' objectives and complaints. Ball was wont to give public sermons in churchyards on Sundays, insisting 'We all be come from one father and one mother, Adam and Eve: whereby can they say or show that they be greater lords than we be, saving by what they cause us to win and labour for what they dispense?' Another goal in common with the rebels was the belief they should call on King Richard as their champion. 'Let us go to the king, he is young, and show him what servage we be in, and show him how we will have it otherwise, or else we will provide us of some remedy.'[16] Although he would reappear later in the summer, there is no evidence to tie him to events in London.

It was on 10 June that Wat Tyler firmly emerged as a leader of the rebels in Kent. Whether he was a former soldier in France or his name obscured some other origin, he seemed to possess a gift for inspiring, organising, and leading men. Tyler was at the head of a large contingent of rebels welcomed into Canterbury on Monday 10 June. As the county's capital, the focus for its government, and the seat of the archbishop of Canterbury, who was also the chancellor, it was an obvious local target. If there was already a plan to take their complaints to London, and the rebels seem from the outset to have wished to get their grievances before the young king, then dealing with Canterbury made sense. If the county were to be mobilised against the rebels, efforts would originate from Canterbury that might catch the rebels up and pin them between London and Kent. On arrival, the insurgents captured Willaim Septvans, Sheriff of Kent, and forced him to hand over all of his documents. They particularly targeted estreat rolls, the record of outstanding fines kept by the sheriff. Canterbury's prison was also broken open, and everyone within set free. The rebels entered the cathedral and forced their way into the archbishop's chambers. '"Ah, this Chancellor of England has had a good market to get together all these riches," the astonished rebels proclaimed. "He shall give us now account of the revenues of England and of the great profits that he hath gathered since the king's coronation."' [17] The sight of the archbishop's riches may have increased the suspicion of corruption and certainly intensified feelings of inequity.

On the same day, 10 June, the real revolt began in Essex, suggesting once more a sophisticated level of coordination. The focal point initially was Bocking and a few miles south-east of the village, Cressing Temple was targeted. The complex was a preceptory of the Knights Hospitaller. Like Canterbury, there were a number of reasons for selecting this site. The Hospitallers were local landlords, and Cressing Temple held their manorial court records, so frequently used to impose villeinage on tenants and deny them freedom or the chance to better themselves. That meant there were documents to burn. Alongside this, the prior of the Knights Hospitaller in England was Sir Robert Hales, a long-standing royal advisor who had become treasurer when Richard II had been declared of age to govern. This meant that Hales was intimately associated not only with the financial corruption the rebels insisted proliferated the kingdom, but also the tax regime. Some of this was unfair, given that he had only taken office some eighteen months earlier, but it was long enough for him to be held responsible. Aside from anything else, Hales had been behind the appointment of commissioners for the re-assessment of the third Poll Tax. That was enough to attract the attention of the rebels. Cressing Temple was looted, and its records put to the flame.

The mob then moved on to Coggleshall, perhaps under the leadership of Jack Straw, though this is far from certain. Essex shared a sheriff and an escheator with Hertfordshire, the two counties frequently lumped together for administrative purposes. The escheator, John Ewell, was chased down, cornered and beheaded. On 11 June, the Essex contingent was at Chelmsford for a bonfire of records. It was just one day later, and only two days after Tyler's arrival in Canterbury, that the two groups appeared outside London. The Essex rebels gathered to the north of the city, and the Kentish men rallied at Blackheath, a large, open space just to the south. It was only ten days since Whitsunday when the revolt proper had begun, and thousands of rebels were already at London's gates looking for redress. It is here that John Ball is supposed to have given his famous address in which he asked 'When Adam delved, and Eve span, Who was then a gentleman?' The phrase highlighted the common argument that the Bible did not set out social structures like lordship and villeinage, so they should not exist.[18] The sermon may be apocryphal, and no contemporary legal source places Ball at Blackheath at all. If he was with the rebels, he was far more likely to have been with the Essex contingent to the north, but he is not noted there either. Whatever the truth, Ball's name may have been added to provide a touch of colour from a known heretical, but popular, preacher. It would serve to add the taint of heresy and wrong-thinking to the revolt, particularly as it moved towards a murder all clerics deemed horrific as Simon Sudbury, Archbishop of Canterbury came into the rebels' sights.

On the same day they arrived at Blackheath, 12 June, the Kentish force sent Sir John Newenton to the Tower of London. Sir John had been the constable of Rochester Castle, and the ease with which the fortress had been taken may be explained by his assertion that the rebels had taken his children hostage and threatened their lives.[19] Sir John was known to the king and gained access to the Tower. The royal party lodged there were likely to have been keen for news of what was happening. Only once they understood this mob's aims could they work out how to deal with them. With the 14-year-old king were his mother the princess of Wales, his two half-brothers, the earls of Salisbury, Warwick, and Oxford, the archbishop of Canterbury, the mayor of London, and others. Two of Froissart's associates were also within the Tower, so he is likely to have had good intelligence of what happened. Sir John explained to the king that the commons wished only to speak with him, 'to show him how all they had done or would do was for him and his honour, and how the realm of England had not been well governed a great space for the honour of the realm nor for the common profit, by his uncles and by the clergy, and specially by the archbishop of Canterbury'.[20] The knight seems to have been able to explain his loss of Rochester Castle without resistance, perhaps with the news that his children were still hostages for his return to Blackheath.

With an assurance from Sir John that he believed the rebels' insistence that they meant the king no harm, and that 'they hold and will hold you for their king',[21] Richard agreed to speak with them. On the following day, 13 June, those wishing to address the king should gather at Rotherhithe. This spot was about halfway between the Tower and Blackheath, as close to neutral territory as was available. Sir John took the news back to Blackheath, doubtless relieved to be able to return with goodtidings. On Thursday 13 June, Richard was rowed along the Thames in his royal barge, his entourage taking up a further four boats. Precisely what Richard and his advisors had expected in unclear, but they were disconcerted to find themselves confronted by some 10,000 men raucously awaiting his arrival. If they had been under the impression this was to be a small meeting with a handful of leaders, they were quickly disabused of the notion. The rebels called on the king to land and speak with them, but the king's advisors refused to permit it, fearing for Richard's safety. The earl of Salisbury ordered the barges to be rowed back to the Tower immediately.[22] Feeling betrayed and robbed of their chance to petition their king by the very advisors they believed were the root of corruption, the mob unleashed a frenzy of violence.

The rebels crossed London Bridge unopposed. Plenty within London immediately joined their cause, sharing many of their grievances. London was a favourite place for villeins looking to escape bondage to abscond to since it offered not only more prospects but also a greater chance of evading notice for the prescribed year and a day among the crowds. Goldsmiths and innkeepers joined weavers and cobblers in a demonstration of the appeal of the revolt's aims across demographics. As they passed through Southwark on the south bank of the Thames, the rebels broke into the prisons there, the Marshalsea and King's Bench, and freed anyone held within. As they went, they also targeted the houses of 'advocates and men of the court', searching out legal records that they might wish to destroy.[23] With London before them, it is striking that the rebels continued to limit their targets, though the willingness with which Londoners joined them perhaps aided in this. They made straight for the symbol of the power of the man they despised the most.

The Savoy Palace lay along a bend in the Thames on the Strand, a desirable location perfectly placed for access to the city and the government at Westminster. The Savoy took its name from Henry III's grant of the property to his wife's uncle Peter, Count of Savoy. Now owned by Gaunt, it was the most magnificent noble residence in England, packed with tapestries, gold, and jewels that screamed its owner's vast wealth to the city. Given that he was primarily blamed for government corruption and mismanagement, foreign policy and military disasters, Gaunt's house was a beacon to the rebels. Some accounts describe the thefts from the Savoy,[24] but Henry Knighton, a monk in Leicester who knew some of Gaunt's household, told a different story. He claimed that nothing was stolen from the palace at all. The place was set on fire with all the duke's riches inside. His tapestries, his clothes, and his furniture were consumed by the flames. All the gold, silver and jewels they found which would not burn was smashed up and thrown into the Thames, causing thousands of pounds of losses to Gaunt. One man caught trying to steal something was thrown back into the flames as the rebels insisted they were not common thieves. Over thirty men were reportedly trapped in Gaunt's wine cellar by the collapse of the burning building above them. It was claimed that their desperate pleas for help were audible among the smouldering wreckage for a week before they finally died.[25]

The truth of this episode can only be guessed at. The revolt in the counties had seen goods taken from local officials, so either the rebels changed their stance to reassure Londoners and the king of their intentions, or Knighton heard an incorrect version of events. The magnificent Savoy Palace was utterly consumed by the fire the rebels set. The destruction was so entire that it was never rebuilt. Gaunt, perhaps not wishing to risk rubbing London's nose in his continuing wealth, left it as it was. The Savoy Palace stood as a blackened reminder of the chilling events of the Great Insurrection for years to come. Although Gaunt took a financial hit from the episode, his written records, as one of England's greatest magnates, were also a target for the rebels. Not yet sated, the crowds made their way to their next target. After their attack on Cressing Temple the selection of Clerkenwell, the London headquarters of the Knights Hospitaller, was not a surprise. The buildings there were burned so completely they smouldered for seven days. Some rebels were accused of going into the church of St Martin's le Grand and forcibly removing those in the sanctuary to kill them.[26]

The violence continued as lawyers were sought out next. The rebels 'came to the Temple, and to all other inns of men of law, and despoiled them and robbed them of their goods, and also their books of law; and they came to London and broke up the prison of Newgate, and drove out all the prisoners, felons, and others of both counties, and all the people that were within them, and destroyed all the books of both counties'.[27] The billowing black smoke from so many great fires must have been visible all across London, and the royal party within the Tower became increasingly nervous as numbers of the angry mob gathered at St Katherine's just outside the fortress's walls. 'Thus,' Froissart complained, 'these ungracious people demeaned themselves like people enraged and mad, and so that day they did much sorrow in London.'[28] It was now that the decision was made to agree to a meeting with the rebels again. What is unclear is whether the choice was Richard's, or one taken by his advisors. The latter seems unlikely given their cautious response to the mob at Rotherhithe. Salisbury's decision to leave had inflamed the crowds and driven widespread attacks so that putting the 14-year-old king on a plate before them was not a risk they were likely to wish to take. The Tower could withstand such a poorly armed horde indefinitely, so it may well have been Richard that determined to meet his people face to face and understand their complaints.

Precisely what happened next, and in what order, is frustratingly unclear and the chroniclers only add to the muddle. Richard offered to meet the rebels at Mile End on Friday 14 June, doubtless hoping to stop the chaos and to draw all the rioters back together. The *Anonimale* describes the crowd kneeling before Richard and reiterating that 'we will not have any other king but you'. Wat Tyler stepped forward as the rebels' leader and explained to Richard that they wished the men they suspected of being traitors around him to be arrested and dealt with. Richard agreed, so long as due process was followed, and the accused had fair trials. The more contentious and far-reaching demand was that 'henceforward no man should be a serf nor make homage or any type of service to any lord, but should give four pence for an acre of land. They asked also that no one should serve any man except at his own will and by means of regular covenant.'[29] Froissart has Richard ride among the people at Mile End asking, '"Ah, ye good people, I am your king: what lack ye? what will ye say?", to which the crowd replied "We will that ye make us free for ever, ourselves, our heirs, and our lands, and that we be called no more bond nor so reputed."'[30]

Richard agreed to the rebels' demand to abolish serfdom and villein tenure. They must have expected some resistance or negotiation, but the king simply told them to return home, and it would be done. Two or three people from each community were to remain behind to await the letters patent the king would provide, and several of the king's banners were given to groups to take away to demonstrate their victory. A group of clerks were immediately set to work producing the letters patent under the Great Seal, which Richard had in his possession because Simon Sudbury had resigned as chancellor just before the king had left the Tower. Oddly, there was no mention anywhere of the Statute of Labourers or the third Poll Tax, two of the central issues that had sparked the revolt. The wind had, perhaps, been sucked from their sails by the king's enthusiastic agreement to their first and more revolutionary request. Those speaking for the crowd, whether Wat Tyler or others, may have feared asking any more and risking what they had already won against the odds.

Amid all this, the Tower of London was breached. Froissart reported that the mob at St Katherine's waited for the king to leave and slipped through the gate. He places Wat Tyler, Jack Straw, and John Ball in this group of around 400. They poured through the Tower's outer walls toward the White Tower, accessed by a steep staircase as it still is today. Crashing through the rooms, they hunted down their prey, who must have grown increasingly fearful as the commotion grew ever closer. Simon Sudbury, Archbishop of Canterbury, along with Sir Robert Hales of the Knights Hospitaller, and a friar who provided medical services to John of Gaunt were all dragged out to Tower Hill and beheaded. John Legge, a sergeant-at-arms to the king, and a lawyer named Richard Somenour of Stepney were also executed, their otherwise obscure selection suggesting some local hatred of them personally. One person who escaped was Henry of Bollingbroke, the oldest son and heir of John of Gaunt. The same age as his cousin the king, the 14-year-old may have been a target of the hatred his father engendered, but he was either hidden or protected by his age. The heads of those less fortunate were put on spikes on London Bridge as traitors.[31] A more plausible explanation than Froissart's of the rebels' easy access to the Tower and their unopposed executions of two of the most prominent figures of both government and church in England is that they undertook it with the king's approval.

It is unlikely that Richard directly authorised the killings of Sudbury and Hales, but if a group from Mile End, perhaps including Tyler and Straw, arrived with letters patent from the king, sealed with his Great Seal, none would stand in their way. If they marched with the king's banners before them, it would only reinforce their apparent authority. The rebels could legitimately believe the king had given them the power to deal with those they considered traitors, though if Richard added the caveat of giving them a fair trial, it was ignored. This scenario would explain how they were able to get into the Tower so quickly, seize two prominent figures and execute them without being challenged. It also allows for Wat Tyler to be at Mile End and at the Tower, which chroniclers are otherwise unable to reconcile if the events took place simultaneously. It is even possible that some of the wealthier Londoners among the crowd were familiar to the Tower's guards and so were able to smooth their entry. The correct sequence of events is impossible to prove but is vital in distinguishing continuing unlawful violent murders from executions carried out with the sanction of the king. The only thing that was certain was that it was not over yet.

Flemish weavers were targeted and brutally attacked, many murdered by Londoners who despised their presence in a ghetto in the city. A significant number of the rebels had not gone home after the meeting at Mile End, and their continuing presence caused Richard to offer to meet them again on Saturday 15 June at Smithfield. Buoyed by his easy success the previous day, and by the affection and deference the crowd had shown him, the king sought to complete the work by calming the remaining mob. Reports of precisely what happened are again frustratingly muddled. Froissart thought Richard happened to be out riding when he noticed a large number of men gathered at Smithfield. This scenario seems unlikely, given that trouble was still gripping the capital. It is usually asserted that Wat Tyler addressed the king, perhaps again if he had done so at Mile End, but Jack Straw takes on the role in other accounts.[32]

The course of the meeting seems to have been similar to that at Mile End, with Richard demanding to know what they still wanted that prevented them from returning home. Tyler (if it was him) asked for more concessions, perhaps regrouping from the shock of the previous day to deliver the rest of the rebels' agenda that had not been put to the king. They asked for the abolition of monopolies on hunting and asked that there should be no law but that of Winchester. The most likely aim of this latter demand was to restructure local society, where the corruption that gnawed at daily life had been a key driver for rebellion. The Statute of Winchester, issued by Edward I in 1285, had made local communities responsible for policing themselves. Any crime committed within a hundred was to be solved by the residents, and the perpetrator handed over for trial, or the community would pay a fine for their failure to find or expose the criminal. What the rebels wanted was a return to less interference from central government, which necessarily meant strangers invasively involving themselves in the community's business. There was possibly a desire wrapped within this to repeal the Statute of Labourers by insisting on a return to a time before it existed.

The rebels also spoke of reforming the church, complaining of absentee priests receiving tithes and cruel landlords. Richard cautiously offered to do what he could to meet these new demands. He must have been aware that things were in danger of getting out of hand. Would there be a new list tomorrow, and the day after? Had these people taken for granted the good grace he had shown them the day before, and in so doing, deprived the young king of his victory? The sources agree that there was then a scuffle, though the cause is less clear. Whether Tyler spoke too familiarly to the king, or grabbed his horse's reins, or threatened violence, a fight broke out. The mayor, William Walworth struck Tyler with his dagger and dragged him from his horse as a royal esquire named Ralph Standish drew his sword and ran Tyler through, killing him. It is at this point that Richard displayed great personal bravery. As the crowd noticed Tyler had been killed and grew agitated, the king spurred his horse forward and rode to them. His entourage must have been stunned as they tried to calculate how this could end well. Richard tried to calm the mob around him, saying, 'Sirs, what aileth you? Ye shall have no captain but me: I am your king: be all in rest and peace.' Shocked to be addressed by the king, the rebels fell silent and took the instruction to return home.[35] Whether Tyler's fate made them wary of pressing matters further and losing all, or they genuinely believed the young king was sincere, they dispersed and returned to their homes.

Just over a fortnight later, Chief Justice Robert Treselian oversaw the king's withdrawal of the letters patent he had granted at Mile End. Some may have been collected from the rebels at Smithfield before they were allowed to leave, but in early July, they were all revoked. In the days after Mile End, those who returned to the countryside carrying the king's letters and displaying his banners carried on their work. Essex saw continued moves against stores of records, including at the archbishop of Canterbury's manor of Tring. There was trouble in St Albans, Cambridge, Norwich, and Bury St Edmonds. It is striking how much was aimed at rich local abbeys and priories which were considered some of the worst landlords for imposing villeinage and villein tenure. Records were burned, and officials deemed corrupt were killed. Long-running legal battles over the status of tenancies and petty feuds over money were likewise pursued to a settlement.

Many rebels were hunted down and prosecuted, sued for their thefts and damage, or executed as traitors. John Ball was tried before the chief justice at St Albans before being executed and his body quartered. There is no real evidence he ever went to London as part of the revolt. He may have remained active in the counties, rallying and organising, but he may just as likely have been made a scapegoat. A convicted heretic with a long history of opposition to the murdered archbishop of Canterbury, his enrolment in the list of chief rebels allowed the uprising to be brushed with the stench of heresy. It warned against listening to critics of the church and made speaking out in favour of the insurrection a whisker away from promulgating Ball's heresy. The delay between the issue of letters patent and their withdrawal meant that those convicted of crimes, including treason, had acted with the king's permission. The reversal of a document given by the king using his Great Seal was highly unusual and verged on dishonourable behaviour on the part of the teenager. Richard's part in the events of June 1381 has often been seen as both personally brave and politically cynical, pacifying and dispersing the mob by pretending to be their champion only to hunt them down once the immediate danger to London was over. There is a hint, though, that he was more genuine and became a victim of those too powerful to accept change, just as his subjects did.

When parliament met in November 1381, the events of the summer were naturally high on the agenda. On Wednesday 13 November, the new treasurer, Sir Hugh Seagrave, delivered an opening speech that outlined the government's desire to understand why the Great Insurrection had happened. Richard's actions were neatly explained away: 'it is not unknown to you indeed that our lord the king, during the said troubles, was constrained to make and grant letters of franchise and manumission under his great seal to the villeins of his kingdom and others, knowing full well that he should not do so in good faith and according to the law of the land, but that he did for the best, to stop and put an end to their clamour and malice, for he did not then enjoy his rightful power as king.' Richard is essentially patted on the head for well-meant naivety. The address went on to ask an interesting question. 'And now the king wishes to know the will of you, my lords, prelates, lords and commons here present, and whether it seems to you that he acted well in that repeal and pleased you, or not. For he says that if you wish to enfranchise and make free the said villeins by your common agreement, as he has been informed some of you wish to do, he will assent to your request.' The clear implication is that Richard had heard rumblings that the manumission should be upheld, either to avoid breaching his word or to avert a repeat of the uprising. Rather than anger at his actions being questioned, Richard asked for their agreed opinion, making it clear he would uphold the grant of freedom if parliament wished it.

The members of parliament were sent away to discuss their answer. When they returned on Monday 18 November, the speaker Sir Richard Walgrave begged the king to excuse him the office, but Richard demanded that he continue. No decision had been reached, Walgrave admitted, asking for a discussion in session on the matter. With a sudden unity, parliament concluded 'with one voice, that the repeal was well made'. The assembly added that 'such a manumission or enfranchisement of the villeins could not be made without the assent of those who had the chief interest in the matter: and they had never agreed to it, either voluntarily or otherwise, nor would they ever do so, even if it were their dying day'.[36] The repeal was upheld, and Richard was chastised for making such a significant decision without consulting parliament, which was made up of those 'who had the chief interest in the matter'. These were the very landlords against whose rights the uprising had pushed so hard, and it was they who were permitted to decide whether to lose a substantial part of their wealth.

The decision was unsurprising, but the episode throws into question the king's motives in thrusting it before an assembly clearly hesitant to offer an opinion despite claiming 'the chief interest'. It is possible that Richard, well aware of the unpopularity in the country of the repeal, and the position he was placed in by going back on his word, sought to bind parliament to the decision so that its members shared the blame too. The other explanation is that Richard held out hope he might still see the manumission of serfs implemented permanently. The king had been quick to grant the abolition of serfdom and slow to withdraw the speedily drawn up letters patent. Parliament heard that some lords believed it should stand and Richard latched onto this to ask parliament for its opinion. Either he was keen to ensure none could later claim they had opposed the repeal, or he still wanted it to happen and hoped parliament might agree with him. It would have been a paradigm shift in English society with no parallel in Europe. The creation of a free-market economy that also allowed freedom of movement within the kingdom would have radically altered the way industry, commerce, and land ownership operated and might have spread wealth far more evenly through society. Richard would have sealed his place in history, but he may also have genuinely believed it was a positive measure. For an idealistic 14-year-old king, giving his subjects what so many of them wanted so much that they rioted to the capital held strong appeal.

The rebels' continual insistence that they regarded Richard as their only lord, and that they sought to erode the layers that separated them and serve only him would have made Richard more powerful. After the Norman Conquest, William the Conqueror had radically redefined land ownership throughout England by making every landowner directly pay homage to him. Uncertainty as to who they might serve in any rebellion was washed away because anyone who held land and might have the power to make a difference was now the king's man, not that of a local lord or national magnate. What Richard offered his people in 1381 would have extended this principle to give every single person in the kingdom a direct link, and corresponding responsibility, to the crown. If Richard knew the problems that had led to the Great Insurrection had been corrupt officials and bad government at the centre, he could have discerned that these layers between him and his people were the real risk to the crown. Sweeping them away removed the problem, made the king more powerful, and ensured Richard would be celebrated for all eternity. The problem was that those men in between had enough leverage to stop it happening.

Whether because it would make them significantly poorer and less powerful or for fear of vesting too much authority in the crown after almost two centuries of wresting it away, parliament would not allow manumission. Cynicism would suggest it was an act of self-preservation, but that may be unfair to those working with a body that had slowly been accruing power that was less reliant on the personality and quality of someone born to their position. Magna Carta had been about the barons sharing the crown's power, just as the Second Barons' War had been. Edward II's reign had been one long episode of trying to compensate for a man utterly unsuited to the position at the pinnacle of society his birth had gifted him or cursed him with. Richard may have felt a genuine commitment to the abolition of serfdom and villein tenure, either because it made him more popular and more powerful, made his barons less so, or because he believed it was the right thing to do. If the king felt the cause keenly, being defeated from his course would have taken a devastating toll on the teenager.

Propelled to the throne in 1377 at the age of 10 following the death of his father then his grandfather, Richard was thrust into nominal charge of a kingdom in turmoil. His uncles only seemed to make it worse, and the continual council did such a poor job it was abolished. In 1380 parliament heard that he was ready to rule for himself because his age was 'very nearly that of his noble grandfather' at his coronation. Edward III had been 14 but had endured three years of regency because of his youth. Now, parliament wished a 13-year-old to be told he was of age to govern. When, a year later, he made his first big, independent decision, Richard was treated like a naughty child and his will undermined by the government and parliament. It must have dawned on the king that he was no more than a puppet to these people who professed to serve him and that he could do nothing about it. The confusion and frustration he felt at 14 would have left an impact as he considered that the people he ruled would hate him and mistrust him for breaking his word while the lords of his kingdom felt impervious to his regal authority. The impact could have been profound enough to affect his relationship with parliament, the nobility and his people for the rest of his reign. The events of the eighteen years that followed the Great Insurrection would suggest that this might have been the case.

Chapter 9

The Rise and Fall of the House of Lancaster

Rebels are rarely revolutionaries. Rebellion seeks to right
a specific perceived wrong, to adjust the seating plan at
the banquet, not to overturn the carefully laid table of
government.

There are moments when this is true, yet the table is overturned anyway. Richard II spent the rest of his reign desperately trying to claw free from the control of his uncles and England's nobility. By 1386, Richard had become unpopular with his barons, who felt he lavished far too much attention and money on a handful of favourites. They were oblivious to the fact that his treatment in the wake of the Great Insurrection may have made him wary of trusting them when they had so readily marginalised his opinions. If he chose instead to find people he could draw close to him by tying their fortunes to his favour, it was both a symptom of his experiences and a dangerous reminder of the way his great-grandfather, Edward II, had ruled.

The parliament that met in November 1386 became known as the Wonderful Parliament. Richard initially refused to engage with the assembly, which openly set about limiting his authority. He was only forced to cooperate when his uncle Thomas of Woodstock 'sent for the statute by which Edward [II] had been adjudged',[1] clearly threatening to depose his nephew. This marked a new and confident high in parliament's authority against that of the crown, feeling it within the assembly's remit and power to decide whether the king was fit to continue in his role. Michael de la Pole, Earl of Suffolk, Richard's chosen chancellor, bore the brunt of parliament's wrath at the king's style of government but escaped severe punishment. A Commission of Government was established, against the wishes of the furious 19-year-old king. Fourteen lords, only one or two of whom were sympathetic to Richard, were to be given full authority to govern the kingdom and to control expenditure for a year. The grant of taxation approved by the session was made conditional on this body taking and retaining control.

Richard protested vehemently at the imposition. His response insisted it could only last for a year, against calls it should remain in place until the next time parliament met, and that he be allowed to appoint his own steward. The final item on the parliament rolls before the session was closed was another reiteration of the king's displeasure, this time made by Richard himself. The king 'made open protest by his own mouth that he willed that nothing done in the said parliament should harm him or his crown; and that his prerogative and the liberties of his said crown should be saved and kept'.[2] He must have felt under assault. As the Commission established itself, the king and his household left London for the Midlands, remaining there for the term of the Commissioners' power. Richard consulted judges in an effort to understand the legality of what had been done to him against his will, and they suggested parliament lacked the authority to behave as it had. Once he returned to the capital in November 1387, Richard tried to gather support but found little. Seeing the way the wind was blowing, two of his favourites, Michael de la Pole, Earl of Suffolk, and Alexander Neville, Archbishop of York, fled abroad. Robert de Vere, created Duke of Ireland by the king, raised an army in Cheshire, but found himself faced by the joined forces of the king's uncle Thomas and the earls of Arundel, Warwick, Nottingham, and Derby. The latter was Henry Bollingbroke, Richard's first cousin and the son and heir of John of Gaunt who had survived the assault on the Tower in 1381.

The two sides clashed at the Battle of Radcot Bridge, a bridge over the River Thames in Oxfordshire, on 20 December 1387. The royal army led by de Vere's was crushed. He fled into exile abroad as his victorious opponents made for London. Richard had summoned parliament to open in February 1388, hoping to correct the injustice done to him and to punish those responsible. When the session opened, the king was not in control. The chronicler Henry Knighton would dub this session the Merciless Parliament, as the lords who had opposed de Vere at Radcot Bridge came to the fore. They presented a document known as the Appeal of Treason, which accused most of the king's household and his favourites of treason. These magnates; Thomas, Duke of Gloucester, along with Arundel, Warwick, Nottingham, and Derby became known as the Lords Appellant on account of this Appeal. There were disturbing parallels to the Lords Ordainer who had sought to restrain Edward II. Three of Richard's favourites were beyond parliament's reach on the Continent. Those who could be tried, including the judges who had responded to Richard's questions about the legality of the Wonderful Parliament, were rounded up, convicted of treason, and eight were executed. A further seven were sent into exile to join the three already out of the kingdom.[3] The Lords Appellant were firmly in the ascendant.

The remainder of Richard's reign proved difficult. Throughout the 1390s he made efforts to assert his authority while accepting some degree of conciliar government was necessary. He had not forgotten the slight to his majesty done by the Lords Appellant, though. When the moment came, he saw to it that they paid for what they had done. In 1397, Richard struck. Thomas Beauchamp, Earl of Warwick, was seized and accused of treason. He pleaded guilty, perhaps saving his life. He forfeited all his lands and titles and was sentenced to life imprisonment. Richard Fitzalan, Earl of Arundel was arrested in July 1397, tried and convicted of treason, and beheaded on 21 September. Parliament also tried the king's uncle Thomas of Woodstock, Duke of Gloucester. He was found guilty of acts 'prejudicial to the king and his crown and a usurpation of his regality and royal power'.[4] Sent to Calais as a prisoner, Thomas was killed in early September 1397 amid speculation that the king had ordered his uncle's murder.

Thomas Mowbray, Earl of Nottingham, had rebuilt his relationship with the king, a parliament would hear in 1399 that he had been tasked with ensuring the death of Thomas of Woodstock. A William Rickhill received instructions to go to Calais 'in the company of our dearest kinsman Thomas, earl marshal and earl of Nottingham, the captain of the aforesaid town, and there that you do and perform each and every thing which is enjoined on you by the aforesaid earl on our behalf'.[5] The accusation was that this commission required the murder of Thomas, and it is perhaps no coincidence that before the end of September 1397, Mowbray had been created Duke of Norfolk. The other Lord Appellant, Henry Bollingbroke, also reconstructed his relationship with the king, perhaps protected by the looming presence of his father John of Gaunt.

In 1398, Richard found a way to deal with the remaining two Lords Appellant. A dispute broke out between Mowbray and Bollingbroke that provided the perfect solution to Richard's desire for vengeance. Mowbray accused Bollingbroke before the king of having 'thought evil and spoken otherwise than ye ought against your natural lord the king of England, when ye said that he was not worthy to hold land or realm'. Mowbray challenged his foe to a duel to 'prove with my body against yours that ye are an evil, false traitor'. Bollingbroke responded by asserting that it was Mowbray, not he, who was the traitor, accepting his challenge to prove the matter in combat. The two met at Eltham Palace on Monday 29 April 1398, the spectacle to be watched by the king and the gathered, fascinated nobility. Just as the duel was about to begin, King Richard sent word that he had changed his mind. There would be no trial by combat. Instead, he had decided Mowbray would be exiled from England for life and Bollingbroke for ten years.[6] With that,

Richard's revenge was complete.[7] Mowbray died of the plague in Venice on 22 September 1399, but Bollingbroke was not done yet.

John of Gaunt, Duke of Lancaster, died on 3 February 1399 aged 58. He was the wealthiest and most powerful man in England after his nephew the king and had accrued a great deal of resentment for what many saw as his malign and selfish influence on government in Richard's younger years. With his son and heir Bollingbroke in exile, Richard spied an opportunity to enhance his position even further after his long-awaited defeat of the Lords Appellant. The king took the vast inheritance of his uncle into royal hands. Although Froissart believed the archbishop of Canterbury had already travelled to Bollingbroke in exile to encourage him to depose Richard,[8] it is more likely that the king's policy was the catalyst for what followed. Oblivious to any trouble, Richard travelled to Ireland, leaving his last surviving uncle Edmund of Langley, Duke of York as Lieutenant of England in his absence. His trip was successful, with Irish lords submitting quickly so that 'he conquered the most part of Ireland in a little time'.[9]

Once his back was turned, Henry Bollingbroke landed at Ravenspur in Yorkshire. He claimed he had returned to claim his duchy of Lancaster and the inheritance that was rightfully his from his father.[10] Whether he had been in communication with Richard's enemies in England is unclear, but almost as soon as he arrived, he realised the country was ripe for change. The north of England may have been selected to allow time, while he travelled south, for his plan to take form depending on how he was received. Bollingbroke met little resistance as he travelled south and Edmund, Duke of York, saw little option but to allow matters to take their course. Richard heard that his cousin had returned to England and was making his way to the capital and immediately sailed from Ireland to Wales. At Conway on 12 August, Henry Percy, Earl of Northumberland, met with the king,[11] and a week later at Flint Castle, it was Northumberland's brother Thomas, Earl of Worcester, who sent away the king's household.[12] Richard, left with little option, surrendered himself to Bollingbroke. He may have seen it as just another episode during which a council of some kind would be forced upon him. A repeat of history that he would endure until it could be undone. Froissart reported a story that Richard had a greyhound named Math who accompanied the king everywhere and would always run to Richard when released. When the king met his cousin, Math supposedly left the king's side and made a fuss of Bollingbroke instead.[13]

Richard was taken to London and installed at the Tower. He resigned his kingdom to his cousin, though how willingly he did so is unclear. Froissart paints a convivial picture in which Richard reflects on all his failures and declares himself happy to be rid of the burden of ruling.[14] If Richard appeared willing, it can only have been because he saw no other option and felt his honour would be better preserved, and his life saved, by appearing to make the choice himself. When parliament opened at Westminster on 6 October 1399, it was to manage the transfer of royal authority from King Richard II to his cousin, King Henry IV, the first monarch of the House of Lancaster. A document was produced by which Richard absolved anyone who had sworn loyalty to him of their fealty. He added 'verbally to the aforesaid renunciation and cession, that if it was in his power, the said duke of Lancaster should succeed him in the realm'.[15] A long list of Richard's mismanagement of the kingdom was rehearsed to demonstrate his unsuitability to continue as king, and commissioners were appointed to depose him. Those gathered perhaps looked to the precedent of 1327 when parliament had removed Edward II as king, and it was ominous that Lord Berkeley was among the commissioners.[16]

The throne of England then being declared vacant, Henry set out his claim. He told parliament, '"In the name of the Father, Son, and Holy Ghost, I, Henry of Lancaster claim this realm of England, and the crown with all its members and its appurtenances, inasmuch as I am descended by right line of the blood from the good lord King Henry the third, and through that right that God in his grace has sent me, with the help of my kin and of my friends in recovering it; which realm was at the point of ruin for lack of governance and destruction of the good laws.'"[17] When the archbishop of Canterbury preached a sermon, it was no accident that his theme was lifted from Kings 9. He told the assembly 'no longer, as was the case before, will boys rule in the realm, but the lord says to you that "a man will rule the people"'.[18] Henry was not Richard's heir. The king had remained childless, and so there was room to debate who should succeed him. Henry's case rested on the fact that just before his death, Edward III had settled the crown in the male line, placing John of Gaunt and his heirs in line after Richard. The legality of this measure was wide open to debate, and the will of a deceased king rarely held sway in the face of the law. Many considered the Mortimer family to be Richard's heirs. The grandson of Roger Mortimer, 1st Earl of March who had acted as regent to Edward III had restored the family to favour to such an extent that his son Edmund had married a granddaughter of Edward III. Philippa was the only child of Lionel of Antwerp, Duke of Clarence, the second son of Edward III. Edmund and Philippa's son Roger was the 4th Earl of March and had served Richard in Ireland before dying there in 1398. Roger left behind two sons, Edmund and Roger, both under

8 years old in 1399. The archbishop's sermon was squarely aimed at negating their potential support and reminding the kingdom of the perils of minority rule.

There was no bar to female rule in England, and Edward III had based his claim to the throne of France on his mother's transmission of the right from his grandfather. In 1399, few were willing to take up the mantle of two small boys against the duke of Lancaster, who had the wind in his sails, but that would not be the end of the Mortimer name, for it would haunt Lancastrian rule of the next sixty years. Richard's single biggest mistake had been to tamper with the laws of inheritance. His cousin Bollingbroke had not been attainted or deprived of his lands and titles when he had been sent into exile. Henry, therefore, had every right to expect to inherit from his father. Whether Richard feared making his cousin so powerful, or simply wanted to bring the vast wealth of the duke of Lancaster under royal control matters less than his lack of justification to act the way he did. In inserting the crown between a deceased magnate and his heir, Richard made anyone in the kingdom with property and titles to leave to their heir nervous. Unfortunately for the king, that meant everyone with power and wealth. This final act alienated anyone who might have felt a lingering affection for or loyalty to Richard.

Henry IV of England was crowned at Westminster Abbey on 13 October 1399. There had been little in the way of rebellion in the immediate leadup to Richard's deposition. Like Edward II, his entire rule had seen a power struggle with ascendancy swinging back and forth from a king who believed in his divine right and a body politic, particularly in parliament, who sought to correct perceived defects. Henry would find his reign dogged by threats that were the natural consequence of his usurpation of the throne. In Wales, Owain Glyndŵr proclaimed himself Prince of Wales and sought support from France and the schismatic pope at Avignon for an independent Wales. Edmund and Roger Mortimer were abducted, and an attempt made to take them to Wales, where Edmund would be declared king in Henry's place.

Although the boys were quickly recovered, the Percy family, disillusioned with their lot under Lancastrian rule, had joined the scheme. They united with Glyndŵr in a plan that would divide the kingdom in three, with Glyndŵr in Wales, the Percy family controlling the north, and Edmund Mortimer ruling the rest of England. Henry faced the Percy family at the Battle of Shrewsbury on 21 July 1403 where the royal army was victorious. Henry's 16-year-old son and heir Prince Henry was seriously wounded, struck by an arrow in his cheek that had to be very carefully removed. The earl of Northumberland's son and heir Henry Percy, known as 'Hotspur' was killed in the fighting and Thomas Percy, Earl of Worcester, was captured and executed two days after the battle. Henry IV's later years were marked by illness from 1405 onwards. He may have suffered from leprosy or psoriasis, eventually succumbing on 20 March 1413 aged 45.

The second Lancastrian king, Henry V, the man who had been wounded at the Battle of Shrewsbury, succeeded his father aged 26. Recognising the persistent opposition his father had faced, Henry resolved to renew the war with France as a diversion from domestic tensions. As the summer of 1415 progressed, an army gathered at Southampton ready to sail to France. On 31 July, Edmund Mortimer, the 8-year-old overlooked in 1399, who was now the 23-year-old 5th Earl of March, approached the king with disturbing news. Richard of Conisbrough, Earl of Cambridge, the younger son of Edmund, Duke of York, along with Henry, Lord Scrope of Masham, and a Northumberland knight named Sir Thomas Grey had concocted a plan to murder the king and his brothers and place Edmund on the throne. That Edmund was the one to expose the Southampton Plot is striking. He had spent time in Henry's household as Prince of Wales and had been given his freedom when Henry became king. The care he must have received, and the relationship fostered with Henry V, had made the unwilling claimant to the throne loyal to the Lancastrian regime. The three conspirators were executed.

Henry V departed on what was to become one of the most famous military campaigns in English history, culminating at the Battle of Agincourt on 25 October 1415. Henry wore a crown on his helm during the battle, an act that not only broadcast his location to his men and the enemy but also placed the Lancastrian right to the throne before God for judgement. The campaign had the desired effect of galvanising England behind the second Lancastrian king, focusing attention on potential glory and riches overseas instead of incessant squabbling at home. Henry's relentless push continued, and on 21 May 1420, when the Treaty of Troyes was sealed, he became regent of France and heir to the throne of his father-in-law King Charles VI. Like his great-grandfather, Henry was to leave his work dangerously incomplete through no fault of his own. On 31 August 1422, aged just 35, Henry succumbed to dysentery on campaign in France. His reputation was sealed by his death at the height of his powers. Henry was never required to face the reality of trying to rule a dual monarchy, or of resisting the efforts of Charles's son, who would not be disinherited quietly.

All of those problems fell on the narrow, infant shoulders of Henry's only child, his son, who became King Henry VI. The problem for England, and for France when Charles VI died on 21 October, less than two months after Henry V, was that Henry VI was just 9 months old when his father died. England had endured minorities before, for Henry III, Richard II, and briefly for Edward III, but the youngest of these had been 9 years old. The kingdom faced many years of minority government while distracted by the war in France that lacked the figurehead who had driven success to date. The minority government that ruled for Henry VI nurtured faction that became endemic. One group at court wanted peace with France, an end to the war that was proving cripplingly expensive, unwinnable, and which stifled trade. The leader of this faction was Cardinal Henry Beaufort, Bishop of Winchester. Cardinal Beaufort was the king's great uncle, a half-brother of Henry IV. The Beaufort family began as the children of John of Gaunt and his mistress Katherine Swynford. When Gaunt married Katherine as his third wife, the children were legitimised by the king and the pope, though no act that passed before parliament barred them from the throne as has long been contended.

Leading the group urging the continued prosecution of the war was the king's uncle Humphrey, Duke of Gloucester. On the death of Henry V, his will had provided for his brother John, Duke of Bedford, to act as regent in France. John would perform admirably in the role until his death in 1435. Henry had wished his youngest brother Humphrey to become regent in England, but the royal council resisted its exclusion from authority and instead implemented a separation of power. The person of the king was made the responsibility of men charged with raising and educating him. Humphrey was made Protector of the Realm, an invented position that gave him the responsibility for the military protection of England, and council would rule on the king's behalf until he came of age. Humphrey's reputation has long been of a man unsuited to the authority his brother wished him to wield; rash, bellicose, and lacking a broad support base. Of at least equal concern to those sitting on the royal council was the danger that their voices would be side lined and they would be deprived of the opportunities to prosper during a long minority.

The feud between Cardinal Beaufort and his nephew Humphrey, Duke of Gloucester, was a precursor to the Wars of the Roses that would consume the second half of the fifteenth century. The two men traded accusations, particularly in parliament, but as Henry VI emerged from his youth and began to take authority in his kingdom, it became clear that he had no taste for his father's war. Henry wished for peace with all his heart. That gave Cardinal Beaufort the upper hand, alongside his funding of the perpetually bankrupt government with endless loans funded by his rich bishopric of Winchester. Henry handed back swathes of territory in France in return for a marriage to Margaret of Anjou, a niece of the queen of France, in 1445. He kept the terms of his marriage secret for as long as possible, aware that they would prove explosively unpopular. He was correct. Henry gave up the counties of Maine and Anjou, driving back the frontier of the English kingdom in France. It may have been a realistic concession to the increasingly unavoidable assessment that the war was too expensive, unmanageable, and unwinnable, but it looked like defeat.

Humphrey, Duke of Gloucester, as the figurehead of the faction committed to maintaining the war effort, took it particularly badly. Richard, Duke of York, whom Gloucester had frequently identified as another prince being roundly ignored by Henry and his court, was demoted as matters came to a head. He had replaced John, Duke of Bedford, in France with reduced powers as Lieutenant-General. When his term of service ended, York had made it known he did not wish to be reappointed, and the office was passed to Richard Beauchamp, Earl of Warwick. When Warwick died in 1439, York was offered increased authority to return, and he served again from 1440–45. At the end of his five-year term, he returned to England, appearing to have expected to return for a further period in office. Instead, he discovered on 24 December 1446 that the position had been given to Edmund Beaufort, Duke of Somerset, a nephew of Cardinal Beaufort. The two men had already grated against each other when Beaufort and his older brother John had been given men and money denied to York to undertake a campaign in France which had gone horrendously wrong in 1443. York was appointed Lieutenant of Ireland in what is often viewed as a form of exile, but he had family links there that made him a suitable candidate and, after France, it remained the second most prestigious post available.

York was a hugely problematical figure for the Lancastrian regime.[20] He was a grandson of Edmund, 1st Duke of York, the fourth son of Edward III. His father was Richard of Conisbrough, the man executed in 1415 for plotting to kill Henry V and place Edmund Mortimer on the throne. When Conisbrough's older brother Edward, 2nd Duke of York was killed at the Battle of Agincourt a few weeks later without children, his nephew Richard became 3rd Duke of York. This connection meant that York was a royal prince, and while Henry VI, now in his mid-twenties and married, remained childless, York was his heir presumptive. At the heart of his enmity with the Beaufort family may have been their potential rivalry to his position as descendants of John of Gaunt. York's status was made more complex by the fact that his mother, who had died shortly after his birth, was Anne Mortimer, sister to Edmund Mortimer, 5thEarl of March, who had been touted as an alternative to the Lancastrian kings since 1399. Edmund had died in 1425 without children, so his rich and extensive lands on the Welsh borders and in Ireland had gone to his nephew, York. The inheritance had made York incredibly wealthy and powerful, but it also meant he had acquired the Mortimer claim to the throne through John of Gaunt's older brother Lionel, Duke of Clarence. In his mid-teens, York had become the focus of a collection of inheritances and claims that presented a possible threat to a regime nervous, in particular, about the Mortimer name.

Henry had avoided handing over the lands he had promised in France for as long as possible, but Charles VII made it known in December 1446 that there would be no more truces unless the counties were returned to the French crown by April 1447. This deadline became the panicked focus for activities that would prove disastrous for the Lancastrian crown. The appointment of Edmund Beaufort to France must have been to smooth the handover it was feared York would oppose. Beaufort proved abrasive, handing Charles VII the excuse he had been looking for to renew hostilities. Writs were sent out on 14 December 1446 summoning parliament to meet at Cambridge on 10 February 1447, but on 20 January the location was suddenly changed to Bury St Edmunds. Cambridge was sympathetic to Humphrey, a patron of literature and learning, and Bury St Edmunds sat nestled in the heartlands of William de la Pole, Duke of Suffolk, Henry's chief advisor. What followed proved a catastrophic miscalculation. As the Tudor chronicler Richard Grafton later noted when retelling the story, 'There is an old saying, that a man intending to avoid the smoke often falls into the fire.'

Humphrey arrived at Bury St Edmunds on 18 February, eight days after parliament had opened. His late arrival may have been a pointed comment on the change of location, but he may also have been aware that he was riding into hostile territory that had been selected to intimidate him. Whether it occurred to him that he was in physical danger is uncertain, but if he was aware of the threat, he took a small retinue and travelled to face it. On his arrival, the duke was told to remain in his lodgings and not to make any effort to see his nephew the king. Two days later, he was arrested by a delegation led by Viscount Beaumont as constable of England and including the duke of Buckingham, Edmund Beaufort, the earl of Salisbury, and Lord Sudeley. Either that evening or the next day, Humphrey collapsed. He may have suffered a stroke from the shock of his arrest, but rumours abounded almost immediately that he had been killed by poison, suffocation, or, lifting a flourish from the stories of Edward II, by a hot poker inserted into his fundament.[21] Humphrey lingered until 23 February when he died. His body was displayed to the public, no doubt to quash rumours of his murder before it was sent to St Albans to be buried as he had wished.[22]

The duke's death meant that he was never tried for what were surely accusations of treason. There was talk of a plan to raise Wales, kill his nephew, and take the throne for himself, but the 56-year-old childless Humphrey can have had little interest in the idea. That had been, perhaps, what Henry and his advisors had meant to form the basis of their charge against Gloucester. At least one commentator was clear that the real reason lay in the imminent revelation of Henry's promise to Charles VII, which 'they knew well they should never bring about until he [Humphrey] were dead'.[23] Henry had either allowed himself to become so paranoid that he believed stories his uncle planned to assassinate him, or he was willing to sacrifice his remaining paternal uncle to win peace with France. Either way, it plunged the House of Lancaster into a spiral that would culminate in its destruction. In a sense, the arrest and death of Humphrey, Duke of Gloucester, was an act of rebellion against the crown by the king.

Although Humphrey had been an outspoken critic of the desire to secure peace with France at the expense of all his brother had died to win, he had never wavered in his loyalty to his nephew. What might be described as loyal opposition to the king was contained and restrained by Humphrey's leadership. There was no question that Henry was king, all Humphrey and his supporters hoped to do was to change policy. War with France was something many in England wanted and believed was both just and potentially profitable, if properly prosecuted. With the duke's death, and rumours it was murder, his popular support cast about for a new champion. They did not have to look far. Humphrey had all but anointed his successor by associating him so closely with Humphrey's ideals, policies, and complaints of exclusion from government. Richard, Duke of York, by Humphrey's hand rather than any effort of his own, became the new figurehead for the mounting opposition to Henry. As Henry's heir presumptive, but also with the Mortimer name clinging to him, he also became the intense focus of the king's paranoia. For the first time in Henry VI's quarter of a century on the throne, the opposition had a rallying point outside the House of Lancaster. It was a shift that would shape the rest of the century.

By 1450, England was starkly aware that the king had given away territory won in blood and using tax-payers' money. As the English kingdom in France contracted, unpaid, disgruntled soldiers and families who had settled in the surrendered territories were squeezed back to England. They brought their resentment and frustration with them and, having no money or work, were blamed for outbreaks of lawlessness all along the south coast.

The year was to prove both a testing and pivotal one. As early as 9 January there were signs of trouble. Adam Moleyns, Bishop of Chichester, had been serving Henry's government for years and had secured permission to make a pilgrimage. Moleyns represented many of the king's less popular policies, but to muddy the waters, he had also quarrelled with York, laying charges of financial mismanagement against the duke that probably formed part of the excuse not to reappoint him to France. Although the former is a far more likely explanation of what happened, the latter may have gnawed away at the back of Henry's mind. As he waited to board a ship at Portsmouth on 9 January, the bishop of Chichester encountered a group of disgruntled soldiers. One chronicle suggests he had been tasked with delivering their wages, but in the violence that erupted, the bishop was beaten to death by a captain named Cuthbert Coalville.[25] A year that began with the violent murder of a bishop would only get worse.

When parliament reopened after a Christmas recess, there was only one matter that dominated proceedings. The Commons demanded the arrest and trial for treason of the king's chief advisor William de la Pole, Duke of Suffolk. The duke was accused of a catalogue of crimes, including colluding with the French and trying to get his son onto the throne by marrying him to Lady Margaret Beaufort.[26] When the Commons refused to back down, Henry was forced to accept Suffolk's arrest, though he sacked John Stafford, Archbishop of Canterbury, as chancellor in a fury. Suffolk denied each of the specific charges laid before him, but on 17 March, the new chancellor John Kemp, Archbishop of York, was forced to deliver the king's verdict. Henry intervened to prevent a trial, finding Suffolk innocent of all the major charges laid before him. Realising he could not entirely exonerate Suffolk, not least without risk to his favourite's life, Henry found the duke guilty of some minor financial indiscretions and exiled him for five years, to begin on 1 May.

On 15 April 1450, the Battle of Formigny saw the English forces in Normandy roundly defeated and pushed even further back in the duchy. It would be followed on 1 July by Somerset's surrender of the city of Caen after a gun stone landed between his wife and his children. The town belonged to York, and his representative opposed the submission but was overruled in another moment that fuelled the feud between York and Beaufort. On 1 May, William de la Pole took ship to sail into five years of exile, but he would never see land alive again. His boat was intercepted, boarded, and he was dragged into a small rowboat where he was ignominiously beheaded by a sailor. Rumours sprang up that York may have arranged the attack from Ireland, but of more concern to the south-east was the story that the king blamed Kent for the murder of his favourite and planned to level the county in vengeance.

For the second time in seventy years, a swirling collection of issues, setbacks, and personalities combined to give rise to a popular rebellion, with tens of thousands of Kentishmen marching on the capital. King Henry was still in the Midlands after the closure of parliament at Leicester on 7 June. The previous day he had despatched the duke of Buckingham and the earls of Oxford, Devon, and Arundel to London to deal with the insurrection being reported. By 10 June, the king was adding Viscount Beaumont, and lords Lovell, Rivers, Scales, and Dudley to go 'against the traitors and rebels in Kent and to punish and arrest the same'.[27] The bulking up of the royal response must have been in reactionto increased news of the rebellion's scale, and it is striking that those involved were already described as traitors. When the royal officers arrived in London, they were made aware that tens of thousands of men were reported to have gathered at Blackheath just south of the capital. Gregory's Chronicle, written by a merchant in London at the time, gave the rebels 46,000 men, though numbers reported are often exaggerated.[28]

The delegation that left London to find out what the rebels wanted included the archbishop of Canterbury, who was a significant landowner in Kent and so well known to those camped at Blackheath. When they met on 16 June, the leader of the force from Kent was identified as Jack Cade. Nothing is known of this mercurial figure. He kept the horde at Blackheath in good order, suggesting some military experience that may have been gained in France. He would also use the name John Amendall, a traditional popular rebel name that promised the fixing of problems. There would be another, far more disturbing development concerning his identity soon, but some sources hinted he was an Irishman, and that inevitably directed attention towards York. Cade presented the king's representatives with a document outlining the complaints that had led these thousands of men to Blackheath. The document represented an organised manifesto and set of solutions for the problems the rebels identified. They aimed their criticism, as was traditional, at the king's advisors, who were insatiable, covetous, and malicious so that the king is daily informed 'that good is evil and evil is good'.[30]

Perhaps aware of the events of 1381 and the attempts of the Great Insurrection, those at Blackheath, who described themselves as the king's petitioners rather than rebels, were careful to distance themselves from such grandiose designs. Their Complaint clearly stated 'we blame not all the lords, nor all those that are about the king's person, nor all gentlemen nor yeomen, nor all men of law, nor all bishops, nor all priests, but all such as may be found guilty by just and true enquiry and by the law'.[31] It is striking that this provision overtly shuns the sweeping societal changes of the Great Insurrection, listing those classes targeted in 1381. Cade's men were here to help the king and his country, not to enforce radical, frightening change. The hope must have been that this would make their aims seem more attainable and palatable. *An English Chronicle* summarised the objective of Cade's band: 'he and his fellowship were assembled and gathered there, forto redress and reform the wrongs that were done in the realm, and to withstand the malice of them that were destroyers of the common profit; and forto correct and amend the defaults of them that were the king's chief counsellors'.

The document complained about the losses in France, but perhaps most worryingly of all, directly referenced Richard, Duke of York. The king's evil counsellors were working to convince Henry, the petition claimed, that the people of England planned to destroy the king's friends and then bring the duke of York to be king in Henry's place.[33] This was an inflammatory statement that went right to the heart of Henry's worst fears. The king was urged to rid himself of anyone associated with the duke of Suffolk and instead 'to take about his noble person his true blood of the royal realm, that is to say, the high and mighty prince the duke of York, exiled from our sovereign lord's person by the noising of the false traitor the duke of Suffolk and his affinity'.[34] If Henry needed any more reason to suspect York's involvement in everything that was going wrong for him, here it was. The Great Insurrection of 1381 had explicitly explained that it was an uprising of the king's men against some amorphous mass of landowning classes. In 1450, Cade's document appeared careful to restrict its aims, but it also gave vocal support to a man Henry was suspicious of and who could easily appear a threat. If Richard II took the rebels' support in 1381 personally and positively, Henry VI took this rising personally, and in bad grace as a challenge.

As Henry moved south towards London, he was gathering an armed force of around 20,000. Unlike Richard II, Henry had no intention of going before this baying mob as their sympathetic champion. The royal army made its way through London and onto Blackheath prepared for a fight, only to find the wide-open space empty. Cade and the thousands of rebels had vanished like mist. Thinking he had won, Henry retired to Greenwich Palace and encamped his men on Blackheath. Sir Humphrey Stafford and his brother William, distant kinsmen of the duke of Buckingham, were sent with a portion of the army to chase down any stragglers. The rebels had withdrawn to Sevenoaks, and as the Stafford brothers made their way there, they were ambushed in the forest, and their men slaughtered. Neither of the Stafford brothers returned, and Sir Humphrey's fine armour was presented to Jack Cade as a trophy. The withdrawal had been a tactical feint, and the rebels now regrouped and headed back towards Blackheath. If the king and court had believed they were going up against a disorganised rabble, they were shocked into the realisation that this was a far more severe threat.

The king took the astonishing decision to flee London. He returned to the safety of the Midlands at Kenilworth Castle, though Queen Margaret appears to have remained behind at Greenwich. The capital was thrown into turmoil, the city officials realising that the king's abandonment also lifted any restraints from the rebels. Just like the uprising of 1381, the problems unsettling the populace in 1450 were not restricted to one county. On 29 June, William Ayscough, Bishop of Salisbury, was celebrating Mass at one of his churches at Edington, Wiltshire. The bishop was Henry's confessor and had officiated at the royal wedding in 1445. He had also been involved in the witchcraft trial of Eleanor Cobham, the wife of Humphrey, Duke of Gloucester, who had been convicted, forcibly divorced from the duke, and declared legally dead in parliament after Humphrey's death to prevent her claiming any of his property. He had left London to ride west and stopped at one of his parish churches to perform Mass. As soon as the service was over, the congregation pounced on Ayscough and hauled him from the church, still wearing all his vestments. He was dragged to the top of a nearby hill and beaten to death by the mob. Stripped naked, he was left there as his killers tore his bloodied shirt into shreds and took pieces as trophies as his goods were stolen.[35] Two bishops in six months had now been murdered, as well as a duke, for their association with the king and his government.

On 1 July, Cade and his rebels returned to Blackheath. The men following the nobles of the court faction had been voicing their lack of willingness to attack Englishmen, and particularly ones with whom they had sympathy. Gregory noted an odd claim that escaped the attention of other commentators. He said that 'the same captain came again, as the Kentishmen said, but it was another that named himself captain, and he came to Blackheath'.[36] The London merchant claimed the man who led the rebels back onto Blackheath on 1 July was not the same man who had been there before. Was Gregory's information mistaken, or did this mark an increase in the rebels' organisation? Had Jack Cade been killed in the attack on the Stafford brothers and his place smoothly taken by another to cover over the loss? Did this point to the duke of York's involvement? In the Midlands, that might have been a question preoccupying Henry's mind, but in London, there were more pressing matters to worry about, even if Gregory was correct.

The following day, Cade entered Southwark on the south bank of the Thames. He took up residence at the White Hart Inn. Cade kept tight control of his men, and the lack of rioting or wanton violence soothed London enough to look favourably on them. On 3 July, Cade crossed London Bridge, cutting the ropes that operated the drawbridge so that it could not be closed against them. He and his men were cautiously welcomed, and Cade promised to take his force out of the city every evening. Just as in 1381, some Londoners were keen to join the rising, and one of the aldermen, Philip Malpas, was targeted and robbed, suggesting some personal animosity toward him dealt with under the guise of the rebellion.[37] It was on this day that one of the most dangerous and shocking moments of the uprising occurred. According to legend, Cade rode into the city and struck the London stone with his knife. The stone has ancient and obscure origins, and part of it remains on the north side of Cannon Street to this day, but as he made the gesture, Cade supposedly declared, 'Now is Mortimer lord of this city.' Whether this particular incident happened is uncertain, but the leader of the force now effectively occupying London did adopt the name John Mortimer. *An English Chronicle* says he 'called himself Mortimer to gain the favour of the people'. Gregory recorded that he arrived 'calling himself John Mortimer'. *The Brut* goes further and describes him as 'an Irish man, who named himself Mortimer, cousin to the duke of York'.[38]

The involvement of the Mortimer name gave a whole new dimension to the uprising that almost certainly doomed any hope it may have had of success. The Lancastrian kings had been acutely aware of the Mortimer threat since the beginning of their rule in 1399. York was considered such a threat not because of his Yorkist lineage, but because of his Mortimer heritage. Whatever the rebels gave as their reasons, Henry grew increasingly fearful York was making his move, a bid for Henry's throne that Humphrey had been preparing for in 1447. This was not, as far as the king was concerned, a popular uprising to highlight injustice as the rebels claimed but a coup d'etat with the aim of placing York onto Henry's throne. Whether York had any involvement in Cade's Rebellion is far from clear. The revolt's manifesto aligned startlingly with York's concerns and seemed to believe he was the solution. To a suspicious king already wary of a powerful magnate, it was more than enough. However, the rebels also made frequent reference to the duke of Gloucester, his unfair arrest, and disastrous death. The aims of the uprising were Gloucester's complaints, with York as a figurehead because Gloucester was dead and had named York his political heir. It is not certain that York embraced the role, not least because it appeared to have cost him his job in France and the favour of the king. It is hard to see York as someone desperate for the throne over the following decade, which suggests that deposing Henry was not part of his agenda in 1450. There was more than enough uncertainty, though, for York to become dangerously linked to Cade's Rebellion.

At the end of 3 July, Cade led his men out of the city and back to Southwark as promised. On the following morning, Saturday 4 July, they crossed London Bridge again and reoccupied the city. Cade set up a headquarters at the Guildhall. He demanded that James Fiennes, Lord Saye and Seale, and his son-in-law William Crowmer be handed over. The two had been detained in the Tower on Henry's orders, though more likely to protect the men than to punish them. They were pushed out of the Tower with little attempt to protect them. Lord Saye and Seale was a figure well-known to the Kentish rebels and disliked intensely by all of them. He had been sheriff of Kent in 1436 and in surrounding counties afterwards. He was still constable of Dover Castle and warden of the Cinque Ports, and he must have been a harsh officer to retain the ire of the people. His son-in-law was under-sheriff of Kent, and so it seems the selection of these two men was highly personal. Lord Saye and Seale had also been Treasurer since 1447, a position that had cost Sir Robert Hales his life in 1381. If many of the rebels were soldiers returning from France, or those affected by the crime spree that coincided with it, the man who held the purse strings that had been drawn tightly against the effort in France was an obvious target. As in 1381, charges of financial mismanagement and unreasonable taxation to fund failure were high on the rebels' list of complaints.

Lord Saye complained bitterly at the Guildhall that he was entitled to trial by his peers rather than some rabble from Kent. It can hardly have softened the crowd gathered to see him condemned to death. They laughed off his demand, and a perfunctory trial took place before the inevitable guilty verdict was delivered. Lord Saye was taken immediately to the Standard at Cheapside and beheaded before a baying audience. His son-in-law Crowmer suffered the same fate at Mile End, and another man named John Bayle was beheaded at Whitechapel. The heads were reunited at London Bridge, where Lord Saye and Crowmer were set on spikes kissing each other. Some others escaped this fate; the alderman Robert Horne was sent to Newgate jail by Cade for unspecified transgressions. As in 1381, it may have been a signal that Londoners were pursuing their own agendas alongside the rebels' activities.[39] The violence seemed to be a turning point for the authorities in the capital. Cade withdrew to Southwark that night and returned on Sunday 5 July. Another man was beheaded, identified only as Thomas Mayne, a squire from Hampton,[40] but plans were afoot to begin resisting the rebels. It is unclear whether Cade lost control of the men he commanded or the Londoners who joined him began settling vendettas that led to widespread violence, but word was sent to the Tower that London was ready to fight back.

As Cade and his men left the city on Sunday evening, a force crept out of the Tower under the leadership of Lord Scales, a veteran of the wars in France, and Matthew Gough, a similarly experienced captain from Wales. The 10 o'clock bell was the signal to move,[41] and the men led by Scales and Gough poured onto London Bridge. They drove off Cade's guards and shut the city's gates as they set about repairing the severed ropes so that the drawbridge could be raised. Word reached Cade at the White Hart in Southwark, and he rallied his men. To swell their numbers further, he broke open the prisons of King's Bench and Marshalsea, just as the 1381 rebels had done, and conscripted the prisoners. They rushed onto London Bridge, and a battle began that would last all night. London Bridge in the fifteenth century was a narrow passage lined with tall buildings that included shops and shrines, so it was cramped conditions for combat. The fighting raged in the dark, and 'many a man was slain and cast into the Thames, harness, body, and all'. Eventually, the wooden drawbridge was fired. Cade was blamed for this, though he can only have sought to destroy his one way into London if he was losing the fight and needed to cover a retreat. It was 9 o'clock in the morning before the encounter ended as the bridge blazed and the wounded moaned to drown out any cock crows. Matthew Gough was amongst the dead, as was one of the city's aldermen John Sutton. Countless bodies had plummeted into the Thames below, dragged away on the sliding current.[42]

Three senior churchmen rowed across the river to make an offer of peace to the rebels. John Stafford, Archbishop of Canterbury, was joined by John Kemp, Archbishop of York, and William Waynflete, Bishop of Winchester. Like the queen, they must have remained in the capital when the king left, both secure in the knowledge they were not the target of the rebels' rage and recognising the mediation and peace-making required by their offices. The Kentishmen were offered full pardons if they would leave immediately and return to their homes. Cade took his charter in the name of John Mortimer and the host melted away back into Kent. One story relates that Cade had all his plunder put into a barge and rowed to Rochester while he and a few men who remained at his side tried half-heartedly to attack Queenborough Castle on the Isle of Sheppey, but were quickly and easily repulsed.[43]

Within a few days, in another parallel to 1381, the pardons were withdrawn, at least from Cade and his chief associates. The reasoning for denying the captain his pardon was that he had taken it in the name John Mortimer when everyone knew his name was Cade. A price of 1,000 marks (£666) was put on Cade's head, dead or alive, with a further 500 marks (£333) for any of his senior allies.[44] On 12 July he was tracked down to the village of Heathfield in East Sussex where he was cornered in a garden by men led by Alexander Iden, a future sheriff of Kent. Cade was killed in the scuffle that followed and his body taken back to London. At Southwark, they stopped at the White Hart Inn and forced the lady who had hosted Cade to identify his body. She confirmed that this was the men who had stayed with her, at which point his corpse was deposited at the prison of King's Bench, where it stayed for four days. On Thursday, 16 July, the body was beheaded and quartered. The pieces were strapped to a hurdle, dragged by horse throughout Southwark, over London Bridge and through the streets to Newgate prison. His head was then taken and placed on a spike on London Bridge.

When parliament met in November 1450, Cade was attainted of treason posthumously. It is striking that the act asserts Cade 'falsely and traitorously plotted your death, and the destruction and subversion of this your said realm' because the rebels never threatened Henry's life or crown. Parliament heard that 'although he is dead and destroyed, he has not yet been punished by the law of your said land' and that this should be completed to discourage those who contemplate rebellion in the future. To that end, he was attainted and would 'forfeit to you all his goods, lands, tenements, rents and possessions which he had on the said 8 July or after, and his blood issue corrupted and made legally incapable forever, and to be called a false traitor within your said realm forevermore'.[45] The parliamentary attainder of a common rebel who was already dead was unnecessary, and seizing all his goods and lands implies it was believed Cade might have been a reasonably wealthy man.

The provision that draws the most attention, though, is that Cade's 'blood issue' should be declared corrupted and 'made legally incapable forever'. Incapable of what? Was this measure a precaution because the government either knew, or at least could not be sure, that Cade was not this man's real name? The act also referred to Cade 'calling himself John Mortimer', so that there could be no question that he was attainted by both names. Could Jack Cade have been a scion of the Mortimer family, driven to take up arms by the parlous state of Henry VI's England and his own dusty claim to the throne? Perhaps it was no more than a rallying cry, or a note of support to the duke of York, but there was clearly some doubt, and Cade's children were declared legally incapable just in case.

Cade's Rebellion drew strong parallels with the Great Insurrection of 1381. There was a list of complaints directed at the management of the government, though the king was excused blame for the evil counsel he received. It was a popular uprising that lacked any noble leadership or support yet was well organised and had a defined aim. Cade was careful to distance his efforts from the wholesale societal reforms demanded in 1381. It was perhaps felt that such changes were a step too far and that by targeting smaller reforms, such as the removal of specific officers around the king, they might have something they could achieve without putting the entire body politic on the defensive. If this did figure in their thinking, it means they were aware of the demands made in 1381 and the reasons King Richard II's initial enthusiasm was overturned. They must also have been acutely aware of the punishments meted out to those involved in 1381 and must have believed they had taken steps to avoid them.

The aims of Cade's Rebellion had seemed reasonable and may have chimed with some of the nobility as much as those further down the social ladder. Had it stuck to an agenda of limited reform for the good of the realm, success may have remained within reach. The addition of the Mortimer name radically altered the face of the uprising and the nature of its threat. Ultimately, it doomed the revolt as a dynastic challenge to Henry personally rather than a call for attainable governmental reform. By drawing in the spectre of the duke of York alongside the Mortimer name, the other causes for revolt became drowned out in Henry's mind. In February 1451, the king toured Kent with his justices chasing down anyone associated with Cade. Four days of hearings were conducted in Canterbury where a large number of men were condemned to be drawn, hanged, and quartered 'for their taking against the king, having more favour unto the duke of York than unto the king'. Nine more men were beheaded at Rochester, closely followed by another twelve. As Gregory watched this grim parade of heads being posted on London Bridge, he lamented, 'Men call it in Kent the harvest of the heads.'[46]

The lack of noble support may have meant that Cade's Rebellion was doomed from the outset, just as that of 1381 was. The disturbing parallel lay in the turmoil that had followed the Great Insurrection. For years afterwards, Richard II had found himself at odds with his own nobility, perhaps in part because he had wanted to give the rebels what they wanted to the detriment of those nobles, who found themselves unable to trust their king. As Gregory watched the decapitated heads of those blamed for the rebellion of 1450 fill up the spikes on London Bridge reserved for traitors, he may have mused on what might come next. Experience suggested this was not the end, but the beginning of something else.

Chapter 10

The Wars of the Roses

*Rebellion is the bitter medicine government should hold its
nose and take for the good of the body.*

The same parliament that attainted Jack Cade in November 1450 did make
efforts to address some of the problems the rebels had highlighted. Financial
issues were reaching a point at which they could no longer be ignored,
even by the king and those who profited from his open-handed generosity.
The king was in debt to the tune of £372,000 (equivalent to roughly
£170,000,000 today). His annual income was £5,000, and his household
expenses alone totalled £24,000. He had been living so far beyond his means
for so long that suppliers were refusing to deliver to his palaces for fear of
never receiving payment. An act of resumption was passed, taking back
into royal hands lands and incomes granted away in an effort to balance the
royal finances. Such measures were never popular, not least because those
sitting in parliament were frequently amongst the hardest hit. A long list of
exceptions followed, including the queen, Henry's foundations at Eton and
Cambridge, and plenty of other people and institutions.[1] Still, there was at
least some acknowledgement that a problem existed.

The duke of York had returned from Ireland in the wake of Cade's
Rebellion. He would claim he came only to help the king restore order,
but Henry posted guards to watch against his return and made efforts to
seize him. The duke arrived in London for parliament two weeks after it
had opened, either looking to make a dramatic entrance or wary of placing
his head into the lion's mouth. It is possible he had begun to fear meeting
the same fate as the duke of Gloucester, and so travelling to parliament
became dangerous. On 2 December, there was more rioting in the streets
of London. Edmund Beaufort, Duke of Somerset, was attacked and robbed
at Blackfriars. York sought to restore order, and one of the attackers was
arrested and executed. York rode through the streets of London, ordering
the rioters to cease. Gregory recorded that York 'made to be cried in divers
places that what manner a man that robbed or rifled any person should have
as hasty justice as the said man had'.[2] The burning question, as unanswerable

to most of England in 1450 as it is today was what happened at Blackfriars and why. Was York a competent governor with the experience and authority to fill the void created by Henry's feeble rule, or was he an ambitious man who saw a chance to grab the ultimate prize for himself?

One thing that was certain was that York and Somerset were at each other's throats. Whether York had arranged the attack on his rival so that he could appear to come to the rescue of the embattled Somerset as his better or genuinely sought to restore order cannot be known. Before parliament closed, it was presented with a petition to rehabilitate Humphrey, Duke of Gloucester, and another to condemn Suffolk as a traitor and bar his descendants from succession.[3] The session was abruptly ended by the king when an MP named Thomas Young, who had links to the duke of York, tried to introduce a motion recognising York as the king's heir until he had a son. Young was thrown in the Tower and would claim recompense for the breach of his parliamentary privilege of free speech in 1455.[4] Suspicion that York was behind the motion only turned Henry further against the duke. Whether York drove the move, it was done by his supporters to improve his position, or was simply a reaction to the uncertainty flooding London and the recognition that stability was required and York was the best candidate began to matter less and less. As the rivalry between York and Somerset intensified, it began to impact the kingdom because King Henry was incapable of reconciling the feuding dukes and instead took one side.

As the summer of 1451 cooled into autumn, there was open warfare in England. The earl of Devon confronted the earl of Wiltshire at Lackham in Wiltshire as part of Devon's ongoing feud with Lord Bonville, who was allied to Wiltshire. After defeating Wiltshire, Devon turned back into Somerset and laid siege to Taunton Castle where Lord Bonville had taken refuge. Noblemen tearing through the countryside settling personal feuds in pitched battles was another symptom of the disintegration of Henry's authority. The rivalry between the Courtenay earls of Devon and the Bonville family had been simmering for a long time, but it bubbled to the surface in Somerset's territory, yet the duke did nothing. He was at the king's right hand, having taken that position in preference to York. Lacking a robust landed base or much wealth that wasn't reliant on the king's favour, Somerset grew increasingly nervous at the thought of leaving Henry's side and had no intention of travelling into the west country to settle a private dispute.

York had retired to his lands on the Welsh Marches after parliament had ended, brooding on his continued exclusion from power. It was York who left his fortress at Ludlow and marched 100 miles south to Taunton where he forced Devon and Bonville to come to terms and ended the siege. Devon had been closely aligned with York during the parliament. Bonville's rise after he had become close to the duke of Suffolk had diminished Devon's influence in the south-west, and so Devon had turned to York as the leader of the opposition. It is perhaps telling that York showed no favour in settling the matter. He did not take Devon's side but forced the two men to cease their action against each other. There was a period of quiet after this dispute had been settled. York remained away from court and watched as the kingdom continued to be poorly run and mismanaged.

In the early days of 1452, York was suddenly moved into action. On 9 January he wrote a letter to the king complaining that the king was 'greatly displeased with me, and hath in me a distrust by sinister information of mine enemies'. He complained that this campaign against him was unjustified, affirming that 'I am, and have been, and ever will be, his true liegeman'. York had asked the bishop of Hereford and the earl of Shrewsbury to make his case to the king and he offered to make an oath on the sacrament that 'I am a true liegeman to my King my sovereign lord, ever have been, and shall be to my dying day.'[5] York was aware, or at least afraid, of a whispering campaign against him, turning Henry even further against the duke. Less than a month later on 3 February York sent a letter to the city of Shrewsbury, and probably to other towns along the Welsh Marches. His efforts to find a way back to the king's favour had fallen on deaf ears. The letter reminded Shrewsbury how glorious it had once been when England had enjoyed success in France, 'what laud, what worship, honour, and manhood, was ascribed of all nations unto the people of this realm'. Now, he complained, 'derogation, loss of merchandise, lesion of honour, and villainy, is said and reported generally unto the English nation for loss of the same'.[6] The despatch of such letters marked a stepping onto the front foot of York's efforts to impose himself on the government.

France had ultimately been lost on Somerset's watch after York had kept it secure for many years. It was clear who had the 'honour, and manhood' and who was responsible for the 'lesion of honour'. This letter marked the first occasion on which York openly named the person he blamed for his woes and those of the entire kingdom. Edmund Beaufort, Duke of Somerset, was accused of treason in the loss of Normandy, of encouraging Henry to give up Gascony and for putting Calais at risk by encouraging the French with his weak response to their aggression. York protested that he had tried to do all he could to help the king correct the realm's problems by dealing with 'certain articles concerning the weal and safeguard, as well of his most royal person, as the tranquillity and conservation of all this his realm'. The reason he was ignored was, he claimed, 'the envy, malice, and untruth of the said Duke of Somerset' who 'laboureth continually about the king's highness for my undoing'. York stated that he planned to take action, but that he would do so in the open, unlike his opponents, 'to the intent that every man shall know my purpose and desire'.[7]

Whether York was, in fact, genuine and open in his dealings or had some agenda carefully hidden behind his words cannot be known. His enemies saw propaganda to excuse his darker motives, while those few who supported him at this stage believed he had been treated unfairly and was a better candidate to advise the king than Somerset. York asked Shrewsbury to send him men to take to London as part of an armed force to impose himself on the king. He must have known he risked panicing the king and capital so soon after Cade's occupation and that he would be walking a very fine line that might easily be crossed into treason. When York marched out of Ludlow shortly after writing his letter to Shrewsbury, he must have been turning all of these things over in his mind. King Henry had withdrawn to the Midlands, perhaps on the advice of the queen and Somerset, who feared London was still unstable and unfriendly after the king had abandoned the city to Cade. By the time York arrived at Dartford, south-east of London, he had around 23,000 men and was basing himself in Kent, amidst those who had suffered in the aftermath of Cade Rebellion.

York camped on the south bank of the Thames, and one detailed record of his force says that he had 3,000 gunners and 8,000 men-at-arms in his entourage. The earl of Devon had joined York, clearly unperturbed by York's impartial intervention in his dispute with Lord Bonville, and Devon had brought 6,000 men. Lord Cobham had also turned out for York with a further 6,000 troops. Seven ships floated on the Thames beside them 'with their stuff', a supply line that could track them along the river to London.[8] The king gathered an army and made his way back to London. York, making it obvious he had no desire to provoke an armed confrontation, remained defensibly arrayed at Dartford and waited for the court party to make a move. Although Henry rode through the streets of London to display his royal power, there was a strong sense that he was not driving policy any longer, since 'the lords both spiritual and temporal took the matter in hand'.[9] A delegation was appointed to visit York and ascertain his demands. The bishops of Winchester and Ely were joined by the father and son earls of Salisbury and Warwick, the duchess of York's brother and nephew, as well as lords Beauchamp and Sudeley. Despite their relationship to the duke of York, it is telling that Salisbury and Warwick were very much in the royal camp at this point.

The demands laid out by York were a disturbing mirror of Cade's manifesto. York insisted 'that he nor none of the company intended hurt unto the king's person, nor to any of his council, being lovers of the common weal and of him and his land'. There were a few people York wanted to be removed from the king's side 'by whose means the common people are grievously oppressed, and the commonalty greatly impoverished; of the which he named for principal the duke of Somerset'.[10] The delegation took this request, which amounted to Somerset's arrest, to the king, who sent back word that he agreed to the terms. Somerset would be arrested and would face the charges York would lay against him. Demonstrating his lack of desire for aggression, on 1 March 1452 York disbanded his force and sent his men home. He then went before the king, only to be horrified to find Somerset not only free but still firmly at the king's right hand. Instead, York was taken into custody. Having acted in good faith, York found he had been tricked, and his openness repaid with dishonesty.

On 10 March, York rode into London in front of the king, very clearly a royal prisoner. He was taken to St Paul's Cathedral, the huge medieval church capable of holding thousands of people. Richard, 3rd Duke of York was forced to stand before the altar in front of a fascinated crowd and swear an oath. Promising to be loyal to Henry VI was not particularly novel. Indeed York had tried to offer assurances before he left Ludlow that he was nothing other than Henry's liegeman. The shame for a duke came in the very public manner in which he was forced to give the pledge and his status as a prisoner of the state. The oath aimed to tie York's hands. He promised never to raise an armed force without the king's express permission. If he ever felt aggrieved, he was to submit his complaints to the king as his only means of satisfaction. He was required to give his oath on the Bible, the cross and the sacrament to ensure that he was utterly bound by it. What must have enraged York most of all is that he could be almost certain none of this came from Henry, who was on good personal terms with everyone. He had been undone by Somerset and the queen.

York was only released from custody in response to rumours reaching London that his 9-year-old son Edward, Earl of March, was coming to the capital at the head of 10,000 Welshmen to free his father.[12] The tale seems unlikely, but it may have been propagated by the Duchess of York or others of York's supporters to put pressure on the court to release the duke. York was allowed to return to Ludlow, but he was under a darkening political cloud, and the episode at Dartford had seen the gloves removed in the feud between York and Somerset. York had made an open play and seen it crash down around him as Somerset's position at the king's right hand was reinforced.

The view of Richard, Duke of York, has long been that of a man driven by an insatiable ambition to take the throne and Dartford in 1452 as his opening gambit. His willingness to send away his army for the simple concession of Somerset's arrest gives the lie to this notion. He clearly wanted to impose himself on government and believed he would be a better minister to Henry than Somerset was. Many at the time would probably have agreed based on his record in France and Ireland, and Somerset's problematical period in France. That was not York's decision to make, though.

When Cecily, Duchess of York, gave birth to the couple's last child who would survive infancy in October 1452, she was at the Yorkist seat of Fotheringhay Castle in Northamptonshire. This child was named for his father and would become one of the most controversial figures in medieval history as King Richard III, but he was born into a family and a country in turmoil. It is telling that his father was at Fotheringhay too. King Henry undertook a tour through the Welsh Marches in a conspicuous effort to show himself in the Mortimer heartlands that had just supported York. There was also a marked change of policy that may have been a recognition that York had a point. Men were sent to reinforce Calais, and there were whispers of a new campaign in Normandy, perhaps led by Somerset. John Talbot, Earl of Shrewsbury, now in his sixties but the kingdom's premier general, was brought out of retirement and indented to serve with 5,000 men. An embassy arrived from Gascony complaining of the weight of French rule and offering to submit to the English king again if he would liberate them. Talbot's force was diverted south and took Bordeaux quickly.

If 1452 had been a positive year for the king, with York subdued and an encouraging renewal of the French wars, the following year was to continue this upward progression. In the early months of 1453, it became clear that Queen Margaret was pregnant. After almost eight years of marriage, the 31-year-old king finally had the promise of an heir. If there were questions and tensions over who might succeed Henry, with York and Somerset both doubtless certain it should be them, then if the child were a son, the uncertainty would be ended and the Lancastrian dynasty secured into another generation. When parliament met in March, Lord Lisle indented to serve alongside his father the earl of Shrewsbury and Henry continued to bolster those closest to him. Whether the king drove this policy or the queen and Somerset felt the need to sure up their own positions in unclear. Somerset was promoted in dignity to have precedence in the realm above the duke of Norfolk.[13] Henry's half-brothers Edmund and Jasper Tudor, two of the children of his mother's second, secret, marriage to Owen Tudor were summoned to parliament as the earls of Richmond and Pembroke respectively.

York was summoned, but he stayed away. The precarious nature of his position was made clear by the session's return to Jack Cade and his uprising. Described as 'the most abominable tyrant, dreadful, odious and errant false traitor' who had used the name Mortimer, Cade's 'name, reputation, acts and deeds ought to be eradicated from every true Christian man's language and memory forever'. Despite being dead for three years now, parliament heard that Cade should be 'be taken, seized, called and declared a false traitor' and that 'all his tyranny, acts, deeds and false beliefs be void, quashed, annulled, destroyed and be removed from memory forever'.[15] Unless this was a veiled assault on York, which would mean he was correct to be wary of his standing, it was oddly malicious to rake over Cade Rebellion and the personal reputation of a single, lowly commoner again. There may have been some lingering support for his aims that Henry was worried about, but it could also point to continued concern that he had been a Mortimer who had found support for a claim that was now embodied by Richard, Duke of York.

Feeling his position was a strong one, Henry continued to move against York. He was deprived of his position as steward and justice in eyre of royal forests south of the Trent, and on 12 May he was replaced as Lord Lieutenant of Ireland by James Butler, Earl of Wiltshire, an ally of the court party. On 2 July 1453 parliament was prorogued until 12 November. Henry planned to use the break, he explained, 'to travel to various parts of the realm to the intention and end that maintenance, extortion, oppression, riots and other misdeeds accustomed in his realm of England for so long a time might be destroyed and the doers or perpetrators of the same be punished and corrected according to their demerits'.[16] York could at least reflect that with renewed efforts in France and a focus on domestic unrest, his concerns were being addressed, even if he was still being excluded from the actions.

There were two main flashpoints to which Henry might travel first. In the north, the ongoing feud between the Percy family of the earl of Northumberland and the Neville family of the earls of Salisbury and Warwick had erupted into violence. During a Neville family wedding, the earl of Northumberland's second son had attacked the Neville party at Heworth Moor, though no casualties were reported from the brief skirmish. In the west, there was a similar threat to the king's peace focussed on Cardiff Castle. There, the earl of Warwick was engaged in a bitter dispute over the apportioning of the Beauchamp inheritance of his wife. Warwick owed his earldom to his wife, but now her half-sister's husband was claiming part of the legacy that Warwick had held uncontested for years, including Cardiff Castle. The fact that Henry chose to focus on this incident above any other is best explained by the fact that Warwick's opponent, the man married to his wife's sister, was Edmund Beaufort, Duke of Somerset. When the king found in Somerset's favour and ordered Warwick to vacate the properties, the earl refused and dug himself in at Cardiff Castle. This was the final straw in driving the Neville family into an alliance with York. Henry was determined to continue bolstering the layer of insulation between himself and opposition provided by Somerset and others around him.

In August 1453, Henry arrived at the royal hunting lodge at Clarendon, Wiltshire on his way west. During his stay, Henry collapsed. Why and what happened is unclear, but it sent the government into a panic. On 17 July, Talbot had lost the Battle of Castillon, a disastrous outcome that had seen the earl killed and any hope of a revival in France gone. It is possible new of this reached Henry at Clarendon and combined with the other stresses caused a breakdown. Henry fell into a catatonic state, unable to stand or speak, and no one knew how long the illness might last. Henry's paternal grandfather, Charles VI, had been prone to mental illness, though his manifested as violent episodes or long periods in which he recognised nobody, refused to bathe or change his clothes, and ran through the corridors of his palaces in a manic state. Henry showed none of these symptoms, becoming utterly unresponsive. On 13 October, Queen Margaret delivered a baby, the son for which the kingdom had been waiting. Born on the feast day of St Edward the Confessor, he was named for the sainted king of England in a departure from the Lancastrian name of Henry. The king was required to recognise his son and claim him as his own before he would be formally recognised as the heir to the throne. This was ostensibly to ensure that he was legitimate, but Henry was utterly unable to perform even this basic function. Despite being presented with the baby by Queen Margaret and by the duke of Buckingham, Henry failed to respond. This failure to claim his son would leave the door open to charges that he was not the king's and that Somerset had fathered the queen's baby, but accusations of illegitimacy were thrown like confetti at enemies since there was no way to prove the matter definitively.

When parliament reopened in November, York was recalled to act as Henry's lieutenant, and the session was prorogued again until February 1454. York did manage to secure the arrest and imprisonment of Somerset. In response to this setback, Queen Margaret made her own bid for regency powers on behalf of her husband and infant son. John Stodeley wrote a newsletter on 19 January 1454 recorded amongst the Paston Letters that details the unsettled situation in London. He reported that the queen had requested authority to 'have the whole rule of this land', as well as the power to appoint the chancellor, treasurer, privy seal, and other officers of the government. She also wanted to be able to appoint bishops and to be given an income sufficient to support the royal household of herself, her husband, and their son.[17] It was not unusual in France for a woman to exercise regency powers during the minority or incapacity of the king, but Margaret had failed to allow for the distaste of the English polity for female rule. It was perhaps a reaction to York's sudden pre-eminence, but it was misjudged.

Parliament reconvened with York as the king's lieutenant. To the horror of Somerset and the queen, they turned to Richard, Duke of York, to resolve the problem. It made sense. He was the senior nobleman in the country and an experienced governor, but it meant Somerset and the court party losing their grip on the government to their enemy. The issue of Henry's incapacity was brought to a head on 22 March 1454 when John Kemp, Archbishop of Canterbury and Lord Chancellor, died. The king's approval was required to appoint a successor, and this was unknown territory for everyone. York took control of the situation, though he did not act unilaterally. Parliament appointed York, the bishops of Winchester, Ely and Chester, the earls of Warwick, Oxford and Shrewsbury, Viscounts Beaumont and Bourchier, the Prior of St John's, and the lords Fauconberg, Dudley and Stourton to a commission to ascertain the king's capacity to be involved. The commission contained some allies of York, including his nephew Warwick and his brother-in-law Viscount Bourchier, but also many who were close to the king. They designed a painstaking process to ensure that the king was given every chance to show his capability.[18]

Five articles were set out. The first, assuring the king of their allegiance to him and that 'there is no earthly thing that they desire more, or set closer to their hearts than to hear of his welfare'. Next, the king would be informed that parliament was underway with York as his lieutenant working for 'the repudiation of misgovernance'. The remaining three articles were only to be read if the king showed signs of comprehending the first two. The third article was to inform the king of the archbishop's passing, 'by whose death the said archbishopric is vacant and his highness remains without a chancellor', and to ask for his guidance in the matter. Next, the king was to be reassured that his seals were being kept safely so that they might not be abused. They were 'enclosed in a chest and sealed with the seals of various lords and stored in the treasury where they remain in the keeping of his treasurer and chamberlain'. Finally, the king was to be consulted on the establishment of a 'learned and wise council' to handle government while he was ill.

The commission visited the king at Windsor on Saturday 23 March. York was the only one not to make the journey, perhaps acutely aware that he might later be accused of falsifying the outcome to gather and keep more power for himself. The delegation found the king being fed his dinner by his servants. Waiting patiently until the spectacle was complete, the bishop of Chester spoke on their behalf. He recited the first two articles. Henry showed no sign at all of comprehending them, or even of being aware of their presence. Despite this, they continued to read the other three articles, deciding it was safer to have read them all than to be accused later of keeping things from the king. The men returned to Westminster to tell parliament 'they could get no sign or answer' from the king. They had asked for him to be moved to another room in the hopes that it might provoke a response but had watched as 'he was led between two men into the chamber where he lies' to no avail. Eventually, they had left because they 'could have no answer, word or sign; and therefore with sorrowful hearts they came away'.

All of this was recorded in minute detail in the parliament rolls, doubtless to avoid later charges that they had taken upon themselves royal authority without justification. The decision was made that a protector ought to be appointed. It was falling back on the example of Henry's minority and was felt to be the least risky option to explain to the king when and if he recovered. The question of who might undertake the role had been answered as long ago as November. York was the senior adult male in the kingdom, was already Henry's lieutenant in parliament and had a strong track record of capable administration. Somerset might have been an option, but he was in the Tower awaiting trial for treason. The queen had made her play in January, and it was clear the nobility would not accept a woman in charge. Appointing anyone but York risked upsetting him, but the use of the template of Henry's childhood meant that the Protector only really had military authority. Council would continue to rule with York envisaged as having a leading role among the members. The duke protested, his assertion that 'I myself am insufficient in wisdom, learning or ability to assume that worthy name of protector and defender of this land'[19] little more than caution against future charges of undue willingness to take on the authority. In response to his request for clarification, the lords confirmed he would not be tutor, which meant having responsibility for the person of the king, nor regent, holding all of the rights to rule the kingdom. He was to be 'protector and defender, which implies a personal duty of attention to the actual defence of this land against both the enemies overseas, if required, and against rebels at home'.[20] With all of this resolved, Richard accepted the post of Protector and Defender of the Realm and Church on 27 March, and it was ratified in parliament on 3 April.[21]

Many, not least the queen, were anxious to see what York's ascendancy would mean. York oversaw his first council meeting on 30 March 1454. He recommended Thomas Bourchier, Bishop of Ely, for the vacancy at Canterbury. The duke appointed his brother-in-law Viscount Bourchier, Thomas's brother, to the council along with John Tiptoft, Earl of Worcester, who also had connections to York. The remainder of those gathered demonstrates the balance he was careful to show. Humphrey Stafford, Duke of Buckingham, was half-brother to Viscount and Bishop Bourchier but was fiercely loyal to the court party. Lords Scales, Beaumont, Dudley, and Fiennes were not allies of York. The duke was trying to show that he intended to be fair and inclusive rather than divisive. On 15 March, almost a fortnight before he was confirmed as Protector, parliament had created Henry's infant son Edward, Prince of Wales. The appointment offered some security to everyone that York understood he was not acting as Henry's heir. The duke's complicity in seeing it through parliament, if he was not the driving force behind it, demonstrates that he was keen to make that very point. Considering his later reputation as a man burning to be king, it is a surprising measure.

Council met regularly, gathering on 30 March, 1 April, 8 April, 15 April, 29 May, and 31 May. There were usually more than twenty attendees, and all decisions were countersigned by all present. York was taking no chances that he might appear to be assuming too much power, or that he might later be hung out to dry by the rest of the council. When a great council was summoned to discuss the defence of Calais, not only Buckingham was called, but also the earl of Northumberland, the enemy of York's key allies the Neville family, and the king's half-brothers Edmund and Jasper Tudor. York tried to run a tighter ship than the previous government, acutely aware that this was his opportunity to prove what he had been asserting for years; that he would do better than Somerset had. On 13 November 1454, York oversaw the signing off of a new set of ordinances for the royal households, including those of the queen and prince of Wales. The king's household was to be made up of 385 individuals, rising to 398 on feast days. It would return the royal household to the levels the king's father Henry V had kept, so it was not restrictive or without precedent, but was meant to tackle head-on the financial problems that were dogging Henry's court. The king's half-brothers were amongst those to be about the king's person, so there was no effort to surround the king with York's men. Queen Margaret was assigned 120 members of her household, and the infant prince of Wales would have thirty-eight.[22] The queen was unimpressed with what she saw as York mandating a reduction in her estate and honour.

On Christmas Day 1454, nine months into York's Protectorate, a miracle occurred. Many at court had given up on Henry and were looking at another prolonged minority until his son came of age to rule. As Christ's birthday was being celebrated, the king suddenly stirred and began to move and speak. His son was quickly brought to him, and a jubilant Henry claimed the boy, amazed that he had not known until that moment that he had a son. The news of archbishop Kemp's death came as a shock to the king as his court set about filling in sixteen months of missing memories. Six weeks later, on 9 February 1455, York was relieved of his position as Protector. On 4 March, Somerset was released from the Tower and returned to Henry's side. It is worth noting that York had resisted calls to have Somerset tried during Henry's illness. Any move to a trial would surely have ended in Somerset's conviction and would have required his execution. That York avoided taking a step from which there was no return, even against the man he despised most in the kingdom, suggests he was wary of doing anything too drastic. York was stripped of the Captaincy of Calais he had been granted and the Lord Lieutenancy of Ireland he had taken back. His ally Salisbury was sacked as chancellor and replaced with the new Archbishop of Canterbury, Thomas Bourchier. It was plain to see the direction of travel.

York retreated north to his castle at Sandal and Salisbury returned to the Neville seat at Middleham. A great council was summoned to meet in the Midlands, the Lancastrian heartland, and York and his allies must have turned their minds once more to the fate of Humphrey, Duke of Gloucester, in 1447. York, Salisbury, and Warwick gathered an armed force, in contravention of York's previous oath never to do so again and moved south to intercept the royal party as it moved out of London. York studiously wrote to the king at each stop to explain that he was coming to prove his innocence of any crime, complaining about Somerset, who one chronicler explained was the man 'by whom at that time the king was principally guided and governed, as he had been before by the duke of Suffolk'.[23] When York reached Key Fields outside St Albans, just north of London, on 21 May, he had some 6,000 men with him compared to the 2,000 accompanying the king. The gates of St Albans were closed and barricaded with Henry, Somerset, Buckingham, Northumberland, and others within.

On the morning of 22 May, York opened a parlay. He sent a herald to the king to request the arrest of Somerset and a handful of others. Showing that he still smarted from the bad faith demonstrated at Dartford, the duke insisted he would not accept any promises and would not leave until the men were in his custody. Henry replied in a sharp tone, ordering the men outside the walls to 'void the field, and not be so hardy to make any resistance against me in my own realm'. He warned that if they failed to do as he said, he would 'destroy them every mother's son, and they be hanged, and drawn, and quartered, that may be taken afterward'.[24] It is plausible that this response came from the lips of Somerset rather than the king. He knew that if Henry wavered now, it would mean his death. When no solution was forthcoming by midday, York's army began its assault on the gates.

Warwick detached himself from the main force and skirted the walls until he found a weak point that allowed entry into some gardens. Leading his men into the streets, Warwick worked his way towards the market square where the royal standard flew. Those around the king were unprepared as Warwick's men unleashed a hail of arrows onto them. The duke of Buckingham was wounded to the face, but to the horror of all, King Henry was struck in the neck by an arrow and was hauled into a tanner's shop for treatment. The commotion in the market square diverted attention from the gates, which were breached as men left their posts. Lord Clifford was killed near the gates. The 62-year-old earl of Northumberland was cut down in the streets, no doubt targeted by his Neville rivals. Somerset was cornered outside the Castle Inn and overwhelmed, fighting bravely to the end. York found the king in the tanner's shop and fell to his knees, pledging his continued allegiance to Henry. Had York wanted the throne in 1455, he was presented with the perfect opportunity to do away with Henry in that moment. Instead, he renewed his fealty and had the king taken to the abbey to receive better care.

Although the First Battle of St Albans on 22 May 1455 is often used as a starting date for the Wars of the Roses, it was little more than the settling of personal vendettas that swirled around the ineffective Henry. There was no suggestion at this point of deposing him, and York had been at pains to have Henry's son created Prince of Wales and to try to negotiate his way out of a confrontation. The Neville family had rid themselves of a Percy, and York had seen Somerset killed, but no one even mooted the idea of removing Henry from the throne. When they rode back into London the following day, Warwick carried the sword of state before the king, who was flanked by York and Salisbury. It was clear who was in charge now, but when York arranged the ceremonial re-crowning of Henry at St Paul's, it was also plain to see who was king.

York and his allies took back the reins of government, picking up where the protectorate had been abruptly cut off. Henry, Margaret, and Prince Edward were installed at Hertford Castle as summonses to parliament were sent out. When it met in July, it continued to address pressing problems but also heard the justification for the action taken at St Albans, including a claim that Somerset had kept York's letters from the king and replied himself in Henry's name, thus escalating the problem.[25] A pardon was put on record for all those involved on York's side so that they could not be 'impeached, sued, grieved, vexed, harmed or molested in their bodies, goods or lands'.[26] Strikingly, there was also a petition for the rehabilitation of the duke of Gloucester, eight years after his death. It was granted in the king's name, proclaiming Humphrey 'the king's true liegeman until his death'.[27] Parliament was prorogued until November, and when it returned, the king had sent word he was not able to attend in person 'for certain just and reasonable causes'.[28] There was suspicion that Henry might have been ill again, but no evidence that this was any more than York keeping a tight grip on proceedings. The Commons submitted a request for a protector to be appointed again and there was little doubt who would take on the role. York was reappointed on 18 November, but this time there was a hint that it was to be a longer-term change to remove Henry from front line politics. Prince Edward was to be offered the protectorate when he came of age, but otherwise, York might remain in post for decades to come.[29]

An act of resumption, the unpopular taking back of royal grants to balance crown finances, was laid before parliament. The Commons wanted it enacted, but it was probably this that led to Henry's sudden reappearance in Westminster on 25 February 1456. The lords were simply unwilling to lose all they had gained from Henry's naïve generosity, and he was once more the pawn of others as he arrived to formally dissolve York's second protectorate. York was pushed into another period in the political wilderness and an edgy, nervous peace settled on England. In 1458, Henry gathered the feuding nobility of the country to London, packing them all into a melting pot which risked escalating rather than resolving problems. The Yorkist lords arrived 'only with their household men in peaceable manner, thinking none harm, and were lodged within the city'. In comparison, the other party, described as 'the young lords whose fathers were slain at St Albans', arrived with large numbers of heavily armed men.[30]

London was tense as Henry arranged several days of mediation. The vengeful young lords were accused of organising ambushes against the Yorkist leaders, but on 24 March, Henry joyfully announced that a settlement had been reached. It essentially blamed the Yorkist lords for the events at St Albans despite their previous pardon in parliament. They were forced to pay reparation to the families of the noblemen killed, with 5,000 marks from York to Somerset's family, Warwick to pay 1,000 marks to Lord Clifford's heir and Salisbury required to cancel a raft of fines owed to him by the Percy family. The Yorkist lords were also required to fund prayers for the souls of the dead at St Albans Abbey to the tune of £45. The day after the arrangement was publicised, Henry, who genuinely believed he had found a way to lasting peace, organised a Love Day in the streets of London to celebrate. The nobles paraded through the city hand in hand. York walked beside the queen, Salisbury held the hand of the new duke of Somerset, then Warwick walked with the earl of Northumberland. Henry was the only one in the city who thought this was an end to the matter. Others may have hoped but seen through the sham.

As 1459 progressed, a cold war settled on England. Each side waited for the other to make a move or provide an excuse for action. The chronicles bemoan the state of the kingdom. 'In this same time, the realm of England was out of all good governance, as it had been many days before, for the king was simple and led by covetous council, and owed more than he was worth.' The same writer was clear who was to blame. 'The queen with such as were of her affinity ruled the realm as she liked, gathering riches innumerable.'[31] As the summer drew to an end, York called Salisbury and Warwick to Ludlow. On 23 September 1459 as the earl of Salisbury moved south from his Yorkshire base, he was confronted by a royal army raised by the queen at Blore Heath in Staffordshire. Lord Audley, who led the force, was killed and his men massacred by Salisbury's army, who arrived in Ludlow a few days later bearing news of the engagement. Warwick came from Calais, where he had managed to hold onto his office as Captain. He brought the garrison of the town, the closest thing to a professional standing army the crown had at this time.

In early October, York led this army out of Ludlow heading south. They reached Worcester and turned east towards London. With the queen in the Midlands, York might have felt he had a chance to speak to the king without the whispering of his enemies poisoning Henry to him. He may well have planned a repeat of his appearance at Dartford in 1452, flexing his muscles to impose himself, but much more wary now of any promises Henry might offer. As they left Worcester, though, news arrived that a royal army was approaching. It was double their strength, and Henry himself rode at the front wearing his armour and flying royal banners. Even at this stage, confronting Henry was a step too far for York, and the numbers were not on his side. He withdrew back to Ludlow and ordered defensive earthworks dug just outside the town at Ludford Meadows. On 10 October, the Yorkist lords wrote to the king protesting their loyalty.[32] The king's response was blunt. Surrender now, and all but Salisbury would be pardoned, his exclusion insisted on because he had attacked the queen's army at Blore Heath. Warwick could hardly accept such terms, and York would lose honour and hope if he abandoned his most high-ranking ally.

On 12 October, the royal army came into view outside Ludlow and made camp. Whatever the Yorkist plans at this point, they unravelled during the night. Andrew Trollope, leader of the Calais garrison brought by Warwick, took his men over the earthworks at Ludford Meadows and fled into the king's pardon, securing their wages from the crown in the process.[33] York, Salisbury, Warwick, and York's two oldest sons Edward, Earl of March, now 17, and Edmund, Earl of Rutland, who was 16, retired to Ludlow Castle to work out their next move. In the morning, as the camp stirred in Ludford Meadows, none of their leaders could be found. The noblemen had slipped away in the night, York and Edmund making for Ireland and Salisbury, Warwick, and Edward heading to the south coast and on to Calais. The Yorkist army immediately submitted to the king, but the royal army was allowed to attack the town of Ludlow to punish the residents for supporting their lord. *An English Chronicle* records that 'the town of Ludlow, belonging then to the duke of York, was robbed to the bare walls, and the noble duchess of York unmanly and cruelly treated and spoiled'. Gregory vividly recounted 'The misrule of the king's gallants at Ludlow, when they had drunk enough of the wine that was in the taverns and in other places, they full ungodly broke open the barrels of wine, and then they robbed the town, and bore away bedding, cloth, and other stuff, and defouled many women.'[35]

Parliament met at Coventry in November 1459 and would later be dubbed the Parliament of Devils. York, Salisbury, Warwick, and their families were attainted for treason, deprived of all their lands and offices and left with nothing to hand to their heirs.[36] The York and Neville families were utterly ruined. It was placed on record that York had planned to go to Kenilworth to assassinate the king only to be thwarted by those who loved Henry.[37] The dismantling of the Yorkist lords' power was swift and complete, with those around the court finding a new well of patronage to ask from the king. Left with nothing to lose, the Yorkist lords made a desperate bid to win back what had been taken from them. In early 1460, Warwick led a raid on Sandwich during which part of the royal fleet was snatched. In June, Salisbury, Warwick, and Edward landed on the south coast and were warmly welcomed into London, where Warwick in particular was very popular. As Salisbury laid siege to the Tower of London, which held out under the command of Lord Scales, Warwick and Edward took an army north to challenge the royal forces. The two sides met at the Battle of Northampton on 10 July 1460. In driving rain, the royal artillery failed and Lord Grey of Ruthin, for reasons that remain unclear, defected from the royal army and allowed Edward to pass through Grey's defensive position. The royal army was destroyed. Amongst the dead were the duke of Buckingham, the earl of Shrewsbury, and Lord Beaumont. The most important outcome of the day was the capture of King Henry after the battle. He was escorted back to London, where the Tower had been secured, and everyone held their breath to await the return of the duke of York.

It was not until 10 October, three months after the Battle of Northampton, that York arrived in London. The delay may have been because he was torn on the path to take. He entered Westminster Hall, walked through the lords gathered there, climbed the steps to the dais and placed his hand on the cushion that sat on the empty throne. The meaning was clear: the duke of York was claiming the throne of England. He was met by a confused and worried silence. If he had hoped for a rapturous welcome for his claim, he was to be disappointed. After a decade in opposition to a crown he professed to wish only to serve, York may have decided his options had narrowed by 1460. It is telling that it took his attainder and the loss of all his lands and titles before he took this fateful step. York has long been considered a man whose burning ambition for the crown drove the nation into civil war, but this step came after ten years trying to make his case and fend off a whispering campaign against him. Combined with his Mortimer heritage, he was viewed with the highest suspicion before he moved into opposition, so he was never likely to succeed in his efforts to impose himself on Henry, yet for a decade he persisted in trying without ever questioning Henry's right to the crown.

On 16 October, York's claim to the throne was presented to parliament. The suit centred not on Richard's position as heir to the House of York, but his credentials as a Mortimer heir to the crown.[39] Richard traced his lineage back to Lionel, Duke of Clarence, and asserted that this connection to the second son of Edward III was senior to the House of Lancaster's descent from Edward's third son, John of Gaunt. During the course of reciting this title, York described himself as 'Richard Plantagenet',[40] the first written use of the name that would be ascribed to the dynasty begun by Henry II in 1154. The name must have held meaning for York to call upon it, but this is the first record of the royal family being called Plantagenet. Parliament descended into comical, farcical panic. No one knew what to do or how to make the decision. Refusing York risked the wrath of the man now in political control of the country by force of arms. Yet there was no real will to deprive Henry, a man anointed king who had ruled for almost forty years, of his position. Unlike the depositions of Edward II and Richard II, parliament was caught suddenly lacking in confidence. The difference in this case was the reason for the uncertainty. Edward II had been deposed in favour of his son. Richard II's removal had been ratified in parliament after it had taken place. Now, parliament was to judge royal credentials and possibly depose a king in favour not of his heir, but his cousin.

The Lords referred the problem to the king's justices, only for those officials to return on 20 October to state that they could not judge such a weighty matter because 'it touched the king's high estate and regality'. Next, the lords summoned the king's attorney and sergeants-at-law, who protested that 'since the said matter was so high that it surpassed the learning of the justices, it must needs exceed their learning'. With their options narrowing, the chancellor instructed the Lords to go away and return with at least one objection to York's claim each. The first problem cited was the frequency with which they had sworn oaths of allegiance to King Henry, but York retorted that oaths made to a king who had no right to his crown were invalid. When they raised the issue of the numerous acts of parliament passed confirming the Lancastrian title, York replied that if they had been undisputed kings with unimpeachable right, no such acts would have been required. The duke was also able to point out that there had only been one such act anyway, in 1406.

The Lords next challenged York as to why he had never used the arms of Lionel of Antwerp, always using those of York. The duke responded that the arms of the duke of Clarence and Mortimer had always been his to use, but he had refrained in deference to Henry VI, adding that 'although right for a time rests and is silenced, yet it does not rot nor shall not perish'. Exhausting their objections, the Lords could not deny the rightfulness of York's claim but remained reticent to expel the ineffective but inoffensive Henry. They provided a compromise, known as the Act of Accord. This would allow Henry to stay on the throne for the rest of his life with York acting as regent. On Henry's death, the crown would not pass to his son Prince Edward, but to York and his heirs. The parliament rolls recorded that when the king was told of the arrangement, Henry, 'to avoid the shedding of Christian blood, by good and serious deliberation and the advice of all his lords spiritual and temporal, agreed to the settlement'. He was not even willing to fight for his own cause.

York was now legally heir to the throne of England. He was granted the duchy of Cornwall from Henry's son along with an income of 10,000 marks. York and his oldest sons Edward and Edmund each took an oath to protect Henry VI and in return, it was made treason to plot against the duke and his family. York was almost a decade older than Henry. His willingness to accept this unsatisfactory compromise adds weight to the notion that he was not driven by an insatiable desire to rule as King Richard III. It would better benefit his children, who would be heirs after him, though Henry's frail health meant the crown was still a possibility for York. He had tried for ten years to secure the position he felt his birth and abilities deserved at the head of Henry's government. It is telling that even now, he was willing to settle for that role rather than the throne.

All of the manoeuvring in London had utterly failed to take account of one person. Queen Margaret had no intention of accepting the disinheritance of her son Prince Edward. Margaret had been in Wales under the protection of her husband's half-brother Jasper Tudor, Earl of Pembroke. She sailed to Scotland and managed to secure an army to accompany her south, though she lacked funds to pay them so conceded the strategically sensitive border town of Berwick and offered the Scots soldiers whatever plunder they could take in lieu of wages. As this force crossed the border, York led an army of around 5,000 north to confront them. He reached his castle at Sandal and received news that the queen's army vastly outnumbered his, so installed himself in Sandal Castle and awaited reinforcements from his oldest son Edward, who was in the Welsh Marches. Precisely why what happened next took place is a mystery.

On 30 December 1460, York led his force out of Sandal Castle and confronted the queen's army, led by the duke of Somerset. The most convincing explanation for the decision appears in *An English Chronicle*.[41] John, Baron Neville, a half-brother of the earl of Salisbury, arrived at Sandal Castle and 'went to the said duke of York, desiring a commission of him for to raise an army for to chastise the rebels of the country'. This side of the Neville family was in conflict with Salisbury's branch, but York permitted Baron Neville to raise a force, and he soon returned with 8,000 men. Out of the blue, Andrew Trollope also appeared and offered to serve York, apologising for his actions at Ludlow. York took him at his word and welcomed the Calais garrison. Feeling that the numbers had swung in his favour, lacking provisions for a long siege, and realising he needed to prevent the queen's army getting past him and making for London, York led his men out to battle. As soon as they were outside the castle, Baron Neville and Andrew Trollope turned on York, and as Somerset piled in too, the duke's army was torn apart, with up to 2,000 men dying in the bitter cold. York was killed during the fighting. His 17-year-old son Edmund, Earl of Rutland, was captured trying to flee and slain by Lord Clifford, whose father had died at St Albans in 1455. Salisbury was captured and imprisoned at Pontefract Castle, only for a mob to break into his prison cell, drag him outside, and behead him. York and Rutland's corpses were posthumously beheaded, and all three heads were set on spikes on Micklegate Bar, one of the gates into the city of York. A paper crown was fixed to York's head to mock his pretensions as a king.

Within ten weeks of the Battle of Wakefield, York's oldest son Edward, Earl of March, and, on his father's death, Duke of York and heir to the throne, was proclaimed King Edward IV of England in London. Having won a crushing victory against Jasper Tudor, Earl of Pembroke, that prevented an army coming out of Wales from joining up with the queen, Edward regrouped with his cousin Warwick, who had lost the Second Battle of St Albans, and they entered London together. The attack on York at Sandal was declared an act of treason as specified by parliament, and when the crowds in the capital were asked if they wished Edward to be their king instead of Henry, there was rapturous agreement. Edward delayed his coronation until after he had confronted the army that had killed his father and brother and on Palm Sunday 29 March 1461, the two sides met at the decisive Battle of Towton. Fought in a swirling blizzard of wind and snow, the battle involved huge numbers of men and was an evenly balanced contest all morning. Eventually, Edward won the day, with some chroniclers numbering the dead at a staggering 28,000. Edward was crowned at Westminster on 28 June 1461, the first king of a new, Yorkist, dynasty.

The wheel continued to turn.

Conclusion

Rebellion against the crown did not begin with Hereward the Exile, or end with the deposition of King Henry VI. Neither are the examples examined above anywhere near a full catalogue of the continual rising of men and women against their monarch during the period. This book has tried to investigate some of the incidents that had the most impact on the crown, leaving a deep scar, a lesson, or a precedent for future generations. Oddly, none would prove as successful as Hereward had been during William the Conqueror's reign. William is considered a hard, ruthless king, and undoubtedly those in the north of England felt the lash of his temper after they rebelled against him. Hereward managed to evade, frustrate, and resist William, but also to emerge reconciled with the Norman crown and in possession of the lands he had been fighting to recover. Few would learn from Hereward's example, which, it occurs to me, is that rebellion can succeed if the aims are narrow, specific, and can be conceded without tarnishing royal authority. Hereward wanted his family lands back. He never sought more than that and never threatened to topple William from the throne. The Conqueror found an adversary he could admire, however irritating he was, and whose demands could ultimately be granted with no real harm done to William. The other critical element to Hereward's success, then, was a roadmap back to favour. Hereward offered a settlement that both could live with and move forward as king and liegeman.

From the succession of Stephen onwards, the incidents covered within these pages all came too close to the royal dignity for a compromise to be acceptable, which only left death for one party or the other. The Anarchy was a struggle for the crown itself between two rival claimants, neither of whom could be defeated by the other. As the second decade of Stephen's rule drew to an end, and the arrival of Empress Matilda's son Henry of Anjou ensured that the fight would continue into the next generation, it was the barons who set about limiting the conflict and trying to bring the two sides together. Despite centuries of being depicted as bloodthirsty, lawless men who enjoyed chaos, it made them poorer and gained them nothing. The truth of the Anarchy is that it was a private dispute over succession that just happened to be about the crown, giving it a national dimension and impact. Stephen was an anointed king. He claimed his uncle had wanted him to take the throne on his deathbed, but once anointed, as Henry I himself has shown, the how and the why no longer mattered. The ceremony of coronation, and particularly the religious element of anointing, transformed a man into a king. Empress Matilda's claim lay in blood and oaths, which made it impossible to dismiss, and the military support of her half-brother Robert, Earl of Gloucester, made it impossible to ignore. There was no room for either side to step back or concede anything, and it was only when chance and tragedy aligned to allow Stephen to adopt Henry and appoint him heir unopposed that an end was reached. Stephen's reign demonstrated very clearly the unassailability of the institute of the crown, irrespective of the head on which it currently rested.

Thomas Becket, once he became Archbishop of Canterbury, set himself on a collision course with the crown that risked bringing into sharp focus the boundaries of royal and ecclesiastical authority that were usually deliberately blurred to avoid such confrontations. In doing so, he left no path to reconciliation that avoided an embarrassing loss of power for the two great monoliths of medieval England; the crown and the church. By 1170, it is possible that Becket saw his only victory in martyrdom, his death not only sealing his eternal future as a saint but also pressing Henry II back into a corner. If that was his plan, then it did work. Although it cost Becket his life, Henry was forced to give up his attempts to gain supremacy over the church in England, and his reign crashed off the rails until he made his peace with the archbishop at his shrine in Canterbury. Becket achieved his aims, but at the cost of his life. Henry's fractious relationship with his sons presented the same problem.

Often accused of an unwillingness to hand off power to the next generation, Henry was happy to make Richard Duke of Aquitaine, Geoffrey Duke of Brittany, and John Lord of Ireland, though he retained a degree of control over all as their liege lord. The issue seems to have been with Henry the Young King. Whether Henry II resisted loosening his grip on the crown of England because it was a different matter than duchies and lordships, or whether he judged his oldest son unsuited, or at least never quite ready, for such responsibility is less clear. Henry the Young King pressed claims to things his father would not give him until it caused his own death. After that, Henry watched Geoffrey head the same way, so his reluctance to repeat the coronation of an heir in his lifetime or to define what would happen on his death becomes understandable. He feared it had become a curse, and he was right. In Richard, his wife's favourite son, Henry met his match.

The two were, perhaps, too much alike to get on well, as is often the case with parents and children at odds. The next death it caused was Henry's, and despite the venomous words reputed to him the last time he saw Richard, he would probably have accepted that fate rather than watch another son perish.

The First Barons' War was a reaction to an objectionable man lacking in ability, making bad choices and indulging in cruelty. The question was, what could be done against an anointed king. Stephen had shown the difficulty in unmaking a king once he had undergone a coronation. The problems of his reign had only endured because a viable rival claim existed. It is striking that the barons gave no recorded consideration to sweeping away the monarchy, or even to promoting one of their own number to challenge John. They looked to the example of the Anarchy and found a royal claimant capable of challenging the king. Dauphin Louis was invited to take the throne, unlike Empress Matilda, who had insisted on her right to it. It is perhaps telling that Louis's wife Blanche of Castile was a granddaughter of Henry II, so the old king's bloodline was being considered in finding a viable alternative, but Louis also had the wealth and military might of France behind him. As with Henry II, it was ultimately the king's death that prevented further disaster. Had John lived, Louis may well have conquered the rest of England and had himself crowned. The barons' quarrel had been with John personally, and the prospect of his 9-year-old son, untouched by all the scandal and needing a guiding hand from the nobility to steer him towards adulthood, had a sudden appeal. The removal of a sitting king would not be achieved for more than a century, so it remained an untried and unknown process.

Henry III suffered the Second Barons' War, which saw him in his older years defeated in battle and held prisoner for a year before his son rescued him. A reaction to what was viewed as weak rule and foreign favourites, Simon de Montfort was both the obvious leader and the wrong one. He had charm, ability, and was driven. As the king's brother-in-law and erstwhile friend, he had a better route than most to Henry's ear and his sympathies had he sought to negotiate reform. Stories of Simon's method of government in Gascony should have offered a warning, but more than this, his family background made him a disastrous champion for the disgruntled barons. Simon transformed the desire for reform of the king's policies into a crusade. It was what Simon understood, it was how his family had made their name in France, and he looked to join his father and brothers in eternal glory. The problem with crusading is that it is an utterly uncompromising form of conflict. It requires the complete dismissal of an opponent's position as heresy and an effort to correct it that can only be ended by death. Instead of following Hereward's example of a defined manifesto that could be delivered and pointed to a resolution all could live with, Simon polarised the revolt until it became a crusade. Like Thomas Becket, he may not have objected to dying the death of a martyr in pursuit of a holy cause, but his approach did nothing to resolve the kingdom's problems.

It was apparent from the outset of Edward II's reign that he was not suited to kingship. Easily led, quickly infatuated, distracted by pursuits deemed unbefitting for a king, his nobility saw trouble coming. Efforts were made from the earliest moment of his reign with the Boulogne Agreement to mitigate the risks the collective memory of the kingdom saw in bad kingship. The reluctance to move toward deposing a king, even one as problematical as Edward II, is striking. Matters only came to a head when Hugh Despenser the Younger emerged as a new favourite but with a harder edge than others had shown the realm. Controlling Edward to get money and distracting his attention from the business of ruling his kingdom was an annoyance, but Hugh was cruel and acquisitive, making him a threat to the rest of the nobility. Queen Isabella gave no sign of distress at other favourites her husband took, and the couple worked together well and showed genuine signs of love and affection within their marriage. If Edward's relationships with his male friends were ever sexual, it was not to the exclusion of Isabella from his affections, nor him from hers.

It was Hugh Despenser that Isabella found objectionable. Despite a long belief that she went to France in a temper with her husband, launched into an affair with Roger Mortimer, and returned to depose her husband to gain power for herself and her lover, the truth is less dramatic and far more tragic. Isabella wanted her husband to rid himself of Hugh Despenser before she returned to him. His refusal must have stung. She had indulged him in so much, but he would not allow her this one request. When she returned to England, removing Edward as king was unlikely to have been her intention, but by now, Mortimer was driving events, and he knew all too well that he would receive the sharp end of Edward's vengeance, not Isabella. Nevertheless, Edward was deposed in favour of his son, the lesser of all evils being to speed up the natural process of succession. For the first time, an anointed king was deprived of his kingdom. The uncertainty as to how it could be done legally and what the consequences might be demonstrate the magnitude of the step. Pandora's Box was open, and a dangerous precedent had been set. It was no longer enough to be a king; there was a requirement to be a good king with the approval of his subjects.

With the forced abdication of Richard II in 1399, the model was extended beyond accelerating the succession into selecting a better candidate to replace an unpopular king. Henry IV might have been considered by some measures to have been Richard's heir presumptive, but by as many, if not more, he was not. By extending the precedent set in 1327, Henry created the potential for problems for his own dynasty. If a new royal house could replace a failing one, the pressure was firmly on the Lancastrian monarchy to deliver or risk being hoist by its own petard. Henry IV would stave off incessant threats and plots, but his son would see the path to removing the tarnish from Lancastrian kingship. Henry V sought and found glory and approval in the fields of France, uniting the kingdom behind him in the prosecution of a successful war with England's old foe. Death at the height of his achievements sealed Henry V's reputation for centuries to come, but he had left a job dangerously incomplete, as both Edward I had done in Scotland and Edward III in France. The longest minority in English history now loomed. The last, that of Richard II, had been significantly shorter but had ended in the deposition of a king verging on tyranny. The problems and expense of prosecuting a war without a king combined with the personality of Henry VI as he grew to adulthood to create the potential for disaster. The focus on the former had perhaps led to the latter. After a lifetime of failing to control his fractious nobles, now grown increasingly powerful on a personal level by the retention of huge armed retinues that operated as private armies, Henry lumbered through a decade of intense problems with York before facing the same fate his grandfather had meted out to Richard II. York appears, much as Isabella had in 1327, to have been reluctant to take the final step of deposing Henry. It is, in many ways, touching that when it came to the crunch no one, not even York, could bring themselves to hate Henry enough to cast him aside. He was useless, but ultimately inoffensive, and deposing a king was still a monumental step to take.

Rebellions did not end there. In 1470, Edward IV would be ejected from his kingdom by his cousin the earl of Warwick, who earned the epithet The Kingmaker. Henry VI was restored only for Edward to return in 1471 and retake the crown by force. Warwick was killed at the Battle of Barnet and shortly afterwards Henry's only son, Prince Edward, was slain at the Battle of Tewkesbury. Henry died, probably murdered, in the immediate aftermath and the Lancastrian dynasty was ended. The House of York would go on to implode, Edward executing his brother George in 1478 and dying unexpectedly in 1483, leaving a minor as his heir. Edward V never ruled, but was declared illegitimate and replaced by his uncle as Richard III, who would be killed two years later at the Battle of Bosworth, ushering in the dawn of the Tudor era. The second half of the fifteenth century saw a terrifying acceleration in the turnover of kings, royal houses, and revolts.

The accession of Henry Tudor as Henry VII can hardly have seemed to end the problems. Another battle at Stoke Field in 1487 saw an attempt to unseat Henry and the pretender Perkin Warbeck would trouble him for much of the 1490s. The sixteenth century is no less littered with rebellion, from the Pilgrimage of Grace to the Spanish Armada, but the Tudors proved hard to dislodge, eventually losing out to nature rather than revolution.

The two popular uprisings during the period, the Peasants' Revolt, or Great Insurrection, and Cade's Rebellion are more unique. Cade's Rebellion had more in common with many baronial uprisings in seeking to remove evil advisors from about the king for the benefit of the realm. Still, it stuck to the idea of a closed, clearly defined list of objectives that could be delivered and then opposition withdrawn. The fault lay in believing the king could be brought to heel by his subjects. The nobility occupied a distinctive position, beneath the king, but close enough to try to hold him to account with authority, and to some extent responsibility, to do so. The same indulgence was not extended to the general populace, and they lacked the power to enforce their will. The Peasants' Revolt was the one incident of rebellion that aimed for a seismic change to the structures of society, and it seemed to win the support of the young King Richard II. Had he been more mature and able to embrace the policy fully, England might have been a very different place by the end of the fourteenth century. As it was, those with power over the king and government stood to lose too much and could pass the concessions Richard made to the rebels off as the naïve actions of a boy under terrible pressure. The reversal cost many their lives, even when they had acted under the authority of letters patent from the king, and it probably left deep scars on Richard that ultimately led to his deposition eighteen years later. The manifesto of the Great Insurrection was simply too broad and deep to be permitted to succeed.

The Peasants' Revolt was also one of the rare occasions when a rebellion sought genuine change. It sought to redefine the nature of England and its peoples. It was the closest medieval England came to a full-blown revolution. Most examples of noblemen rising against the crown were attempts to preserve the status quo, not least because the nobility was the class within society that benefitted the most from that equilibrium. Hereward demanded the return of his family's lands to restore him to the position in which he should have been. When the barons worked to end the civil strife of Stephen's reign, it was so that they could return to the peaceful normality that made them rich. Becket sought to preserve the rights of the church and prevent change, the barons of the thirteenth century protested against styles of rule they disapproved of and sought to impose regulations that would minimise if not negate change. The same issue appeared in Edward II's reign when his unbalanced reliance on favourites made government unpredictable and the position of the nobility uncertain. By the middle of the fifteenth century, three kings had been deposed in sixty-two years. The rate of acceleration in these once-unheard-of occurrences must have been startling to those who gave it any thought. It would happen four more times between 1470 and 1485.

Perhaps the other most striking element these outbursts of rebellion shared in common was the lack of an explosive eruption with no warning or build up. Most were years, if not decades, in the making before the final step of open rebellion was taken. As many of the stories demonstrate, there was a slow burn to all of these, even if the conclusion was dramatic and sudden; the murder of an archbishop, or the deposition of a king. Even the Peasants' Revolt was the result of decades of labour suppression and years of harsh taxation. This perhaps illustrates the most troubling dimension of rebellion against the crown. It invariably led to the death of the rebel or rebels. With the exception of Hereward, and narratives that allow for the longer life of Edward II and Richard II than is usually accepted, the leaders of uprisings against the crown paid with their lives. Even if the two monarchs survived, stories were put about that they were dead. Roger Mortimer paid for unseating Edward II with his life as soon as Edward III was old enough. Henry IV managed to overthrow a king and found a dynasty, but his precedent would ultimately doom his grandson. Stephen's reign and that of Edward II would see two decades of sustained opposition. The Becket affair lasted for eight years. York was in a position of what he might have described as loyal opposition for ten years until, left with nothing to lose, he took the ultimate step, only to die for it weeks later. Rebellion without a pathway to peace must have been a desperate last resort because it was likely to cost those who took that route dearly. It suggests they must have been driven by conviction in their cause and belief in their ability to fight for it successfully, or else a willingness to die rather than accept the wrong they perceived. Whether the cause was just or otherwise, there is something noble in that.

The crown as an institution remained remarkably robust against these persistent storms. Even when the person wearing it at any given moment was challenged, there was never any sense of abolishing the monarchy. King Stephen is widely considered an inept king who failed dismally, yet his period in captivity in 1141 and his emergence still wearing his crown served to strengthen the institution rather than weaken it. For all of their revolutionary aims, the men and women of the Great Insurrection began and ended by insisting they wanted Richard as their king. Their grievances were with those who were inserted between the crown and its people and the corruption these layers heaped down onto the lowest. They never intended to be rid of the crown, only to connect more directly to it. Even failed rebellions could give kings pause for thought. The persistent problems suffered by Henry III, Edward II, and Henry VI reflected an unwillingness to accept that there might be genuine problems that could reasonably easily be addressed. There was no better student of this than Henry V, and it is no accident that his confrontation of the issues around Lancastrian kingship has left him with an enviable royal reputation in the popular consciousness for centuries. He would tolerate no dissent, as the Southampton Plot and the swift executions showed, but he would also find a way to unite the country in a common cause behind the crown.

One constant from the thirteenth century onwards was a vehicle for rebellion that not only worked but gathered to itself ever-increasing power and authority in parallel to the crown. Parliament was a nascent idea under Norman rule. The Anglo-Saxon Witenagamot had been a council of elders, nobles, and churchmen that not only advised the king but took responsibility for selecting the next ruler. William the Conqueror swept away such conciliar rule, but the idea lingered that England did not want absolutist monarchs with no mechanism to hold them to account. Magna Carta was a narrow attempt to impose the rule of law on the crown, though it only served the barons and was only to be applied to free people, around 40 percent of the population. During Henry III's reign, the rebuilding of royal authority after the disasters of John's rule took place in parallel to the emergence of a body referred to for the first time as a parliament. By using its power to grant, or withhold, direct taxation as both carrot and stick, the assembly was able to coerce the crown into meeting criteria or making reforms to get what it wanted. Over the decades, it became a method for moderating or compensating for a bad king's shortcomings. By 1327, it was viewed as a forum for deposing and appointing a monarch, taking a tentative and nervous step back in time towards the Witan. After the Peasants' Revolt, the nobility used parliament as a cage around what they viewed as the risks posed by Richard II. When he was removed as king, it was parliament that was seen as the vehicle to complete the dynastic change legally.

By 1460 and the Act of Accord, parliament was viewed as the place to weigh competing claims to the throne, the arbiter of titles. Parliament had worked itself into a position of equal authority to the monarch. It still required a royal summons to gather, but once it sat for whatever reason, it was, by the middle of the fifteenth century, increasingly confident in its dealings with the crown. It was the perfect forum for rebellion because the king only summoned it when he wanted something from it. That gave the Lords and, increasingly, the Commons the leverage to extract concessions, reforms and actions from the crown in return. There was always a quid pro quo that meant neither side gave away anything without gaining in equal measure what they required. As the Commons came to the fore, the country moved closer to something like the aims of the Peasants' Revolt, with the representatives of the people making a direct connection to the king to make their grievances heard, often complaints levelled at the Lords. It was far from perfect, with rigged elections and corrupt officials still prevalent, but it was a shift. It is from this that the parliamentary democracy of the United Kingdom was nurtured. It may remain imperfect, but it was born of rebellion, a forum to hold the highest powers in the land to account, and to decide who should wield that ultimate authority. By the fifteenth century, the monarch would have struggled to operate without parliament. In the seventeenth century, parliament would demonstrate that it could not function without a monarch. The ability to adjust and readjust this relationship is perhaps the single greatest reason the United Kingdom has never had a successful revolution that has overthrown either institution permanently.

Centuries in the development and slow-moving like glacial ice, the Houses of Parliament are, perhaps, the ultimate example of the potential for medieval rebellion to succeed.

Bibliography

A Shorter Froissart, ed. F.J. Tickner, Thomas Nelson & Sons

An English Chronicle, ed. J.S. Davies, The Camden Society, 1856

Annales Londonienses, Chronicles of the Reigns of Edward I and Edward II, ed. W. Stubbs, Cambridge Library Collection, 1882

Annales Monastici, Vol IV, 'The Chronicle of Thomas Wyke', ed. H.R. Luard, London, 1869

Annales Paulini, Chronicles of the Reigns of Edward I and Edward II, Vol I, W. Stubbs, London, 1882

Annals of Roger de Hoveden, Vols I and II, trans. H.T. Riley, London, 1853

Aymer de Valence, Earl of Pembroke 1307–1324, J.R.S. Phillips, Oxford University Press, 1972

Calendar of the Close Rolls, Edward II, 1307–13, London, 1892

Calendar of the Close Rolls, Edward II, 1323–1327, London, 1898

Calendar of the Patent Rolls, Henry VI, 1446–52 The Public Record Office, 1909

Calendar of the Patent Rolls, Henry VI, Vol VI, 1452–1461, Public Record Office, 1971

Chronicles of the Reigns of Stephen, Henry II and Richard I, Vol I, ed. R. Howlett, London, 1884

Chronicles of the Reigns of Stephen, Henry II and Richard I, Vol IV, ed. R. Howlett, London, 1889

Chronicon Angliae Petriburgense AD 1069, ed. J.A. Giles, Caxton Society, 1845

Danmonii Orientales Illustres or The Worthies of Devon, J. Prince, London, 1810

Edward II: The Unconventional King, K. Warner, Amberley Publishing, 2014

England, Arise: The People, The King & The Great Revolt of 1381, J. Barker, Abacus, 2014

Flores Historiarum, Vol III, ed. H.R. Luard, London, 1890

Gesta Stephani, ed. K.R. Potter, Oxford Medieval Texts, 1976

Hereward of the Fens, *De Gestis Herewardi Saxoni*, T. Bevis, 1995

Ingulph's Chronicle of the Abbey of Croyland, trans. H.T. Riley, London, 1908

King Stephen, D. Matthew, Hambledon and London, 2002

L'Histoire de Guillaume le Maréchal, P. Meyer, Paris, 1894

Letters of Royal and Illustrious Ladies of Great Britain, Vol I, M.A. Everett Wood, London, 1846

Liber Eliensis, trans. J. Fairweather, The Boydell Press, 2005

Materials for the History of Thomas Becket, Vol I, ed. J.C. Robertson, London, 1875

Materials for the History of Thomas Becket, Vol II, ed. J.C. Robertson, London, 1876

Materials for the History of Thomas Becket, Vol III, ed. J.C. Robertson, London, 1877

Materials for a History of Thomas Becket, Vol V, ed. J.C. Robertson, London, 1881

Matthew Paris's English History, Vol I, trans. J.A. Giles, London, 1852

Matthew Paris's English History, Vol II, trans. J.A. Giles, London, 1853

Matthew Paris's English History, Vol III, trans. J.A. Giles, London, 1854

Original Papal Documents in England and Wales, J.E. Sayers, Oxford University Press, 1999

Polychronicon Ranulphi Higden, Vol VIII, ed. J. Lumby, London, 1882

Proceedings and Ordinances of the Privy Council of England, Vol VI, ed. H. Nicolas, 1837

Registrum Abbatiae Johannis Whethamstede abbatis monasterii Sancti Albani, ed. H.T. Riley, Vol I, London, 1872

Roger of Wendover's Flowers of History, Vol II, trans. J.A. Giles, London, 1849

Rymer's Foedera, Vol I, ed. T. Rymer, London, 1739

St Thomas of Canterbury: An Account of his Life and Fame from The Contemporary Biographers and other Chroniclers, ed. Rev W.H. Hutton, London, 1899

Scalacronica: By Sir Thomas Gray of Heton, Knight: A Chronicle of England and Scotland from AD MLXVI to AD MCCCLXII, ed. J. Stevenson, Edinburgh, 1836

Select Historical Documents of the Middle Ages, trans. E.F. Henderson, London, 1896

Simon de Montfort and His Cause, W.H. Hutton, London, 1907

Source Problems in English History, A.B. White and W. Notestein, Harper and Brothers, 1915

The Anglo-Saxon Chronicle, trans. E.E.C. Gomme, London, 1909

The Anonimalle Chronicle, ed. W.R. Childs & J. Taylor, Yorkshire Archaeological Society Record Series, 1991

The Brut or The Chronicles of England, Part 1, ed. F.W.D. Brie, London, 1906

The Chronicle of Florence of Worcester, trans. T. Forester, London, 1854

The Chronicle of Henry of Huntingdon, ed. T. Forester, London, 1853

The Chronicle of Lanercost 1272–1346, trans. Herbert Maxwell, Glasgow, 1913

The Chronicle of the kings of England: From William the Norman to the Death of George III, R. Dodsley, London, 1821

The Church Historians of England, Vol IV, Part II, *William of Newburgh*, trans. Rev J. Stevenson, London, 1856

The Church Historians of England, Vol V, Part I, *Gerald of Wales on the Instruction of Princes*, trans. Rev J. Stevenson, London, 1858

The Ecclesiastical History of England and Normandy by Orderic Vitalis, Vol I, trans. T. Forester, London, 1853

The Ecclesiastical History of England and Normandy by Orderic Vitalis, Vol II, trans. T. Forester, London, 1854

The Ecclesiastical History of England and Normandy by Orderic Vitalis, Vol IV, trans. T. Forester, London, 1856

The First Century of English Feudalism, F.M. Stenton, Oxford, 1961

The Greatest Knight, T. Asbridge, Simon and Schuster, London, 2015

The Greatest Traitor: The Life of Sir Roger Mortimer, Ruler of England 1327 to 1330, Ian Mortimer, Pimlico, 2003

The Historical Collections of A Citizen of London in the Fifteenth Century, ed. J. Gairdner, The Camden Society, 1876

The Historical Works of Gervase of Canterbury, Vol II, ed. W. Stubbs, Roll Series, 1880

The Last Hours of Simon de Montfort: An Account of the Battle of Evesham, S. English, A Lion Occasional Paper, 2015

The New Chronicles of England and France by Robert Fabyan, ed. H. Ellis, London, 1811

The Origins of the English Parliament, 924–1327, J.R. Maddicott, Oxford University Press, 2012

The Paston Letters A.D. 1422–1509, ed. J. Gairdner, London, 1904

The Paston Letters, Vol I, ed. J. Gairdner, 1872

The Peasants' Revolt of 1381, R.B. Dobson, Macmillian, 1970

The Song of Lewes, C.L. Kingsford, Oxford, 1890

Thomas Becket, F. Barlow, Phoenix Press, London, 1986

Thomas of London Before His Consecration, L.B. Radford, Cambridge, 1894

Three Fifteenth-Century Chronicles, ed. J. Gairdner, The Camden Society, 1880

Vita Edwardi Secundi: The Life of Edward the Second, N. Denholm-Young, Thomas Nelson & Sons, 1957

William de Nangis: An Account of the Battle of Evesham, trans. R. Leamon and T. Spicer, A Lion Occasional Paper, 2011

William of Malmesbury Historia Novella, ed. E. King, Oxford Medieval Texts, 1956

Endnotes

1. Hereward the Exile

1. *The Ecclesiastical History of England and Normandy by Orderic Vitalis*, Vol I, trans. T. Forester, London, 1853, pp. 490–1 for an account of William I's coronation.
2. *Chronicon Angliae Petriburgense AD 1069*, ed. J.A. Giles, Caxton Society, 1845, p. 55.
3. *The Anglo-Saxon Chronicle*, trans. E.E.C. Gomme, London, 1909, p. 163.
4. *Ingulph's Chronicle of the Abbey of Croyland*, trans. H.T. Riley, London, 1908, pp. 134–5.
5. Ibid, p. 141.
6. Ibid, p. 142.
7. For more on Hereward's identity, see; *Hereward*, P. Rex, Amberley Publishing, 2013. Rex's research is vital in shining a light on the Danish connections of Hereward and his likely family.
8. Hereward of the Fens, *De Gestis Herewardi Saxoni*, T. Bevis, Cambs, 1995, p. 11.
9. *Ingulph's Chronicle*, p. 135.
10. Ibid.
11. Hereward of the Fens, *De Gestis Herewardi Saxoni*, pp. 13–4.
12. Ibid, p. 19.
13. Ibid, p. 20.
14. Ibid, p. 21.
15. Ibid, p. 22.
16. Ibid, and *Ingulph's Chronicle*, p. 141.
17. Orderic Vitalis, *The Ecclesiastical History of England*, p. 28.
18. *The Anglo-Saxon Chronicle*, p. 183.
19. Orderic Vitalis, *The Ecclesiastical History of England*, pp. 31–2.
20. *Liber Eliensis*, trans. J. Fairweather, Woodbridge, 2005, p. 204: 'In particular, he caused the monasteriesof all England to be thoroughly searched and gave orders that he money which the wealthier men of

England had deposited in them, because of his harshness and pillaging, should be removed and transferred to his treasury.'

21. *The Anglo-Saxon Chronicle*, p. 184.
22. *Ingulph's Chronicle*, p. 143.
23. *The Anglo-Saxon Chronicle*, p. 185.
24. *Liber Eliensis*, pp. 204–5.
25. Hereward of the Fens, *De Gestis Herewardi Saxoni*, p. 24 and *Liber Eliensis*, p. 205.
26. *Liber Eliensis*, p. 205.
27. Ibid, p. 210.
28. Hereward of the Fens, *De Gestis Herewardi Saxoni*, p. 28.
29. Ibid, p. 30.
30. Ibid, pp. 30–1 *and Liber Eliensis*, pp. 219–20 (p. 220 for quote).
31. Orderic Vitalis, *The Ecclesiastical History of England*, p. 45.
32. Hereward of the Fens, *De Gestis Herewardi Saxoni*, p. 31.
33. Ibid, p. 32.
34. Ibid, p. 33.
35. Ibid.
36. Ibid, p. 34.
37. Ibid, p. 35
38. Ibid, p. 36.
39. Ibid, p. 37.

2. The Anarchy

1. *Gesta Stephani*, ed. K.R. Potter, Oxford Medieval Texts, 1976, p. 5.
2. Ibid, p. 37.
3. Orderic Vitalis, *The Ecclesiastical History of England*, p. 174.
4. *The Anglo-Saxon Chronicle*, p. 248.
5. *Gesta Stephani*, p. 67.
6. *The Chronicle of Henry of Huntingdon*, ed. T. Forester, London, 1853, p. 266.
7. Ibid, pp. 269–70.
8. *Gesta Stephani*, p. 69.
9. William of Malmesbury, *Historia Novella*, ed. E. King, Oxford Medieval Texts, 1956, p. 61.
10. *King Stephen*, D. Matthew, Hambledon and London, 2002, pp. 88–9.
11. *Gesta Stephani*, p. 87.
12. William of Malmesbury, *Historia Novella*, p. 63.

13. Ibid, p. 47.
14. *Gesta Stephani*, p. 73.
15. Ibid, p. 77.
16. William of Malmesbury, *Historia Novella*, p. 49.
17. *Gesta Stephani*, p. 101.
18. William of Malmesbury, *Historia Novella*, pp. 75–7.
19. Ibid, p. 71.
20. Ibid, pp. 73–5.
21. Henry of Huntingdon's is not the only account of the battle, and details differ across those provided by William of Malmesbury and the *Gesta Stephani*.
22. *The Chronicle of Henry of Huntingdon*, pp. 274–80 for his account of the battle used here.
23. *Chronicles of the Reigns of Stephen, Henry II and Richard I*, Vol IV, ed. R. Howlett, London, 1889, pp. 139–41.
24. *The Chronicle of Henry of Huntingdon*, p. 280.
25. *Gesta Stephani*, p. 115.
26. Ibid, p. 117.
27. William of Malmesbury, *Historia Novella*, p. 87.
28. *Gesta Stephani*, p. 119.
29. Ibid, p. 121.
30. *The Chronicle of Henry of Huntingdon*, p. 280.
31. William of Malmesbury, *Historia Novella*, p. 91.
32. Ibid.
33. Ibid, p. 93.
34. *Gesta Stephani*, p. 121.
35. Ibid, pp. 121–3.
36. Ibid, p. 123.
37. Ibid.
38. William of Malmesbury, *Historia Novella*, p. 101.
39. *Gesta Stephani*, pp. 119 and 125.
40. William of Malmesbury, *Historia Novella*, p. 101.
41. Ibid, p. 103.
42. *The Chronicle of Florence of Worcester*, trans. T. Forester, London, 1854, p. 284.
43. William of Malmesbury, *Historia Novella*, pp. 117–9.
44. Ibid, p. 123.
45. Ibid, p. 127.
46. *The Anglo-Saxon Chronicle*, pp. 247-8.
47. *Chronicles of the Reigns of Stephen, Henry II and Richard I*, p. 282.

48. *Gesta Stephani*, pp. 205–7.
49. *The First Century of English Feudalism*, F.M. Stenton, Oxford, 1961, pp. 250–6, 286–8.
50. *Chronicles of the Reigns of Stephen, Henry II and Richard I*, p. 88 for William of Newburgh and, p. 171 for Robert of Torigni.
51. *Gesta Stephani*, p. 239.
52. Ibid, and *The Chronicle of Henry of Huntingdon*, p. 293.
53. *Chronicles of the Reigns of Stephen, Henry II and Richard I*, p. 177.

3. The Becket Affair

1. *Materials for the History of Thomas Becket*, Vol I, *William of Canterbury*, ed. J.C. Robertson, London, 1875, p. 3 and *Materials for the History of Thomas Becket*, Vol II, *Edward Grimm*, ed. J.C. Robertson, London, 1876, pp. 359–61 and *Materials for the History of Thomas Becket*, Vol III, *William Fitz Stephen*, ed. J.C. Robertson, London, 1877, p. 17.
2. *Thomas Becket*, F. Barlow, Phoenix Press, London, 1986, p. 36.
3. *Materials for the History of Thomas Becket*, Vol III, pp. 29–33.
4. Ibid.
5. Ibid, pp. 24–5.
6. St Thomas of Canterbury, *An Account of his Life and Fame from The Contemporary Biographers and other Chroniclers*, ed. Rev W.H. Hutton, London, 1899, pp. 26–7 (from Herbert of Bosham).
7. *Materials for a History of Thomas Becket*, Vol V, Epistles I.-CCXXVI. ed. J.C. Robertson, London, 1881, pp. 410, 516–7.
8. *The Ecclesiastical History of England and Normandy by Orderic Vitalis*, Vol II, trans. T. Forester, London, 1854, pp. 125–130 lists the 46 canons of the Decrees of Lillebonne.
9. *Thomas of London Before His Consecration*, L.B. Radford, Cambridge, 1894, p. 222.
10. Ibid, p. 223.
11. Ibid.
12. St Thomas of Canterbury, An account of his *Life and Fame from The Contemporary Biographers and other*, p. 29.
13. *Chronicles of the Reigns of Stephen, Henry II, and Richard I*, Vol IV, p. 322.
14. *Annals of Roger de Hoveden*, Vol I, trans. H.T. Riley, London, 1853, p. 259.

15. Ibid, p. 258.
16. *Select Historical Documents of the Middle Ages*, trans. E.F. Henderson, London, 1896, pp. 11–16.
17. *Annals of Roger de Hoveden*, Vol I, p. 259.
18. Ibid, p. 261.
19. Ibid.
20. Ibid.
21. Ibid, pp. 262–7 for Roger's account of the trial at Northampton.
22. Ibid, p. 278.
23. *Letters of Royal and Illustrious Ladies of Great Britain*, Vol I, M.A. Everett Wood, London, 1846, pp. 9–11.
24. *Annals of Roger de Hoveden*, Vol I, p. 279.
25. Ibid, pp. 279–81.
26. Ibid, pp. 281–2 for Pope Alexander's letter, and pp. 282–7 for the reply of Gilbert, Bishop of London.
27. Ibid, p. 287.
28. Ibid, pp. 312–3.
29. Ibid, p. 333.
30. *The Chronicle of the Kings of England: From William the Norman to the Death of George III*, R. Dodsley, London, 1821, p. 27. A longer version of the quote appears in a footnote on the same page, with the briefer rendering in the main text. Also, *The History of King Henry the Second*, Vol IV, G. Lyttelton, London, 1777, p. 353. The 1964 film Becket uses the same phrase as Henry bellows, 'Will no one rid me of this meddlesome priest?'
31. *The Church Historians of England*, Vol IV, Part II, *William of Newburgh*, trans. Rev J. Stevenson, London, 1856, p. 479.
32. Barlow, *Thomas Becket*, p. 235.
33. *Materials for the History of Thomas Becket, Archbishop of Canterbury*, Vol II, pp. 430–8.
34. *Annals of Roger de Hoveden*, Vol I, pp. 339–40 and pp. 342–3.
35. *The Church Historians of England*, Vol IV, Part II, *William of Newburgh*, p. 493.
36. Gospel of John 18:8.

4. The Eaglets

1. *Annals of Roger de Hoveden*, Vol I, p. 367.
2. Ibid, p. 525.

3. Ibid, p. 374.

4. Ibid, p. 375.

5. *The Church Historians of England*, Vol IV, Part II, *William of Newburgh*, pp. 266–8.

6. *Annals of Roger de Hoveden*, Vol I, p. 385.

7. *Annals of Roger de Hoveden*, Vol II, trans. H.T. Riley, London, 1853, p. 23.

8. Ibid, p. 24.

9. *The Church Historians of England*, Vol V, Part I, *Gerald of Wales on the Instruction of Princes*, trans. Rev J. Stevenson, London, 1858, p. 151.

10. Ibid.

11. *Annals of Roger de Hoveden*, Vol II, pp. 63–4.

12. Ibid.

13. Ibid, p. 99.

14. Henry's final days are described in several sources: *Annals of Roger de Hoveden*, Vol II, pp. 106–11; *The Church Historians of England*, Vol IV, Part II, *William of Newburgh*, p. 552; *The Church Historians of England*, Vol V, Part I, *Gerald of Wales on the Instruction of Princes*, pp. 214–22; *The Historical Works of Gervase of Canterbury*, Vol II, ed. W. Stubbs, Roll Series, 1880, pp. 447–9.

15. *The Greatest Knight*, T. Asbridge, Simon and Schuster, London, 2015, p. 201 quoting *The History of William Marshal*.

16. *The Church Historians of England*, Vol V, Part I, *Gerald of Wales on the Instruction of Princes*, p. 222.

17. *Annals of Roger de Hoveden*, Vol II, p. 100.

18. Ibid, p. 111.

19. Ibid, p. 23

20. *The Church Historians of England*, Vol V, Part I, *Gerald of Wales on the Instruction of Princes*, p. 221.

5. The First Barons' War

1. The National Archive Currency Converter only runs back to 1270, but equates £40,000 to around £29,000,000 in modern money. https://www.nationalarchives.gov.uk/currency-converter/#currency-result, accessed 19/09/2020.

2. *The Brut or The Chronicles of England*, Part 1, ed. F.W.D. Brie, London, 1906, pp. 163–4 for John's letter to Rome.

3. Ibid.

4. *Source Problems in English History*, A.B. White and W. Notestein, London, 1915, pp. 367–70 for Henry I's Charter of Liberties of 1100.
5. *The Brut or The Chronicles of England*, Part 1, pp. 166–7.
6. *Original Papal Documents in England and Wales*, J.E. Sayers, Oxford University Press, 1999, pp. 31–2.
7. *The Brut or The Chronicles of England*, Part 1, p. 167.
8. *L'Histoire de Guillaume le Maréchal*, ed. P. Meyer, Paris, 1894, pp. 235–6.
9. *Roger of Wendover's Flowers of History*, Vol II, trans. J.A. Giles, London, 1849, p. 395.
10. Ibid, p. 398.
11. Ibid, pp. 402–4.
12. The case of the Braose family was not unique. John ordered others starved, including a group of twenty-two French prisoners at Corfe Castle.

6. The Second Barons' War

1. *Matthew Paris's English History*, Vol I, trans. J.A. Giles, London, 1852, p. 117.
2. Ibid, pp. 121–3.
3. Ibid, p. 160.
4. Ibid, p. 194.
5. *Matthew Paris's English History*, Vol II, trans. J.A. Giles, London, 1853, pp. 420–1.
6. Ibid, p. 507.
7. *Matthew Paris's English History*, Vol III, trans. J.A. Giles, London, 1854, pp. 294–5.
8. Ibid, p. 341.
9. *Rymer's Foedera*, Vol I, ed. T. Rymer, London, 1739, pp. 433–4.
10. *Annales Monastici*, Vol IV, 'The Chronicle of Thomas Wyke', ed. H.R. Luard, London, 1869, p. 141. Quoted in Hutton, *Simon de Montfort and His Cause*, pp. 116–8.
11. *Matthew Paris's English History*, Vol III, pp. 344–5.
12. Ibid, p. 345.
13. Ibid, pp. 345–6.
14. Ibid, pp. 347–9 for Matthew Paris's account of the Battle of Lewes.
15. Ibid, and *Chronicle of Melrose*, ed. B. Club, p. 193 quoted in Hutton, *Simon de Montfort and His Cause*, pp. 124–5.

16. *Chronicle of* Melrose, ed. B. Club, p. 193 quoted in Hutton, *Simon de Montfort and His Cause*, p. 128.
17. *William Rishanger's Chronicle*, p. 37, quoted in Hutton, *Simon de Montfort and His Cause*, pp. 131–3, and *Matthew Paris's English History*, Vol III, 1854, p. 349.
18. *The Song of Lewes*, C.L. Kingsford, Oxford, 1890, pp. 33–54 for the English translation.
19. Ibid, p. 46.
20. Ibid, p. 47.
21. William de Nangis, *An Account of the Battle of Evesham, From Historiae Francorum Scriptores Coaetanei (Biographies of Three Kings) by William de Nangis*, Tome V, 1649, starting at page 372, trans. R. Leaman and T. Spicer, A Lion Occasional Paper, 2011, p. 15.
22. *Matthew Paris's English History*, Vol III, p. 351.
23. *Select Charters*, W. Stubbs, Oxford, 1905, pp. 412–4 translated in Hutton, *Simon de Montfort and His Cause*, pp. 138–41.
24. *Matthew Paris's English History*, Vol III, p. 350.
25. Ibid, p. 351.
26. There is plenty of discussion on this issue. e.g. *The Origins of the English Parliament, 924–1327*, J.R. Maddicott, Oxford University Press, 2012, pp. 234–57 and http://sussexpast.co.uk/wp-content/uploads/2012/05/Simon-de-Montfort-the-Battle-of-Lewes-and-the-development-of-Parliament.pdf.
27. *Matthew Paris's English History*, Vol III, pp. 349–50.
28. *Annales Monastici*, Vol IV, 'The Chronicle of Thomas Wyke', pp. 157–8.
29. *Matthew Paris's English History*, Vol III, p. 350.
30. Ibid, p. 352.
31. Ibid, p. 353 and *Robert of Gloucester*, II, p. 756, quoted in Hutton, *Simon de Montfort and His Cause*, pp. 145–6.
32. *Matthew Paris's English History*, Vol III, p. 353–4.
33. William de Nangis, *An Account of the Battle of Evesham*, pp. 16–7.
34. *The Last Hours of Simon de Montfort: An Account of the Battle of Evesham*, S. English, A Lion Occasional Paper, 2015, pp. 16–7.
35. Ibid, p. 17.
36. Ibid, pp. 18–9, and William de Nangis, *An Account of the Battle of Evesham*, p. 18.
37. Robert of Gloucester, II, p. 762, quoted in Hutton, *Simon de Montfort and His Cause*, p. 149.

38. Ibid.
39. *Chronicle of Melrose*, ed. Stevenson, p. 200, quoted in Hutton, *Simon de Montfort and His Cause*, pp. 150–1.
40. I would argue that almost all rebels are driven by self-interest rather than unrestrained altruism. Hereward fought for what he had lost, but managed to lash his own complaints and aims to those of others, including a populace buckling under the Norman yoke. Simon had no such devastating opponent, and used the power he gained exclusively to better his own position.

7. I Could Not Be Other Than I Am

1. *The Chronicle of Lanercost 1272–1346*, trans. Herbert Maxwell, Glasgow, 1913, p. 222.
2. *Polychronicon Ranulphi Higden*, Vol VIII, ed. J. Lumby, London, 1882, p. 299.
3. *Vita Edwardi Secundi: The Life of Edward the Second*, N. Denholm-Young, Thomas Nelson & Sons, 1957, p. 3.
4. *Aymer de Valence, Earl of Pembroke 1307–1324*, J.R.S. Phillips, Oxford University Press, 1972, pp. 316–7 provides a transcription of the Agreement.
5. *Vita Edwardi Secundi*, p. 4.
6. Ibid, p. 9.
7. *Annales Londonienses, Chronicles of the Reigns of Edward I and Edward II*, ed. W. Stubbs, Cambridge Library Collection, 1882, pp. 169–74.
8. *Calendar of the Close Rolls*, Edward II, 1307–13, London, 1892, pp. 448–9.
9. *Vita Edwardi Secundi*, p. 25.
10. Ibid, p. 26.
11. Ibid, p. 27.
12. *Scalacronica: By Sir Thomas Gray of Heton, knight. A Chronicle of England and Scotland from AD MLXVI to AD MCCCLXII*, ed. J. Stevenson, Edinburgh, 1836, p. 51.
13. Ibid, p. 60.
14. *The Anonimalle Chronicle*, ed. W.R. Childs and J. Taylor, Yorkshire Archaeological Society Record Series, 1991, p. 92.
15. *Vita Edwardi Secundi*, p. 109.

16. *The Brut or The Chronicles of England*, p. 219. The language is similar to the stories told of Edward II's death, which are almost certainly untrue.
17. Ibid, p. 223.
18. Ibid, p. 231.
19. *The Anonimalle Chronicle*, p. 120.
20. *Vita Edwardi Secundi*, pp. 142–3.
21. *Calendar of the Close Rolls*, Edward II, 1323–27, London, 1898, p. 543.
22. Ibid, p. 578.
23. Ibid, pp. 578–9.
24. Ibid, pp. 650–1.
25. *Danmonii Orientales Illustres or The Worthies of Devon*, J. Prince, London, 1810, p. 724.
26. *Calendar of the Close Rolls*, Edward II, 1323–27, p. 655.
27. *The Brut or The Chronicles of England*, p. 240 and *Annales Paulini, Chronicles of the Reigns of Edward I and Edward II*, Vol I, W. Stubbs, London, 1882, pp. 317–8.
28. *The Brut or The Chronicles of England*, pp. 239–40 *and Annales Paulini, Chronicles of the Reigns of Edward I and Edward II*, Vol I, W. Stubbs, London, 1882, pp. 319–20.
29. *Flores Historiarum*, Vol III, ed. H.R. Luard, London, 1890, p. 235.
30. 'The Conspiracy of Thomas Dunheved, 1327', F.J. Tanqueray, *English Historical Review* 31, 1916, pp. 119–24.
31. *Edward II: The Unconventional King*, K. Warner, Amberley Publishing, 2014, p. 248. From Warwickshire County Record Office, CR136/C2027. As someone who has written a book on *The Survival of the Princes in the Tower*, this facet of Edward's story intrigues me. Kathryn Warner and Ian Mortimer make compelling cases for believing Edward was not dead in 1330 and beyond.
32. 'Edward III: March 1330', in *Parliament Rolls of Medieval England*, ed. Chris Given-Wilson, Paul Brand, Seymour Phillips, Mark Ormrod, Geoffrey Martin, Anne Curry and Rosemary Horrox (Woodbridge, 2005), British History Online http://www.british-history.ac.uk/no-series/parliament-rolls-medieval/march-1330 [accessed 17 November 2020].
33. 'Edward III: November 1330, C 65/2, mm.7-5', in Given-Wilson et al, *Parliament Rolls of Medieval England*, British History Online http://www.british-history.ac.uk/no-series/parliament-rolls-medieval/november-1330-c-65 [accessed 17 November 2020].
34. *The Greatest Traitor: The Life of Sir Roger Mortimer, Ruler of England 1327 to 1330*, I. Mortimer, Pimlico, 2003, pp. 251–62.

8. The Peasants' Revolt

1. *A Shorter Froissart*, ed. F.J. Tickner, Thomas Nelson & Sons, p. 154.
2. White and Notestein, *Source Problems in English History*, pp. 141–6.
3. Ibid, pp. 146–52.
4. *England, Arise: The People, The King & The Great Revolt of 1381*, J. Barker, Abacus, 2014, pp. 113–4.
5. 'Richard II: April 1379', in Given-Wilson et al, *Parliament Rolls of Medieval England*, British History Online http://www.british-history.ac.uk/no-series/parliament-rolls-medieval/april-1379 [accessed 23 November 2020].
6. 'Richard II: January 1380', in Given-Wilson et al, *Parliament Rolls of Medieval England*, British History Online http://www.british-history.ac.uk/no-series/parliament-rolls-medieval/january-1380 [accessed 23 November 2020].
7. 'Richard II: November 1380', in Given-Wilson et al, *Parliament Rolls of Medieval England*, British History Online http://www.british-history.ac.uk/no-series/parliament-rolls-medieval/november-1380 [accessed 23 November 2020].
8. Ibid.
9. Barker, *England, Arise*, pp. 134–5.
10. Ibid, p. 144.
11. Tickner, *A Shorter Froissart*, p. 148.
12. Ibid, pp. 148–9.
13. *The Peasants' Revolt of 1381*, R.B. Dobson, Macmillian, 1970, pp. 126–7.
14. *The Brut or The Chronicles of England*, p. 336.
15. Barker, *England, Arise*, p. 166.
16. Tickner, *A Shorter Froissart*, p. 149.
17. Ibid, p. 152.
18. Dobson, *The Peasants' Revolt of 1381*, pp. 374–5 for Walsingham's account of the sermon.
19. Tickner, *A Shorter Froissart*, pp. 152–3.
20. Ibid, p. 153.
21. Ibid, p. 154.
22. Ibid, p. 155.
23. *The Brut or The Chronicles of England*, p. 336 and Tickner, *A Shorter Froissart*, p. 156.
24. *The Brut or The Chronicles of England*, p. 336 and Tickner, *A Shorter Froissart*, p. 157.
25. Barker, *England, Arise*, pp. 230–1.

26. *The Brut or The Chronicles of England*, pp. 336–7.
27. Ibid, p. 337.
28. Tickner, *A Shorter Froissart*, p. 158.
29. Dobson, *The Peasants' Revolt of 1381*, p. 161.
30. Tickner, *A Shorter Froissart*, pp. 160–1.
31. Ibid, p. 157.
32. Ibid, p. 163–6. Froissart has Tyler, Straw, and Ball present with Tyler approaching the king. *The Brut or The Chronicles of England*, p. 337 has Jack Straw taking the leading role.
33. Dobson, *The Peasants' Revolt of 1381*, pp. 164–7.
34. Tickner, *A Shorter Froissart*, pp. 165–6. *The Brut or The Chronicles of England*, p. 337 has Jack Straw killed William Walworth.
35. Tickner, *A Shorter Froissart*, p. 166.
36. 'Richard II: November 1381', in Given-Wilson et al, *Parliament Rolls of Medieval England*, British History Online http://www.british-history.ac.uk/no-series/parliament-rolls-medieval/november-1381 [accessed 24 November 2020].

9. The Rise and Fall of the House of Lancaster

1. 'Richard II: October 1386', in Given-Wilson et al, *Parliament Rolls of Medieval England*, British History Online http://www.british-history.ac.uk/no-series/parliament-rolls-medieval/october-1386 [accessed 25 November 2020].
2. Ibid.
3. 'Richard II: February 1388', in Given-Wilson et al, *Parliament Rolls of Medieval England*, British History Online http://www.british-history.ac.uk/no-series/parliament-rolls-medieval/february-1388 [accessed 26 November 2020].
4. 'Richard II: September 1397, Part 1', in Given-Wilson et al, *Parliament Rolls of Medieval England*, British History Online http://www.british-history.ac.uk/no-series/parliament-rolls-medieval/september-1397-pt-1 [accessed 26 November 2020].
5. 'Henry IV: October 1399, Part 1', in Given-Wilson et al, *Parliament Rolls of Medieval England*, British History Online http://www.british-history.ac.uk/no-series/parliament-rolls-medieval/october-1399-pt-1 [accessed 26 November 2020], Item 92.
6. Tickner, *A Shorter Froissart*, pp. 228–9.
7. 'Richard II: September 1397, Part 2', in Given-Wilson et al, *Parliament Rolls of Medieval England*, British History Online http://www.british-

history.ac.uk/no-series/parliament-rolls-medieval/september-1397-pt-2 [accessed 26 November 2020] deals with Richard's actions against the Lord Appellant and the issue of the trial by combat.

8. Tickner, *A Shorter Froissart*, pp. 230–3.
9. *The Brut or The Chronicles of England*, p. 357.
10. Ibid.
11. *Richard II*, N. Saul, Yale University Press, 1997, pp. 412–3.
12. *The Brut or The Chronicles of England*, p. 358.
13. Tickner, *A Shorter Froissart*, pp. 239–40.
14. Ibid, pp. 245–8.
15. 'Henry IV: October 1399, Part 1', in Given-Wilson et al, *Parliament Rolls of Medieval England*, British History Online http://www.british-history.ac.uk/no-series/parliament-rolls-medieval/october-1399-pt-1 [accessed 26 November 2020], Item 13–4.
16. Ibid, Item 51.
17. Ibid, Item 53.
18. Ibid, Item 55.
19. 'Henry V: November 1415', in Given-Wilson et al, *Parliament Rolls of Medieval England*, British History Online http://www.british-history.ac.uk/no-series/parliament-rolls-medieval/november-1415 [accessed 26 November 2020], Item 6.
20. The reasons for this are far deeper and more complex than room permits here. I have written a biography of *York: Richard Duke of York, King By Right*, Amberley, 2016.
21. *The Brut or The Chronicles of England*, pp. 512–3.
22. *An English Chronicle*, ed. J.S. Davies, The Camden Society, 1856, pp. 62–3 *and The Brut or The Chronicles of England*, pp. 512–3 and *Registrum Abbatiae Johannis Whethamstede abbatis monasterii Sancti Albani*, ed. H.T. Riley, Vol I, London, 1872, pp. 178–9 for accounts of Gloucester's arrest and death.
23. *An English Chronicle*, p. 63.
24. Ibid, p. 64.
25. 'Henry VI: November 1449', in Given-Wilson et al, *Parliament Rolls of Medieval England*, British History Online http://www.british-history.ac.uk/no-series/parliament-rolls-medieval/november-1449 [accessed 27 November 2020].
26. Ibid, Items 14-51. It is also telling that in 1450, Lady Margaret Beaufort, the future mother of Henry Tudor, was seen as a key to the succession, though parliament describes the claim as false (Item 19).
27. *Calendar of the Patent Rolls*, Henry VI, 1446–52 The Public Record Office, 1909, p. 385.

28. *The Historical Collections of A Citizen of London in the Fifteenth Century*, ed. J. Gairdner, The Camden Society, 1876, p. 190.
29. e.g. *An English Chronicle*, p. 64.
30. *Three Fifteenth-Century Chronicles*, ed. J. Gairdner, The Camden Society, 1880, pp. 94–9 for the entire document.
31. Ibid, p. 96.
32. *An English Chronicle*, p. 65.
33. Gairdner, *Three Fifteenth-Century Chronicles*, p. 95.
34. Ibid, p. 97.
35. *An English Chronicle*, p. 64.
36. Gairdner, *The Historical Collections of A Citizen of London*, p. 191.
37. Ibid, p. 192.
38. *An English Chronicle*, p. 64 *and* Gairdner, *The Historical Collections of A Citizen of London*, p. 193 *and The Brut or The Chronicles of England*, p. 517.
39. *The Brut or The Chronicles of England*, pp. 518–9 suggest neighbours were robbing neighbours.
40. Gairdner, *The Historical Collections of A Citizen of London*, p. 193.
41. Gregory sets the time at 10pm, though *The Brut* and *An English Chronicle* say 9pm. I have gone with Gregory's assertion simply on the basis that he was in the city when it happened.
42. Gairdner, *The Historical Collections of A Citizen of London*, p. 193 *and The Brut or The Chronicles of England*, p. 519, and *An English Chronicle*, p. 67 for accounts of the battle.
43. *An English Chronicle*, p. 67.
44. Gairdner, *The Historical Collections of A Citizen of London*, p. 194.
45. 'Henry VI: November 1450', in Given-Wilson et al, *Parliament Rolls of Medieval England*, British History Online http://www.british-history.ac.uk/no-series/parliament-rolls-medieval/november-1450 [accessed 28 November 2020], Item 19.
46. Gairdner, *The Historical Collections of A Citizen of London*, p. 197.

10. The Wars of the Roses

1. 'Henry VI: November 1450', in Given-Wilson et al, *Parliament Rolls of Medieval England*, British History Online http://www.british-history.ac.uk/no-series/parliament-rolls-medieval/november-1450 [accessed 28 November 2020], Item 17.
2. Gairdner, *The Historical Collections of A Citizen of London*, p. 196.

3. 'Henry VI: November 1450', in Given-Wilson et al, *Parliament Rolls of Medieval England*, British History Online http://www.british-history. ac.uk/no-series/parliament-rolls-medieval/november-1450 [accessed 28 November 2020], Appendices 9 and 6.

4. 'Henry VI: July 1455', in Given-Wilson et al, *Parliament Rolls of Medieval England*, British History Online http://www.british-history. ac.uk/no-series/parliament-rolls-medieval/july-1455 [accessed 28 November 2020], Appendix 14.

5. *The Paston Letters A.D. 1422–1509*, ed. J. Gairdner, London, 1904, p. 96.

6. Ibid, pp. 97–8.

7. Ibid.

8. Ibid, p. 99.

9. Gairdner, *Three Fifteenth-Century Chronicles*, p. 69.

10. *The New Chronicles of England and France by Robert Fabyan*, ed. H. Ellis, London, 1811, p. 627

11. Gairdner, *The Paston Letters A.D. 1422–1509*, pp. 101–2 for the full oath.

12. *The Brut or The Chronicles of England*, p. 520.

13. 'Henry VI: March 1453', in Given-Wilson et al, *Parliament Rolls of Medieval England*, British History Online http://www.british-history.ac.uk/no-series/parliament-rolls-medieval/march-1453 [accessed 29 November 2020], Appendix 36.

14. Ibid, Item 50.

15. Ibid, Item 63.

16. Ibid, Item 20.

17. *The Paston Letters*, Vol I, ed. J. Gairdner, 1872, p. 265.

18. 'Henry VI: March 1453', in Given-Wilson et al, *Parliament Rolls of Medieval England*, British History Online http://www.british-history.ac.uk/no-series/parliament-rolls-medieval/march-1453 [accessed 29 November 2020], Item 31 for the commission and the articles drawn up as well as the account of the visit to the king.

19. Ibid, Item 34.

20. Ibid, Item 36.

21. *Calendar of the Patent Rolls*, Henry VI, Vol VI, 1452–1461, Public Record Office, 1971, p. 159.

22. *Proceedings and Ordinances of the Privy Council of England*, Vol VI, ed. H. Nicolas, 1837, p. 220–33.

23. *An English Chronicle*, p. 71.

24. Gairdner, *The Paston Letters*, Vol I, pp. 328–9.

25. 'Henry VI: July 1455', in Given-Wilson et al, *Parliament Rolls of Medieval England*, British History Online http://www.british-history.ac.uk/no-series/parliament-rolls-medieval/july-1455 [accessed 29 November 2020], Item 21.
26. Ibid, Item 24.
27. Ibid, Appendix 12.
28. Ibid, Item 30.
29. Ibid, Item 31.
30. *An English Chronicle*, p. 77.
31. Ibid, p. 79.
32. Ibid, pp. 81–3.
33. *The Brut or The Chronicles of England*, p. 527.
34. *An English Chronicle*, p. 83.
35. Gairdner, *The Historical Collections of A Citizen of London*, p. 207.
36. 'Henry VI: November 1459', in Given-Wilson et al, *Parliament Rolls of Medieval England*, British History Online http://www.british-history.ac.uk/no-series/parliament-rolls-medieval/november-1459 [accessed 29 November 2020], Items 21-3.
37. Ibid, Item 14.
38. 'Henry VI: October 1460', Given-Wilson et al, *Parliament Rolls of Medieval England*, British History Online http://www.british-history.ac.uk/no-series/parliament-rolls-medieval/october-1460 [accessed 29 November 2020], Items 10-30.
39. Ibid, Item 11 in particular.
40. Ibid.
41. *An English Chronicle*, p. 106–7.

Index